DATE DUE			
3-20			
GAYLORD 234			PRINTED IN U. S. A.

HISTORY OF DOGMA

BY

Dr. ADOLPH HARNACK

ORDINARY PROF. OF CHURCH HISTORY IN THE UNIVERSITY, AND FELLOW OF
THE ROYAL ACADEMY OF SCIENCE, BERLIN

*TRANSLATED
FROM THE THIRD GERMAN
EDITION*

BY

NEIL BUCHANAN

VOLUME I

GLOUCESTER, MASS.

PETER SMITH

1976

Published in the United Kingdom by Constable
and Company, Ltd., 10 Orange Street, London WC 2.

The new Dover edition, first published in 1961,
is an unabridged republication of the English translation of the third German edition that appeared
circa 1900. This Dover edition is an unaltered republication except that minor typographical errors
in Volume VII have been corrected.

The original English edition appeared as seven
separate volumes, whereas this Dover edition is
published complete in four separate volumes.

ISBN 0-8446-2207-9
Reprinted, 1976

Library of Congress Catalog Card Number: 61-4455

VORWORT ZUR ENGLISCHEN AUSGABE.

Ein theologisches Buch erhält erst dadurch einen Platz in der Weltlitteratur, dass es Deutsch und Englisch gelesen werden kann. Diese beiden Sprachen zusammen haben auf dem Gebiete der Wissenschaft vom Christenthum das Lateinische abgelöst. Es ist mir daher eine grosse Freude, dass mein Lehrbuch der Dogmengeschichte in das Englische übersetzt worden ist, und ich sage dem Uebersetzer sowie den Verlegern meinen besten Dank.

Der schwierigste Theil der Dogmengeschichte ist ihr Anfang, nicht nur weil in dem Anfang die Keime für alle späteren Entwickelungen liegen, und daher ein Beobachtungsfehler beim Beginn die Richtigkeit der ganzen folgenden Darstellung bedroht, sondern auch desshalb, weil die Auswahl des wichtigsten Stoffs aus der Geschichte des Urchristenthums und der biblischen Theologie ein schweres Problem ist. Der Eine wird finden, dass ich zu viel in das Buch aufgenommen habe, und der Andere zu wenig—vielleicht haben Beide recht; ich kann dagegen nur anführen, dass sich mir die getroffene Auswahl nach wiederholtem Nachdenken und Experimentiren auf's Neue erprobt hat.

Wer ein theologisches Buch aufschlägt, fragt gewöhnlich zuerst nach dem "Standpunkt" des Verfassers. Bei geschichtlichen Darstellungen sollte man so nicht fragen. Hier handelt es sich darum, ob der Verfasser einen Sinn hat für den Gegenstand den er darstellt, ob er Originales und Abgeleitetes zu unterscheiden versteht, ob er seinen Stoff volkommen kennt, ob er sich der Grenzen des geschichtlichen Wissens bewusst ist, und ob er wahrhaftig ist. Diese Forderungen erhalten den kategorischen Imperativ für den Historiker; aber nur indem man rastlos an sich selber arbeitet, sind sie zu erfüllen, — so ist jede geschichtliche Darstellung eine ethische Aufgabe. Der Historiker soll in jedem Sinn *treu* sein: ob er das gewesen ist, darnach soll mann fragen.

Berlin, am 1. Mai, 1894.

ADOLF HARNACK.

THE AUTHOR'S
PREFACE TO THE ENGLISH EDITION.

No theological book can obtain a place in the literature of the world unless it can be read both in German and in English. These two languages combined have taken the place of Latin in the sphere of Christian Science. I am therefore greatly pleased to learn that my "History of Dogma" has been translated into English, and I offer my warmest thanks both to the translator and to the publishers.

The most difficult part of the history of dogma is the beginning, not only because it contains the germs of all later developments, and therefore an error in observation here endangers the correctness of the whole following account, but also because the selection of the most important material from the history of primitive Christianity and biblical theology is a hard problem. Some will think that I have admitted too much into the book, others too little. Perhaps both are right. I can only reply that after repeated consideration and experiment I continue to be satisfied with my selection.

In taking up a theological book we are in the habit of enquiring first of all as to the "stand-point" of the Author. In a historical work there is no room for such enquiry. The question here is, whether the Author is in sympathy with the subject about which he writes, whether he can distinguish original elements from those that are derived, whether he has a thorough acquaintance with his material, whether he is conscious of the limits of historical knowledge, and whether he is truthful. These requirements constitute the categorical imperative for the historian: but they can only be fulfilled by an unwearied self-discipline. Hence every historical study is an ethical task. The historian ought to be faithful in every sense of the word; whether he has been so or not is the question on which his readers have to decide.

Berlin, 1st May, 1894.

ADOLF HARNACK.

FROM THE
AUTHOR'S PREFACE TO THE FIRST EDITION.

The task of describing the genesis of ecclesiastical dogma which I have attempted to perform in the following pages, has hitherto been proposed by very few scholars, and, properly speaking, undertaken by one only. I must therefore crave the indulgence of those acquainted with the subject for an attempt which no future historian of dogma can avoid.

At first I meant to confine myself to narrower limits, but I was unable to carry out that intention, because the new arrangement of the material required a more detailed justification. Yet no one will find in the book, which presupposes the knowledge of Church history so far as it is given in the ordinary manuals, any repertory of the theological thought of Christian antiquity. The diversity of Christian ideas, or of ideas closely related to Christianity, was very great in the first centuries. For that very reason a selection was necessary; but it was required, above all, by the aim of the work. The history of dogma has to give an account only of those doctrines of Christian writers which were authoritative in wide circles, or which furthered the advance of the development; otherwise it would become a collection of monographs, and thereby lose its proper value. I have endeavoured to subordinate everything to the aim of exhibiting the development which led to the ecclesiastical dogmas, and therefore have neither, for example, communicated the details of the gnostic systems, nor brought forward in detail the theological ideas of Clemens Romanus, Ignatius, etc. Even a history of Paulinism will be sought for in the book in vain. It is a task by itself, to trace the after-effects of the theology of Paul in the post-Apostolic age. The History of Dogma can only furnish fragments here; for it is not consistent with its task to give an accurate account of the history of a theology the effects of which were at first very limited. It is certainly no easy matter to determine what was authoritative in wide circles at the time when dogma was first being developed, and I may confess that I have found the working out of the third chapter of the first book very difficult. But I hope that the severe limitation in the material will be of service to the subject. If the result of this limitation should be to lead students to read connectedly the manual which has grown out of my lectures, my highest wish will be gratified.

There can be no great objection to the appearance of a text-book on the history of dogma at the present time. We now know in what direction we have to work; but we still want a history of Christian theological ideas in their relation to contemporary philosophy. Above all, we have nct got an exact knowledge of the Hellenistic philosophical terminologies in their development up to the fourth century. I have keenly felt this want, which can only be remedied by well-directed common labour. I have made a plentiful use of the contro-versial treatise of Celsus against Christianity, of which little use has hitherto been made for the history of dogma. On the other hand, except in a few cases, I have deemed it in-admissible to adduce parallel passages, easy to be got, from Philo, Seneca, Plutarch, Epictetus, Marcus Aurelius, Porphyry, etc.; for only a comparison strictly carried out would have been of value here. I have been able neither to borrow such from others, nor to furnish it myself. Yet I have ventured to submit my work, because, in my opinion, it is possible to prove the dependence of dogma on the Greek spirit, without being compelled to enter into a discussion of all the details.

The Publishers of the Encyclopædia Brittannica have allowed me to print here, in a form but slightly altered, the articles on Neoplatonism and Manichæism which I wrote for their work, and for this I beg to thank them.

It is now eighty-three years since my grandfather, Gustav Ewers, edited in German the excellent manual on the earliest history of dogma by Münter, and thereby got his name associated with the history of the founding of the new study. May the work of the grandson be found not unworthy of the clear and disciplined mind which presided over the beginnings of the young science.

Giessen, 1st August, 1885.

AUTHOR'S
PREFACE TO THE SECOND EDITION.

In the two years that have passed since the appearance of the first edition I have steadily kept in view the improvement of this work, and have endeavoured to learn from the reviews of it that have appeared. I owe most to the study of Weizsäcker's work on the Apostolic Age, and his notice of the first edition of this volume in the Göttinger gelehrte Anzeigen, 1886, No. 21. The latter, in several decisive passages concerning the general conception, drew my attention to the fact that I had emphasised certain points too strongly, but had not given due prominence to others of equal importance, while not entirely overlooking them. I have convinced myself that these hints were, almost throughout, well founded, and have taken pains to meet them in the new edition. I have also learned from Heinrici's commentary on the Second Epistle to the Corinthians, and from Bigg's "Lectures on the Christian Platonists of Alexandria." Apart from these works there has appeared very little that could be of significance for my historical account; but I have once more independently considered the main problems, and in some cases, after repeated reading of the sources, checked my statements, removed mistakes and explained what had been to briefly stated. Thus, in particular, Chapter II. §§ 1-3 of the "Presuppositions," also the Third Chapter of the First Book (especially Section 6), also in the Second Book, Chapter I. and Chapter II. (under B), the Third

Chapter (Supplement 3 and excursus on "Catholic and Romish"),
the Fifth Chapter (under 1 and 3) and the Sixth Chapter
(under 2) have been subjected to changes and greater additions.
Finally, a new excursus has been added on the various modes
of conceiving pre-existence, and in other respects many things
have been improved in detail. The size of the book has thereby
been increased by about fifty pages. As I have been misrepre-
sented by some as one who knew not how to appreciate the
uniqueness of the Gospel history and the evangelic faith, while
others have conversely reproached me with making the history
of dogma proceed from an "apostasy" from the Gospel to
Hellenism, I have taken pains to state my opinions on both
these points as clearly as possible. In doing so I have only
wrought out the hints which were given in the first edition,
and which, as I supposed, were sufficient for readers. But it
is surely a reasonable desire when I request the critics in
reading the paragraphs which treat of the "Presuppositions,"
not to forget how difficult the questions there dealt with are,
both in themselves and from the nature of the sources, and
how exposed to criticism the historian is who attempts to
unfold his position towards them in a few pages. As is self-
evident, the centre of gravity of the book lies in that which
forms its subject proper, in the account of the origin of
dogma within the Græco-Roman empire. But one should not
on that account, as many have done, pass over the beginning
which lies before the beginning, or arbitrarily adopt a starting-
point of his own; for everything here depends on where
and how one begins. I have not therefore been able to
follow the well-meant counsel to simply strike out the "Presuppositions."

I would gladly have responded to another advice to work
up the notes into the text; but I would then have been
compelled to double the size of some chapters. The form of
this book, in many respects awkward, may continue as it is
so long as it represents the difficulties by which the subject
is still pressed. When they have been removed—and the
smallest number of them lie in the subject matter—I will
gladly break up this form of the book and try to give it

another shape. For the friendly reception given to it I have to offer my heartiest thanks. But against those who, believing themselves in possession of a richer view of the history here related, have called my conception meagre, I appeal to the beautiful words of Tertullian: "Malumus in scripturis minus, si forte, sapere quam contra."

Marburg, 24th December, 1887.

AUTHOR'S
PREFACE TO THE THIRD EDITION.

In the six years that have passed since the appearance of the second edition I have continued to work at the book, and have made use of the new sources and investigations that have appeared during this period, as well as corrected and extended my account in many passages. Yet I have not found it necessary to make many changes in the second half of the work. The increase of about sixty pages is almost entirely in the first half.

Berlin, 31st December, 1893.

Τὸ δόγματος ὄνομα τῆς ἀνθρωπίνης ἔχεται βουλῆς τε καὶ γνώμης. Ὅτι δὲ τοῦθ' οὕτως ἔχει, μαρτυρεῖ μὲν, ἱκανῶς ἡ δογματικὴ τῶν ἰατρῶν τέχνη μαρτυρεῖ δὲ καὶ τὰ τῶν φιλοσόφων καλούμενα δόγματα. Ὅτι δὲ καὶ τὰ συγκλήτῳ δόξαντα ἔτι καὶ νῦν δόγματα συγκλήτου λέγεται, οὐδένα ἀγνοεῖν οἶμαι.

MARCELLUS OF ANCYRA.

Die Christliche Religion hat nichts in der Philosophie zu thun, Sie ist ein mächtiges Wesen für sich, woran die gesunkene und leidende Menschheit von Zeit zu Zeit sich immer wieder emporgearbeitet hat; und indem man ihr diese Wirkung zugesteht, ist sie über aller Philosophie erhaben und bedarf von ihr keine Stütze.

Gespräche mit GOETHE VON ECKER-
MANN, 2 Th. p. 39.

CONTENTS.

SUPPLEMENTARY.

DIVISION I.—THE GENESIS OF ECCLESIASTICAL DOGMA, OR THE GENESIS OF THE CATHOLIC APOSTOLIC DOGMATIC THEOLOGY, AND THE FIRST SCIENTIFIC ECCLESIASTICAL SYSTEM OF DOCTRINE.

BOOK I.

THE PREPARATION.

I

PROLEGOMENA TO THE DISCIPLINE OF THE HISTORY OF DOGMA.

II

THE PRESUPPOSITIONS OF THE HISTORY OF DOGMA.

CHAPTER I

PROLEGOMENA TO THE DISCIPLINE OF THE HISTORY

OF DOGMA.

§ 1. *The Idea and Task of the History of Dogma.*

1. THE History of Dogma is a discipline of general Church History, which has for its object the dogmas of the Church. These dogmas are the doctrines of the Christian faith logically formulated and expressed for scientific and apologetic purposes, the contents of which are a knowledge of God, of the world, and of the provisions made by God for man's salvation. The Christian Churches teach them as the truths revealed in Holy Scripture, the acknowledgment of which is the condition of the salvation which religion promises. But as the adherents of the Christian religion had not these dogmas from the beginning, so far, at least, as they form a connected system, the business of the history of dogma is, in the first place, to ascertain the origin of Dogmas (of Dogma), and then secondly, to describe their development (their variations).

2. We cannot draw any hard and fast line between the time of the origin and that of the development of dogma; they rather shade off into one another. But we shall have to look for the final point of division at the time when an article of faith logically formulated and scientifically expressed, was first raised to the *articulus constitutivus ecclesiæ*, and as such was universally enforced by the Church. Now that first happened when the doctrine of Christ, as the pre-existent and personal Logos of God, had obtained acceptance everywhere in the confederated Churches as the revealed and

fundamental doctrine of faith, that is, about the end of the
third century or the beginning of the fourth. We must therefore, in our account, take this as the final point of division. [1]
As to the development of dogma, it seems to have closed in
the Eastern Church with the seventh Œcumenical Council (787).
After that time no further dogmas were set up in the East as
revealed truths. As to the Western Catholic, that is, the
Romish Church, a new dogma was promulgated as late as the
year 1870, which claims to be, and in point of form really
is, equal in dignity to the old dogmas. Here, therefore, the
History of Dogma must extend to the present time. Finally,
as regards the Protestant Churches, they are a subject of special difficulty in the sphere of the history of dogma; for at the
present moment there is no agreement within these Churches
as to whether, and in what sense, dogmas (as the word was
used in the ancient Church) are valid. But even if we leave
the present out of account and fix our attention on the Protestant Churches of the 16th century, the decision is difficult.
For, on the one hand, the Protestant faith, the Lutheran as
well as the Reformed (and that of Luther no less), presents
itself as a doctrine of faith which, resting on the Catholic
canon of scripture, is, in point of form, quite analogous to the
Catholic doctrine of faith, has a series of dogmas in common
with it, and only differs in a few. On the other hand, Pro-

---

[1] Weizsäcker, Gött. Gel. Anz. 1886, p. 823 f. says, "It is a question whether
we should limit the account of the genesis of Dogma to the Antenicene period
and designate all else as a development of that. This is undoubtedly correct so
long as our view is limited to the history of dogma of the Greek Church in the
second period, and the development of it by the Œcumenical Synods. On the other
hand, the Latin Church, in its own way and in its own province, becomes productive from the days of Augustine onwards; the formal signification of dogma in
the narrower sense becomes different in the middle ages. Both are repeated in a
much greater measure through the Reformation. We may therefore, in opposition
to that division into genesis and development, regard the whole as a continuous
process, in which the contents as well as the formal authority of dogma are in
process of continuous development." This view is certainly just, and I think is
indicated by myself in what follows. We have to decide here, as so often elsewhere in our account, between rival points of view. The view favoured by me has
the advantage of making the nature of dogma clearly appear as a product of the
mode of thought of the early church, and that is what it has remained, in spite
of all changes both in form and substance, till the present day.

testantism has taken its stand in principle on the Gospel exclusively, and declared its readiness at all times to test all doctrines afresh by a true understanding of the Gospel. The Reformers, however, in addition to this, began to unfold a conception of Christianity which might be described, in contrast with the Catholic type of religion, as a new conception, and which indeed draws support from the old dogmas, but changes their original significance materially and formally. What this conception was may still be ascertained from those writings received by the Church, the Protestant symbols of the 16th century, in which the larger part of the traditionary dogmas are recognised as the appropriate expression of the Christian religion, nay, as the Christian religion itself.[1] Accordingly, it can neither be maintained that the expression of the Christian faith in the form of dogmas is abolished in the Protestant Churches—the very acceptance of the Catholic canon as the revealed record of faith is opposed to that view—nor that its meaning has remained absolutely unchanged.[2] The history of dogma has simply to recognise this state of things, and to represent it exactly as it lies before us in the documents.

But the point to which the historian should advance here still remains an open question. If we adhere strictly to the definition of the idea of dogma given above, this much is certain, that dogmas were no longer set up after the Formula of Concord, or in the case of the Reformed Church, after the decrees of the Synod of Dort. It cannot, however, be maintained that they have been set aside in the centuries that

---

[1] See Kattenbusch. Luther's Stellung zu den ökumenischen Symbolen, 1883.

[2] See Ritschl. Geschichte des Pietismus, I. p. 80 ff.: 93 ff., II. p. 60 f.: 88 f. "The Lutheran view of life did not remain pure and undefiled, but was limited and obscured by the preponderance of dogmatic interests. Protestantism was not delivered from the womb of the Western Church of the middle ages in full power and equipment, like Athene from the head of Jupiter. The incompleteness of its ethical view, the splitting up of its general conceptions into a series of particular dogmas, the tendency to express its beliefs as a hard and fast whole, are defects which soon made Protestantism appear to disadvantage in comparison with the wealth of mediæval theology and asceticism... The scholastic form of pure doctrine is really only the provisional, and not the final form of Protestantism."

have passed since then; for apart from some Protestant National-
al and independent Churches, which are too insignificant and
whose future is too uncertain to be taken into account here,
the ecclesiastical tradition of the 16th century, and along with
it the tradition of the early Church, have not been abrogated
in authoritative form. Of course, changes of the greatest
importance with regard to doctrine have appeared everywhere
in Protestantism from the 17th century to the present day.
But these changes cannot in any sense be taken into account
in a history of dogma, because they have not as yet attained
a form valid for the Church. However we may judge of these
changes, whether we regard them as corruptions or improve-
ments, or explain the want of fixity in which the Protestant
Churches find themselves, as a situation that is forced on them,
or the situation that is agreeable to them and for which they
are adapted, in no sense is there here a development which
could be described as history of dogma.

These facts would seem to justify those who, tike Thomasius
and Schmid, carry the history of dogma in Protestantism to
the Formula of Concord, or, in the case of the Reformed Church,
to the decrees of the Synod of Dort. But it may be objected
to this boundary line; (1) That those symbols have at all times
attained only a partial authority in Protestantism; (2) That as
noted above, the dogmas, that is, the formulated doctrines of
faith have different meanings on different matters in the Protestant and in the Catholic Churches. Accordingly, it seems
advisable within the frame-work of the history of dogma, to
examine Protestantism only so far as this is necessary for
obtaining a knowledge of its deviations from the Catholic dogma
materially and formally, that is, to ascertain the original
position of the Reformers with regard to the doctrine of the
Church, a position which is beset with contradictions. The more
accurately we determine the relation of the Reformers to
Catholicism, the more intelligible will be the developments
which Protestantism has passed through in the course of its
history. But these developments themselves (retrocession and
advance) do not belong to the sphere of the history of dogma,
because they stand in no comparable relation to the course

of the history of dogma within the Catholic Church. As history of Protestant doctrines they form a peculiar independent province of Church history.

As to the division of the history of dogma, it consists of two main parts. The first has to describe the origin of dogma, that is, of the Apostolic Catholic system of doctrine based on the foundation of the tradition authoritatively embodied in the creeds and Holy Scripture, and extends to the beginning of the fourth century. This may be conveniently divided into two parts, the first of which will treat of the preparation, the second of the establishment of the ecclesiastical doctrine of faith. The second main part, which has to portray the development of dogma, comprehends three stages. In the first stage the doctrine of faith appears as Theology and Christology. The Eastern Church has never got beyond this stage, although it has to a large extent enriched dogma ritually and mystically (see the decrees of the seventh council). We will have to shew how the doctrines of faith formed in this stage have remained for all time in the Church dogmas κατ' ἐξοχήν. The second stage was initiated by Augustine. The doctrine of faith appears here on the one side completed, and on the other re-expressed by new dogmas, which treat of the relation of sin and grace, freedom and grace, grace and the means of grace. The number and importance of the dogmas that were, in the middle ages, really fixed after Augustine's time, had no relation to the range and importance of the questions which they raised, and which emerged in the course of centuries in consequence of advancing knowledge, and not less in consequence of the growing power of the Church. Accordingly, in this second stage which comprehends the whole of the middle ages, the Church as an institution kept believers together in a larger measure than was possible to dogmas. These in their accepted form were too poor to enable them to be the expression of religious conviction and the regulator of Church life. On the other hand, the new decisions of Theologians, Councils and Popes, did not yet possess the authority which could have made them incontestable truths of faith. The third stage begins with the Reformation, which compelled the Church to fix its faith on

the basis of the theological work of the middle ages. Thus
arose the Roman Catholic dogma which has found in the Vatican
decrees its provisional settlement.   This Roman Catholic dogma,
as it was formulated at Trent, was moulded in express opposition to the Theses of the Reformers.   But these Theses
themselves represent a peculiar conception of Christianity, which
has its root in the theology of Paul and Augustine, and includes
either explicitly or implicitly a revision of the whole ecclesiastical tradition, and therefore of dogma also.   The History of
Dogma in this last stage, therefore, has a twofold task.   It
has, on the one hand, to present the Romish dogma as a
product of the ecclesiastical development of the middle ages
under the influence of the Reformation faith which was to be
rejected, and on the other hand, to portray the conservative new
formation which we have in original Protestantism, and determine
its relation to dogma.   A closer examination, however, shews
that in none of the great confessions does religion live in
dogma, as of old.   Dogma everywhere has fallen into the background; in the Eastern Church it has given place to ritual,
in the Roman Church to ecclesiastical instructions, in the
Protestant Churches, so far as they are mindful of their origin,
to the Gospel.   At the same time, however, the paradoxical
fact is unmistakable that dogma as such is nowhere at this
moment so powerful as in the Protestant Churches, though by
their history they are furthest removed from it.   Here, however,
it comes into consideration as an object of immediate religious
interest, which, strictly speaking, in the Catholic Church is not
the case. [1]   The Council of Trent was simply wrung from the
Romish Church, and she has made the dogmas of that council

---

[1] It is very evident how the mediæval and old catholic dogmas were transformed
in the view which Luther originally took of them. In this view we must remember
that he did away with all the presuppositions of dogma, the infallible Apostolic
Canon of Scripture, the infallible teaching function of the Church, and the infallible
Apostolic doctrine and constitution.   On this basis dogmas can only be utterances
which do not support faith, but are supposed by it.   But, on the other hand, his
opposition to all the Apocryphal saints which the Church had created, compelled
him to emphasise faith alone, and to give it a firm basis in Scripture, in order to
free it from the burden of tradition.   Here then, very soon, first by Melanchthon,
a summary of *articuli fidei* was substituted for the faith, and the Scriptures recovered

in a certain sense innocuous by the Vatican decrees.[1] In this sense, it may be said that the period of development of dogma is altogether closed, and that therefore our discipline requires

their place as a rule. Luther himself, however, is responsible for both, and so it came about that very soon the new evangelic standpoint was explained almost exclusively by the "abolition of abuses," and by no means so surely by the transformation of the whole doctrinal tradition. The classic authority for this is the Augsburg confession ("hæc fere summa est doctrina apud suos, in qua cerni potest nihil inesse, quod discrepet a scripturis vel ab ecclesia Catholica vel ab ecclesia Romana .... sed dissensio est de quibusdam abusibus"). The purified catholic doctrine has since then become the palladium of the Reformation Churches. The refuters of the Augustana have justly been unwilling to admit the mere "purifying," but have noted in addition that the Augustana does not say everything that was urged by Luther and the Doctors (see Ficker, Die Konfutation des Augsburgischen Bekenntnisse, 1891). At the same time, however, the Lutheran Church, though not so strongly as the English, retained the consciousness of being the true Catholics. But, as the history of Protestantism proves, the original impulse has not remained inoperative. Though Luther himself all his life measured his personal Christian standing by an entirely different standard than subjection to a law of faith; yet, however presumptuous the words may sound, we might say that in the complicated struggle that was forced on him, he did not always clearly understand his own faith.

[1] In the modern Romish Church, dogma is, above all, a judicial regulation which one has to submit to, and in certain circumstances submission alone is sufficient, *fides implicita*. Dogma is thereby just as much deprived of its original sense and its original authority as by the demand of the Reformers, that every thing should be based upon a clear understanding of the Gospel. Moreover, the changed position of the Romish Church towards dogma is also shewn by the fact that it no longer gives a plain answer to the question as to what dogma is. Instead of a series of dogmas definitely defined, and of equal value, there is presented an infinite multitude of whole and half dogmas, doctrinal directions, pious opinions, probable theological propositions, etc. It is often a very difficult question whether a solemn decision has or has not already been taken on this or that statement, or whether such a decision is still necessary. Everything that must be believed is nowhere stated, and so one sometimes hears in Catholic circles the exemplary piety of a cleric praised with the words that "he believes more than is necessary." The great dogmatic conflicts within the Catholic Church, since the Council of Trent, have been silenced by arbitrary Papal pronouncements and doctrinal directions. Since one has simply to accommodate oneself to these as laws, it once more appears clear that dogma has become a judicial regulation, administered by the Pope, which is carried out in an administrative way and loses itself in an endless casuistry. We do not mean by this to deny that dogma has a decided value for the pious Catholic as a summary of the faith. But in the Catholic Church it is no longer piety, but obedience that is decisive. The solidarity with the orthodox Protestants may be explained by political reasons, in order, from political reasons again, to condemn, where it is necessary, all Protestants as heretics and revolutionaries.

a statement such as belongs to a series of historical phenomena
that has been completed.

3. The Church has recognised her faith, that is religion
itself, in her dogmas. Accordingly, one very important business of the History of Dogma is to exhibit the unity that exists
in the dogmas of a definite period, and to shew how the several
dogmas are connected with one another and what leading
ideas they express. But, as a matter of course, this undertaking
has its limits in the degree of unanimity which actually existed
in the dogmas of the particular period. It may be shewn without much difficulty, that a strict though by no means absolute
unanimity is expressed only in the dogmas of the Greek Church.
The peculiar character of the western post-Augustinian ecclesiastical conception of Christianity, no longer finds a clear
expression in dogma, and still less is this the case with the
conception of the Reformers. The reason of this is that
Augustine, as well as Luther, disclosed a new conception
of Christianity, but at the same time appropriated the old
dogmas.[1] But neither Baur's nor Kliefoth's method of writing
the history of dogma has done justice to this fact. Not
Baur's, because, notwithstanding the division into six periods,
it sees a uniform process in the development of dogma, a
process which begins with the origin of Christianity and has
run its course, as is alleged, in a strictly logical way. Not
Kliefoth's, because, in the dogmas of the Catholic Church
which the East has never got beyond, it only ascertains the
establishment of one portion of the Christian faith, to which
the parts still wanting have been successively added in later
times.[2] In contrast with this, we may refer to the fact that
we can clearly distinguish three styles of building in the
history of dogma, but only three; the style of Origen, that of
Augustine, and that of the Reformers. But the dogma of the
post-Augustinian Church, as well as that of Luther, does not

---

[1] See the discussions of Biedermann (Christliche Dogmatik. 2 Ed. p. 150 f.) about
what he calls the law of stability in the history of religion.

[2] See Ritschl's discussion of the methods of the early histories of dogma in the
Jahrb. f. Deutsche Theologie, 1871, p. 181 ff.

in any way represent itself as a new building, not even as the mere extension of an old building, but as a complicated rebuilding, and by no means in harmony with former styles, because neither Augustine nor Luther ever dreamed of building independently. [1] This perception leads us to the most peculiar phenomenon which meets the historian of dogma, and which must determine his method.

Dogmas arise, develop themselves and are made serviceable to new aims; this in all cases takes place through Theology. But Theology is dependent on innumerable factors, above all on the spirit of the time; for it lies in the nature of theology that it desires to make its object intelligible. Dogmas are the product of theology, not inversely; of a theology of course which, as a rule, was in correspondence with the faith of the time. The critical view of history teaches this: first we have the Apologists and Origen, then the councils of Nice and Chalcedon; first the Scholastics, and the Council of Trent. In consequence of this, dogma bears the mark of all the factors on which the theology was dependent. That is one point. But the moment in which the product of theology became dogma, the way which led to it must be obscured; for, according to the conception of the Church, dogma can be nothing else than the revealed faith itself. Dogma is regarded not as the exponent, but as the basis of theology, and therefore the product of theology having passed into dogma limits, and criticises the work of theology both past and future. [2] That is the second point. It follows from this that the history of the Christian religion embraces a very complicated relation of ecclesiastical dogma and theology, and that the

---

[1] In Catholicism, the impulse which proceeded from Augustine has finally proved powerless to break the traditional conception of Christianity, as the Council of Trent and the decrees of the Vatican have shewn. For that very reason the development of the Roman Catholic Church doctrine belongs to the history of dogma. Protestantism must, however, under all circumstances be recognised as a new thing, which indeed in none of its phases has been free from contradictions.

[2] Here then begins the ecclesiastical theology which takes as its starting-point the finished dogma it strives to prove or harmonise, but very soon, as experience has shewn, loses its firm footing in such efforts and so occasions new crises.

ecclesiastical conception of the significance of theology cannot
at all do justice to this significance. The ecclesiastical scheme
which is here formed and which denotes the utmost concession
that can be made to history, is to the effect that theology gives
expression only to the form of dogma, while so far as it is
ecclesiastical theology, it presupposes the unchanging dogma,
i.e., the substance of dogma. But this scheme, which must
always leave uncertain what the form really is, and what the
substance, is in no way applicable to the actual circumstances.
So far, however, as it is itself an article of faith it is an object
of the history of dogma. Ecclesiastical dogma when put on
its defence must at all times take up an ambiguous position towards theology, and ecclesiastical theology a corresponding position towards dogma; for they are condemned to
perpetual uncertainty as to what they owe each other, and
what they have to fear from each other. The theological
Fathers of dogma have almost without exception failed to
escape being condemned by dogma, either because it went
beyond them, or lagged behind their theology. The Apologists, Origen and Augustine may be cited in support of this;
and even in Protestantism, *mutatis mutandis*, the same thing
has been repeated, as is proved by the fate of Melanchthon
and Schleiermacher. On the other hand, there have been
few theologians who have not shaken some article of the
traditional dogma. We are wont to get rid of these fundamental facts by hypostatising the ecclesiastical principle or
the common ecclesiastical spirit, and by this normal hypostasis, measuring, approving or condemning the doctrines of
the theologians, unconcerned about the actual conditions and
frequently following a hysteron-proteron. But this is a view
of history which should in justice be left to the Catholic
Church, which indeed cannot dispense with it. The critical
history of dogma has, on the contrary, to shew above all how
an ecclesiastical theology has arisen; for it can only give
account of the origin of dogma in connection with this main
question. The horizon must be taken here as wide as possible; for the question as to the origin of theology can only
be answered by surveying all the relations into which the

Christian religion has entered in naturalising itself in the world and subduing it. When ecclesiastical dogma has once been created and recognised as an immediate expression of the Christian religion, the history of dogma has only to take the history of theology into account so far as it has been active in the formation of dogma. Yet it must always keep in view the peculiar claim of dogma to be a criterion and not a product of theology. But it will also be able to shew how, partly by means of theology and partly by other means—for dogma is also dependent on ritual, constitution, and the practical ideals of life, as well as on the letter, whether of Scripture, or of tradition no longer understood— dogma in its development and re-expression has continually changed, according to the conditions under which the Church was placed. If dogma is originally the formulation of Christian faith as Greek culture understood it and justified it to itself, then dogma has never indeed lost this character, though it has been radically modified in later times. It is quite as important to keep in view the tenacity of dogma as its changes, and in this respect the Protestant way of writing history, which, here as elsewhere in the history of the Church, is more disposed to attend to differences than to what is permanent, has much to learn from the Catholic. But as the Protestant historian, as far as possible, judges of the progress of development in so far as it agrees with the Gospel in its documentary form, he is still able to shew, with all deference to that tenacity, that dogma has been so modified and used to the best advantage by Augustine and Luther, that its Christian character has in many respects gained, though in other respects it has become further and further alienated from that character. In proportion as the traditional system of dogmas lost its stringency it became richer. In proportion as it was stripped by Augustine and Luther of its apologetic philosophic tendency, it was more and more filled with Biblical ideas, though, on the other hand, it became more full of contradictions and less impressive.

This outlook, however, has already gone beyond the limits fixed for these introductory paragraphs and must not be pur-

sued further. To treat *in abstracto* of the method of the
history of dogma in relation to the discovery, grouping and
interpretation of the material is not to be recommended; for
general rules to preserve the ignorant and half instructed from
overlooking the important, and laying hold of what is not
important, cannot be laid down. Certainly everything depends
on the arrangement of the material; for the understanding of
history is to find the rules according to which the phenomena
should be grouped, and every advance in the knowledge of
history is inseparable from an accurate observance of these
rules. We must, above all, be on our guard against preferring
one principle at the expense of another in the interpretation
of the origin and aim of particular dogmas. The most diverse
factors have at all times been at work in the formation of
dogmas. Next to the effort to determine the doctrine of religion according to the *finis religionis*, the blessing of salvation,
the following may have been the most important. (1) The
conceptions and sayings contained in the canonical Scriptures.
(2) The doctrinal tradition originating in earlier epochs of the
Church, and no longer understood. (3) The needs of worship
and organisation. (4) The effort to adjust the doctrine of
religion to the prevailing doctrinal opinions. (5) Political and
social circumstances. (6) The changing moral ideals of life.
(7) The so-called logical consistency, that is the abstract ana-
logical treatment of one dogma according to the form of another.
(8) The effort to adjust different tendencies and contradictions
in the Church. (9) The endeavour to reject once for all a
doctrine regarded as erroneous. (10) The sanctifying power of
blind custom. The method of explaining everything wherever
possible by "the impulse of dogma to unfold itself," must be
given up as unscientific, just as all empty abstractions whatsoever
must be given up as scholastic and mythological. Dogma has
had its history in the individual living man and nowhere else.
As soon as one adopts this statement in real earnest, that
mediæval realism must vanish to which a man so often thinks
himself superior while imbedded in it all the time. Instead of
investigating the actual conditions in which believing and intelligent men have been placed, a system of Christianity has been

constructed from which, as from a Pandora's box, all doctrines which in course of time have been formed, are extracted, and in this way legitimised as Christian. The simple fundamental proposition that that only is Christian which can be established authoritatively by the Gospel, has never yet received justice in the history of dogma. Even the following account will in all probability come short in this point; for in face of a prevailing false tradition the application of a simple principle to every detail can hardly succeed at the first attempt.

Explanation as to the Conception and Task of the History of Dogma.

No agreement as yet prevails with regard to the conception of the history of dogma. Münscher (Handbuch der Christl. D. G. 3rd ed. I. p. 3 f.) declared that the business of the history of dogma is "To represent all the changes which the theoretic part of the Christian doctrine of religion has gone through from its origin up to the present, both in form and substance," and this definition held sway for a long time. Then it came to be noted that the question was not about changes that were accidental, but about those that were historically necessary, that dogma has a relation to the Church, and that it represents a rational expression of the faith. Emphasis was put sometimes on one of these elements and sometimes on the other. Baur, in particular, insisted on the first; V. Hofmann, after the example of Schleiermacher, on the second, and indeed exclusively (Encyklop. der theol. p. 257 f.: "The history of dogma is the history of the Church confessing the faith in words"). Nitzsch (Grundriss der Christl. D. G. I. p. 1) insisted on the third: "The history of dogma is the scientific account of the origin and development of the Christian system of doctrine or that part of historical theology which presents the history of the expression of the Christian faith in notions, doctrines and doctrinal systems." Thomasius has combined the second and third by conceiving the history of dogma as the history of the development of the ecclesiastical system of doctrine.

But even this conception is not sufficiently definite, inasmuch as it fails to do complete justice to the special peculiarity of the subject.

Ancient and modern usage does certainly seem to allow the word dogma to be applied to particular doctrines, or to a uniform system of doctrine, to fundamental truths, or to opinions, to theoretical propositions or practical rules, to statements of belief that have not been reached by a process of reasoning, as well as to those that bear the marks of such a process. But this uncertainty vanishes on closer examination. We then see that there is always an authority at the basis of dogma, which gives it to those who recognise that authority the signification of a fundamental truth "*quæ sine scelere prodi non poterit*" (Cicero Quæst. Acad. IV. 9). But therewith at the same time is introduced into the idea of dogma a social element (see Biedermann, Christl. Dogmatik. 2 Edit. I. p. 2 f.); the confessors of one and the same dogma form a community.

There can be no doubt that these two elements are also demonstrable in Christian dogma, and therefore we must reject all definitions of the history of dogma which do not take them into account. If we define it as the history of the understanding of Christianity by itself, or as the history of the changes of the theoretic part of the doctrine of religion or the like, we shall fail to do justice to the idea of dogma in its most general acceptation. We cannot describe as dogmas, doctrines such as the Apokatastasis, or the Kenosis of the Son of God, without coming into conflict with the ordinary usage of language and with ecclesiastical law.

If we start, therefore, from the supposition that Christian dogma is an ecclesiastical doctrine which presupposes revelation as its authority, and therefore claims to be strictly binding, we shall fail to bring out its real nature with anything like completeness. That which Protestants and Catholics call dogmas, are not only ecclesiastical doctrines, but they are also: (1) theses expressed in abstract terms, forming together a unity, and fixing the contents of the Christian religion as a knowledge of God, of the world, and of the sacred history under the aspect of a proof of the truth. But (2) they have also emerged at a definite stage of the history of the Christian religion; they shew in their conception as such, and in many details, the influence of that stage, viz., the Greek period, and they have preserved this character in spite of all their reconstructions and additions in after periods. This view of dogma cannot be shaken by the fact that particular historical facts, miraculous or not miraculous are described as dogmas; for here they are regarded as such only in so far as they have got the value of doctrines which have been inserted in the complete structure of doctrines and are, on the other hand, members of a chain of proofs, viz., proofs from prophecy.

But as soon as we perceive this, the parallel between the ecclesiastical dogmas and those of ancient schools of philosophy appears to be in point of form complete. The only difference is that revelation is here put as authority in the place of human knowledge, although the later philosophic schools appealed to revelation also. The theoretical as well as the practical doctrines which embraced the peculiar conception of the world and the ethics of the school, together with their rationale, were described in these schools as dogmas. Now, in so far as the adherents of the Christian religion possess dogmas in this sense, and form a community which has gained an understanding of its religious faith by analysis and by scientific definition and grounding, they appear as a great philosophic school in the ancient sense of the word. But they differ from such a school in so far as they have always eliminated the process of thought which has led to the dogma, looking upon the whole system of dogma as a revelation and therefore, even in respect of the reception of the dogma, at least at first, they have taken account not of the powers of human understanding, but of the Divine enlightenment which is bestowed on all the willing and the virtuous. In later times, indeed, the analogy was far more complete, in so far as the Church reserved the full possession of dogma to a circle of consecrated and initiated individuals. Dogmatic Christianity is therefore a definite stage in the history of the development of Christianity. It corresponds to the antique mode of thought, but has nevertheless continued to a very great extent in the following epochs, though subject to great transformations. Dogmatic Christianity stands between Christianity as the religion of the Gospel, presupposing a personal experience and dealing with disposition and conduct, and Christianity as a religion of cultus, sacraments, ceremonial and obedience, in short of superstition, and it can be united with either the one or the other. In itself and in spite of all its mysteries it is always intellectual Christianity, and therefore there is always the danger here that as knowledge it may supplant religious faith, or connect it with a doctrine of religion, instead of with God and a living experience.

If then the discipline of the history of dogma is to be what its name purports, its object is the very dogma which is so formed, and its fundamental problem will be to discover how it has arisen. In the history of the canon our method of procedure has for long been to ask first of all, how the canon originated, and then to examine the changes through which it has passed. We must proceed in the same way with the history of dogma, of which the history of the canon is simply a part. Two objections will be raised against this. In the first place, it will be said that from the very first the Christian religion has included a definite religious faith as well as a definite ethic, and that therefore Christian dogma is as original as Christianity itself, so that there can be no question about a genesis, but only as to a development or alteration of dogma within the Church. Again it will be said, in the second place, that dogma as defined above, has validity only for a definite epoch in the history of the Church, and that it is therefore quite impossible to write a comprehensive history of dogma in the sense we have indicated.

As to the first objection, there can of course be no doubt that the Christian religion is founded on a message, the contents of which are a definite belief in God and in Jesus Christ whom he has sent, and that the promise of salvation is attached to this belief. But faith in the Gospel and the later dogmas of the Church are not related to each other as theme and the way in which it is worked out, any more than the dogma of the New Testament canon is only the explication of the original reliance of Christians on the word of their Lord and the continuous working of the Spirit; but in these later dogmas an entirely new element has entered into the conception of religion. The message of religion appears here clothed in a knowledge of the world and of the ground of the world which had already been obtained without any reference to it, and therefore religion itself has here become a doctrine which has, indeed, its certainty in the Gospel, but only in part derives its contents from it, and which can also be appropriated by such as are neither poor in spirit nor weary and heavy laden. Now, it may of course be shewn that a philosophic conception of the Christian religion is possible, and began to make its appearance from the very first, as in the case of Paul. But the Pauline gnosis has neither been simply identified with the Gospel by Paul himself (1 Cor. III. 2 f.: XII. 3: Phil. I. 18) nor is it analogous to the later dogma, not to speak of being identical with it. The characteristic of this dogma is that it represents itself in no sense as foolishness, but as wisdom, and at the same time desires to be regarded as the contents of revelation itself. Dogma in its conception and development is a work of the Greek spirit on the soil of the Gospel. By comprehending in itself and giving excellent expression to the religious conceptions contained in Greek philosophy and the Gospel, together with its Old Testament basis; by meeting the search for a revelation as well as the desire for a universal knowledge; by subordinating itself to the aim of the Christian religion to bring a Divine life to humanity as well as to the aim of philosophy to know the world: it became the instrument by which the Church conquered the ancient world and educated the modern nations. But this dogma—one cannot but admire its formation or fail to regard it as a great achievement of the spirit, which never again in the history of Christianity has made itself at home with such freedom and boldness in religion—is the product of a comparatively long history which needs to be deciphered; for it is obscured by the completed dogma. The Gospel itself is not dogma, for belief in the Gospel provides room for knowledge only so far as it is a state of feeling and

course of action, that is a definite form of life. Between
practical faith in the Gospel and the historico-critical account
of the Christian religion and its history, a third element can
no longer be thrust in without its coming into conflict with
faith, or with the historical data—the only thing left is the
practical task of defending the faith. But a third element
has been thrust into the history of this religion, viz., dogma,
that is, the philosophical means which were used in early
times for the purpose of making the Gospel intelligible
have been fused with the contents óf the Gospel and raised
to dogma. This dogma, next to the Church, has become a
real world power, the pivot in the history of the Christian
religion. The transformation of the Christian faith into dogma
is indeed no accident, but has its reason in the spiritual character of the Christian religion, which at all times will feel the
need of a scientific apologetic. [1] But the question here is not
as to something indefinite and general, but as to the definite
dogma formed in the first centuries, and binding even yet.

This already touches on the second objection which was
raised above, that dogma, in the given sense of the word, was
too narrowly conceived, and could not in this conception be
applied throughout the whole history of the Church. This
objection would only be justified, if our task were to carry
the history of the development of dogma through the whole
history of the Church. But the question is just whether we
are right in proposing such a task. The Greek Church has
no history of dogma after the seven great Councils, and it is
incomparably more important to recognise this fact than to

---

[1] Weizsäcker, Apostolic Age, Vol. I. p. 123. "Christianity as religion is
absolutely inconceivable without theology; first of all, for the same reasons which
called forth the Pauline theology. As a religion it cannot be separated from the
religion of its founder, hence not from historical knowledge. And as Monotheism
and belief in a world purpose, it is the religion of reason with the inextinguish-
able impulse of thought. The first gentile Christians therewith gained the proud
consciousness of a gnosis." But of ecclesiastical Christianity which rests on dogma
ready made, as produced by an earlier epoch, this conception holds good only in
a very qualified way; and of the vigorous Christian piety of the earliest and of
every period, it may also be said that it no less feels the impulse to think against
reason than with reason.

register the theologoumena which were later on introduced by individual Bishops and scholars in the East, who were partly influenced by the West. Roman Catholicism in its dogmas, though, as noted above, these at present do not very clearly characterise it, is to-day essentially—that is, so far as it is religion—what it was 1500 years ago, viz., Christianity as understood by the ancient world. The changes which dogma has experienced in the course of its development in western Catholicism are certainly deep and radical: they have, in point of fact, as has been indicated in the text above, modified the position of the Church towards Christianity as dogma. But as the Catholic Church herself maintains that she adheres to Christianity in the old dogmatic sense, this claim of hers cannot be contested. She has embraced new things and changed her relations to the old, but still preserved the old. But she has further developed new dogmas according to the scheme of the old. The decrees of Trent and of the Vatican are formally analogous to the old dogmas. Here, then, a history of dogma may really be carried forward to the present day without thereby shewing that the definition of dogma given above is too narrow to embrace the new doctrines. Finally, as to Protestantism, it has been briefly explained above why the changes in Protestant systems of doctrine are not to be taken up into the history of dogma. Strictly speaking, dogma, as dogma, has had no development in Protestantism, inasmuch as a secret note of interrogation has been here associated with it from the very beginning. But the old dogma has continued to be a power in it, because of its tendency to look back and to seek for authorities in the past, and partly in the original unmodified form. The dogmas of the fourth and fifth centuries have more influence to-day in wide circles of Protestant Churches than all the doctrines which are concentrated around justification by faith. Deviations from the latter are borne comparatively easy, while as a rule, deviations from the former are followed by notice to quit the Christian communion, that is, by excommunication. The historian of to-day would have no difficulty in answering the question whether the power of Protestantism as a Church lies at present in the elements which it has in common with the old dogmatic Christianity, or in that by which it is distinguished from it. Dogma, that is to say, that type of Christianity which was formed in ecclesiastical antiquity, has not been suppressed even in Protestant Churches, has really not been modified or replaced by a new conception of the Gospel. But, on the other hand, who could deny that the Reformation began to disclose such a conception, and that this new conception was related in a very different way to the traditional dogma from that of the new propositions of Augustine to the dogmas handed down to him? Who could further call in question that, in consequence of the reforming impulse in Protestantism, the way was opened up for a conception which does not identify Gospel and dogma, which does not disfigure the latter by changing or paring down its meaning while failing to come up to the former? But the historian who has to describe the formation and changes of dogma can take no part in these developments. It is a task by itself more rich and comprehensive than that of the historian of dogma, to portray the diverse conceptions that have been formed of the Christian religion, to portray how strong men and weak men, great and little minds have explained the Gospel outside and inside the frame-work of dogma, and how under the cloak, or in the province of dogma, the Gospel has had its own peculiar history. But the more limited theme must not be put aside. For it can in no way be conducive to historical knowledge to regard as indifferent the peculiar character of the expression of Christian faith as dogma, and allow the history of dogma to be absorbed in a general history of the various conceptions of Christianity. Such a "liberal" view would not agree either with the teaching of history or with the actual situation of the Protestant Churches of the present day: for it is, above all, of crucial importance to perceive that it is a peculiar stage in the development of the human spirit which is described by dogma. On this stage, parallel with dogma and inwardly united with it, stands a definite psychology, metaphysic and natural philosophy, as well as a view of history of a definite type. This is the conception of the

world obtained by antiquity after almost a thousand years'
labour, and it is the same connection of theoretic perceptions
and practical ideals which it accomplished. This stage on
which the Christian religion has also entered we have in no
way as yet transcended, though science has raised itself above
it. [1] But the Christian religion, as it was not born of the culture of the ancient world, is not for ever chained to it. The
form and the new contents which the Gospel received when
it entered into that world have only the same guarantee of
endurance as that world itself. And that endurance is limited.
We must indeed be on our guard against taking episodes for
decisive crises. But every episode carries us forward, and
retrogressions are unable to undo that progress. The Gospel
since the Reformation, in spite of retrograde movements which
have not been wanting, is working itself out of the forms
which it was once compelled to assume, and a true comprehension of its history will also contribute to hasten this process.

1. The definition given above, p. 17: "Dogma in its conception and development is a work of the Greek spirit on
the soil of the Gospel," has frequently been distorted by my
critics, as they have suppressed the words "on the soil of the
Gospel." But these words are decisive. The foolishness of
identifying dogma and Greek philosophy never entered my
mind; on the contrary, the peculiarity of ecclesiastical dogma
seemed to me to lie in the very fact that, on the one hand,
it gave expression to Christian Monotheism and the central
significance of the person of Christ, and, on the other hand,
comprehended this religious faith and the historical knowledge

[1] In this sense it is correct to class dogmatic theology as historical theology,
as Schleiermacher has done. If we maintain that for practical reasons it must be
taken out of the province of historical theology, then we must make it part of
practical theology. By dogmatic theology here, we understand the exposition of
Christianity in the form of Church doctrine, as it has been shaped since the
second century. As distinguished from it, a branch of theological study must be
conceived which harmonises the historical exposition of the Gospel with the
general state of knowledge of the time. The Church can as little dispense with
such a discipline as there can be a Christianity which does not account to itself
for its basis and spiritual contents.

connected with it in a philosophic system. I have given quite as little ground for the accusation that I look upon the whole development of the history of dogma as a pathological process within the history of the Gospel. I do not even look upon the history of the origin of the Papacy as such a process, not to speak of the history of dogma. But the perception that "everything must happen as it has happened" does not absolve the historian from the task of ascertaining the powers which have formed the history, and distinguishing between original and later, permanent and transitory, nor from the duty of stating his own opinion.

2. Sabatier has published a thoughtful treatise on "Christian Dogma: its Nature and its Development," I agree with the author in this, that in dogma—rightly understood—two elements are to be distinguished, the religious proceeding from the experience of the individual or from the religious spirit of the Church, and the intellectual or theoretic. But I regard as false the statement which he makes, that the intellectual element in dogma is only the symbolical expression of religious experience. The intellectual element is itself again to be differentiated. On the one hand, it certainly is the attempt to give expression to religious feeling, and so far is symbolical; but, on the other hand, within the Christian religion it belongs to the essence of the thing itself, inasmuch as this not only awakens feeling, but has a quite definite content which determines and should determine the feeling. In this sense Christianity without dogma, that is, without a clear expression of its content, is inconceivable. But that does not justify the unchangeable permanent significance of that dogma which has once been formed under definite historical conditions.

3. The word "dogmas" (Christian dogmas) is, if I see correctly, used among us in three different senses, and hence spring all manner of misconceptions and errors. By dogmas are denoted: (1) The historical doctrines of the Church. (2) The historical facts on which the Christian religion is reputedly or actually founded. (3) Every definite exposition of the contents of Christianity is described as dogmatic. In contrast with this the attempt has been made in the following presentation to

use dogma only in the sense first stated.   When I speak, therefore, of the decomposition of dogma, I mean by that, neither the historical facts which really establish the Christian religion, nor do I call in question the necessity for the Christian and the Church to have a creed.   My criticism refers not to the general genus dogma, but to the species, viz., the defined dogma, as it was formed on the soil of the ancient world, and is still a power, though under modifications.

§ 2. *History of the History of Dogma.*

The history of dogma as a historical and critical discipline had its origin in the last century through the works of Mosheim, C. W. F. Walch, Ernesti, Lessing and Semler.   Lange gave to the world in 1796 the first attempt at a history of dogma as a special branch of theological study.   The theologians of the Early and Mediæval Churches have only transmitted histories of Heretics and of Literature, regarding dogma as unchangeable. [1] This presupposition is so much a part of the nature of Catholicism that it has been maintained till the present day.   It is there-fore impossible for a Catholic to make a free, impartial and scientific investigation of the history of dogma. [2]   There have, indeed, at almost all times before the Reformation, been critical efforts in the domain of Christianity, especially of western Christianity, efforts which in some cases have led to the proof

---

[1] See Eusebius' preface to his Church History. Eusebius in this work set himself a comprehensive task, but in doing so he never in the remotest sense thought of a history of dogma. In place of that we have a history of men "who from generation to generation proclaimed the word of God orally or by writing," and a history of those who by their passion for novelties, plunged themselves into the greatest errors.

[2] See for example, B. Schwane, Dogmengesch. d. Vornicänischen Zeit, 1862, where the sense in which dogmas have no historical side is first expounded, and then it is shewn that dogmas, "notwithstanding, present a certain side which permits a historical consideration, because in point of fact they have gone through historical developments." But these historical developments present themselves simply either as solemn promulgations and explications, or as private theological speculations.

of the novelty and inadmissibility of particular dogmas. But, as a rule, these efforts were of the nature of a polemic against the dominant Church. They scarcely prepared the way for, far less produced a historical view of, dogmatic tradition. [1] The progress of the sciences [2] and the conflict with Protestantism could here, for the Catholic Church, have no other effect than that of leading to the collecting, with great learning, of material for the history of dogma, [3] the establishing of the *consensus patrum et doctorum*, the exhibition of the necessity of a continuous explication of dogma, and the description of the history of heresies pressing in from without, regarded now as unheard-of novelties, and again as old enemies in new masks. The modern Jesuit-Catholic historian indeed exhibits, in certain circumstances, a manifest indifference to the task of establishing the *semper idem* in the faith of the Church, but this indifference is at present regarded with disfavour, and, besides, is only an apparent one, as the continuous though inscrutable

---

[1] If we leave out of account the Marcionite gnostic criticism of ecclesiastical Christianity, Paul of Samosata and Marcellus of Ancyra may be mentioned as men who, in the earliest period, criticised the apologetic Alexandrian theology which was being naturalised (see the remarkable statement of Marcellus in Euseb. C. Marc. i. 4: τὸ τοῦ δόγματος ὄνομα τῆς ἀνθρωπίνης ἔχεται βουλῆς τε καὶ γνώμης κ.τ.λ., which I have chosen as the motto of this book). We know too little of Stephen Gobarus (VI. cent.) to enable us to estimate his review of the doctrine of the Church and its development (Photius Bibl. 232). With regard to the middle ages (Abelard "Sic et Non"), see Reuter, Gesch. der relig. Aufklärung im MA., 1875. Hahn Gesch. der Ketzer, especially in the 11th, 12th and 13th centuries, 3 vols., 1845. Keller, Die Reformation und die alteren Reform-Parteien, 1885.

[2] See Voigt, Die Wiederbelebung des classischen Alterthums, 2 vols., 1881, especially vol. II. p. 1 ff. 363 ff. 494 ff. ("Humanism and the science of history"). The direct importance of humanism for illuminating the history of the middle ages is very little, and least of all for the history of the Church and of dogma. The only prominent works here are those of Saurentius Valla and Erasmus. The criticism of the scholastic dogmas of the Church and the Pope began as early as the 12th century. For the attitude of the Renaissance to religion, see Burckhardt, Die Cultur der Renaissance, 2 vols., 1877.

[3] Baronius, Annals Eccles. XII. vol. 1588-1607. Chief work: Dionysius Petavius, Opus de theologicis dogmatibus. 4 vols. (incomplete) 1644-1650. See further Thomassin, Dogmata theologica. 3 vols. 1684-1689.

guidance of the Church by the infallible teaching of the Pope
is the more emphatically maintained. [1]

It may be maintained that the Reformation opened the way
for a critical treatment of the history of dogma. [2] But even
in Protestant Churches, at first, historical investigations remained

[1] See Holtzmann, Kanon und Tradition, 1859. Hase, Handbuch der protest,
Polemik. 1878. Joh. Delitszch, Das Lehrsystem der röm. Kirche, 1875. New
revelations, however, are rejected, and bold assumptions leading that way are not
favoured: See Schwane, above work p. 11 : "The content of revelation is not
enlarged by the decisions or teaching of the Church, nor are new revelations added
in course of time.... Christian truth cannot therefore in its content be completed
by the Church, nor has she ever claimed the right of doing so, but always where
new designations or forms of dogma became necessary for the putting down of
error or the instruction of the faithful, she would always teach what she had
received in Holy Scripture or in the oral tradition of the Apostles." Recent
Catholic accounts of the history of dogma are Klee, Lehrbuch der D.G. 2 vols.
1837, (Speculative). Schwane, Dogmengesch. der Vornicänischen Zeit, 1862, der
patrist. Zeit, 1869; der Mittleren Zeit, 1882. Bach, Die D.G. des MA. 1873. There
is a wealth of material for the history of dogma in Kuhn's Dogmatik, as well as
in the great controversial writings occasioned by the celebrated work of Bellarmin;
Disputationes de controversiis Christianæ fidei adversus hujus temporis hæreticos,
1581–1593. It need not be said that, in spite of their inability to treat the history
of dogma historically and critically, much may be learned from these works, and
some other striking monographs of Roman Catholic scholars. But everything in
history that is fitted to shake the high antiquity and unanimous attestation of the
Catholic dogmas, becomes here a problem, the solution of which is demanded,
though indeed its carrying out often requires a very exceptional intellectual
subtlety.

[2] Historical interest in Protestantism has grown up around the questions as to
the power of the Pope, the significance of Councils, or the Scripturalness of the
doctrines set up by them, and about the meaning of the Lord's supper, of the
conception of it by the Church Fathers; (see Œcolampadius and Melanchthon.)
Protestants were too sure that the doctrine of justification was taught in the
scriptures to feel any need of seeking proofs for it by studies in the history of
dogma, and Luther also dispensed with the testimony of history for the dogma of
the Lord's supper. The task of shewing how far and in what way Luther and
the Reformers compounded with history has not even yet been taken up. And yet
there may be found in Luther's writings surprising and excellent critical comments
on the history of dogma and the theology of the Fathers, as well as genial conceptions which have certainly remained inoperative; see especially the treatise
"Von den Conciliis und Kirchen," and his judgment on different Church Fathers.
In the first edition of the *Loci* of Melanchthon we have also critical material for
estimating the old systems of dogma. Calvin's depreciatory estimate of the Trinitarian and Christological Formula, which, however, he retracted at a later period
is well known,

under the ban of the confessional system of doctrine and were used only for polemics.[1] Church history itself up to the 18th century was not regarded as a theological discipline in the strict sense of the word; and the history of dogma existed only within the sphere of dogmatics as a collection of testimonies to the truth, *theologia patristica*. It was only after the material had been prepared in the course of the 16th and 17th centuries by scholars of the various Church parties, and, above all, by excellent editions of the Fathers,[2] and after Pietism had exhibited the difference between Christianity and Ecclesiasticism, and had begun to treat the traditional confessional structure of doctrine with indifference,[3] that a critical investigation was entered on.

The man who was the Erasmus of the 18th century, neither orthodox nor pietistic, nor rationalistic, but capable of appreciating all these tendencies; familiar with English, French and Italian literature; influenced by the spirit of the new English

---

[1] Protestant Church history was brought into being by the Interim, Flacius being its Father; see his Catalogus Testium Veritatis, and the so-called Magdeburg Centuries, 1559–1574; also Jundt., Les Centuries de Magdebourg, Paris, 1883. Von Engelhardt (Christenthum Justin's, p. 9 ff.) has drawn attention to the estimate of Justin in the Centuries, and has justly insisted on the high importance of this first attempt at a criticism of the Church Fathers. Kliefoth (Einl. in d. D.G. 1839) has the merit of pointing out the somewhat striking judgment of A. Hyperius on the history of dogma. Chemnitz, Examen concilii Tridentini, 1565. Forbesius a Corse (a Scotsman). Instructiones historico-theologiæ de doctrina Christiana, 1645.

[2] The learning, the diligence in collecting, and the carefulness of the Benedictines and Maurians, as well as of English, Dutch and French theologians, such as Casaubon, Vossius, Pearson, Dalläus, Spanheim, Grabe, Basnage, etc. have never since been equalled, far less surpassed. Even in the literary, historical and higher criticism these scholars have done splendid work, so far as the confessional dogmas did not come into question.

[3] See especially, G. Arnold, Unpartheyische Kirchen- und Ketzerhistorie, 1699: also Baur, Epochen der kirchlichen Geschichtsschreibung, p. 84 ff.; Floring, G. Arnold als Kirchenhistoriker, Darmstadt, 1883. The latter determines correctly the measure of Arnold's importance. His work was the direct preparation for an impartial examination of the history of dogma, however partial it was in itself. Pietism, here and there, after Spener, declared war against scholastic dogmatics as a hindrance to piety, and in doing so broke the ban under which the knowledge of history lay captive.

Science,[1] while avoiding all statements of it that would endanger positive Christianity: John Lorenz Mosheim, treated Church history in the spirit of his great teacher Leibnitz,[2] and by impartial analysis, living reproduction, and methodical artistic form raised it for the first time to the rank of a science. In his monographic works also, he endeavours to examine impartially the history of dogma, and to acquire the historic standpoint between the estimate of the orthodox dogmatics and that of Gottfried Arnold. Mosheim, averse to all fault-finding and polemic, and abhorring theological crudity as much as pietistic narrowness and undevout Illuminism, aimed at an actual correct knowledge of history, in accordance with the principle of Leibnitz, that the valuable elements which are everywhere to be found in history must be sought out and recognised. And the richness and many-sidedness of his mind qualified him for gaining such a knowledge. But his latitudinarian dogmatic standpoint as well as the anxiety to awaken no controversy or endanger the gradual naturalising of a new science and culture, caused him to put aside the most important problems of the history of dogma and devote his attention to political Church history as well as to the more indifferent historical questions. The opposition of two periods which he endeavoured peacefully to reconcile could not in this way be permanently set aside.[3] In Mosheim's sense, but without the

[1] The investigations of the so-called English Deists about the Christian religion contain the first, and to some extent a very significant free-spirited attempt at a critical view of the history of dogma (see Lechler, History of English Deism, 1841). But the criticism is an abstract, rarely a historical one. Some very learned works bearing on the history of dogma were written in England against the position of the Deists, especially by Lardner : see also at an earlier time Bull, Defensio fidei nic.

[2] Calixtus of Helmstädt was the forerunner of Leibnitz with regard to Church history. But the merit of having recognised the main problem of the history of dogma does not belong to Calixtus. By pointing out what Protestantism and Catholicism had in common he did not in any way clear up the historical-critical problem. On the other hand the *Consensus repetitus* of the Wittenberg theologians shews what fundamental questions Calixtus had already stirred.

[3] Among the numerous historical writings of Mosheim may be mentioned specially his Dissert. ad hist. Eccles. pertinentes. 2 vols. 1731–1741, as well as the work: "De rebus Christianorum ante Constantinum M. Commentarii," 1753: see also "Institutiones hist. Eccl." last Edition, 1755.

spirit of that great man, C. W. F. Walch taught on the subject
and described the religious controversies of the Church with
an effort to be impartial, and has thus made generally accessible the abundant material collected by the diligence of earlier
scholars.[1] Walch, moreover, in the "Gedanken von der Geschichte der Glaubenslehre," 1756, gave the impulse that was
needed to fix attention on the history of dogma as a special
discipline. The stand-point which he took up was still that
of subjection to ecclesiastical dogma, but without confessional
narrowness. Ernesti in his programme of the year 1759, "De
theologiæ historicæ et dogmaticæ conjungendæ necessitate,"
gave eloquent expression to the idea that Dogmatic is a positive science which has to take its material from history, but
that history itself requires a devoted and candid study, on
account of our being separated from the earlier epochs by a
complicated tradition.[2] He has also shewn in his celebrated
"Antimuratorius," that an impartial and critical investigation
of the problems of the history of dogma, might render the
most effectual service to the polemic against the errors of
Romanism. Besides, the greater part of the dogmas were already
unintelligible to Ernesti, and yet during his lifetime the way
was opened up for that tendency in theology, which, prepared
in Germany by Chr. Thomasius, supported by English writers,
drew the sure principles of faith and life from what is called

---

[1] Walch, "Entwurf einer vollständigen Historie der Ketzereien, Spaltungen und
Religionsstreitigkeiten bis auf die Zeiten der Reformation." 11 Thle (incomplete),
1762–1785. See also his "Entwurf einer vollständigen Historie der Kirchenver-
sammlungen," 1759, as well as numerous monographs on the history of dogma.
Such were already produced by the older Walch, whose "Histor. theol. Einleitung
in die Religionsstreitigkeiten der Ev. Luth. Kirche," 5 vols. 1730–1739, and
"Histor.-theol. Einleit. in die Religionsstreitigkeiten welche sonderlich ausser der
Ev. Luth. Kirche entstanden sind 5 Thle," 1733–1736, had already put polemics
behind the knowledge of history (see Gass. "Gesch. der protest. Dogmatik," 3rd
Vol. p. 205 ff.).

[2] Opusc. p. 576 f.: "Ex quo fit, ut nullo modo in theologicis, quæ omnia e
libris antiquis hebraicis, græcis, latinis ducuntur, possit aliquis bene in definiendo
versari et a peccatis multis et magnis sibi cavere, nisi litteras et historiam assumat."
The title of a programme of Crusius, Ernesti's opponent, "De dogmatum Christianorum historia cum probatione dogmatum non confundenda," 1770, is significant
of the new insight which was steadily making way.

reason, and therefore was not only indifferent to the system of dogma, but felt it more and more to be the tradition of unreason and of darkness. Of the three requisites of a historian; knowledge of his subject, candid criticism, and a capacity for finding himself at home in foreign interests and ideas, the Rationalistic Theologians who had outgrown Pietism and passed through the school of the English Deists and of Wolf, no longer possessed the first, a knowledge of the subject, to the same extent as some scholars of the earlier generation. The second, free criticism, they possessed in the high degree guaranteed by the conviction of having a rational religion; the third, the power of comprehension, only in a very limited measure. They had lost the idea of positive religion, and with it a living and just conception of the history of religion.

In the history of thought there is always need for an apparently disproportionate expenditure of power, in order to produce an advance in the development. And it would appear as if a certain self-satisfied narrow-mindedness within the progressing ideas of the present, as well as a great measure of inability even to understand the past and recognise its own dependence on it, must make its appearance, in order that a whole generation may be freed from the burden of the past. It needed the absolute certainty which Rationalism had found in the religious philosophy of the age, to give sufficient courage to subject to historical criticism the central dogmas on which the Protestant system as well as the Catholic finally rests, the dogmas of the canon and inspiration on the one hand, and of the Trinity and Christology on the other. The work of Lessing in this respect had no great results. We to-day see in his theological writings the most important contribution to the understanding of the earliest history of dogma, which that period supplies; but we also understand why its results were then so trifling. This was due, not only to the fact that Lessing was no theologian by profession, or that his historical observations were couched in aphorisms, but because, like Leibnitz and Mosheim, he had a capacity for appreciating the history of religion which forbade him to do violence to that history or to sit in judgment on it, and because his philosophy in its bearings on the case allowed him to seek no more from his materials than an assured understanding of them; in a word again, because he was no theologian. The Rationalists, on the other hand, who within certain limits were no less his opponents than the orthodox, derived the strength of their opposition to the systems of dogma, as the Apologists of the second century had already done with regard to polytheism, from their religious belief and their inability to estimate these systems historically. That, however, is only the first impression which one gets here from the history, and it is everywhere modified by other impressions. In the first place, there is no mistaking a certain latitudinarianism in several prominent theologians of the rationalistic tendency. Moreover, the attitude to the canon was still frequently, in virtue of the Protestant principle of scripture, an uncertain one, and it was here chiefly that the different types of rational supernaturalism were developed. Then, with all subjection to the dogmas of Natural religion, the desire for a real true knowledge was unfettered and powerfully excited. Finally, very significant attempts were made by some rationalistic theologians to explain in a real historical way the phenomena of the history of dogma, and to put an authentic and historical view of that history in the place of barren pragmatic or philosophic categories.

The special zeal with which the older rationalism applied itself to the investigation of the canon, either putting aside the history of dogma, or treating it merely in the frame-work of Church history, has only been of advantage for the treatment of our subject. It first began to be treated with thoroughness when the historical and critical interests had become more powerful than the rationalistic. After the important labours of Semler, which here, above all, have wrought in the interests of freedom,[1] and after some monographs on the history

---

[1] Semler, Einleitung zu Baumgartens evang. Glaubenslehre, 1759: also Geschichte der Glaubenslehre, zu Baumgartens Untersuch. theol. Streitigkesten, 1762-1764. Semler paved the way for the view that dogmas have arisen and been gradually developed under definite historical conditions. He was the first to grasp the problem of the relation of Catholicism to early Christianity, because he freed the early Christian documents from the letters of the Canon. Schröckh (Christl.

of dogma, [1] S. G. Lange for the first time treated the history
of dogma as a special subject. [2] Unfortunately, his compre-
hensively planned and carefully written work, which shews a
real understanding of the early history of dogma, remains incomplete. Consequently, W. Münscher, in his learned manual,
which was soon followed by his compendium of the history
of dogma, was the first to produce a complete presentation
of our subject. [3] Münscher's compendium is a counterpart
to Giesler's Church history; it shares with that the merit of
drawing from the sources, intelligent criticism and impartiality,
but with a thorough knowledge of details it fails to impart
a real conception of the development of ecclesiastical dogma.
The division of the material into particular *loci*, which, in three
sections, is carried through the whole history of the Church,
makes insight into the whole Christian conception of the different epochs impossible, and the prefixed "General History

Kirchengesch., 1786) in the spirit of Semler described with impartiality and care
the changes of the dogmas.

[1] Rössler, Lehrbegriff der Christlichen Kirche in den 3 ersten Jahrb., 1775;
also, Arbeiten by Burscher, Heinrich, Stäudlin, etc., see especially, Löffler's "Ab-
handlung welche eine kurze Darstellung der Entstehungsart der Dreieinigkeit
enthält, 1792, in the translation of Souverain's Le Platonisme devoilé, 1700. The
question as to the Platonism of the Fathers, this fundamental question of the
history of dogma, was raised even by Luther and Flacius, and was very vigorously
debated at the end of the 17th and beginning of the 18th centuries, after the
Socinians had already affirmed it strongly. The question once more emerges on
German soil in the church history of G. Arnold, but cannot be said to have
received the attention it deserves in the 150 years that have followed (see the
literature of the controversy in Tzschirner, Fall des Heidenthums, p. 580 f.). Yet
the problem was first thrust aside by the speculative view of the history of
christianity.

[2] Lange. Ausführ. Gesch. der Dogmen, oder der Glaubenslehre der Christl.
Kirche nach den Kirchenväter ausgearbeitet. 1796.

[3] Münscher, Handb. d. Christl. D. G. 4 vols. first 6 Centuries 1797–1809; Lehrbuch, 1st Edit. 1811; 3rd Edit. edited by v. Cölln, Hupfeld and Neudecker, 1832–
1838. Planck's epoch-making work: Gesch. der Veränderungen und der Bildung
unseres protestantischen Lehrbegriffs. 6 vols. 1791–1800, had already for the most
part appeared. Contemporary with Münscher are Wundemann, Gesch. d. Christl.
Glaubenslehren vom Zeitalter des Athanasius bis auf Gregor. d. Gr. 2 Thle.
1789–1799; Münter, Handbuch der alteren Christl. D. G. hrsg. von Ewers. 2 vols.
1802–1804; Stäudlin, Lehrbuch der Dogmatik und Dogmengeschichte, 1800, last
Edition 1822, and Beck, Comment. hist. decretorum religionis Christianæ, 1801.

of Dogma," is far too sketchily treated to make up for that
defect. Finally, the connection between the development of
dogma and the general ideas of the time is not sufficiently
attended to. A series of manuals followed the work of Münscher, but did not materially advance the study.[1] The compendium of Baumgarten Crusius,[2] and that of F. K. Meier,[3]
stand out prominently among them. The work of the former
is distinguished by its independent learning as well as by the
discernment of the author that the centre of gravity of the
subject lies in the so-called general history of dogma.[4] The
work of Meier goes still further, and accurately perceives that
the division into a general and special history of dogma must
be altogether given up, while it is also characterised by an
accurate setting and proportional arrangement of the facts.[5]

The great spiritual revolution at the beginning of our century, which must in every respect be regarded as a reaction
against the efforts of the rationalistic epoch, changed also the
conceptions of the Christian religion and its history. It appears
therefore plainly in the treatment of the history of dogma.
The advancement and deepening of Christian life, the zealous

[1] Augusti, Lehrb. d. Christl. D. G. 1805. 4 Edit. 1835. Berthold, Handb. der
D. G. 2 vols. 1822-1823. Schickedanz, Versuch einer Gesch. d. Christl. Glaubens-
lehre, etc. 1827. Rüperti, Geschichte der Dogmen, 1831. Lenz, Gesch. der Christl.
Dogmen. 2 parts. 1834-1835. J. G. V. Engelhardt, Dogmengesch. 1839. See also
Giesler, Dogmengesch. 2 vols. edited by Redepenning, 1855: also Illgen, Ueber
den Werth der Christl. D. G. 1817.

[2] Baumgarten Crusius, Lehrb. d. Christl. D. G. 1852: also conpendium d. Christl.
D. G. 2 parts 1830-1846, the second part edited by Hase.

[3] Meier, Lehrb. d. D. G, 1840, 2nd Edit. revised by G. Baur 1854.

[4] The "Special History of Dogma," in Baumgarten Crusius, in which every
particular dogma is by itself pursued through the whole history of the Church, is
of course entirely unfruitful But even the opinions which are given in the
"General History of Dogma," are frequently very far from the mark (Cf. *e.g.*, § 14
and p. 67), which is the more surprising as no one can deny that he takes a
scholarly view of history.

[5] Meier's Lehrbuch is formally and materially a very important piece of work,
the value of which has not been sufficiently recognised, because the author followed
neither the track of Neander nor of Bauer. Besides the excellences noted in the
text, may be further mentioned, that almost everywhere Meier has distinguished
correctly between the history of dogma and the history of theology, and has given
an account only of the former.

study of the past, the new philosophy which no longer thrust
history aside, but endeavoured to appreciate it in all its phenomena as the history of the spirit, all these factors co-operated in begetting a new temper, and accordingly, a new
estimate of religion proper and of its history. There were
three tendencies in theology that broke up rationalism; that
which was identified with the names of Schleiermacher and
Neander, that of the Hegelians, and that of the Confession-
alists. The first two were soon divided into a right and a left,
in so far as they included conservative and critical interests
from their very commencement. The conservative elements
have been used for building up the modern confessionalism,
which in its endeavours to go back to the Reformers has never
actually got beyond the theology of the Formula of Concord,
the stringency of which it has no doubt abolished by new
theologoumena and concessions of all kinds. All these tendencies have in common the effort to gain a real comprehension of history and be taught by it, that is, to allow the idea
of development to obtain its proper place, and to comprehend
the power and sphere of the individual. In this and in the
deeper conception of the nature and significance of positive
religion, lay the advance beyond Rationalism. And yet the
wish to understand history, has in great measure checked the
effort to obtain a true knowledge of it, and the respect for
history as the greatest of teachers, has not resulted in that
supreme regard for facts which distinguished the critical rationalism. The speculative pragmatism, which, in the Hegelian
School, was put against the "lower pragmatism," and was
rigorously carried out with the view of exhibiting the unity
of history, not only neutralised the historical material, in so
far as its concrete definiteness was opposed, as phenomenon,
to the essence of the matter, but also curtailed it in a suspicious way, as may be seen, for example, in the works of
Baur. Moreover, the universal historical suggestions which the
older history of dogma had given were not at all, or only
very little regarded. The history of dogma was, as it were,
shut out by the watchword of the immanent development of
the spirit in Christianity. The disciples of Hegel, both of the

right and of the left, were, and still are, agreed in this watchword, [1] the working out of which, including an apology for the
course of the history of dogma, must be for the advancement
of conservative theology. But at the basis of the statement
that the history of Christianity is the history of the spirit,
there lay further a very one-sided conception of the nature
of religion, which confirmed the false idea that religion is
theology. It will always, however, be the imperishable merit
of Hegel's great disciple, F. Chr. Baur, in theology, that he
was the first who attempted to give a uniform general idea
of the history of dogma, and to live through the whole process
in himself, without renouncing the critical acquisitions of the
18th century. [2] His brilliantly written manual of the history of
dogma, in which the history of this branch of theological
science is relatively treated with the utmost detail, is, however,
in material very meagre, and shews in the very first proposition of the historical presentation an abstract view of history. [3]
Neander, whose "Christliche Dogmengeschichte," 1857, is distin-

---

[1] Biedermann (Christl. Dogmatik. 2 Edit. 1 vol. p. 332 f.) says, "The history
of the development of the Dogma of the Person of Christ will bring before us
step by step the ascent of faith in the Gospel of Jesus Christ to its metaphysical
basis in the nature of his person. This was the quite normal and necessary way
of actual faith, and is not to be reckoned as a confused mixture of heterogeneous
philosophical opinions. ... The only thing taken from the ideas of contemporary
philosophy was the special material of consciousness in which the doctrine of Christ's
Divinity was at any time expressed. The process of this doctrinal development
was an inward necessary one."

[2] Baur, Lehrbuch der Christl. D. G. 1847. 3rd Edit. 1867: also Vorles. über
die Christl. D. G. edited by F. Baur, 1865-68. Further the Monographs, "Ueber
die Christl. Lehre v. d. Versöhnung in ihrer gesch. Entw." 1838: Ueber die Christl.
Lehre v. d. Dreieinigkeit u. d. Menschwerdung." 1841: etc. D. F. Strauss, preceded
him with his work: Die Christl. Glaubenslehre in ihrer gesch. Entw. 2 vols. 1840-41.
From the stand-point of the Hegelian right we have: Marheineke, Christl. D. G.
edited by Matthias and Vatke, 1849. From the same stand-point, though at the
same time influenced by Schleiermacher, Dorner wrote "The History of the Person
of Christ."

[3] See p. 63: "As Christianity appeared in contrast with Judaism and Heathenism,
and could only represent a new and peculiar form of the religious consciousness
in distinction from both, reducing the contrasts of both to a unity in itself, so
also the first difference of tendencies developing themselves within Christianity,
must be determined by the relation in which it stood to Judaism on the one hand,
and to Heathenism on the other." Compare also the very characteristic introduction to the first volume of the "Vorlesungen."

guished by the variety of its points of view, and keen apprehension of particular forms of doctrine, shews a far more lively
and therefore a far more just conception of the Christian religion. But the general plan of the work, (General history of
dogma—*loci*, and these according to the established scheme),
proves that Neander has not succeeded in giving real expression to the historical character of the study, and in attaining
a clear insight into the progress of the development. [1]

Kliefoth's thoughtful and instructive, "Einleitung in die Dogmengeschichte," 1839, contains the programme for the conception of the history of dogma characteristic of the modern
confessional theology. In this work the Hegelian view of
history, not without being influenced by Schleiermacher, is
so represented as to legitimise a return to the theology of
the Fathers. In the successive great epochs of the Church
several circles of dogmas have been successively fixed, so
that the respective doctrines have each time been adequately formulated. [2] Disturbances of the development are due
to the influence of sin. Apart from this, Kliefoth's conception
is in point of form equal to that of Baur and Strauss, in so
far as they also have considered the theology represented by
themselves as the goal of the whole historical development.
The only distinction is that, according to them, the next following stage always cancels the preceding, while according to
Kliefoth, who, moreover, has no desire to give effect to mere
traditionalism, the new knowledge is added to the old. The
new edifice of true historical knowledge, according to Kliefoth,
is raised on the ruins of Traditionalism, Scholasticism, Pietism,
Rationalism and Mysticism. Thomasius (Das Bekenntniss der

---

[1] Hagenbach's Manual of the history of dogma, might be put alongside of
Neander's work. It agrees with it both in plan and spirit. But the material of
the history of dogma, which it offers in superabundance, seems far less connectedly
worked out than by Neander. In Shedd's history of Christian doctrine the Ameri-
cans possess a presentation of the history of dogma worth noting, 2 vols. 3 Edit.
1883. The work of Fr. Bonifas. Hist. des Dogmes. 2 vols. 1886, appeared after
the death of the author and is not important.

[2] No doubt Kliefoth also maintains for each period a stage of the disintegration
of dogma, but this is not to be understood in the ordinary sense of the word.
Besides, there are ideas in this introduction which would hardly obtain the approval
of their author to-day.

evang.-luth. Kirche in der Consequenz seines Princips, 1848) has, after the example of Sartorius, attempted to justify by history the Lutheran confessional system of doctrine from another side, by representing it as the true mean between Catholicism and the Reformed Spiritualism. This conception has found much approbation in the circles of Theologians related to Thomasius, as against the Union Theology. But Thomasius is entitled to the merit of having produced a Manual of the history of dogma which represents in the most worthy manner [1] the Lutheran confessional view of the history of dogma. The introduction, as well as the selection and arrangement of his material, shews that Thomasius has learned much from Baur. The way in which he distinguishes between central and peripheral dogmas is, accordingly, not very appropriate, especially for the earliest period. The question as to the origin of dogma and theology is scarcely even touched by him. But he has an impression that the central dogmas contain for every period the whole of Christianity, and that they must therefore be apprehended in this sense. [2] The presentation is dominated throughout by the idea of the self-explication of dogma, though a malformation has to be admitted for the middle ages, [3] and therefore the formation of dogma is almost everywhere justified as the testimony of the Church represented as completely hypostatised, and the outlook on the history of the time is put into the

[1] Thomasius' Die Christl. Dogmengesch. als Entwickel. Gesch des Kirchl. Lehrbegriffs. 2 vols. 1874-76. 2nd Edit. intelligently and carefully edited by Bonwetsch. and Seeberg, 1887. (Seeberg has produced almost a new work in vol. II.) From the same stand-point is the manual of the history of dogma by H. Schmid, 1859, (in the 4th Ed. revised and transformed into an excellent collection of passages from the sources by Hauck, 1887) as well as the Luther. Dogmatik (Vol. II. 1864: Der Kirchenglaube) of Kahnis, which, however, subjects particular dogmas to a freer criticism.

[2] See Vol. I. p. 14.

[3] See Vol. I. p. 11. " The first period treats of the development of the great main dogmas which were to become the basis of the further development (the Patristic age). The problem of the second period was, partly to work up this material theologically, and partly to develop it. But this development, under the influence of the Hierarchy, fell into false paths, and became partly, at least, corrupt (the age of Scholasticism), and therefore a reformation was necessary. It was reserved for this third period to carry back the doctrinal formation, which had become abnormal, to the old sound paths, and on the other hand, in virtue of the

background. But narrow and insufficient as the complete view
here is, the excellences of the work in details are great, in
respect of exemplary clearness of presentation, and the discriminating knowledge and keen comprehension of the author for
religious problems. The most important work done by Thomasius is contained in his account of the history of Christology.

In his outlines of the history of Christian dogma (Grundriss
der Christl. Dogmengesch. 1870), which unfortunately has not
been carried beyond the first part (Patristic period), F.
Nitzsch, marks an advance in the history of our subject. The
advance lies, on the one hand, in the extensive use he makes
of monographs on the history of dogma, and on the other
hand, in the arrangement. Nitzsch has advanced a long way
on the path that was first entered by F. K. Meier, and has
arranged his material in a way that far excels all earlier
attempts. The general and special aspects of the history of
dogma are here almost completely worked into one, [1] and in
the main divisions, "Grounding of the old Catholic Church doctrine," and "Development of the old Catholic Church doctrine,"
justice is at last done to the most important problem which
the history of dogma presents, though in my opinion the
division is not made at the right place, and the problem is
not so clearly kept in view in the execution as the arrangement would lead one to expect. [2] Nitzsch has freed himself
from that speculative view of the history of dogma which
reads ideas into it. No doubt idea and motive on the one
hand, form and expression on the other, must be distinguished
for every period. But the historian falls into vagueness as

regeneration of the Church which followed, to deepen it and fashion it according
to that form which it got in the doctrinal systems of the Evangelic Church, while
the remaining part fixed its own doctrine in the decrees of Trent (period of the
Reformation.)." This view of history, which from the Christian stand-point, will
allow absolutely nothing to be said against the doctrinal formation of the early
Church, is a retrogression from the view of Luther and the writers of the "Centuries," for these were well aware that the corruption did not first begin in the
middle ages.

[1] This fulfils a requirement urged by Weizsäcker (Jahrb. f. Deutsche Theol.
1866, p. 170 ff.).

[2] See Ritschl's Essay, "Ueber die Methode der älteren Dogmengeschichte"
(Jahrb. f. deutsche Theol. 1871. p. 191 ff.) in which the advance made by Nitzsch

soon as he seeks and professes to find behind the demonstrable
ideas and aims which have moved a period, others of which,
as a matter of fact, that period itself knew nothing at all.
Besides, the invariable result of that procedure is to concentrate the attention on the theological and philosophical points
of dogma, and either neglect or put a new construction on
the most concrete and important, the expression of the religious faith itself. Rationalism has been reproached with
"throwing out the child with the bath," but this is really
worse, for here the child is thrown out while the bath is

is estimated, and at the same time an arrangement proposed for the treatment of
the earlier history of dogma which would group the material more clearly and
more suitable than has been done by Nitzsch. After having laid the foundation
for a correct historical estimate of the development of early Christianity in his
work "Entstehung der Alt-Katholischen Kirche," 1857, Ritschl published an epoch-
making study in the history of dogma in his "History of the doctrine of justification and reconciliation," 2 edit. 1883. We have no superabundance of good
monographs on the history of dogma. There are few that give such exact information regarding the Patristic period as that of Von Engelhardt "Ueber das
Christenthum Justin's," 1878, and Zahn's work on Marcellus, 1867. Among the
investigators of our age, Renan above all has clearly recognised that there are
only two main periods in the history of dogma, and that the changes which
Christianity experienced after the establishment of the Catholic Church bear no
proportion to the changes which preceded. His words are as follows (Hist. des
origin. du Christianisme T. VII. p. 503 f.):—the division about the year 180 is
certainly placed too early, regard being had to what was then really authoritative
in the Church.—"Si nous comparons maintenant le Christianisme, tel qu'il exis-
tait vers l'an 180, au Christianisme du IVe et du Ve siècle, au Christianisme du
moyen âge, au Christianisme de nos jours, nous trouvons qu'en réalité il s'est
augmenté des très peu de chose dans les siècles qui ont suivis. En 180, le nouveau
Testament est clos: il ne s'y ajoutera plus un seul livre nouveau(?). Lentement,
les Épitres de Paul ont conquis leur place à la suite des Evangiles, dans le code
sacré et dans la liturgie. Quant aux dogmes, rien n'est fixé; mais le germe de
tout existe; presque aucune idée n'apparaitra qui ne puisse faire valoir des autorités
du 1er et du 2e siècle. Il y a du trop, il y a des contradictions; le travail théo-
logique consistera bien plus á émonder, à écarter des superfluités qu'à inventer du
nouveau. L'Église laissera tomber une foule de choses mal commencées, elle
sortira de bien des impasses. Elle a encore deux cœurs, pour ainsi dire; elle a
plusieurs têtes; ces anomalies tomberont; mais aucun dogme vraiment original ne
se formera plus." Also the discussions in chapter 28-34 of the same volume.
H. Thiersch (Die Kirche im Apostolischen Zeitalter, 1852) reveals a deep insight
into the difference between the spirit of the New Testament writers and the post-
Apostolic Fathers, but he has overdone these differences, and sought to explain
them by the mythological assumption of an Apostasy. A great amount of material
for the history of dogma may be found in the great work of Böhringer, Die Kirche
Christi und ihre Zeugen, oder die Kirchengeschichte in Biographien. 2 Edit. 1864.

retained. Every advance in the future treatment of our subject will further depend on the effort to comprehend the
history of dogma without reference to the momentary opinions
of the present, and also on keeping it in closest connection
with the history of the Church, from which it can never be
separated without damage. We have something to learn on
this point from rationalistic historians of dogma. [1] But progress
is finally dependent on a true perception of what the Christian
religion originally was, for this perception alone enables us to
distinguish that which sprang out of the inherent power of
Christianity from that which it has assimilated in the course
of its history. For the historian, however, who does not wish
to serve a party, there are two standards in accordance with

[1] By the connection with general church history we must, above all, understand,
a continuous regard to the world within which the church has been developed,
The most recent works on the history of the church and of dogma, those of Renan,
Overbeck (Anfänge der patristischen Litteratur). Aube, Von Engelhardt (Justin),
Kühn (Minucius Felix). Hatch ("Organization of the Early Church," and especially
his posthumous work "The influence of Greek ideas and usages upon the Christian
Church," 1890, in which may be found the most ample proof for the conception
of the early history of dogma which is set forth in the following pages), are in
this respect worthy of special note. Deserving of mention also is R. Rothe, who,
in his "Vorlesungen über Kirchengeschichte," edited by Weingarten," 1875, 2
vols., gave most significant suggestions towards a really historical conception of
the history of the church and of dogma. To Rothe belongs the undiminished
merit of realising thoroughly the significance of a nationality in church history.
But the theology of our century is also indebted for the first scientific conception
of Catholicism, not to Marheineke or Winer, but to Rothe (see Vol. II. pp. 1-11
especially ;p. 7 f.). "The development of the Christian Church in the Græco-
Roman world was not at the same time a development of that world by the Church
and further by Christianity. There remained, as the result of the process, nothing
but the completed Church. The world which had built it had made itself bank-
rupt in doing so." With regard to the origin and development of the Catholic
cultus and constitution, nay, even of the Ethic (see Luthardt, Die antike Ethik,
1887, preface), that has been recognised by Protestant scholars, which one always
hesitates to recognise with regard to catholic dogma: see the excellent remarks of
Schwegler, Nachapostolisches Zeitalter, Vol. 1. p. 3 ff. It may be hoped that an
intelligent consideration of early christian literature will form the bridge to a broad
and intelligent view of the history of dogma. The essay of Overbeck mentioned
above (Histor. Zeitschrift N. F. XII. p. 417 ff.) may be most heartily recommended
in this respect. It is very gratifying to find an investigator so conservative as
Sohm, now fully admitting that "Christian theology grew up in the second and
third centuries, when its foundations were laid for all time (?), the last great production of the Hellenic Spirit." (Kirchengeschichte im Grundriss. 1888, p. 37).
The same scholar in his very important Kirchenrecht. Bd. I. 1892. has transferred

which he may criticise the history of dogma. He may either, as far as this is possible, compare it with the Gospel, or he may judge it according to the historical conditions of the time and the result. Both ways can exist side by side, if only they are not mixed up with one another. Protestantism has in principle expressly recognised the first, and it will also have the power to bear its conclusions; for the saying of Tertullian still holds good in it; "Nihil veritas erubescit nisi solummodo abscondi." The historian who follows this maxim, and at the same time has no desire to be wiser than the facts, will, while furthering science, perform the best service also to every Christian community that desires to build itself upon the Gospel.

After the appearance of the first and second editions of this Work, Loofs published, "Leitfaden für seine Vorlesungen über Dogmengeschichte," Halle, 1889, and in the following year, "Leitfaden zum Studium der Dogmengeschichte, zunächst für seine Vorlesungen," (second and enlarged edition of the first-named book). The work in its conception of dogma and its history comes pretty near that stated above, and it is distinguished by independent investigation and excellent selection of material. I myself have published a "Grundriss der Dogmengeschichte," 2 Edit. in one vol. 1893. (Outlines of the History of Dogma, English translation. Hodder and Stoughton). That this has not been written in vain, I have the pleasure of seeing from not a few notices of professional colleagues. I may mention the Church history of Herzog in the new revision by Koffmane, the first vol. of the Church history of Karl Müller, the first vol. of the Symbolik of Kattenbusch, and Kaftan's work. "The truth of the Christian religion." Wilhelm Schmidt, "Der alte Glaube und die Wahrheit des Christenthums," 1891, has attempted to furnish a refutation in principle of Kaftan's work.

to the history of the origin of Church law and Church organization, the points of view which I have applied in the following account to the consideration of dogma. He has thereby succeeded in correcting many old errors and prejudices; but in my opinion he has obscured the truth by exaggerations connected with a conception, not only of original Christianity, but also of the Gospel in general, which is partly a narrow legal view, partly an enthusiastic one. He has arrived *ex errore per veritatem ad errorem;* but there are few books from which so much may be learned about early church history as from this paradoxical "Kirchenrecht."

CHAPTER II

§ 1. *Introductory.*

THE Gospel presents itself as an Apocalyptic message on the soil of the Old Testament, and as the fulfilment of the law and the prophets, and yet is a new thing, the creation of a universal religion on the basis of that of the Old Testament. It appeared when the time was fulfilled, that is, it is not without a connection with the stage of religious and spiritual development which was brought about by the intercourse of Jews and Greeks, and was established in the Roman Empire; but still it is a new religion because it cannot be separated from Jesus Christ. When the traditional religion has become too narrow the new religion usually appears as something of a very abstract nature; philosophy comes upon the scene, and religion withdraws from social life and becomes a private matter. But here an overpowering personality has appeared—the Son of God. Word and deed coincide in that personality, and as it leads men into a new communion with God, it unites them at the same time inseparably with itself, enables them to act on the world as light and leaven, and joins them together in a spiritual unity and an active confederacy.

2. Jesus Christ brought no new doctrine, but he set forth in his own person a holy life with God and before God, and gave himself in virtue of this life to the service of his brethren in order to win them for the Kingdom of God, that is, to lead them out of selfishness and the world to God, out of

the natural connections and contrasts to a union in love, and prepare them for an eternal kingdom and an eternal life. But while working for this Kingdom of God he did not withdraw from the religious and political communion of his people, nor did he induce his disciples to leave that communion. On the contrary, he described the Kingdom of God as the fulfilment of the promises given to the nation, and himself as the Messiah whom that nation expected. By doing so he secured for his new message, and with it his own person, a place in the system of religious ideas and hopes, which by means of the Old Testament were then, in diverse forms, current in the Jewish nation. The origin of a doctrine concerning the Messianic hope, in which the Messiah was no longer an unknown being, but Jesus of Nazareth, along with the new temper and disposition of believers was a direct result of the impression made by the person of Jesus. The conception of the Old Testament in accordance with the *analogia fidei*, that is, in accordance with the conviction that this Jesus of Nazareth is the Christ, was therewith given. Whatever sources of comfort and strength Christianity, even in its New Testament, has possessed or does possess up to the present, is for the most part taken from the Old Testament, viewed from a Christian stand-point, in virtue of the impression of the person of Jesus. Even its dross was changed into gold; its hidden treasures were brought forth, and while the earthly and transitory were recognised as symbols of the heavenly and eternal, there rose up a world of blessings, of holy ordinances, and of sure grace prepared by God from eternity. One could joyfully make oneself at home in it; for its long history guaranteed a sure future and a blessed close, while it offered comfort and certainty in all the changes of life to every individual heart that would only raise itself to God. From the positive position which Jesus took up towards the Old Testament, that is, towards the religious traditions of his people, his Gospel gained a footing which, later on, preserved it from dissolving in the glow of enthusiasm, or melting away in the ensnaring dream of antiquity, that dream of the indestructible Divine nature of the human spirit, and the nothingness and baseness of all material things.[1] But from the positive attitude of Jesus to the Jewish tradition, there followed also, for a generation that had long been accustomed to grope after the Divine active in the world, the summons to think out a theory of the media of revelation, and so put an end to the uncertainty with which speculation had hitherto been afflicted. This, like every theory of religion, concealed in itself the danger of crippling the power of faith ; for men are ever prone to compound with religion itself by a religious theory.

3. The result of the preaching of Jesus, however, in the case of the believing Jews, was not only the illumination of the Old Testament by the Gospel and the confirmation of the Gospel by the Old Testament, but not less, though indirectly, the detachment of believers from the religious community of the Jews from the Jewish Church. How this came about cannot be discussed here : we may satisfy ourselves with the fact that it was essentially accomplished in the first two generations of believers. The Gospel was a message for humanity even when there was no break with Judaism ; but it seemed impossible to bring this message home to men who were not Jews in any other way than by leaving the Jewish Church. But to leave that Church was to declare it to be worthless, and that could only be done by conceiving it as a malformation from its very commencement, or assuming that it had temporarily or completely fulfilled its mission. In either case it was necessary to put another in its place, for, according to the Old Testament, it was unquestionable that God had not only given revelations, but through these revelations had founded a nation, a religious community. The result, also, to which the conduct of the unbelieving Jews, and the social union of the disciples of Jesus required by that conduct, led, was carried home with irresistible power: be-

---

[1] The Old Testament of itself alone could not have convinced the Græco-Roman world. But the converse question might perhaps be raised as to what results the Gospel would have had in that world without its union with the Old Testament. The Gnostic Schools and the Marcionite Church are to some extent the answer. But would they ever have arisen without the presupposition of a Christian community which recognised the Old Testament?

lievers in Christ are the community of God, they are the true Israel, the ἐκκλησία τοῦ θεοῦ: but the Jewish Church persisting in its unbelief is the Synagogue of Satan. Out of this consciousness sprang—first as a power in which one believed, but which immediately began to be operative, though not as a commonwealth—the Christian Church, a special communion of hearts on the basis of a personal union with God, established by Christ and mediated by the Spirit; a communion whose essential mark was to claim as its own the Old Testament and the idea of being the people of God, to sweep aside the Jewish conception of the Old Testament and the Jewish Church, and thereby gain the shape and power of a community that is capable of a mission for the world.

4. This independent Christian community could not have been formed had not Judaism, in consequence of inner and outer developments, then reached a point at which it must either altogether cease to grow or burst its shell. This community is the presupposition of the history of dogma, and the position which it took up towards the Jewish tradition is, strictly speaking, the point of departure for all further developments, so far as with the removal of all national and ceremonial peculiarities it proclaimed itself to be what the Jewish Church wished to be. We find the Christian Church about the middle of the third century, after severe crisis, in nearly the same position to the Old Testament and to Judaism as it was 150 or 200 years earlier.[1] It makes the same claim to the Old Testament, and builds its faith and hope upon its teaching. It is also, as before, strictly anti-national; above all, antijudaic, and sentences the Jewish religious community to the abyss of hell. It might appear, then, as though the basis for the further development of Christianity as a church was completely given from the moment in which the first breach of believers with the synagogue and the formation of indepen-

---

[1] We here leave out of account learned attempts to expound Paulinism. Nor do we take any notice of certain truths regarding the relation of the Old Testament to the New, and regarding the Jewish religion, stated by the Antignostic church teachers, truths which are certainly very important, but have not been sufficiently utilised.

dent Christian communities took place. The problem, the solution of which will always exercise this church, so far as it reflects upon its faith, will be to turn the Old Testament more completely to account in its own sense, so as to condemn the Jewish Church with its particular and national forms.

5. But the rule even for the Christian use of the Old Testament lay originally in the living connection in which one stood with the Jewish people and its traditions, and a new religious community, a religious commonwealth, was not yet realised, although it existed for faith and thought. If again we compare the Church about the middle of the third century with the condition of Christendom 150 or 200 years before, we shall find that there is now a real religious commonwealth, while at the earlier period there were only communities who believed in a heavenly Church, whose earthly image they were, endeavoured to give it expression with the simplest means, and lived in the future as strangers and pilgrims on the earth, hastening to meet the Kingdom of whose existence they had the surest guarantee. We now really find a new commonwealth, politically formed and equipped with fixed forms of all kinds. We recognise in these forms few Jewish, but many Græco-Roman features, and finally we perceive also in the doctrine of faith on which this commonwealth is based, the philosophic spirit of the Greeks. We find a Church as a political union and worship institute, a formulated faith and a sacred learning; but one thing we no longer find, the old enthusiasm and individualism which had not felt itself fettered by subjection to the authority of the Old Testament. Instead of enthusiastic independent Christians, we find a new literature of revelation, the New Testament, and Christian priests. When did these formations begin? How and by what influence was the living faith transformed into the creed to be believed, the surrender to Christ into a philosophic Christology, the Holy Church into the *corpus permixtum*, the glowing hope of the Kingdom of heaven into a doctrine of immortality and deification, prophecy into a learned exegesis and theological science, the bearers of the spirit into clerics, the brethren into laity held in tutelage, miracles and

healings into nothing or into priestcraft, the fervent prayers into a solemn ritual, renunciation of the world into a jealous dominion over the world, the "spirit" into constraint and law?

There can be no doubt about the answer: these formations are as old in their origin as the detachment of the Gospel from the Jewish Church. A religious faith which seeks to establish a communion of its own in opposition to another, is compelled to borrow from that other what it needs. The religion which is life and feeling of the heart cannot be converted into a knowledge determining the motley multitude of men without deferring to their wishes and opinions. Even the holiest must clothe itself in the same existing earthly forms as the profane if it wishes to found on earth a confederacy which is to take the place of another, and if it does not wish to enslave, but to determine the reason. When the Gospel was rejected by the Jewish nation, and had disengaged itself from all connection with that nation, it was already settled whence it must take the material to form for itself a new body and be transformed into a Church and a theology. National and particular, in the ordinary sense of the word, these forms could not be: the contents of the Gospel were too rich for that; but separated from Judaism, nay, even before that separation, the Christian religion came in contact with the Roman world and with a culture which had already mastered the world, viz., the Greek. The Christian Church and its doctrine were developed within the Roman world and Greek culture in opposition to the Jewish Church. This fact is just as important for the history of dogma as the other stated above, that this Church was continuously nourished on the Old Testament. Christendom was of course conscious of being in opposition to the empire and its culture, as well as to Judaism; but this from the beginning—apart from a few exceptions—was not without reservations. No man can serve two masters; but in setting up a spiritual power in this world one must serve an earthly master, even when he desires to naturalise the spiritual in the world. As a consequence of the complete break with the Jewish Church there followed not only the strict necessity of quarrying the stones for the building of the Church from the Græco-Roman world, but also the idea that Christianity has a more positive relation to that world than to the synagogue. And, as the Church was being built, the original enthusiasm must needs vanish. The separation from Judaism having taken place, it was necessary that the spirit of another people should be admitted, and should also materially determine the manner of turning the Old Testament to advantage.

6. But an inner necessity was at work here no less than an outer. Judaism and Hellenism in the age of Christ were opposed to each other, not only as dissimilar powers of equal value, but the latter having its origin among a small people, became a universal spiritual power, which, severed from its original nationality, had for that very reason penetrated foreign nations. It had even laid hold of Judaism, and the anxious care of her professional watchmen to hedge round the national possession, is but a proof of the advancing decomposition within the Jewish nation. Israel, no doubt, had a sacred treasure which was of greater value than all the treasures of the Greeks,—the living God; but in what miserable vessels was this treasure preserved, and how much inferior was all else possessed by this nation in comparison with the riches, the power, the delicacy and freedom of the Greek spirit and its intellectual possessions. A movement like that of Christianity, which discovered to the Jew the soul whose dignity was not dependent on its descent from Abraham, but on its responsibility to God, could not continue in the framework of Judaism however expanded, but must soon recognise in that world which the Greek spirit had discovered and prepared, the field which belonged to it: εἰκότως Ἰουδαίοις μὲν νόμος, Ἕλλεσι δὲ φιλοσοφία μέχρις τῆς παρουσίας ἐντεῦθεν δὲ ἡ κλῆσις ἡ καθολική [to the Jews the law, to the Greeks Philosophy, up to the Parousia; from that time the catholic invitation]. But the Gospel at first was preached exclusively to the lost sheep of the house of Israel, and that which inwardly united it with Hellenism did not yet appear in any doctrine or definite form of knowledge.

On the contrary, the Church doctrine of faith, in the preparatory

stage, from the Apologists up to the time of Origen, hardly
in any point shews the traces, scarcely even the remembrance
of a time in which the Gospel was not detached from Judaism.
For that very reason it is absolutely impossible to understand
this preparation and development solely from the writings that
remain to us as monuments of that short earliest period. The
attempts at deducing the genesis of the Church's doctrinal
system from the theology of Paul, or from compromises
between Apostolic doctrinal ideas, will always miscarry;
for they fail to note that to the most important premises
of the Catholic doctrine of faith belongs an element which
we cannot recognise as dominant in the New Testament. [1]

[1] There is indeed no single writing of the new Testament which does not
betray the influence of the mode of thought and general conditions of the culture
of the time which resulted from the Hellenising of the east: even the use of the
Greek translation of the Old Testament attests this fact. Nay, we may go further,
and say that the Gospel itself is historically unintelligible, so long as we compare
it with an exclusive Judaism as yet unaffected by any foreign influence. But on
the other hand, it is just as clear that, specifically, Hellenic ideas form the presuppositions neither for the Gospel itself, nor for the most important New Testament writings. It is a question rather as to a general spiritual atmosphere created
by Hellenism, which above all strengthened the individual element, and with it
the idea of completed personality, in itself living and responsible. On this foundation we meet with a religious mode of thought in the Gospel and the early
Christian writings, which so far as it is at all dependent on an earlier mode of
thought, is determined by the spirit of the Old Testament (Psalms and Prophets)
and of Judaism. But it is already otherwise with the earliest Gentile Christian
writings. The mode of thought here is so thoroughly determined by the Hellenic
spirit that we seem to have entered a new world when we pass from the synoptists, Paul and John, to Clement, Barnabas, Justin or Valentinus. We may therefore
say, especially in the frame-work of the history of dogma, that the Hellenic element has exercised an influence on the Gospel first on Gentile Christian soil, and
by those who were Greek by birth, if only we reserve the general spiritual
atmosphere above referred to. Even Paul is no exception; for in spite of the
well-founded statement of Weizsäcker (Apostolic Age, vol. I. Book 11) and Heinrici
(Das 2 Sendschreiben an die Korinthier, 1887, p. 578 ff.), as to the Hellenism of
Paul, it is certain that the Apostle's mode of religious thought, in the strict sense
of the word, and therefore also the doctrinal formation peculiar to him, are but
little determined by the Greek spirit. But it is to be specially noted that as a
missionary and an Apologist he made use of Greek ideas (Epistles to the Romans
and Corinthians). He was not afraid to put the Gospel into Greek modes of
thought. To this extent we can already observe in him the beginning of the
development which we can trace so clearly in the Gentile Church from Clement
to Justin, and from Justin to Irenæus.

viz., the Hellenic spirit. [1] As far backwards as we can trace
the history of the propagation of the Church's doctrine of
faith, from the middle of the third century to the end of the
first, we nowhere perceive a leap, or the sudden influx of an
entirely new element. What we perceive is rather the gradual disappearance of an original element, the Enthusiastic
and Apocalyptic, that is, of the sure consciousness of an immediate possession of the Divine Spirit, and the hope of the
future conquering the present; individual piety conscious of
itself and sovereign, living in the future world, recognising no
external authority and no external barriers. This piety became
ever weaker and passed away: the utilising of the Codex of
Revelation, the Old Testament, proportionally increased with
the Hellenic influences which controlled the process, for the
two went always hand in hand. At an earlier period the
Churches made very little use of either, because they had in
individual religious inspiration on the basis of Christ's preaching
and the sure hope of his Kingdom which was near at hand,
much more than either could bestow. The factors whose

---

[1] The complete universalism of salvation is given in the Pauline conception of
Christianity. But this conception is singular. Because: (1) the Pauline universalism
is based on a criticism of the Jewish religion as religion, including the Old Testament, which was not understood and therefore not received by Christendom in
general. (2) Because Paul not only formulated no national anti-judaism, but always
recognised the prerogative of the people of Israel as a people. (3) Because his
idea of the Gospel, with all his Greek culture, is independent of Hellenism in its
deepest grounds. This peculiarity of the Pauline Gospel is the reason why little
more could pass from it into the common consciousness of Christendom than the
universalism of salvation, and why the later development of the Church cannot
be explained from Paulinism. Baur, therefore, was quite right when he recognised
that we must exhibit another and more powerful element in order to comprehend
the post-Pauline formations. In the selection of this element, however, he has
made a fundamental mistake by introducing the narrow national Jewish Christianity,
and he has also given much too great scope to Paulinism by wrongly conceiving
it as Gentile Christian doctrine. One great difficulty for the historian of the
early Church is that he cannot start from Paulinism, the plainest phenomenon of
the Apostolic age, in seeking to explain the following development, that in fact
the premises for this development are not at all capable of being indicated in the
form of outlines, just because they were too general. But, on the other hand, the
Pauline theology, this theology of one who had been a Pharisee, is the strongest
proof of the independent and universal power of the impression made by the
Person of Jesus.

co-operation we observe in the second and third centuries, were already operative among the earliest Gentile Christians. We nowhere find a yawning gulf in the great development which lies between the first Epistle of Clement and the work of Origen, Περὶ ἀρχῶν. Even the importance which the "Apostolic" was to obtain, was already foreshadowed by the end of the first century, and enthusiasm always had its limits. [1] The most decisive division, therefore, falls before the end of the first century; or more correctly, the relatively new element, the Greek, which is of importance for the forming of the Church as a commonwealth, and consequently for the formation of its doctrine, is clearly present in the churches even in the Apostolic age. Two hundred years, however, passed before it made itself completely at home in the Gospel, although there were points of connection inherent in the Gospel.

7. The cause of the great historical fact is clear. It is given in the fact that the Gospel, rejected by the majority of the Jews, was very soon proclaimed to those who were not Jews, that after a few decades the greater number of its professors were found among the Greeks, and that, consequently. the development leading to the Catholic dogma took place within Græco-Roman culture. But within this culture there was lacking the power of understanding either the idea of the completed Old Testament theocracy, or the idea of the Mes-

---

[1] In the main writings of the New Testament itself we have a twofold conception of the Spirit. According to the one he comes upon the believer fitfully, expresses himself in visible signs, deprives men of self-consciousness, and puts them beside themselves. According to the other, the spirit is a constant possession of the Christian, operates in him by enlightening the conscience and strengthening the character, and his fruits are love, joy, peace, patience, gentleness, etc. (Gal. V. 22). Paul above all taught Christians to value these fruits of the spirit higher than all the other effects of his working. But he has not by any means produced a perfectly clear view on this point: for "he himself spoke with more tongues than they all." As yet "Spirit" lay within "Spirit." One felt in the spirit of sonship a completely new gift coming from God and recreating life, a miracle of God; further, this spirit also produced sudden exclamations—"Abba, Father;" and thus shewed himself in a way patent to the senses. For that very reason, the spirit of ecstasy and of miracle appeared identical with the spirit of sonship. (See Gunkel, Die Wirkungen d. h. Geistes nach der populären Anschauung der Apostol. Zeit. Zeit. Göttingen, 1888).

siah. Both of these essential elements of the original proclamation, therefore, must either be neglected or remodelled. [1]
But it is hardly allowable to mention details however important, where the whole aggregate of ideas, of religious historical
perceptions and presuppositions, which were based on the old
Testament, understood in a Christian sense, presented itself
as something new and strange. One can easily appropriate
words, but not practical ideas. Side by side with the Old
Testament religion as the presupposition of the Gospel, and
using its forms of thought, the moral and religious views and
ideals dominant in the world of Greek culture could not but
insinuate themselves into the communities consisting of Gentiles. From the enormous material that was brought home
to the hearts of the Greeks, whether formulated by Paul
or by any other, only a few rudimentary ideas could at first
be appropriated. For that very reason, the Apostolic Catholic
doctrine of faith in its preparation and establishment, is no
mere continuation of that which, by uniting things that are
certainly very dissimilar, is wont to be described as "Biblical
Theology of the New Testament." Biblical Theology, even
when kept within reasonable limits, is not the presupposition of
the history of dogma. The Gentile Christians were little able
to comprehend the controversies which stirred the Apostolic age
within Jewish Christianity. The presuppositions of the history
of dogma are given in certain fundamental ideas, or rather
motives of the Gospel, (in the preaching concerning Jesus
Christ, in the teaching of Evangelic ethics and the future
life, in the Old Testament capable of any interpretation, but
to be interpreted with reference to Christ and the Evangelic
history), and in the Greek spirit. [2]

8. The foregoing statements involve that the difference

---

[1] It may even be said here that the ἀθανασία (ζωὴ αἰώνιος), on the one hand,
and the ἐκκλησία, on the other, have already appeared in place of the Βασιλεία
τοῦ θεοῦ, and that the idea of Messiah has been finally replaced by that of the
Divine Teacher and of God manifest in the flesh.

[2] It is one of the merits of Bruno Bauer (Christus und die Cäsaren, 1877),
that he has appreciated the real significance of the Greek element in the Gentile
Christianity which became the Catholic Church and doctrine, and that he has

between the development which led to the Catholic doctrine of religion and the original condition, was by no means a total one. By recognising the Old Testament as a book of Divine revelation, the Gentile Christians received along with it the religious speech which was used by Jewish Christians, were made dependent upon the interpretation which had been used from the very beginning, and even received a great part of the Jewish literature which accompanied the Old Testament. But the possession of a common religious speech and literature is never a mere outward bond of union, however strong the impulse be to introduce the old familiar contents into the newly acquired speech. The Jewish, that is, the Old Testament element, divested of its national peculiarity, has remained the basis of Christendom. It has saturated this element with

appreciated the influence of the Judaism of the Diaspora as a preparation for this Gentile Christianity. But these valuable contributions have unfortunately been deprived of their convincing power by a baseless criticism of the early Christian literature, to which Christ and Paul have fallen a sacrifice. Somewhat more cautious are the investigations of Havet in the fourth volume of Le Christianisme, 1884; Le Nouveau Testament. He has won great merit by the correct interpretation of the elements of Gentile Christianity developing themselves to catholicism, but his literary criticism is often unfortunately entirely abstract, reminding one of the criticism of Voltaire, and therefore his statements in detail are, as a rule, arbitrary and untenable. There is a school in Holland at the present time closely related to Bruno Bauer and Havet, which attempts to banish early Christianity from the world. Christ and Paul are creations of the second century: the history of Christianity begins with the passage of the first century into the second—a peculiar phenomenon on the soil of Hellenised Judaism in quest of a Messiah. This Judaism created Jesus Christ just as the later Greek religious philosophers created their Saviour (Apollonius, for example). The Marcionite Church produced Paul, and the growing Catholic Church completed him. See the numerous treatises of Loman, the Verisimilia of Pierson and Naber (1886), and the anonymous English work "Antiqua Mater" (1887), also the works of Steck (see especially his Untersuchung über den Galaterbrief). Against these works see P. V. Schmidt's "Der Galaterbrief," 1892. It requires a deep knowledge of the problems which the first two centuries of the Christian Church present, in order not to thrust aside as simply absurd these attempts, which as yet have failed to deal with the subject in a connected way. They have their strength in the difficulties and riddles which are contained in the history of the formation of the Catholic tradition in the second century. But the single circumstance that we are asked to regard as a forgery such a document as the first Epistle of Paul to the Corinthians, appears to me, of itself, to be an unanswerable argument against the new hypotheses.

the Greek spirit, but has always clung to its main idea, faith in
God as the creator and ruler of the world. It has in the
course of its development rejected important parts of that
Jewish element, and has borrowed others at a later period
from the great treasure that was transmitted to it. It has
also been able to turn to account the least adaptable features,
if only for the external confirmation of its own ideas. The Old
Testament applied to Christ and his universal Church has
always remained the decisive document, and it was long ere
Christian writings received the same authority, long ere individual doctrines and sayings of Apostolic writings obtained
an influence on the formation of ecclesiastical doctrine.

9. From yet another side there makes its appearance an
agreement between the circles of Palestinian believers in Jesus
and the Gentile Christian communities, which endured for
more than a century, though it was of course gradually effaced.
It is the enthusiastic element which unites them, the consciousness
of standing in an immediate union with God through the Spirit,
and receiving directly from God's hand miraculous gifts, powers
and revelations, granted to the individual that he may turn
them to account in the service of the Church. The depoten-
tiation of the Christian religion, where one may believe in the
inspiration of another, but no longer feels his own, nay, dare
not feel it, is not altogether coincident with its settlements on
Greek soil. On the contrary, it was more than two centuries
ere weakness and reflection suppressed, or all but suppressed,
the forms in which the personal consciousness of God originally expressed itself.[1] Now it certainly lies in the nature of

---

[1] It would be a fruitful task, though as yet it has not been undertaken, to
examine how long visions, dreams and apocalypses, on the one hand, and the
claim of speaking in the power and name of the Holy Spirit, on the other, played
a *rôle* in the early Church; and further to shew how they nearly died out among
the laity, but continued to live among the clergy and the monks, and how, even
among the laity, there were again and again sporadic outbreaks of them. The
material which the first three centuries present is very great. Only a few may be
mentioned here: Ignat. ad. Rom. VII. 2: ad Philad VII. ad. Eph. XX. 1. etc.:
1 Clem. LXIII. 2: Martyr. Polyc.: Acta Perpet. et Felic: Tertull de animo XLVII.:
"Major pæne vis hominum e visionibus deum discunt." Orig. c. Celsum. I. 46:
πολλοὶ ὡσπερεὶ ἄκοντες προσεληλύθασι χριστιανισμῷ, πνεύματός τινος τρέψαντος . . .
καὶ φαντασιώσαντος αὐτοὺς ὕπαρ ἢ ὄναρ (even Arnobius was ostensibly led to

enthusiasm, that it can assume the most diverse forms of expression, and follow very different impulses, and so far it frequently separates instead of uniting. But so long as criticism
and reflection are not yet awakened, and a uniform ideal hov-
ers before one, it does unite, and in this sense there existed
an identity of disposition between the earliest Jewish Christians
and the still enthusiastic Gentile Christian communities.

10. But, finally, there is a still further uniting element
between the beginnings of the development to Catholicism,
and the original condition of the Christian religion as a movement within Judaism, the importance of which cannot be over-
rated, although we have every reason to complain here of the
obscurity of the tradition. Between the Græco-Roman world
which was in search of a spiritual religion, and the Jewish
commonwealth which already possessed such a religion as a national property, though vitiated by exclusiveness, there had
long been a Judaism which, penetrated by the Greek spirit, was,
ex professo, devoting itself to the task of bringing a new religion to the Greek world, the Jewish religion, but that religion
in its kernel Greek, that is, philosophically moulded, spiritualised and secularised. Here then was already consummated
an intimate union of the Greek spirit with the Old Testament
religion, within the Empire and to a less degree in Palestine
itself. If everything is not to be dissolved into a grey mist, we
must clearly distinguish this union between Judaism and Hellenism and the spiritualising of religion it produced, from the

---

Christianity by a dream). Cyprian makes the most extensive use of dreams,
visions, etc., in his letters, see for example Ep. XI. 3–5 : XVI. 4 ("præter nocturnas
visiones per dies quoque impletur apud nos spiritu sancto puerorum innocens ætas,
quæ in ecstasi videt," etc.) ; XXXIX. 1 : LXVI. 10 (very interesting : "quamquam
sciam somnia ridicula et visiones ineptas quibusdam videri, sed utique illis, qui
malunt contra sacerdotes credere quam sacerdoti, sed nihil mirum, quando de
Joseph fratres sui dixerunt : ecce somniator ille," etc.). One who took part in the
baptismal controversy in the great Synod of Carthage writes, "secundum motum
animi mei et spiritus sancti." The enthusiastic element was always evoked with
special power in times of persecution, as the genuine African matyrdoms, from
the second half of the third century, specially shew. Cf. especially the passio
Jacobi, Mariani, etc. But where the enthusiasm was not convenient it was called,
as in the case of the Montanists, dæmonic. Even Constantine operated with dreams
and visions of Christ (see his Vita).

powerful but indeterminable influences which the Greek spirit exercised on all things Jewish, and which have been a historical condition of the Gospel. The alliance, in my opinion, was of no significance at all for the *origin* of the Gospel, but was of the most decided importance, first, for the propagation of Christianity, and then, for the development of Christianity to Catholicism, and for the genesis of the Catholic doctrine of faith. [1] We cannot certainly name any particular personality who was specially active in this, but we can mention three facts which prove more than individual references. (1) The propaganda of Christianity in the Diaspora followed the Jewish propaganda and partly took its place, that is, the Gospel was at first preached to those Gentiles who were already acquainted with the general outlines of the Jewish religion, and who were even frequently viewed as a Judaism of a second order, in which Jewish and Greek elements had been united in a peculiar mixture. (2) The conception of the Old Testament, as we find it even in the earliest Gentile Christian teachers, the method of spiritualising it, etc., agrees in the most surprising way with the methods which were used by the Alexandrian Jews. (3) There are Christian documents in no small number and of unknown origin, which completely agree in plan, in form and contents with Græco-Jewish writings of the Diaspora, as for example, the Christian Sibylline Oracles, and the pseudo-Justinian treatise, "de Monarchia." There are numerous tractates of which it is impossible to say with certainty whether they are of Jewish or of Christian origin.

---

[1] As to the first, the recently discovered "Teaching of the Apostles" in its first moral part, shews a great affinity with the moral philosophy which was set up by Alexandrian Jews and put before the Greek world as that which had been revealed: see Massebieau, L'enseignement des XII. Apôtres. Paris. 1884, and in the Journal "Le Témoignage," 7 Febr. 1885. Usener, in his Preface to the Ges. Abhandl. Jacob Bernays', which he edited, 1885, p. v. f., has, independently of Massebieau, pointed out the relationship of chapters 1-5 of the "Teaching of the Apostles" with the Phocylidean poem (see Bernays' above work, p. 192 ff.). Later Taylor "The teaching of the twelve Apostles," 1886, threw out the conjecture that the Didache had a Jewish foundation, and I reached the same conclusion independently of him: see my Treatise: Die Apostellehre und die jüdischen beiden Wege, 1886.

The Alexandrian and non-Palestinian Judaism is still Judaism. As the Gospel seized and moved the whole of Judaism, it must also have been operative in the non-Palestinian Judaism. But that already foreshadowed the transition of the Gospel to the non-Jewish Greek region, and the fate which it was to experience there. For that non-Palestinian Judaism formed the bridge between the Jewish Church and the Roman Empire, together with its culture. [1] The Gospel passed into the world chiefly by this bridge. Paul indeed had a large share in this, but his own Churches did not understand the way he led them, and were not able on looking back to find it. [2] He indeed

---

[1] It is well known that Judaism at the time of Christ embraced a great many different tendencies. Beside Pharisaic Judaism as the stem proper, there was a motley mass of formations which resulted from the contact of Judaism with foreign ideas, customs and institutions (even with Babylonian and Persian), and which attained importance for the development of the predominant church, as well as for the formation of the so-called gnostic Christian communions. Hellenic elements found their way even into Pharisaic theology. Orthodox Judaism itself has marks which shew that no spiritual movement was able to escape the influence which proceeded from the victory of the Greeks over the east. Besides, who would venture to exhibit definitely the origin and causes of that spiritualising of religions and that limitation of the moral standard of which we can find so many traces in the Alexandrian age? The nations who inhabited the eastern shore of the Mediterranean sea, had from the fourth century B. C., a common history, and therefore had similar convictions. Who can decide what each of them acquired by its own exertions, and what it obtained through interchange of opinions? But in proportion as we see this we must be on our guard against jumbling the phenomena together and effacing them. There is little meaning in calling a thing Hellenic, as that really formed an element in all the phenomena of the age. All our great political and ecclesiastical parties to-day are dependent on the ideas of 1789, and again on romantic ideas. It is just as easy to verify this as it is difficult to determine the measure and the manner of the influence for each group. And yet the understanding of it turns altogether on this point. To call Pharisaism, or the Gospel, or the old Jewish Christianity Hellenic, is not paradox, but confusion.

[2] The Acts of the Apostles is in this respect a most instructive book. It, as well as the Gospel of Luke, is a document of Gentile christianity developing itself to Catholicism: Cf. Overbeck in his Commentar z. Apostelgesch. But the comprehensive judgment of Havet (in the work above mentioned, IV. p. 395 is correct. "L'hellénisme tient assez peu de place dans le N. T., du moins l'hellénisme voulu et réfléchi. Ces livres sont écrits en grec et leurs auteurs vivaient en pays grec; il y a donc eu chez eux infiltration des idées et des sentiments helléniques; quelquefois même l'imagination hellénique y a pénétré comme dans le 3 évangile et dans les Actes.... Dans son ensemble, le N. T. garde le caractère d'un livre hébraïque Le christianisme ne commence avoir une littérature et des doctrines vraiment hellé·

became a Greek to the Greeks, and even began the undertaking of placing the treasures of Greek knowledge at the service of the Gospel. But the knowledge of Christ crucified, to which he subordinated all other knowledge as only of preparatory value, had nothing in common with Greek philosophy, while the idea of justification and the doctrine of the Spirit (Rom. VIII.), which together formed the peculiar contents of his Christianity, were irreconcilable with the moralism and the religious ideals of Hellenism. But the great mass of the earliest Gentile Christians became Christians because they perceived in the Gospel the sure tidings of the benefits and obligations which they had already sought in the fusion of Jewish and Greek elements. It is only by discerning this that we can grasp the preparation and genesis of the Catholic Church and its dogma.

From the foregoing statements it appears that there fall to be considered as presuppositions of the origin of the Catholic Apostolic doctrine of faith, the following topics, though of unequal importance as regards the extent of their influence.

(a). The Gospel of Jesus Christ.

(b). The common preaching of Jesus Christ in the first generation of believers.

(c). The current exposition of the Old Testament, the Jewish speculations and hopes of the future, in their significance for the earliest types of Christian preaching. [1]

(d). The religious conceptions, and the religious philosophy of the Hellenistic Jews, in their significance for the later restatement of the Gospel.

(e). The religious dispositions of the Greeks and Romans of the first two centuries, and the current Græco-Roman philosophy of religion.

---

niques qu'au milieu du second siècle. Mais il y avait un judaïsme, celui d'Alexandrie, qui avait faite alliance avec l'hellénisme avant même qu'il y eût des chrétiens."

[1] The right of distinguishing *(b)* and *(c)* may be contested. But if we surrender this we therewith surrender the right to distinguish kernel and husk in the original proclamation of the Gospel. The dangers to which the attempt is exposed should not frighten us from it, for it has its justification in the fact that the Gospel is neither doctrine nor law,

§ 2. *The Gospel of Jesus Christ according to His own testimony concerning Himself.*

I. The Fundamental Features.

The Gospel entered into the world as an apocalyptic eschatological message, apocalyptical and eschatological not only in its form, but also in its contents. But Jesus announced that the kingdom of God had already begun with his own work, and those who received him in faith became sensible of this beginning; for the "apocalyptical" was not merely the unveiling of the future, but above all the revelation of God as the Father, and the "eschatological" received its counterpoise in the view of Jesus' work as Saviour, in the assurance of being certainly called to the kingdom, and in the conviction that life and future dominion is hid with God the Lord and preserved for believers by him. Consequently, we are following not only the indications of the succeeding history, but also the requirement of the thing itself, when, in the presentation of the Gospel, we place in the foreground, not that which unites it with the contemporary disposition of Judaism, but that which raises it above it. Instead of the hope of inheriting the kingdom, Jesus had also spoken simply of preserving the soul, or the life. In this one substitution lies already a transformation of universal significance, of political religion into a religion that is individual and therefore holy; for the life is nourished by the word of God, but God is the Holy One.

The Gospel is the glad message of the government of the world and of every individual soul by the almighty and holy God, the Father and Judge. In this dominion of God, which frees men from the power of the Devil, makes them rulers in a heavenly kingdom in contrast with the kingdoms of the world, and which will also be sensibly realised in the future æon just about to appear, is secured life for all men who yield themselves to God, although they should lose the world and the earthly life. That is, the soul which is pure and holy in connection with God, and in imitation of the Divine perfection is eternally preserved with God, while those who would gain the world and preserve their life, fall into the hands of the Judge who sentences them to Hell. This dominion of God imposes on men a law, an old and yet a new law, viz., that of the Divine perfection and therefore of undivided love to God and to our neighbour. In this love, where it sways the inmost feeling, is presented the better righteousness (better not only with respect to the Scribes and Pharisees, but also with respect to Moses, see Matt. V.), which corresponds to the perfection of God. The way to attain it is a change of mind, that is, self-denial, humility before God, and heartfelt trust in him. In this humility and trust in God there is contained a recognition of one's own unworthiness; but the Gospel calls to the kingdom of God those very sinners who are thus minded, by promising the forgiveness of the sins which hitherto have separated them from God. But the Gospel which appears in these three elements, the dominion of God, a better right- eousness embodied in the law of love, and the forgiveness of sin, is inseparably connected with Jesus Christ; for in preach- ing this Gospel Jesus Christ everywhere calls men to himself. In him the Gospel is word and deed; it has become his food, and therefore his personal life, and into this life of his he draws all others. He is the Son who knows the Father. In him men are to perceive the kindness of the Lord; in him they are to feel God's power and government of the world, and to become certain of this consolation; they are to follow him the meek and lowly, and while he, the pure and holy one, calls sinners to himself, they are to receive the assurance that God through him forgiveth sin.

Jesus Christ has by no express statement thrust this con- nection of his Gospel with his Person into the foreground. No words could have certified it unless his life, the overpow- ering impression of his Person, had created it. By living, acting and speaking from the riches of that life which he lived with his Father, he became for others the revelation of the God of whom they formerly had heard, but whom they had not known. He declared his Father to be their Father and they understood him. But he also declared himself to be

Messiah, and in so doing gave an intelligible expression to his abiding significance for them and for his people. In a solemn hour at the close of his life, as well as on special occasions at an earlier period, he referred to the fact that the surrender to his Person which induced them to leave all and follow him, was no passing element in the new position they had gained towards God the Father. He tells them, on the contrary, that this surrender corresponds to the service which he will perform for them and for the many, when he will give his life a sacrifice for the sins of the world. By teaching them to think of him and of his death in the breaking of bread and the drinking of wine, and by saying of his death that it takes place for the remission of sins, he has claimed as his due from all future disciples what was a matter of course so long as he sojourned with them, but what might fade away after he was parted from them. He who in his preaching of the kingdom of God raised the strictest self-examination and humility to a law, and exhibited them to his followers in his own life, has described with clear consciousness his life crowned by death as the imperishable service by which men in all ages will be cleansed from their sin and made joyful in their God. By so doing he put himself far above all others, although they were to become his brethren; and claimed a unique and permanent importance as Redeemer and Judge. This permanent importance as the Lord he secured, not by disclosures about the mystery of his Person, but by the impression of his life and the interpretation of his death. He interprets it, like all his sufferings, as a victory, as the passing over to his glory, and in spite of the cry of God-forsakenness upon the cross, he has proved himself able to awaken in his followers the real conviction that he lives and is Lord and Judge of the living and the dead.

The religion of the Gospel is based on this belief in Jesus Christ, that is, by looking to him, this historical person, it becomes certain to the believer that God rules heaven and earth, and that God, the Judge, is also Father and Redeemer. The religion of the Gospel is the religion which makes the highest moral demands, the simplest and the most difficult, and discloses the contradiction in which every man finds himself towards them. But it also procures redemption from such misery, by drawing the life of men into the inexhaustible and blessed life of Jesus Christ, who has overcome the world and called sinners to himself.

In making this attempt to put together the fundamental features of the Gospel, I have allowed myself to be guided by the results of this Gospel in the case of the first disciples. I do not know whether it is permissible to present such fundamental features apart from this guidance. The preaching of Jesus Christ was in the main so plain and simple, and in its application so manifold and rich, that one shrinks from attempting to systematise it, and would much rather merely narrate according to the Gospel. Jesus searches for the point in every man on which he can lay hold of him and lead him to the Kingdom of God. The distinction of good and evil— for God or against God—he would make a life question for every man, in order to shew him for whom it has become this, that he can depend upon the God whom he is to fear. At the same time he did not by any means uniformly fall back upon sin, or even the universal sinfulness, but laid hold of individuals very diversely, and led them to God by different paths. The doctrinal concentration of redemption on sin was certainly not carried out by Paul alone; but, on the other hand, it did not in any way become the prevailing form for the preaching of the Gospel. On the contrary, the antitheses, night, error, dominion of demons, death and light, truth, deliverance, life, proved more telling in the Gentile Churches. The consciousness of universal sinfulness was first made the negative fundamental frame of mind of Christendom by Augustine.

II. Details.

1. Jesus announced the Kingdom of God which stands in opposition to the kingdom of the devil, and therefore also to the kingdom of the world, as a future Kingdom, and yet it is presented in his preaching as present; as an invisible,

and yet it was visible—for one actually saw it. He lived
and spoke within the circle of eschatological ideas which Judaism had developed more than two hundred years before:
but he controlled them by giving them a new content and
forcing them into a new direction. Without abrogating the
law and the prophets he, on fitting occasions, broke through
the national, political and sensuous eudæmonistic forms in
which the nation was expecting the realisation of the dominion of God, but turned their attention at the same time to a
future near at hand, in which believers would be delivered
from the oppression of evil and sin, and would enjoy blessedness and dominion. Yet he declared that even now, every
individual who is called into the kingdom may call on God
as his Father, and be sure of the gracious will of God, the
hearing of his prayers, the forgiveness of sin, and the protection of God even in this present life. [1] But everything
in this proclamation is directed to the life beyond: the
certainty of that life is the power and earnestness of the
Gospel.

2. The conditions of entrance to the kingdom are, in the
first place, a complete change of mind, in which a man renounces the pleasures of this world, denies himself, and is
ready to surrender all that he has in order to save his soul;
then, a believing trust in God's grace which he grants to the
humble and the poor, and therefore hearty confidence in Jesus
as the Messiah chosen and called by God to realise his kingdom on the earth. The announcement is therefore directed
to the poor, the suffering, those hungering and thirsting for
righteousness, not to those who live, but to those who wish
to be healed and redeemed, and finds them prepared for entrance into, and reception of the blessings of the kingdom of

---

[1] Therewith are, doubtless, heavenly blessings bestowed in the present. Historical investigation has, notwithstanding, every reason for closely examining, whether,
and in how far, we may speak of a present for the Kingdom of God, in the
sense of Jesus. But even if the question had to be answered in the negative, it
would make little or no difference for the correct understanding of Jesus' preaching.
The Gospel viewed in its kernel is independent of this question. It deals with
the inner constitution and mood of the soul.

God, [1] while it brings down upon the self-satisfied, the rich and those proud of their righteousness, the judgment of obduracy and the damnation of Hell.

3. The commandment of undivided love to God and the brethren, as the main commandment, in the observance of which righteousness is realised, and forming the antithesis to the selfish mind, the lust of the world, and every arbitrary impulse, [2] corresponds to the blessings of the Kingdom of God, viz., forgiveness of sin, righteousness, dominion and blessedness. The standard of personal worth for the members of the Kingdom is self-sacrificing labour for others, not any technical mode of worship or legal preciseness. Renunciation of the world together with its goods, even of life itself in certain circumstances, is the proof of a man's sincerity and earnestness in seeking the Kingdom of God; and the meekness which renounces every right, bears wrong patiently, requiting it with kindness, is the practical proof of love to God, the conduct that answers to God's perfection.

4. In the proclamation and founding of this kingdom, Jesus summoned men to attach themselves to him, because he had recognised himself to be the helper called by God, and therefore also the Messiah who was promised. [3] He gradually declared

---

[1] The question whether, and in what degree, a man of himself can earn righteousness before God is one of those theoretic questions to which Jesus gave no answer. He fixed his attention on all the gradations of the moral and religious conduct of his countrymen as they were immediately presented to him, and found some prepared for entrance into the kingdom of God, not by a technical mode of outward preparation, but by hungering and thirsting for it, and at the same time unselfishly serving their brethren. Humility and love unfeigned were always the decisive marks of these prepared ones. They are to be satisfied with righteousness before God, that is, are to receive the blessed feeling that God is gracious to them as sinners, and accepts them as his children. Jesus, however, allows the popular distinction of sinners and righteous to remain, but exhibits its perverseness by calling sinners to himself, and by describing the opposition of the righteous to his Gospel as a mark of their godlessness and hardness of heart.

[2] The blessings of the kingdom were frequently represented by Jesus as a reward for work done. But this popular view is again broken through by reference to the fact that all reward is the gift of God's free grace.

[3] Some Critics—most recently Havet, Le Christianisme et ses origines, 1884. T. IV. p. 15 ff.—have called in question the fact that Jesus called himself Messiah. But this article of the Evangelic tradition seems to me to stand the test of the most minute investigation. But, in the case of Jesus, the consciousness of being

himself to the people as such by the names he assumed, [1] for the names "Anointed," "King," "Lord," "Son of David," "Son of Man," "Son of God," all denote the Messianic office, and were familiar to the greater part of the people. [2] But though, at first, they express only the call, office, and power of the Messiah, yet by means of them and especially by the designation Son of God, Jesus pointed to a relation to God the Father, then and in its immediateness unique, as the basis of the office with which he was entrusted. He has, however, given no further explanation of the mystery of this relation than the declaration that the Son alone knoweth the Father, and that this knowledge of God and Sonship to God are secured for all others by the sending of the Son. [3] In the

the Messiah undoubtedly rested on the certainty of being the Son of God, therefore of knowing the Father and being constrained to proclaim that knowledge.

[1] We can gather with certainty from the Gospels that Jesus did not enter on his work with the announcement: Believe in me for I am the Messiah. On the contrary, he connected his work with the baptising movement of John, but carried that movement further, and thereby made the Baptist his forerunner (Mark I. 15: πεπλήρωται ὁ καιρὸς καὶ ἤγγικεν ἡ βασιλεία τοῦ θεοῦ, μετανοεῖτε καὶ πιστεύετε ἐν τῷ εὐαγγελίῳ). He was in no hurry to urge anything that went beyond that message, but gradually prepared, and cautiously required of his followers an advance beyond it. The goal to which he led them was to believe in him as Messiah without putting the usual political construction on the Messianic ideal.

[2] Even "Son of Man" probably means Messiah: we do not know whether Jesus had any special reason for favouring this designation which springs from Dan. VII. The objection to interpreting the word as Messiah really resolves itself into this, that the disciples (according to the Gospels) did not at once recognise him as Messiah. But that is explained by the contrast of his own peculiar idea of Messiah with the popular idea. The confession of him as Messiah was the keystone of their confidence in him, inasmuch as by that confession they separated themselves from old ideas.

[3] The distinction between the Father and the Son stands out just as plainly in the sayings of Jesus, as the complete obedient subordination of the Son to the Father. Even according to John's Gospel, Jesus finishes the work which the Father has given him, and is obedient in everything even unto death. He declares Mat. XIX. 17: εἷς ἐστιν ὁ ἀγαθός. Special notice should be given to Mark XIII. 32, (Matt. XXIV, 36). Behind the only manifested life of Jesus, later speculation has put a life in which he wrought, not in subordination and obedience, but in like independence and dignity with God. That goes beyond the utterances of Jesus even in the fourth Gospel. But it is no advance beyond these, especially in the religious view and speech of the time, when it is announced that the rela-

proclamation of God as Father, [1] as well as in the other proclamation that all the members of the kingdom following
the will of God in love, are to become one with the Son and
through him with the Father, [2] the message of the realised
kingdom of God receives its richest, inexhaustible content: the
Son of the Father will be the first-born among many brethren.

5. Jesus as the Messiah chosen by God has definitely distinguished himself from Moses and all the Prophets: as his
preaching and his work are the fulfilment of the law and the
prophets, so he himself is not a disciple of Moses, but corrects
that law-giver; he is not a Prophet, but Master and Lord. He
proves this Lordship during his earthly ministry in the accomplishment of the mighty deeds given him to do, above all in
withstanding the Devil and his kingdom, [3] and—according

tion of the Father to the Son lies beyond time. It is not even improbable that
the sayings in the fourth Gospel referring to this, have a basis in the preaching
of Jesus himself.

[1] Paul knew that the designation of God as the Father of our Lord Jesus Christ,
was the new Evangelic confession. Origen was the first among the Fathers (though
before him Marcion) to recognise that the decisive advance beyond the Old Testament stage of religion, was given in the preaching of God as Father; see the
exposition of the Lord's Prayer in his treatise *De oratione*. No doubt the Old
Testament, and the later Judaism knew the designation of God as Father; but it
applied it to the Jewish nation, it did not attach the evangelic meaning to the
name, and it did not allow itself in any way to be guided in its religion by this idea.

[2] See the farewell discourses in John, the fundamental ideas of which are, in
my opinion, genuine, that is, proceed from Jesus.

[3] The historian cannot regard a miracle as a sure given historical event: for
in doing so he destroys the mode of consideration on which all historical investigation rests. Every individual miracle remains historically quite doubtful, and
a summation of things doubtful never leads to certainty. But should the historian,
notwithstanding, be convinced that Jesus Christ did extraordinary things, in the
strict sense miraculous things, then, from the unique impression he has obtained
of this person, he infers the possession by him of supernatural power. This conclusion itself belongs to the province of religious faith: though there has seldom
been a strong faith which would not have drawn it. Moreover, the healing miracles
of Jesus are the only ones that come into consideration in a strict historical examination. These certainly cannot be eliminated from the historical accounts without
utterly destroying them. But how unfit are they of themselves, after 1800 years,
to secure any special importance to him to whom they are attributed, unless that
importance was already established apart from them. That he could do with himself what he would, that he created a new thing without overturning the old, that
he won men to himself by announcing the Father, that he inspired without fanaticism, set up a kingdom without politics, set men free from the world without

to the law of the Kingdom of God—for that very reason in
the service which he performs. In this service Jesus also
reckoned the sacrifice of his life, designating it as a "λύτρον"
which he offered for the redemption of man.[1]   But he declared
at the same time that his Messianic work was not yet fulfilled
in his subjection to death. On the contrary, the close is
merely initiated by his death; for the completion of the
kingdom will only appear when he returns in glory in the
clouds of heaven to judgment. Jesus seems to have announced
this speedy return a short time before his death, and to have
comforted his disciples at his departure, with the assurance

asceticism, was a teacher without theology, at a time of fanaticism and politics,
asceticism and theology, is the great miracle of his person, and that he who
preached the Sermon on the Mount declared himself in respect of his life and
death, to be the Redeemer and Judge of the world, is the offence and foolishness
which mock all reason.

[1] See Mark X. 45—That Jesus at the celebration of the first Lord's supper described his death as a sacrifice which he should offer for the forgiveness of sin, is
clear from the account of Paul. From that account it appears to be certain that
Jesus gave expression to the idea of the necessity and saving significance of his
death for the forgiveness of sins, in a symbolical ordinance (based on the conclusion of the covenant, Exod. XXIV. 3 ff., perhaps, as Paul presupposes, on the
Passover), in order that his disciples by repeating it in accordance with the will
of Jesus, might be the more deeply impressed by it.   Certain observations based
on John VI., on the supper prayer in the Didache, nay, even on the report of
Mark, and supported at the same time by features of the earliest practice in which
it had the character of a real meal, and the earliest theory of the supper, which
viewed it as a communication of eternal life and an anticipation of the future
existence, have for years made me doubt very much whether the Pauline account
and the Pauline conception of it, were really either the oldest, or the universal
and therefore only one.   I have been strengthened in this suspicion by the profound
and remarkable investigation of Spitta (z. Gesch. u. Litt. d. Urchristenthums: Die
urchristl. Traditionen ü. den Urspr. u. Sinnd. Abendmahls, 1893). He sees in the
supper as not instituted, but celebrated by Jesus, the festival of the Messianic meal,
the anticipated triumph over death, the expression of the perfection of the Messianic
work, the symbolic representation of the filling of believers with the powers of
the Messianic kingdom and life.   The reference to the Passover and the death of
Christ was attached to it later, though it is true very soon.   How much is thereby
explained that was hitherto obscure—critical, historical, and dogmatico-historical
questions—cannot at all be stated briefly.   And yet I hesitate to give a full recognition to Spitta's exposition: the words I. Cor. XI. 23: ἐγὼ γὰρ παρέλαβον ἀπὸ τοῦ
κυρίου, ὃ καὶ παρέδωκα ὑμῖν κ.τ.λ., are too strong for me.   Cf. besides, Weizsäcker's
investigation in "The Apostolic Age." Lobstein, La doctrine de la s. cène, 1889.
A. Harnack i. d. Texten u. Unters. VII. 2 p. 139 ff.   Schürer, Theol. Lit. Ztg. 1891,
p. 29 ff.   Jülicher Abhandl. f. Weizsäker, 1892, p. 215 ff.

that he would immediately enter into a supramundane position with God. [1]

6. The instructions of Jesus to his disciples are accordingly dominated by the thought that the end,—the day and hour of which, however, no one knows,—is at hand. In consequence of this, also, the exhortation to renounce all earthly good takes a prominent place. But Jesus does not impose ascetic commandments as a new law, far less does he see in asceticism, as such, sanctification [2]—he himself did not live as an ascetic, but was reproached as a wine-bibber—but he prescribed a perfect simplicity and purity of disposition, and a singleness of heart which remains invariably the same in trouble and renunciation, in possession and use of earthly good. A uniform equality of all in the conduct of life is not commanded: "To whom much is given, of him much shall be required." The disciples are kept as far from fanaticism and overrating of spiritual results as from asceticism. "Rejoice not that the spirits are subject to you, but rejoice that your names are written in heaven." When they besought him to teach them to pray, he taught them the "Lord's prayer", a prayer which demands such a collected mind, and such a tranquil, childlike elevation of the heart to God, that it cannot be offered at all by minds subject to passion or preoccupied by any daily cares.

7. Jesus himself did not found a new religious community, but gathered round him a circle of disciples, and chose Apostles whom he commanded to preach the Gospel. His preaching was universalistic inasmuch as it attributed no value to ceremonialism as such, and placed the fulfilment of the Mosaic

[1] With regard to the eschatology, no one can say in detail what proceeds from Jesus, and what from the disciples. What has been said in the text does not claim to be certain, but only probable. The most important, and at the same time the most certain point, is that Jesus made the definitive fate of the individual depend on faith, humility and love. There are no passages in the Gospel which conflict with the impression that Jesus reserved day and hour to God, and wrought in faith and patience as long as for him it was day.

[2] He did not impose on every one, or desire from every one even the outward following of himself: see Mark V. 18-19. The "imitation of Jesus," in the strict sense of the word, did not play any noteworthy rôle either in the Apostolic or in the old Catholic period.

law in the exhibition of its moral contents, partly against or
beyond the letter. He made the law perfect by harmonising
its particular requirements with the fundamental moral requirements which were also expressed in the Mosaic law. He
emphasised the fundamental requirements more decidedly
than was done by the law itself, and taught that all details
should be referred to them and deduced from them. The
external righteousness of Pharisaism was thereby declared to
be not only an outer covering, but also a fraud, and the bond
which still united religion and nationality in Judaism was
sundered. [1] Political and national elements may probably have

---

[1] It is asserted by well-informed investigators, and may be inferred from the
Gospels (Mark XII. 32-34; Luke X. 27, 28), perhaps also from the Jewish original
of the Didache, that some representatives of Pharisaism, beside the pedantic treatment of the law, attempted to concentrate it on the fundamental moral commandments. Consequently, in Palestinian and Alexandrian Judaism at the time of Christ,
in virtue of the prophetic word and the Thora, influenced also, perhaps, by the
Greek spirit which everywhere gave the stimulus to inwardness, the path was
indicated in which the future development of religion was to follow. Jesus entered
fully into the view of the law thus attempted, which comprehended it as a whole
and traced it back to the disposition. But he freed it from the contradiction that
adhered to it, (because, in spite of and alongside the tendency to a deeper perception, men still persisted in deducing righteousness from a punctilious observance
of numerous particular commandments, because in so doing they became self-
satisfied, that is, irreligious, and because in belonging to Abraham, they thought
they had a claim of right on God). For all that, so far as a historical understanding
of the activity of Jesus is at all possible, it is to be obtained from the soil of
Pharisaism, as the Pharisees were those who cherished and developed the Messianic
expectations, and because, along with their care for the Thora, they sought also
to preserve, in their own way, the prophetic inheritance. If everything does not
deceive us, there were already contained in the Pharisaic theology of the age,
speculations which were fitted to modify considerably the narrow view of history,
and to prepare for universalism. The very men who tithed mint, anise and cummin,
who kept their cups and dishes outwardly clean, who, hedging round the Thora,
attempted to hedge round the people, spoke also of the sum total of the law.
They made room in their theology for new ideas which are partly to be described
as advances, and on the other hand, they have already pondered the question even
in relation to the law, whether submission to its main contents was not sufficient
for being numbered among the people of the covenant (see Renan: *Paul*). In
particular the whole sacrificial system, which Jesus also essentially ignored, was
therewith thrust into the background. Baldensperger (Selbstbewusstsein Jesu. p. 46)
justly says, "There lie before us definite marks that the certainty of the nearness
of God in the Temple (from the time of the Maccabees) begins to waver, and the
efficacy of the temple institutions to be called in question. Its recent desecration
by the Romans, appears to the author of the Psalms of Solomon (II. 2) as a kind

been made prominent in the hopes of the future, as Jesus appropriated them for his preaching. But from the conditions to which the realising of the hopes for the individual was attached, there already shone the clearer ray which was to eclipse those elements, and one saying such as Matt. XXII. 31., annulled at once political religion and religious politics.

of Divine requital for the sons of Israel themselves having been guilty of so grossly profaning the sacrificial gifts. Enoch calls the shewbread of the second Temple polluted and unclean ... There had crept in among the pious a feeling of the insufficiency of their worship, and from this side the Essenic schism will certainly represent only the open outbreak of a disease which had already begun to gnaw secretly at the religious life of the nation": see here the excellent explanations of the origin of Essenism in Lucius (Essenism, 75 ff. 109 ff.). The spread of Judaism in the world, the secularization and apostacy of the priestly caste, the desecration of the Temple, the building of the Temple at Leontopolis, the perception brought about by the spiritualising of religion in the empire of Alexander the Great, that no blood of beasts can be a means of reconciling God—all these circumstances must have been absolutely dangerous and fatal, both to the local centralisation of worship, and to the statutory sacrificial system. The proclamation of Jesus (and of Stephen) as to the overthrow of the Temple, is therefore no absolutely new thing, nor is the fact that Judaism fell back upon the law and the Messianic hope, a mere result of the destruction of the Temple. This change was rather prepared by the inner development. Whatever point in the preaching of Jesus we may fix on, we shall find, that—apart from the writings of the Prophets and the Psalms, which originated in the Greek Maccabean periods—parallels can be found only in Pharisaism, but at the same time that the sharpest contrasts must issue from it. Talmudic Judaism is not in every respect the genuine continuance of Pharisaic Judaism, but a product of the decay which attests that the rejection of Jesus by the spiritual leaders of the people had deprived the nation and even the Virtuosi of Religion of their best part: (see for this the expositions of Kuenen "Judaismus und Christenthum," in his (Hibbert) lectures on national religions and world religions). The ever recurring attempts to deduce the origin of Christianity from Hellenism, or even from the Roman Greek culture, are there also rightly, briefly and tersely rejected. Also the hypotheses, which either entirely eliminate the person of Jesus or make him an Essene, or subordinate him to the person of Paul, may be regarded as definitively settled. Those who think they can ascertain the origin of Christian religion from the origin of Christian Theology will indeed always think of Hellenism: Paul will eclipse the person of Jesus with those who believe that a religion for the world must be born with a universalistic doctrine. Finally, Essenism will continue in authority with those who see in the position of indifference which Jesus took to the Temple worship, the main thing, and who, besides, create for themselves an "Essenism of their own finding." Hellenism, and also Essenism, can of course indicate to the historian some of the conditions by which the appearance of Jesus was prepared and rendered possible; but they explain only the possibility, not the reality of the appearance. But this with its historically not deducible power is the decisive thing. If some one has recently said that "the

Supplement 1.—The idea of the inestimable inherent value
of every individual human soul, already dimly appearing in
several psalms, and discerned by Greek Philosophers, though
as a rule developed in contradiction to religion, stands out
plainly in the preaching of Jesus. It is united with the idea
of God as Father, and is the complement to the message of
the communion of brethren realising itself in love. In this
sense the Gospel is at once profoundly individualistic and
Socialistic. The prospect of gaining life, and preserving it
for ever, is therefore also the highest which Jesus has set
forth; it is not, however, to be a motive, but a reward of
grace. In the certainty of this prospect, which is the converse of renouncing the world, he has proclaimed the sure
hope of the resurrection, and consequently the most abundant
compensation for the loss of the natural life. Jesus put an
end to the vacillation and uncertainty which in this respect
still prevailed among the Jewish people of his day. The
confession of the Psalmist, "Whom have I in heaven but thee,
and there is none upon the earth that I desire beside thee ",
and the fulfilling of the Old Testament commandment, "Love
thy neighbour as thyself ", were for the first time presented
in their connection in the person of Jesus. He himself therefore is Christianity, for the "impression of his person convinced
the disciples of the facts of forgiveness of sin and the second

historical speciality of the person of Jesus" is not the main thing in Christianity;
he has thereby betrayed that he does not know how a religion that is worthy of
the name is founded, propagated, and maintained. For the latest attempt to put
the Gospel in a historical connection with Buddhism (Seydel. Das Ev. von Jesus
in seinem Verhältnissen zur Buddha-Sage, 1882: likewise, Die Buddha-Legende
und das Leben Jesu, 1884), see, Oldenburg, Theol. Lit.-Ztg. 1882, Col. 415 f.;
1884, 185 f. However much necessarily remains obscure to us in the ministry of
Jesus when we seek to place it in a historical connection,—what is known is sufficient to confirm the judgment that his preaching developed a germ in the religion
of Israel (see the Psalms) which was finally guarded and in many respects developed
by the Pharisees, but which languished and died under their guardianship. The
power of development which Jesus imported to it was not a power which he himself had to borrow from without; but doctrine and speculation were as far from
him as ecstasy and visions. On the other hand, we must remember we do not
know the history of Jesus up to his public entrance on his ministry, and that
therefore we do not know whether in his native province he had any connection
with Greeks.

birth, and gave them courage to believe in and to lead a new life". We cannot therefore state the "doctrine" of Jesus; for it appears as a supramundane life which must be felt in the person of Jesus, and its truth is guaranteed by the fact that such a life can be lived.

Supplement 2.—The history of the Gospel contains two great transitions, both of which, however, fall within the first century; from Christ to the first generation of believers, including Paul, and from the first, Jewish Christian, generation of these believers to the Gentile Christians; in other words, from Christ to the brotherhood of believers in Christ, and from this to the incipient Catholic Church. No later transitions in the Church can be compared with these in importance. As to the first, the question has frequently been asked, Is the Gospel of Christ to be the authority or the Gospel concerning Christ? But the strict dilemma here is false. The Gospel certainly is the Gospel of Christ. For it has only, in the sense of Jesus, fulfilled its Mission when the Father has been declared to men as he was known by the Son, and where the life is swayed by the realities and principles which ruled the life of Jesus Christ. But it is in accordance with the mind of Jesus and at the same time a fact of history, that this Gospel can only be appropriated and adhered to in connection with a believing surrender to the person of Jesus Christ. Yet every dogmatic formula is suspicious, because it is fitted to wound the spirit of religion; it should not at least be put before the living experience in order to evoke it; for such a procedure is really the admission of the half belief which thinks it necessary that the impression made by the person must be supplemented. The essence of the matter is a personal life which awakens life around it as the fire of one torch kindles another. Early as weakness of faith is in the Church of Christ, it is no earlier than the procedure of making a formulated and ostensibly proved confession the foundation of faith, and therefore demanding, above all, subjection to this confession. Faith assuredly is propagated by the testimony of faith, but dogma is not in itself that testimony.

The peculiar character of the Christian religion is conditioned by the fact that every reference to God is at the same time a reference to Jesus Christ, and *vice versa*. In this sense the Person of Christ is the central point of the religion, and insep-arably united with the substance of piety as a sure reliance on God. Such a union does not, as is supposed, bring a foreign element into the pure essence of religion. The pure essence of religion rather demands such a union; for "the reverence for persons, the inner bowing before the manifest-ation of moral power and goodness is the root of all true religion" (W. Herrmann). But the Christian religion knows and names only one name before which it bows. In this rests its positive character, in all else, as piety, it is by its strictly spiritual and inward attitude, not a positive religion alongside of others, but religion itself. But just because the Person of Christ has this significance is the knowledge and understanding of the "historical Christ" required: for no other comes within the sphere of our knowledge. "The his-torical Christ" that, to be sure, is not the powerless Christ of contemporary history shewn to us through a coloured biograph-ical medium, or dissipated in all sorts of controversies, but Christ as a power and as a life which towers above our own life, and enters into our life as God's Spirit and God's Word, (see Herrmann, Der Verkehr des Christen mit Gott. 2. Edit. 1892, [*i. e.*, "The Fellowship of the Christian with God", an important work included in the present series of translations. Ed.]: Kähler, Der sog. historische Jesus und der geschichtliche biblische Christus, 1892). But historical labour and investiga-tion are needed in order to grasp this Jesus Christ ever more firmly and surely.

As to the second transition, it brought with it the most important changes, which, however, became clearly manifest only after the lapse of some generations. They appear, first, in the belief in holy consecrations, efficacious in themselves, and administered by chosen persons; further, in the conviction, that the relation of the individual to God and Christ is, above all, conditioned on the acceptance of a definite divinely attested law of faith and holy writings; further, in the opinion that God has established Church arrangements, observance of which

is necessary and meritorious, as well as in the opinion that
a visible earthly community is the people of a new covenant.
These assumptions, which formally constitute the essence of
Catholicism as a religion, have no support in the teaching of
Jesus, nay, offend against that teaching.

Supplement 3.—The question as to what new thing Christ
has brought, answered by Paul in the words, "If any man be
in Christ he is a new creature, old things are passed away,
behold all things are become new", has again and again been
pointedly put since the middle of the second century by Apologists, Theologians and religious Philosophers within and
without the Church, and has received the most varied answers.
Few of the answers have reached the height of the Pauline
confession. But where one cannot attain to this confession,
one ought to make clear to oneself that every answer which
does not lie in the line of it is altogether unsatisfactory; for
it is not difficult to set over against every article from the
preaching of Jesus an observation which deprives it of its originality. It is the Person, it is the fact of his life that is
new and creates the new. The way in which he called forth
and established a people of God on earth, which has become
sure of God and of eternal life; the way in which he set up
a new thing in the midst of the old and transformed the religion of Israel into *the religion:* that is the mystery of his
Person, in which lies his unique and permanent position in
the history of humanity.

Supplement 4.—The conservative position of Jesus towards
the religious traditions of his people had the necessary result
that his preaching and his Person were placed by believers
in the frame-work of this tradition, which was thereby very
soon greatly expanded. But, though this way of understanding the Gospel was certainly at first the only possible way,
and though the Gospel itself could only be preserved by such
means (see § 1), yet it cannot be mistaken that a displacement in the conception of the Person and preaching of Jesus,
and a burdening of religious faith, could not but forthwith
set in, from which developments followed, the premises of which
would be vainly sought for in the words of the Lord (see

§§ 3, 4). But here the question arises as to whether the Gospel is not inseparably connected with the eschatological world-renouncing element with which it entered into the world, so that its being is destroyed where this is omitted. A few words may be devoted to this question. The Gospel possesses properties which oppose every positive religion, because they depreciate it, and these properties form the kernel of the Gospel. The disposition which is devoted to God, humble, ardent and sincere in its love to God and to the brethren, is as an abiding habit, law, and at the same time a gift of the Gospel, and also finally exhausts it. This quiet, peaceful element was at the beginning strong and vigorous, even in those who lived in the world of ecstasy and expected the world to come. One may be named for all, Paul. He who wrote 1. Cor. XIII. and Rom. VIII. should not, in spite of all that he has said elsewhere, be called upon to witness that the nature of the Gospel is exhausted in its world-renouncing, ecstatic and eschatological elements, or at least that it is so inseparable united with these as to fall along with them. He who wrote those chapters, and the greater than he who promised the kingdom of heaven to children and to those who were hungering and thirsting for righteousness, he to whom tradition ascribes the words: "Rejoice not that the spirits are subject to you, but rather rejoice that your names are written in heaven" — both attest that the Gospel lies above the antagonisms between this world and the next, work and retirement from the world, reason and ecstasy, Judaism and Hellenism. And because it lies above them it may be united with either, as it originally unfolded its powers under the ruins of the Jewish religion. But still more; it not only can enter into union with them, it must do so if it is otherwise the religion of the living and is itself living. It has only one aim; that man may find God and have him as his own God, in order to gain in him humility and patience, peace, joy and love. How it reaches this goal through the advancing centuries, whether with the co-efficients of Judaism or Hellenism, of renunciation of the world or of culture, of mysticism or the doctrine of predestination, of Gnosticism or

Agnosticism, and whatever other incrustations there may yet be which can defend the kernel, and under which alone living elements can grow—all that belongs to the centuries. However each individual Christian may reckon to the treasure itself the earthly vessel in which he hides his treasure; it is the duty and the right, not only of the religious, but also of the historical estimate to distinguish between the vessel and the treasure; for the Gospel did not enter into the world as a positive statutory religion, and cannot therefore have its classic manifestation in any form of its intellectual or social types, not even in the first. It is therefore the duty of the historian of the first century of the Church, as well as that of those which follow, not to be content with fixing the changes of the Christian religion, but to examine how far the new forms were capable of defending, propagating and impressing the Gospel itself. It would probably have perished if the forms of primitive Christianity had been scrupulously maintained in the Church; but now primitive Christianity has perished in order that the Gospel might be preserved. To study this progress of the development, and fix the significance of the newly received forms for the kernel of the matter, is the last and highest task of the historian who himself lives in his subject. He who approaches from without must be satisfied with the general view that in the history of the Church some things have always remained, and other things have always been changing.

Literature.—Weiss. Biblical Theology of the New Testament. T. and T. Clark. Wittichen. Beitr. z. bibl. Theol. 3. Thle. 1864-72.

Schurer. Die Predigt Jesu in ihrem Verhaltniss z. A. T. u z. Judenthum, 1882.

Wellhausen. Abriss der Gesch. Israels u. Juda's (Skizzen u. Vorarbeiten) 1. Heft. 1884.

Baldensperger. Das Selbstbewusstsein Jesu im Licht der Messianischen Hoffnungen seiner Zeit, 1888, (2 Aufl. 1891). The prize essays of Schmoller and Issel, Ueber die Lehre vom Reiche Gottes im N. Test. 1891 (besides Gunkel in d. Theol. Lit. Ztg. 1893. No. 2).

Wendt. Die Lehre Jesu. (The teaching of Jesus. T. and
T. Clark. English translation.)

Joh. Weiss. Die Predigt Jesu vom Reiche Gottes, 1892.

Bousset. Jesu Predigt in ihrem Gegensatz zum Judenthum, 1892.

C. Holtzman. Die Offenbarung durch Christus und das Neue
Testament (Zeitschr. f. Theol. und Kirche I. p. 367 ff.) The
special literature in the above work of Weiss, and in the recent
works on the life of Jesus, and the Biblical Theology of the
New Testament by Beyschlag. [T. T. Clark]

§ 3.   *The Common Preaching concerning Jesus Christ in the
First Generation of Believers.*

Men had met with Jesus Christ and in him had found the
Messiah. They were convinced that God had made him to be
wisdom and righteousness, sanctification and redemption. There
was no hope that did not seem to be certified in him, no
lofty idea which had not become in him a living reality.
Everything that one possessed was offered to him. He was
everything lofty that could be imagined. Everything that can
be said of him was already said in the first two generations
after his appearance. Nay, more: he was felt and known to
be the ever living one Lord of the world and operative principle
of one's own life. "To me to live is Christ and to die is gain;"
"He is the way, the truth and the life." One could now for
the first time be certain of the resurrection and eternal life,
and with that certainty the sorrows of the world melted away
like mist before the sun, and the residue of this present
time became as a day. This group of facts which the history
of the Gospel discloses in the world, is at the same time the
highest and most unique of all that we meet in that history:
it is its seal and distinguishes it from all other universal religions. Where in the history of mankind can we find anything
resembling this, that men who had eaten and drunk with their
Master should glorify him, not only as the revealer of God,
but as the Prince of life, as the Redeemer and Judge of the
world, as the living power of its existence, and that a choir
of Jews and Gentiles, Greeks and Barbarians, wise and foolish,

should along with them immediately confess that out of the fulness of this one man they have received grace for grace? It has been said that Islam furnishes the unique example of a religion born in broad daylight, but the community of Jesus was also born in the clear light of day. The darkness connected with its birth is occasioned not only by the imperfection of the records, but by the uniqueness of the fact, which refers us back to the uniqueness of the Person of Jesus.

But though it certainly is the first duty of the historian to signalise the overpowering impression made by the Person of Jesus on the disciples, which is the basis of all further developments, it would little become him to renounce the critical examination of all the utterances which have been connected with that Person with the view of elucidating and glorifying it; unless he were with Origen to conclude that Jesus was to each and all whatever they fancied him to be for their edification. But this would destroy the personality. Others are of opinion that we should conceive him, in the sense of the early communities, as the second God who is one in essence with the Father, in order to understand from this point of view all the declarations and judgments of these communities. But this hypothesis leads to the most violent distortion of the original declarations, and the suppression or concealment of their most obvious features. The duty of the historian rather consists in fixing the common features of the faith of the first two generations, in explaining them as far as possible from the belief that Jesus is Messiah, and in seeking analogies for the several assertions. Only a very meagre sketch can be given in what follows. The presentation of the matter in the frame-work of the history of dogma does not permit of more, because as noted above, § 1, the presupposition of dogma forming itself in the Gentile Church is not the whole infinitely rich abundance of early Christian views and perceptions. That presupposition is simply a proclamation of the one God and of Christ transferred to Greek soil, fixed merely in its leading features and otherwise very plastic, accompanied by a message regarding the future, and demands for a holy life. At the

same time the Old Testament and the early Christian Palestinian writings with the rich abundance of their contents, did
certainly exercise a silent mission in the earliest communities, till
by the creation of the canon they became a power in the Church.

1. The contents of the faith of the disciples, [1] and the
common proclamation which united them, may be comprised
in the following propositions. Jesus of Nazareth is the Messiah promised by the prophets. Jesus after his death is by
the Divine awakening raised to the right hand of God, and
will soon return to set up his kingdom visibly upon the earth.
He who believes in Jesus, and has been received into the
community of the disciples of Jesus, who, in virtue of a sincere
change of mind, calls on God as Father, and lives according
to the commandments of Jesus, is a saint of God, and as such
can be certain of the sin-forgiving grace of God, and of a
share in the future glory, that is, of redemption. [2]

A community of Christian believers was formed within
the Jewish national community. By its organisation, the close
brotherly union of its members, it bore witness to the
impression which the Person of Jesus had made on it, and
drew from faith in Jesus and hope of his return, the assurance
of eternal life, the power of believing in God the Father and
of fulfilling the lofty moral and social commands which Jesus
had set forth. They knew themselves to be the true Israel of
the Messianic time (see § 1), and for that very reason lived
with all their thoughts and feelings in the future. Hence the
Apocalyptic hopes which in manifold types were current in
the Judaism of the time, and which Jesus had not demolished,
continued to a great extent in force (see § 4). One guarantee
for their fulfilment was supposed to be possessed in the various

---

[1] See the brilliant investigations of Weizsäcker (Apost. Zeitalter. p. 36) as to
the earliest significant names, self-designations, of the disciples. The twelve were
in the first place "μαθηταί," (disciples and family-circle of Jesus, see also the
significance of James and the brethren of Jesus), then witnesses of the resurrection
and therefore Apostles; very soon there appeared beside them, even in Jerusalem,
Prophets and Teachers.

[2] The christian preaching is very pregnantly described in Acts XXVIII. 31, as
κηρύσσειν τὴν Βασιλείαν τοῦ θεοῦ, καὶ διδάσκειν τὰ περὶ τοῦ κυρίου Ἰησοῦ Χριστοῦ.

manifestations of the Spirit, [1] which were displayed in the members of the new communities at their entrance, with which an act of baptism seems to have been united from the very first, [2] and in their gatherings. They were a guarantee that believers really were the ἐκκλησία τοῦ θεοῦ, those called to be saints, and, as such, kings and priests unto God [3] for whom the world, death and devil are overcome, although they still rule the course of the world. The confession of the God of Israel as the Father of Jesus,

---

[1] On the spirit of God (of Christ) see note, p. 50. The earliest christians felt the influence of the spirit as one coming on them from without.

[2] It cannot be directly proved that Jesus instituted baptism, for Matth. XXVIII. 19, is not a saying of the Lord. The reasons for this assertion are: (1) It is only a later stage of the tradition that represents the risen Christ as delivering speeches and giving commandments. Paul knows nothing of it. (2) The Trinitarian formula is foreign to the mouth of Jesus, and has not the authority in the Apostolic age which it must have had if it had descended from Jesus himself. On the other hand, Paul knows of no other way of receiving the Gentiles into the Christian communities than by baptism, and it is highly probable that in the time of Paul all Jewish Christians were also baptised. We may perhaps assume that the practice of baptism was continued in consequence of Jesus' recognition of John the Baptist and his baptism, even after John himself had been removed. According to John IV. 2, Jesus himself baptised not, but his disciples under his superintendence. It is possible only with the help of tradition to trace back to Jesus a "Sacrament of Baptism," or an obligation to it *ex necessitate salutis*, though it is credible that tradition is correct here. Baptism in the Apostolic age was εἰς ἄφεσιν ἁμαρτιῶν, and indeed εἰς τὸ ὄνομα χριστοῦ (1. Cor. I. 13: Acts XIX. 5). We cannot make out when the formula, εἰς τὸ ὄνομα τοῦ πατρὸς, καὶ τοῦ υἱοῦ, καὶ τοῦ ἁγίου πνεύματος, emerged. The formula, εἰς τὸ ὄνομα, expresses that the person baptised is put into a relation of dependence on him into whose name he is baptised. Paul has given baptism a relation to the death of Christ, or justly inferred it from the εἰς ἄφεσιν ἁμαρτιῶν. The descent of the spirit on the baptised very soon ceased to be regarded as the necessary and immediate result of baptism; yet Paul, and probably his contemporaries also, considered the grace of baptism and the communication of the spirit to be inseparably united. See Scholten. Die Taufformel. 1885. Holtzman, Die Taufe im N. T. Ztsch. f. wiss. Theol. 1879.

[3] The designation of the Christian community as ἐκκλησία originates perhaps with Paul, though that is by no means certain; see as to this "name of honour," Sohm, Kirchenrecht, Vol. I. p. 16 ff. The words of the Lord, Matt. XVI. 18: XVIII. 17, belong to a later period. According to Gal. I. 22, ταῖς ἐν χριστῷ is added to the ταῖς ἐκκλησίαις τῆς Ἰουδαίας. The independence of every individual Christian in and before God is strongly insisted on in the Epistles of Paul, and in the Epistle of Peter, and in the Christian portions of Revelations: ἐποίησεν ἡμᾶς βασιλείαν, ἱερεῖς τῷ θεῷ καὶ πατρὶ αὐτοῦ.

and of Jesus as Christ and Lord [1] was sealed by the testimony
of the possession of the Spirit, which as Spirit of God assured
every individual of his call to the kingdom, united him personally
with God himself and became to him the pledge of future glory. [2]

2. As the Kingdom of God which was announced had not
yet visibly appeared, as the appeal to the Spirit could not
be separated from the appeal to Jesus as Messiah, and as
there was actually nothing possessed but the reality of the
Person of Jesus, so, in preaching, all stress must necessarily
fall on this Person. To believe in him was the decisive fundamental requirement, and, at first, under the presupposition
of the religion of Abraham and the Prophets, the sure guarantee of salvation. It is not surprising then to find that in
the earliest Christian preaching Jesus Christ comes before us
as frequently as the Kingdom of God in the preaching of
Jesus himself. The image of Jesus and the power which proceeded from it were the things which were really possessed.
Whatever was expected was expected only from Jesus the
exalted and returning one. The proclamation that the Kingdom of heaven is at hand must therefore become the proclamation that Jesus is the Christ, and that in him the revelation of God is complete. He who lays hold of Jesus lays hold
in him of the grace of God and of a full salvation. We
cannot, however, call this in itself a displacement: but as soon
as the proclamation that Jesus is the Christ ceased to be
made with the same emphasis and the same meaning that it

[1] Jesus is regarded with adoring reverence as Messiah and Lord, that is, these
are regarded as the names which his Father has given him. Christians are those
who call on the name of the Lord Jesus Christ (1 Cor. 1. 2): every creature must
bow before him and confess him as Lord (Phil. II. 9): see Deissmann on the
N. T. formula "in Christo Jesu."

[2] The confession of Father, Son and Spirit is therefore the unfolding of the
belief that Jesus is the Christ; but there was no intention of expressing by this
confession the essential equality of the three persons, or even the similar relation
of the Christian to them. On the contrary, the Father in it is regarded as the
God and Father over all, the Son as revealer, redeemer and Lord, the Spirit as a
possession, principle of the new supernatural life and of holiness. From the
Epistles of Paul we perceive that the Formula, Father, Son and Spirit, could not
yet have been customary, especially in Baptism. But it was approaching (2 Cor.
XIII. 13).

had in his own preaching, and what sort of blessings they
were which he brought, not only was a displacement inevitable, but even a dispossession. But every dispossession requires the given forms to be filled with new contents. Simple
as was the pure tradition of the confession: "Jesus is the Christ,"
the task of rightly appropriating and handing down entire
the peculiar contents which Jesus had given to his self-wit-
nessing and preaching was nevertheless great, and in its limit
uncertain. Even the Jewish Christian could perform this task only
according to the measure of his spiritual understanding and
the strength of his religious life. Moreover, the external position of the first communities in the midst of contemporaries
who had crucified and rejected Jesus, compelled them to
prove, as their main duty, that Jesus really was the Messiah
who was promised. Consequently, everything united to bring
the first communities to the conviction that the proclamation
of the Gospel with which they were entrusted, resolved itself
into the proclamation that Jesus is the Christ. The διδάσκειν
τηρεῖν πάντα ὅσα ἐνετείλατο ὁ Ἰησοῦς (teaching to observe all
that Jesus had commanded), a thing of heart and life, could
not lead to reflection in the same degree, as the διδάσκειν ὅτι
οὗτός ἐστιν ὁ χριστὸς τοῦ θεοῦ (teaching that this is the Christ
of God); for a community which possesses the Spirit does not
reflect on whether its conception is right, but, especially a
missionary community, on what the certainty of its faith rests.

The proclamation of Jesus as the Christ, though rooted entirely in the Old Testament, took its start from the exaltation
of Jesus, which again resulted from his suffering and death.
The proof that the entire Old Testament points to him, and
that his person, his deeds and his destiny are the actual and
precise fulfilment of the Old Testament predictions, was the
foremost interest of believers, so far as they at all looked
backwards. This proof was not used in the first place for the
purpose of making the meaning and value of the Messianic
work of Jesus more intelligible, of which it did not seem to
be in much need, but to confirm the Messiahship of Jesus.
Still, points of view for contemplating the Person and work
of Jesus could not fail to be got from the words of the Pro-

phets. The fundamental conception of Jesus dominating every-thing was, according to the Old Testament, that God had chosen him and through him the Church. God had chosen him and made him to be both Lord and Christ. He had made over to him the work of setting up the Kingdom, and had led him through death and resurrection to a supramundane position of sovereignty, in which he would soon visibly appear and bring about the end. The hope of Christ's speedy return was the most important article in the "Christology," inasmuch as his work was regarded as only reaching its conclusion by that return. It was the most difficult, inasmuch as the Old Testament contained nothing of a second advent of Messiah. Belief in the second advent became the specific Christian belief.

But the searching in the scriptures of the Old Testament, that is, in the prophetic texts, had already, in estimating the Person and dignity of Christ, given an important impulse to-wards transcending the frame-work of the idea of the theo-cracy completed solely in and for Israel. Moreover, belief in the exaltation of Christ to the right hand of God, caused men to form a corresponding idea of the beginning of his existence. The missionary work among the Gentiles, so soon begun and so rich in results, threw a new light on the range of Christ's pur-pose and work, and led to the consideration of its significance for the whole human race. Finally, the self-testimony of Jesus summoned them to ponder his relation to God the Father, with the presuppositions of that relation, and to give it expression in intelligible statements. Speculation had already begun on these four points in the Apostolic age, and had resulted in very dif ferent utterances as to the Person and dignity of Jesus (§ 4). [1]

[1] The Christological utterances which are found in the New Testament writings, so far as they explain and paraphrase the confession of Jesus as the Christ and the Lord, may be almost entirely deduced from one or other of the four points mentioned in the text. But we must at the same time insist that these declarations were meant to be explanations of the confession that "Jesus is the Lord," which of course included the recognition that Jesus by the resurrection became a heavenly being (see Weizsäcker in above mentioned work, p. 110). The solemn protestation of Paul, 1 Cor. XII. 3; διὸ γνωρίζω ὑμῖν ὅτι οὐδεὶς ἐν πνεύματι θεοῦ λαλῶν λέγει ΑΝΑΘΕΜΑ ΙΗΣΟΥΣ, καὶ οὐδεὶς δύναται εἰπεῖν ΚΥΡΙΟΣ ΙΗΣΟΥΣ εἰ μὴ ἐν πνεύματι ἁγίῳ (cf. Rom. X. 9), shews that he who acknowledged Jesus as the Lord, and accordingly believed in the resurrection of Jesus, was regarded as a full-

3. Since Jesus had appeared and was believed on as the
Messiah promised by the Prophets, the aim and contents of
his mission seemed already to be therewith stated with sufficient clearness. Further, as the work of Christ was not yet
completed, the view of those contemplating it was, above all,
turned to the future. But in virtue of express words of Jesus,
and in the consciousness of having received the Spirit of God,
one was already certain of the forgiveness of sin dispensed
by God, of righteousness before him, of the full knowledge
of the Divine will, and of the call to the future Kingdom as a
present possession. In the procuring of these blessings not a
few perceived with certainty the results of the first advent of
Messiah, that is, his work. This work might be seen in the
whole activity of Christ. But as the forgiveness of sins might
be conceived as *the* blessing of salvation which included with
certainty every other blessing, as Jesus had put his death in
express relation with this blessing, and as the fact of this
death so mysterious and offensive required a special explanation, there appeared in the foreground from the very beginning the confession, in 1 Cor. XV. 3: παρέδωκα ὑμῖν ἐν πρώτοις,
ὃ καὶ παρέλαβον, ὅτι χριστὸς ἀπέθανεν ὑπὲρ τῶν ἁμαρτιῶν ἡμῶν.
"I delivered unto you first of all that which I also received,
that *Christ died for our sins.*" Not only Paul, for whom, in
virtue of his special reflections and experiences, the cross of
Christ had become the central point of all knowledge, but
also the majority of believers, must have regarded the preaching of the death of the Lord as an essential article in
the preaching of Christ, [1] seeing that, as a rule, they placed

born Christian. It] undoubtedly excludes from the Apostolic age the independent
authority of any christological dogma besides that confession and the worship of
Christ connected with it. It is worth notice, however, that those early Christian
men who recognised Christianity as the vanquishing of the Old Testament religion
(Paul, the Author of the Epistle to the Hebrews, John) all held that Christ was a
being who had come down from heaven.

[1] Compare in their fundamental features the common declarations about the
saving value of the death of Christ in Paul, in the Johannine writings, in 1st
Peter, in the Epistle to the Hebrews, and in the Christian portions of the book
of Revelation: τῷ ἀγαπῶντί ἡμᾶς καὶ λύσαντι ἡμᾶς ἐκ τοῦ ἁμαρτιῶν ἐν τῷ αἵματι
αὐτοῦ, αὐτῷ ἡ δόξα: Compare the reference to Isaiah LIII. and the Passover lamb:

it somehow under the aspect of a sacrifice offered to God. Still, there were very different conceptions of the value of the death as a means of procuring salvation, and there may have been many who were satisfied with basing its necessity on the fact that it had been predicted, (ἀπέθανεν κατὰ τὰς γραφάς: "he died for our sins *according to the scriptures*"), while their real religious interests were entirely centered in the future glory to be procured by Christ. But it must have been of greater significance for the following period that, from the first, a short account of the destiny of Jesus lay at the basis of all preaching about him (see a part of this in i. Cor. XV. 1-11). Those articles in which the identity of the Christ who had appeared with the Christ who had been promised stood out with special clearness, must have been taken up into this report, as well as those which transcended the common expectations of Messiah, which for that very reason appeared of special importance, viz., his death and resurrection. In putting together this report, there was no intention of describing the "work" of Christ. But after the interest which occasioned it had been obscured, and had given place to other interests, the customary preaching of those articles must have led men to see in them Christ's real performance, his "work." [1]

4. The firm confidence of the disciples in Jesus was rooted in the belief that he did not abide in death, but was raised by God. That Christ had risen was, in virtue of what they had experienced in him, certainly only after they had seen him, just as sure as the fact of his death, and became the main article of their preaching about him. [2] But in the

the utterances about the "lamb" generally in the early writings: see Westcott, The Epistles of John, p. 34 f.: The idea of the blood of Christ in the New Testament.

[1] This of course could not take place otherwise than by reflecting on its significance. But a dislocation was already completed as soon as it was isolated and separated from the whole of Jesus, or even from his future activity. Reflection on the meaning or the causes of particular facts might easily, in virtue of that isolation, issue in entirely new conceptions.

[2] See the discriminating statements of Weizsäcker, "Apostolic Age," p. 1 f., especially as to the significance of Peter as first witness of the resurrection. Cf. 1 Cor. XV. 5 with Luke XXIV. 34: also the fragment of the "Gospel of Peter" which unfortunately breaks off at the point where one expects the appearance of the Lord to Peter.

message of the risen Lord was contained not only the conviction that he lives again, and now lives for ever, but also
the assurance that his people will rise in like manner and
live eternally. Consequently, the resurrection of Jesus became
the sure pledge of the resurrection of all believers, that is of
their real personal resurrection. No one at the beginning
thought of a mere immortality of the spirit, not even those
who assumed the perishableness of man's sensuous nature. In
conformity with the uncertainty which yet adhered to the
idea of resurrection in Jewish hopes and speculations, the
concrete notions of it in the Christian communities were also
fluctuating. But this could not affect the certainty of the
conviction that the Lord would raise his people from death.
This conviction, whose reverse side is the fear of that God
who casts into hell, has become the mightiest power through
which the Gospel has won humanity. [1]

[1] It is often said that Christianity rests on the belief in the resurrection of
Christ. This may be correct, if it is first declared who this Jesus Christ is, and
what his life signifies. But when it appears as a naked report to which one must
above all submit, and when in addition, as often happens, it is supplemented by
the assertion that the resurrection of Christ is the most certain fact in the history
of the world, one does not know whether he should marvel more at its thought-
lessness or its unbelief. We do not need to have faith in a fact, and that which
requires religious belief, that is, trust in God, can never be a fact which would
hold good apart from that belief. The historical question and the question of
faith must therefore be clearly distinguished here. The following points are
historically certain. (1) That none of Christ's opponents saw him after his death.
(2) That the disciples were convinced that they had seen him soon after his death.
(3) That the succession and number of those appearances can no longer be ascertained with certainty. (4) That the disciples and Paul were conscious of having
seen Christ not in the crucified earthly body, but in heavenly glory—even the later
incredible accounts of the appearances of Christ, which strongly emphasise the
reality of the body, speak at the same time of such a body as can pass through
closed doors, which certainly is not an earthly body. (5) That Paul does not
compare the manifestation of Christ given to him with any of his later visions,
but, on the other hand, describes it in the words (Gal. I. 15: ὅτε εὐδόκησεν ὁ θεὸς
ἀποκαλύψαι τὸν υἱὸν αὐτοῦ ἐν ἐμοί, and yet puts it on a level with the appearances
which the earlier Apostles had seen. But, as even the empty grave on the third
day can by no means be regarded as a certain historical fact, because it appears
united in the accounts with manifest legendary features, and further because it is
directly excluded by the way in which Paul has portrayed the resurrection 1 Cor.
XV. it follows: (1) That every conception which represents the resurrection of
Christ as a simple reanimation of his mortal body, is far from the original conception, and (2) that the question generally as to whether Jesus has risen, can have

5. After the appearance of Paul, the earliest communities were greatly exercised by the question as to how believers obtain the righteousness which they possess, and what significance a precise observance of the law of the Fathers may have in connection with it. While some would hear of no change in the regulations and conceptions which had hitherto existed, and regarded the bestowal of righteousness by God as possible only on condition of a strict observance of the law, others taught that Jesus as Messiah had procured righteousness for his people, had fulfilled the law once for all, and had founded a new covenant, either in opposition to the old, or as a stage above it. Paul especially saw in the death of Christ the end of the law, and deduced righteousness solely from faith in Christ, and sought to prove from the Old Testament itself, by means of historical speculation, the merely temporary validity of the law and therewith the abrogation of the Old

no existence for any one who looks at it apart from the contents and worth of the Person of Jesus. For the mere fact that friends and adherents of Jesus were convinced that they had seen him, especially when they themselves explain that he appeared to them in heavenly glory, gives, to those who are in earnest about fixing historical facts, not the least cause for the assumption that Jesus did not continue in the grave.

History is therefore at first unable to bring any succour to faith here. However firm may have been the faith of the disciples in the appearances of Jesus in their midst, and it was firm, to believe in appearances which others have had is a frivolity which is always revenged by rising doubts. But history is still of service to faith: it limits its scope and therewith shews the province to which it belongs. The question which history leaves to faith is this: Was Jesus Christ swallowed up of death, or did he pass through suffering and the cross to glory, that is, to life, power and honour? The disciples would have been convinced of that in the sense in which Jesus meant them to understand it, though they had not seen him in glory (a consciousness of this is found in Luke XXIV. 26: οὐχὶ ταῦτα ἔδει παθεῖν τὸν χριστὸν καὶ εἰσελθεῖν εἰς τὴν δόξαν αὐτοῦ; and Joh. XX. 29: ὅτι ἑώρακας με πεπίστευκας, μακάριοι οἱ μὴ ἰδόντες καὶ πιστεύσαντας) and we might probably add, that no appearances of the Lord could permanently have convinced them of his life, if they had not possessed in their hearts the impression of his Person. Faith in the eternal life of Christ and in our own eternal life is not the condition of becoming a disciple of Jesus, but is the final confession of discipleship. Faith has by no means to do with the knowledge of the form in which Jesus lives, but only with the conviction that he is the living Lord The determination of the form was immediately dependent on the most varied general ideas of the future life, resurrection, restoration, and glorification of the body, which were current at the time. The idea of the rising again of the body of Jesus appeared comparatively

Testament religion. Others, and this view, which is not everywhere to be explained by Alexandrian influences (see above
p. 72 f.), is not foreign to Paul, distinguished between spirit and
letter in the Mosaic law, giving to everything a spiritual significance, and in this sense holding that the whole law as
νόμος πνευματικός was binding. The question whether righteousness comes from the works of the law or from faith, was
displaced by this conception, and therefore remained in its
deepest grounds unsolved, or was decided in the sense of a
spiritualised legalism. But the detachment of Christianity from
the political forms of the Jewish religion, and from sacrificial
worship, was also completed by the conception, although it
was regarded as identical with the Old Testament religion
rightly understood. The surprising results of the direct mission to the Gentiles would seem to have first called forth
those controversies (but see Stephen) and given them the

early, because it was this hope which animated wide circles of pious people for
their own future. Faith in Jesus, the living Lord, in spite of the death on the
cross, cannot be generated by proofs of reason or authority, but only to-day in
the same way as Paul has confessed of himself: ὅτε εὐδόκησεν ὁ θεὸς ἀποκαλύψαι
τὸν υἱὸν αὐτοῦ ἐν ἐμοί. The conviction of having seen the Lord was no doubt of
the greatest importance for the disciples and made them Evangelists: but what
they saw cannot at first help us. It can only then obtain significance for us when
we have gained that confidence in the Lord which Peter has expressed in Mark
VIII. 29. The Christian even to-day confesses with Paul: εἰ ἐν τῇ ζωῇ ταύτῃ ἐν
χριστῷ ἠλπικότες ἐσμὲν μόνον, ἐλεεινότεροι πάντων ἀνθρώπων ἐσμέν. He believes in
a future life for himself with God because he believes that Christ lives. That is
the peculiarity and paradox of Christian faith. But these are not convictions that
can be common and matter of course to a deep feeling and earnest thinking being
standing amid nature and death, but can only be possessed by those who live with
their whole hearts and minds in God, and even they need the prayer: "I believe,
help thou mine unbelief." To act as if faith in eternal life and in the living Christ
was the simplest thing in the world, or a dogma to which one has just to submit,
is irreligious. The whole question about the resurrection of Christ, its mode and
its significance, has thereby been so thoroughly confused in later Christendom, that
we are in the habit of considering eternal life as certain, even apart from Christ.
That, at any rate, is not Christian. It is Christian to pray that God would give
the Spirit to make us strong to overcome the feelings and the doubts of nature,
and create belief in an eternal life through the experience of "dying to live."
Where this faith, obtained in this way, exists, it has always been supported by the
conviction that the Man lives who brought life and immortality to light. To hold
fast this faith is the goal of life, for only what we consciously strive for is in this
matter our own. What we think we possess is very soon lost.

highest significance. The fact that one section of Jewish Christians, and even some of the Apostles at length recognised the right of the Gentile Christians to be Christians without first becoming Jews, is the clearest proof that what was above all prized was faith in Christ and surrender to him as the Saviour. In agreeing to the direct mission to the Gentiles the earliest Christians, while they themselves observed the law, broke up the national religion of Israel, and gave expression to the conviction that Jesus was not only the Messiah of his people, but the redeemer of humanity. [1] The establishment of the universal character of the Gospel, that is, of Christianity as a religion for the world, became now, however, a problem, the solution of which, as given by Paul, but few were able to understand or make their own.

6. In the conviction that salvation is entirely bound up with faith in Jesus Christ, Christendom gained the consciousness of being a new creation of God. But while the sense of being the true Israel was thereby, at the same time, held fast, there followed, on the one hand, entirely new historical perspectives, and on the other, deep problems which demanded solution. As a new creation of God, ἡ ἐκκλησία τοῦ θεοῦ, the community was conscious of having been chosen by God in Jesus before the foundation of the world. In the conviction of being the true Israel, it claimed for itself the whole

---

[1] Weizsäcker (Apostolic Age, p. 73) says very justly: "The rising of Judaism against believers put them on their own feet. They saw themselves for the first time persecuted in the name of the law, and therewith for the first time it must have become clear to them, that in reality the law was no longer the same to them as to the others. Their hope is the coming kingdom of heaven, in which it is not the law, but their Master from whom they expect salvation. Everything connected with salvation is in him. But we should not investigate the conditions of the faith of that early period, as though the question had been laid before the Apostles whether they could have part in the Kingdom of heaven without circumcision, or whether it could be obtained by faith in Jesus, with or without the observance of the law. Such questions had no existence for them either practically or as questions of the school. But though they were Jews, and the law which even their Master had not abolished, was for them a matter of course, that did not exclude a change of inner position towards it, through faith in their Master and hope of the Kingdom. There is an inner freedom which can grow up alongside of all the constraints of birth, custom, prejudice, and piety. But this only comes into consciousness, when a demand is made on it which wounds it, or when it is assailed on account of an inference drawn not by its own consciousness, but only by its opponents.

historical development recorded in the Old Testament, convinced that all the divine activity there recorded had the
new community in view. The great question which was to
find very different answers, was how, in accordance with this
view, the Jewish nation, so far as it had not recognised Jesus
as Messiah, should be judged. The detachment of Christianity
from Judaism was the most important preliminary condition,
and therefore the most important preparation, for the Mission
among the Gentile nations, and for union with the Greek spirit.

Supplement 1.—Renan and others go too far when they say
that Paul alone has the glory of freeing Christianity from the
fetters of Judaism. Certainly the great Apostle could say in this
connection also: περισσότερον αὐτῶν πάντων ἐκοπίασα, but there
were others beside him who, in the power of the Gospel, transcended
the limits of Judaism. Christian communities, it may now be
considered certain, had arisen in the empire, in Rome for example,
which were essentially free from the law without being in any
way determined by Paul's preaching. It was Paul's merit that
he clearly formulated the great question, established the universalism of Christianity in a peculiar manner, and yet in doing so
held fast the character of Christianity as a positive religion, as
distinguished from Philosophy and Moralism. But the later development presupposes neither his clear formulation nor his peculiar
establishment of universalism, but only the universalism itself.

Supplement 2.—The dependence of the Pauline Theology
on the Old Testament or on Judaism is overlooked in the traditional contrasting of Paulinism and Jewish Christianity, in
which Paulinism is made equivalent to Gentile Christianity.
This theology, as we might *a priori* suppose, could, apart from
individual exceptions, be intelligible as a whole to born Jews,
if to any, for its doctrinal presuppositions were strictly Pharisaic, and its boldness in criticising the Old Testament, rejecting and asserting the law in its historical sense, could be as
little congenial to the Gentile Christians as its piety towards
the Jewish people. This judgment is confirmed by a glance at
the fate of Pauline Theology in the 120 years that followed.
Marcion was the only Gentile Christian who understood Panl,
and even he misunderstood him: the rest never got beyond

the appropriation of particular Pauline sayings, and exhibited
no comprehension especially of the theology of the Apostle,
so far as in it the universalism of Christianity as a religion
is proved, even without recourse to Moralism and without putting a new construction on the Old Testament religion. It
follows from this, however, that the scheme "Jewish Christianity"—"Gentile Christianity" is insufficient. We must rather,
in the Apostolic age, at least at its close, distinguish four
main tendencies that may have crossed each other here and
there, [1] (within which again different shades appear). (1) The
Gospel has to do with the people of Israel, and with the
Gentile world only on the condition that believers attach
themselves to the people of Israel. The punctilious observance of the law is still necessary and the condition on which
the messianic salvation is bestowed (particularism and legalism,
in practice and in principle, which, however, was not to cripple
the obligation to prosecute the work of the Mission). (2) The
Gospel has to do with Jews and Gentiles: the first, as believers in Christ, are under obligation as before to observe the
law, the latter are not; but for that reason they cannot on
earth fuse into one community with the believing Jews. Very
different judgments in details were possible on this stand-point;
but the bestowal of salvation could no longer be thought of
as depending simply on the keeping of the ceremonial commandments of the law [2] (universalism in principle, particularism in practice; the prerogative of Israel being to some
extent clung to). (3) The Gospel has to do with both Jews
and Gentiles; no one is any longer under obligation to observe

---

[1] Only one of these four tendencies—the Pauline, with the Epistle to the Hebrews
and the Johannine writings which are related to Paulinism—has seen in the Gospel
the establishment of a new religion. The rest identified it with Judaism made
perfect, or with the Old Testament religion rightly understood. But Paul, in
connecting Christianity with the promise given to Abraham, passing thus beyond
the actual Old Testament religion, has not only given it a historical foundation,
but also claimed for the Father of the Jewish nation a unique significance for
Christianity. As to the tendencies named 1 and 2, see Book I. chap. 6.

[2] It is clear from Gal. II. 11 ff that Peter then and for long before occupied
in principle the stand-point of Paul: see the judicious remarks of Weizsäcker in
the book mentioned above, p. 75 f.

the law; for the law is abolished (or fulfilled), and the salvation which Christ's death has procured is appropriated by faith. The law (that is the Old Testament religion) in its literal sense is of divine origin, but was intended from the first only for a definite epoch of history. The prerogative of Israel remains, and is shewn in the fact that salvation was first offered to the Jews, and it will be shewn again at the end of all history. That prerogative refers to the nation as a whole, and has nothing to do with the question of the salvation of individuals (Paulinism: universalism in principle and in practice, and Antinomianism in virtue of the recognition of a merely temporary validity of the whole law; breach with the traditional religion of Israel; recognition of the prerogative of the people of Israel; the clinging to the prerogative of the people of Israel was not, however, necessary on this stand-point: see the epistle to the Hebrews and the Gospel of John). (4) The Gospel has to do with Jews and Gentiles: no one need therefore be under obligation to observe the ceremonial commandments and sacrificial worship, because these commandments themselves are only the wrappings or moral and spiritual commandments which the Gospel has set forth as fulfilled in a more perfect form (universalism in principle and in practice in virtue of a neutralising of the distinction between law and Gospel, old and new; spiritualising and universalising of the law). [1]

---

[1] These four tendencies were represented in the Apostolic age by those who had been born and trained in Judaism, and they were collectively transplanted into Greek territory. But we cannot be sure that the third of the above tendencies found intelligent and independent representatives in this domain, as there is no certain evidence of it. Only one who had really been subject to it, and therefore understood it, could venture on a criticism of the Old Testament religion. Still, it may be noted that the majority of non-Jewish converts in the Apostolic age had probably come to know the Old Testament beforehand—not always the Jewish religion, (see Havet, Le Christianisme, T. IV. p. 120: "Je ne sais s'il y est entré, du vivant de Paul, un seul païen: je veux dire un homme, qui ne connût pas déjà, avant d'y entrer, le judaîsm et la Bible "). These indications will shew how mistaken and misleading it is to express the different tendencies in the Apostolic age and the period closely following by the designations "Jewish Christianity—Gentile Christianity." Short watchwords are so little appropriate here that one might even with some justice reverse the usual conception, and maintain that what is usually understood by Gentile Christianity (criticism of the Old Testament religion) was possible only within Judaism, while that which is frequently called Jewish Christianity

Supplement 3.—The appearance of Paul is the most important fact in the history of the Apostolic age. It is impossible
to give in a few sentences an abstract of his theology and
work; and the insertion here of a detailed account is forbidden,
not only by the external limits, but by the aim of this investigation. For, as already indicated (§ 1), the doctrinal formation in the Gentile Church is not connected with the
whole phenomenon of the Pauline theology, but only with
certain leading thoughts which were only in part peculiar to
the Apostle. His most peculiar thoughts acted on the development of Ecclesiastical doctrine only by way of occasional stimulus.
We can find room here only for a few general outlines. [1]

(1) The inner conviction that Christ had revealed himself
to him, that the Gospel was the message of the crucified and
risen Christ, and that God had called him to proclaim that
message to the world, was the power and the secret of his
personality and his activity. These three elements were a
unity in the consciousness of Paul, constituting his conversion and determining his after-life. (2) In this conviction he
knew himself to be a new creature, and so vivid was this
knowledge that he was constrained to become a Jew to the
Jews, and a Greek to the Greeks in order to gain them. (3)
The crucified and risen Christ became the central point of
his theology, and not only the central point, but the one
source and ruling principle. The Christ was not in his
estimation Jesus of Nazareth now exalted, but the mighty
personal spiritual being in divine form who had for a time

is rather a conception which must have readily suggested itself to born Gentiles
superficially acquainted with the Old Testament.

[1] The first edition of this volume could not appeal to Weizsäcker's work, Das
Apostolische Zeitalter der Christlichen Kirche, 1886, [second edition translated in
this series]. The author is now in the happy position of being able to refer the
readers of his imperfect sketch to this excellent presentation, the strength of which
lies in the delineation of Paulinism in its relation to the early Church, and to
early Christian theology (p. 79-172). The truth of Weizsäcker's expositions of the
inner relations (p. 85 f.), is but little affected by his assumptions concerning the
outer relations, which I cannot everywhere regard as just. (The work of Weizsäcker as a whole is, in my opinion, the most important work on Church history
we have received since Ritschl's "Entstehung der alt-katholischen Kirche." 2
Aufl. 1857.)

humbled himself, and who as Spirit has broken up the world
of law, sin and death, and continues to overcome them in
believers. (4) Theology therefore was to him, looking forwards,
the doctrine of the liberating power of the Spirit (of Christ)
in all the concrete relations of human life and need. The
Christ who has already overcome law, sin and death, lives as
Spirit, and through his Spirit lives in believers, who for that
very reason know him not after the flesh. He is a creative
power of life to those who receive him in faith in his redeeming death upon the cross, that is to say, to those who
are justified. The life in the Spirit, which results from union
with Christ, will at last reveal itself also in the body (not in
the flesh). (5) Looking backwards, theology was to Paul a
doctrine of the law and of its abrogation; or more accurately,
a description of the old system before Christ in the light of
the Gospel, and the proof that it was destroyed by Christ. The
scriptural proof, even here, is only a superadded support to
inner considerations which move entirely within the thought
that that which is abrogated has already had its due, by having
its whole strength made manifest that it might then be annulled,—the law, the flesh of sin, death: by the law the
law is destroyed, sin is abolished in sinful flesh, death is destroyed by death. (6) The historical view which followed
from this begins, as regards Christ, with Adam and Abraham;
as regards the law, with Moses. It closes, as regards Christ,
with the prospect of a time when he shall have put all enemies beneath his feet, when God will be all in all; as regards
Moses and the promises given to the Jewish nation, with the
prospect of a time when all Israel will be saved. (7) Paul's
doctrine of Christ starts from the final confession of the primitive Church, that Christ is with the Father as a heavenly
being and as Lord of the living and the dead. Though Paul
must have accurately known the proclamation concerning the
historical Christ, his theology in the strict sense of the word
does not revert to it: but springing over the historical, it
begins with the pre-existent Christ (the Man from heaven),
whose moral deed it was to assume the flesh in self-denying
love, in order to break for all men the powers of nature and

the doom of death. But he has pointed to the words and example of the historical Christ in order to rule the life in the Spirit. (8) Deductions, proofs, and perhaps also conceptions, which in point of form betray the theology of the Pharisaic schools, were forced from the Apostle by Christian opponents, who would only grant a place to the message of the crucified Christ beside the δικαιοσύνη ἐξ ἔργων Both as an exegete and as a typologist he appears as a disciple of the Pharisees. But his dialectic about law, circumcision and sacrifice, does not form the kernel of his religious mode of thought, though, on the other hand, it was unquestionably his very Pharisaism which qualified him for becoming what he was. Pharisaism embraced nearly everything lofty which Judaism apart from Christ at all possessed, and its doctrine of providence, its energetic insistence on making manifest the religious contrasts, its Messianic expectations, its doctrines of sin and predestination, were conditions for the genesis of a religious and Christian character such as Paul.[1] This first Christian of the second generation is the highest product of the Jewish spirit under the creative power of the Spirit of Christ. Pharisaism had fulfilled its mission for the world when it produced this man. (9) But Hellenism also had a share in the making of Paul, a fact which does not conflict with his Pharisaic origin, but is partly given with it. In spite of all its exclusiveness the desire for making proselytes especially in the Diaspora, was in the blood of Pharisaism. Paul continued the old movement in a new way, and he was qualified for his work among the Greeks by an accurate knowledge of the Greek translation of the Old Testament, by considerable dexterity in the use of the Greek language, and by a growing insight into the spiritual life of the Greeks. But the peculiarity of his Gospel as a message from the Spirit of Christ, which was equally near to and equally distant from every religious and moral mode of thought

---

[1] Kabisch, *Die Eschatologie des Paulus*, 1893, has shewn how strongly the eschatology of Paul was influenced by the later Pharisaic Judaism. He has also called attention to the close connection between Paul's doctrine of sin and the fall, and that of the Rabbis.

among the nations of the world, signified much more than
all this. This Gospel—who can say whether Hellenism had
already a share in its conception—required that the missionary to the Greeks should become a Greek and that believers
should come to know, "all things are yours, and ye are Christ's."
Paul, as no doubt other missionaries besides him, connected
the preaching of Christ with the Greek mode of thought;
he even employed philosophic doctrines of the Greeks as
presuppositions in his apologetic,[1] and therewith prepared
the way for the introduction of the Gospel to the Græco-
Roman world of thought. But, in my opinion, he has nowhere
allowed that world of thought to influence his doctrine of
salvation. This doctrine, however, was so fashioned in its
practical aims that it was not necessary to become a Jew in
order to appropriate it. (10) Yet we cannot speak of any
total effect of Paulinism, as there was no such thing. The
abundance of its details was too great and the greatness of
its simplicity too powerful, its hope of the future too vivid,
its doctrine of the law too difficult, its summons to a new
life in the spirit too mighty to be comprehended and adhered
to even by those communities which Paul himself had founded.
What they did comprehend was its Monotheism, its universalism, its redemption, its eternal life, its asceticism; but all
this was otherwise combined than by Paul. The style became
Hellenic, and the element of a new kind of knowledge from
the very first, as in the Church of Corinth, seems to have
been the ruling one. The Pauline doctrine of the incarnate
heavenly Man was indeed apprehended; it fell in with Greek
notions, although it meant something very different from the
notions which Greeks had been able to form of it.

Supplement 4.—What we justly prize above all else in the
New Testament is that it is a union of the three groups,

---

[1] Some of the Church Fathers (see Socr. H. E. III. 16) have attributed to Paul
an accurate knowledge of Greek literature and philosophy: but that cannot be
proved. The references of Heinrici (2 Kor -Brief. p. 537-604) are worthy of our
best thanks; but no certain judgment can be formed about the measure of the
Apostles' Greek culture, so long as we do not know how great was the extent of
spiritual ideas which were already precipitated in the speech of the time.

Synoptic Gospels, Pauline Epistles, [1] and Johannine writings, in which are expressed the richest contents of the earliest history of the Gospel. In the Synodic Gospels and the epistles of Paul are represented two types of preaching the Gospel which mutually supplement each other. The subsequent history is dependent on both, and would have been other than it is had not both existed alongside of each other. On the other hand, the peculiar and lofty conception of Christ and of the Gospel, which stands out in the writings of John, has directly exercised no demonstrable influence on the succeeding development— with the exception of one peculiar movement, the Montanistic which, however, does not rest on a true understanding of these writings—and indeed partly for the same reason that has prevented the Pauline theology as a whole from having such an influence. What is given in these writings is a criticism of the Old Testament as religion, or the independence of the Christian religion, in virtue of an accurate knowledge of the Old Testament through development of its hidden germs. The Old Testament stage of religion is really transcended and over-come in the Johannine Christianity, just as in Paulinism, and in the theology of the epistle to the Hebrews. "The circle of disciples who appropriated this characterisation of Jesus is," says Weizsäcke, "a revived Christ-party in the higher sense." But this transcending of the Old Testament religion was the very thing that was unintelligible, because there were few ripe for such a conception. Moreover, the origin of the Johannine writings is, from the stand-point of a history of literature and dogma, the most marvellous enigma which the early history of Christianity presents: Here we have portrayed a Christ who clothes the indescribable with words, and proclaims as his own self-testimony what his disciples have experienced

---

[1] The epistle to the Hebrews and the first epistle of Peter, as well as the Pastoral epistles belong to the Pauline circle; they are of the greatest value because they shew that certain fundamental features of Pauline theology took effect after-wards in an original way, or received independent parallels, and because they prove that the cosmic Christology of Paul made the greatest impression and was continued. In Christology, the epistle to the Ephesians in particular, leads directly from Paul to the pneumatic Christology of the post-apostolic period. Its non-genuineness is by no means certain to me.

in him, a speaking, acting, Pauline Christ, walking on the
earth, far more human than the Christ of Paul and yet
far more Divine, an abundance of allusions to the historical
Jesus, and at the same time the most sovereign treatment of
the history. One divines that the Gospel can find no loftier
expression than John XVII.: one feels that Christ himself put
these words into the mouth of the disciple, who gives them
back to him, but word and thing, history and doctrine are
surrounded by a bright cloud of the suprahistorical. It is
easy to shew that this Gospel could as little have been written without Hellenism, as Luther's treatise on the freedom of
a Christian man could have been written without the "Deutsche Theologie." But the reference to Philo and Hellenism
is by no means sufficient here, as it does not satisfactorily
explain even one of the external aspects of the problem. The
elements operative in the Johannine theology were not Greek
Theologoumena—even the Logos has little more in common
with that of Philo than the name, and its mention at the beginning of the book is a mystery, not the solution of one [1]—

---

[1] In the Ztschr. für Theol. und Kirche, II. p. 189 ff. I have discussed the relation of the prologue of the fourth Gospel to the whole work and endeavoured to
prove the following: "The prologue of the Gospel is not the key to its comprehension. It begins with a well-known great object, the Logos, re-adapts and
transforms it—implicitly opposing false Christologies—in order to substitute for it
Jesus Christ, the μονογενὴς θεός, or in order to unveil it as this Jesus Christ. The
idea of the Logos is allowed to fall from the moment that this takes place." The
author continues to narrate of Jesus only with the view of establishing the belief
that he is the Messiah, the Son of God. This faith has for its main article the
recognition that Jesus is descended from God and from heaven; but the author is
far from endeavouring to work out this recognition from cosmological, philosophical
considerations. According to the Evangelist, Jesus proves himself to be the Messiah,
the Son of God, in virtue of his self-testimony, and because he has brought a
full knowledge of God and life—purely supernatural divine blessings. (Cf. besides,
and partly in opposition, Holtzmann, i. d. Ztschr. f. wissensch. Theol. 1893.) The
author's peculiar world of theological ideas, is not, however, so entirely isolated
in the early Christian literature as appears on the first impression. If, as is
probable, the Ignatian Epistles are independent of the Gospel of John, further, the
Supper prayer in the Didache, finally, certain mystic theological phrases in the
Epistle of Barnabas, in the second epistle of Clement, and in Hermas: a complex
of Theologoumena may be put together, which reaches back to the primitive period
of the Church, and may be conceived as the general ground for the theology of
John. This complex has on its side a close connection with the final development
of the Jewish Hagiographic literature under Greek influence.

but the Apostolic testimony concerning Christ has created from the old faith of Psalmists and Prophets, a new faith in a man who lived with the disciples of Jesus among the Greeks. For that very reason, in spite of his abrupt Anti-judaism, we must without doubt regard the Author as a born Jew.

Supplement 5.—The authorities to which the Christian communities were subjected in faith and life, were these: (1) The Old Testament interpreted in the Christian sense. (2) The tradition of the Messianic history of Jesus. (3) The words of the Lord: see the epistles of Paul, especially 1 Corinthians. But every writing which was proved to have been given by the Spirit has also to be regarded as an authority, and every tested Christian Prophet and Teacher inspired by the Spirit could claim that his words be received and regarded as the words of God. Moreover, the twelve whom Jesus had chosen had a special authority, and Paul claimed a similiar authority for himself (διατάξεις τῶν ἀποστόλων). Consequently, there were numerous courts of appeal in the earliest period of Christendom, of diverse kinds and by no means strictly defined. In the manifold gifts of the spirit was given a fluid element indefinable in its range and scope, an element which guaranteed freedom of development, but which also threatened to lead the enthusiastic communities to extravagance.

Literature.—Weiss, Biblical Theology of the New Testament, 1884. Beyschlag, New Testament Theology, 1892. Ritschl, Entstehung der Alt-Katholischen Kirche, 2 Edit. 1857. Reuss, History of Christian Theology in the Apostolic Age, 1864. Baur, The Apostle Paul, 1866. Holsten, Zum Evangelium des Paulus und Petrus, 1868. Pfleiderer, Paulinism, 1873 : also, Das Urchristenthum, 1887. Schenkel, Das Christusbild der Apostel, 1879. Renan, Origins of Christianity, Vols. II.—IV. Havet, Le Christianisme et ses orig. T. IV. 1884. Lechler, The Apostolic and Post-Apostolic Age, 1885. Weizsäcker, The Apostolic Age, 1892. Hatch, Article "Paul" in the Encyclopædia Britannica. Everett, The Gospel of Paul. Boston, 1893. On the origin and earliest history of the Christian proofs from prophecy, see my "Texte und Unters. z. Gesch. der Alt-Christl." Lit. I. 3, p. 56 f.

§ 4. *The Current Exposition of the Old Testament, and the*
      Jewish hopes of the future, in their significance for
      the earliest types of Christian preaching.

Instead of the frequently very fruitless investigations about
"Jewish-Christian", and "Gentile-Christian", it should be asked,
What Jewish elements have been naturalised in the Christian
Church, which were in no way demanded by the contents of
the Gospel? Have these elements been simply weakened in
course of the development, or have some of them been strengthened by a peculiar combination with the Greek? We have
to do here, in the first instance, with the doctrine of Demons
and Angels, the view of history, the growing exclusiveness,
the fanaticism; and on the other hand, with the cultus, and
the Theocracy, expressing itself in forms of law.

1. Although Jesus had in principle abolished the methods
of pedantry, the casuistic treatment of the law, and the sub-
tleties of prophetic interpretation, yet the old Scholastic exegesis remained active in the Christian communities above all
the unhistorical local method in the exposition of the Old
Testament, both allegoristic and Haggadic; for in the exposition of a sacred text—and the Old Testament was regarded
as such—one is always required to look away from its historical limitations and to expound it according to the needs
of the present. [1] The traditional view exercised its influence
on the exposition of the Old Testament, as well as on the
representations of the person, fate and deeds of Jesus, especially in those cases where the question was about the proof
of the fulfilment of prophecy, that is, of the Messiahship of
Jesus. (See above § 3, 2.) Under the impression made by
the history of Jesus it gave to many Old Testament passages
a sense that was foreign to them, and, on the other hand,
enriched the life of Jesus with new facts, turning the interest

---

[1] The Jewish religion, specially since the (relative) close of the canon, had
become more and more a religion of the Book.

at the same time to details which were frequently unreal and seldom of striking importance. [1]

2. The Jewish Apocalyptic literature, especially as it flourished since the time of Antiochus Epiphanes, and was impregnated with new elements borrowed from an ethico-religious philosophy, as well as with Babylonian and Persian myths (Greek myths can only be detected in very small number), was not banished from the circles of the first professors of the Gospel, but was rather held fast, eagerly read, and even extended with the view of elucidating the promises of Jesus. [2]

[1] Examples of both in the New Testament are numerous. See above all, Matt. I. II. Even the belief that Jesus was born of a Virgin sprang from Isaiah VII. 14. It cannot, however, be proved to be in the writings of Paul (the two genealogies in Matt. and Luke directly exclude it: according to Dillmann, Jahrb. f. protest. Theol. p. 192 ff. Luke I. 34, 35 would be the addition of a redactor); but it must have arisen very early, as the Gentile Christians of the second century would seem to have unanimously confessed it (see the Romish Symbol. Ignatius, Aristides, Justin, etc.). For the rest, it was long before theologians recognised in the Virgin birth of Jesus more than fulfilment of a prophecy, viz., a fact of salvation. The conjecture of Usener, that the idea of the birth from a Virgin is a heathen myth which was received by the Christians, contradicts the entire earliest development of Christian tradition, which is free from heathen myths so far as these had not already been received by wide circles of Jews, (above all, certain Babylonian and Persian Myths), which in the case of that idea is not demonstrable. Besides, it is in point of method not permissible to stray so far when we have near at hand such a complete explanation as Isaiah VII. 14. Those who suppose that the reality of the Virgin birth must be held fast, must assume that a misunderstood prophecy has been here fulfilled (on the true meaning of the passage see Dillmann [Jesajas, 5 Aufl. p. 69]: "of the birth by a Virgin [*i.e.*, of one who at the birth was still a Virgin.] the Hebrew text says nothing... Immanuel as beginning and representative of the new generation, from which one should finally take possession of the king's throne"). The application of an unhistorical local method in the exposition of the Old Testament—Haggada and Rabbinic allegorism—may be found in many passages of Paul (see, *e.g.*, Gal. III. 16, 19; IV. 22-31; 1 Cor. IX. 9; X. 4; XI. 10; Rom. IV. etc.).

[2] The proof of this may be found in the quotations in early Christian writings from the Apocalypses of Enoch, Ezra, Eldad and Modad, the assumption of Moses and other Jewish Apocalypses unknown to us. They were regarded as Divine revelations beside the Old Testament; see the proofs of their frequent and long continued use in Schürer's "History of the Jewish people in the time of our Lord." But the Christians in receiving these Jewish Apocalypses did not leave them intact, but adapted them with greater or less Christian additions (see Esra, Enoch, Ascension of Isaiah). Even the Apocalypse of John is, as Vischer (Texte u. Unters. 3 altchristl. lit. Gesch. Bd. II. H. 4) has shown, a Jewish Apocalypse adapted to

Though their contents seem to have been modified on Christian soil, and especially the uncertainty about the person of the Messiah exalted to victory and coming to judgment, [1] yet the sensuous earthly hopes were in no way repressed. Green fat meadows and sulphurous abysses, white horses and frightful beasts, trees of life, splendid cities, war and bloodshed filled the fancy, [2] and threatened to obscure the simple and yet, at bottom, much more affecting maxims about the judgment which is certain to every individual soul, and drew the confessors of the Gospel into a restless activity, into politics, and abhorrence of the State. It was an evil inheritance which the Christians took over from the Jews, [3] an inheritance which makes it impossible to reproduce with certainty the eschatological sayings of Jesus. Things directly foreign were mixed up with them, and, what was most serious, delineations of the hopes of the future could easily lead to the undervaluing of the most important gifts and duties of the Gospel. [4]

a Christian meaning. But in this activity, and in the production of little Apocalyptic prophetic sayings and articles, (see in the Epistle to the Ephesians, and in those of Barnabas and Clement) the Christian labour here in the earliest period seems to have exhausted itself. At least we do not know with certainty of any great Apocalyptic writing of an original kind proceeding from Christian circles. Even the Apocalypse of Peter which, thanks to the discovery of Bouriant, we now know better, is not a completely original work as contrasted with the Jewish Apocalypses.

[1] The Gospel reliance on the Lamb who was slain very significantly pervades the Revelation of John, that is, its Christian parts. Even the Apocalypse of Peter shews Jesus Christ as the comfort of believers and as the Revealer of the future. In it (v. 3,) Christ says; " Then will God come to those who believe on me, those who hunger and thirst and mourn, etc."

[2] These words were written before the Apocalypse of Peter was discovered. That Apocalypse confirms what is said in the text. Moreover, its delineation of Paradise and blessedness are not wanting in poetic charm and power. In its delineation of Hell, which prepares the way for Dante's Hell, the author is scared by no terror.

[3] These ideas, however, encircled the earliest Christendom as with a wall of fire, and preserved it from a too early contact with the world.

[4] An accurate examination of the eschatological sayings of Jesus in the synoptists shews that much foreign matter is mixed with them (see Weiffenbach, Der Wiederkunftsgedanke Jesu, 1875). That the tradition here was very uncertain, because influenced by the Jewish Apocalyptic, is shewn by the one fact that Papias (in Iren. V. 33) quotes as words of the Lord which had been handed down by the disciples, a group of sayings which we find in the Apocalypse of Baruch, about the amazing fruitfulness of the earth during the time of the Messianic Kingdom.

3. A wealth of mythologies and poetic ideas was naturalised and legitimised [1] in the Christian communities, chiefly by
the reception of the Apocalyptic literature, but also by the
reception of artificial exegesis and Haggada. Most important for the following period were the speculations about
Messiah, which were partly borrowed from expositions of the
Old Testament and from the Apocalypses, partly formed independently, according to methods the justice of which no
one contested, and the application of which seemed to give
a firm basis to religious faith.

Some of the Jewish Apocalyptists had already attributed
pre-existence to the expected Messiah, as to other precious
things in the Old Testament history and worship, and, without
any thought of denying his human nature, placed him as already existing before his appearing in a series of angelic
beings. [2] This took place in accordance with an established

---

[1] We may here call attention to an interesting remark of Goethe. Among his
Apophthegms (no. 537) is the following : "Apocrypha: It would be important to
collect what is historically known about these books, and to shew that these very
Apocryphal writings with which the communities of the first centuries of our era
were flooded, were the real cause why Christianity at no moment of political or
Church history could stand forth in all her beauty and purity." A historian would
not express himself in this way, but yet there lies at the root of this remark a true
historical insight.

[2] See Schürer, History of the Jewish people. Div. II. vol. II. p. 160 f.; yet the
remarks of the Jew Trypho in the dialogue of Justin shew that the notions of a
pre-existent Messiah were by no means very widely spread in Judaism. (See also
Orig. c. Cels. I. 49: "A Jew would not at all admit that any Prophet had said
the Son of God will come; they avoided this designation and used instead the
saying, the anointed of God will come.") The Apocalyptists and Rabbis attributed
pre-existence, that is, a heavenly origin, to many sacred things and persons, such
as the Patriarchs, Moses, the Tabernacle, the Temple vessels, the city of Jerusalem.
That the true Temple and the real Jerusalem were with God in heaven and would
come down from heaven at the appointed time, must have been a very wide-spread
idea, especially at the time of the destruction of Jerusalem, and even earlier than that
(see Gal. IV. 26 : Rev. XXI. 2 : Heb. XII. 22). In the Assumption of Moses (c. 1)
Moses says of himself: Dominus invenit me, qui ab initio orbis terrarum præpa-
ratus sum, ut sim arbiter (μεσίτης) testamenti illius (τῆς διαθήκης αὐτοῦ). In the
Midrasch Bereschith rabba VIII. 2. we read, "R. Simeon ben Lakisch says, 'The
law was in existence 2000 years before the creation of the world.'" In the Jewish
treatise Προσευχὴ Ἰωσήφ, which Origen has several times quoted, Jacob says of
himself (ap. Orig. tom. II. in Joann. c. 25. Op. IV. 84: "ὁ γὰρ λαλῶν πρὸς ὑμᾶς,
ἐγὼ Ἰακὼβ καὶ Ἰσραήλ, ἄγγελος θεοῦ εἰμὶ ἐγὼ καὶ πνεῦμα ἀρχικὸν καὶ Ἀβραὰμ

method of speculation, so far as an attempt was made thereby
to express the special value of an empiric object, by distinguishing between the essence and the inadequate form of appearance, hypostatising the essence, and exalting it above
time and space. But when a later appearance was conceived
as the aim of a series of preparations, it was frequently hypostatised and placed above these preparations even in time.
The supposed aim was, in a kind of real existence, placed,
as first cause, before the means which were destined to realise it on earth. [1]

καὶ Ἰσαὰκ προεκτίσθησαν προ παντος ἔργου, ἐγὼ δὲ Ἰακὼβ.... ἐγὼ πρωτογονος
παντὸς ζώος ζωουμένου ὑπὸ θεοῦ." These examples could easily be increased. The
Jewish speculations about Angels and Mediators, which at the time of Christ grew
very luxuriantly among the Scribes and Apocalyptists, and endangered the purity
and vitality of the Old Testament idea of God, were also very important for the
development of Christian dogmatics. But neither these speculations, nor the notions
of heavenly Archetypes, nor of pre-existence, are to be referred to Hellenic influence.
This may have co-operated here and there, but the rise of these speculations in
Judaism is not to be explained by it; they rather exhibit the Oriental stamp. But,
of course, the stage in the development of the nations had now been reached, in
which the creations of Oriental fancy and Mythology could be fused with the ideal
conceptions of Hellenic philosophy.

[1] The conception of heavenly ideals of precious earthly things followed from
the first naive method of speculation we have mentioned, that of a pre-existence
of persons from the last. If the world was created for the sake of the people of
Israel, and the Apocalyptists expressly taught that, then it follows that in the
thought of God Israel was older than the world. The idea of a kind of pre-
existence of the people of Israel follows from this. We can still see this process
of thought very plainly in the shepherd of Hermas, who expressly declares that
the world was created for the sake of the Church. In consequence of this he
maintains that the Church was very old, and was created before the foundation of the
world. See Vis. I. 2. 4: II. 4. 11: Διατί οὖν πρεσβυτέρα (scil. ἡ ἐκκλησία): "Ὅτι, φησίν,
πάντων πρώτη ἐκτίσθη διὰ τοῦτο πρεσβυτέρα, καὶ διὰ ταύτην ὁ κόσμος κατηρτίσθη.
But in order to estimate aright the bearing of these speculations, we must observe
that, according to them, the precious things and persons, so far as they are now
really manifested, were never conceived as endowed with a double nature. No
hint is given of such an assumption; the sensible appearance was rather conceived
as a mere wrapping which was necessary only to its becoming visible, or, conversely, the pre-existence or the archetype was no longer thought of in presence
of the historical appearance of the object. That pneumatic form of existence was
not set forth in accordance with the analogy of existence verified by sense, but
was left in suspense. The idea of "existence" here could run through all the
stages which, according to the Mythology and Metaphysic of the time, lay between
what we now call "valid," and the most concrete being. He who nowadays
undertakes to justify the notion of pre-existence, will find himself in a very dif-

Some of the first confessors of the Gospel, though not all
the writers of the New Testament, in accordance with the
same method, went beyond the declarations which Jesus himself had made about his person, and endeavoured to conceive
its value and absolute significance abstractly and speculatively.
The religious convictions (see § 3. 2): (1) That the founding
of the Kingdom of God on earth, and the mission of Jesus
as the perfect mediator, were from eternity based on God's
plan of Salvation, as his main purpose; (2) that the exalted
Christ was called into a position of Godlike Sovereignty belonging to him of right; (3) that God himself was manifested in Jesus, and that he therefore surpasses all mediators
of the Old Testament, nay, even all angelic powers,—these
convictions with some took the form that Jesus pre-existed, and
that in him has appeared and taken flesh a heavenly being
fashioned like God, who is older than the world, nay, its creative principle. [1] The conceptions of the old Teachers, Paul,
the author of the Epistle to the Hebrews, the Apocalypse,
the author of the first Epistle of Peter, the fourth Evangelist, differ in many ways when they attempt to define these
convictions more closely. The latter is the only one who has
recognised with perfect clearness that the premundane Christ
must be assumed to be θεὸς ὤν ἐν ἀρχῇ πρός τὸν θεόν, so as not
to endanger by this speculation the contents and significance
of the revelation of God which was given in Christ. This, in
the earliest period, was essentially a religious problem, that
is, it was not introduced for the explanation of cosmological
problems, (see, especially, Epistle to the Ephesians, 1 Peter;
but also the Gospel of John), and there stood peacefully be-

ferent situation from these earlier times, as he will no longer be able to count on
shifting conceptions of existence. See Appendix I. at the end of this Vol. for a
fuller discussion of the idea of pre-existence.

[1] It must be observed here that Palestinian Judaism, without any apparent
influence from Alexandria, though not independently of the Greek spirit, had
already created a multitude of intermediate beings between God and the world,
avowing thereby that the idea of God had become stiff and rigid. "Its original
aim was simply to help the God of Judaism in his need." Among these intermediate beings should be specially mentioned the Memra of God (see also the
Shechina and the Metatron).

side it, such conception as recognised the equipment of the
man Jesus for his office in a communication of the Spirit at
his baptism, [1] or in virtue of Isaiah VII., found the germ of
his unique nature in his miraculous origin. [2] But as soon as that
speculation was detached from its original foundation, it necessarily withdrew the minds of believers from the consideration of the work of Christ, and from the contemplation of
the revelation of God which was given in the ministry of the
historical person Jesus. The mystery of the person of Jesus
in itself, would then necessarily appear as the true revelation. [3]

A series of theologoumena and religious problems for the
future doctrine of Christianity lay ready in the teaching of
the Pharisees and in the Apocalypses (see especially the fourth
book of Ezra), and was really fitted for being of service to
it; e.g., doctrines about Adam, universal sinfulness, the fall,
predestination, Theodocy, etc., besides all kinds of ideas about
redemption. Besides these spiritual doctrines there were not
a few spiritualised myths which were variously made use of
in the Apocalypses. A rich, spiritual, figurative style, only too
rich and therefore confused, waited for the theological artist
to purify, reduce and vigorously fashion. There really remained
very little of the Cosmico-Mythological in the doctrine of the
great Church.

Supplement.,—The reference to the proof from prophecy, to
the current exposition of the Old Testament, the Apocalyptic

---

[1] See Justin. Dial. 48. fin: Justin certainly is not favourably disposed towards
those who regard Christ as a "man among men," but he knows that there are
such people.

[2] The miraculous genesis of Christ in the Virgin by the Holy Spirit and the
real pre-existence are of course mutually exclusive. At a later period, it is true,
it became necessary to unite them in thought.

[3] There is the less need for treating this more fully here, as no New Testament Christology has become the direct starting-point of later doctrinal developments. The Gentile Christians had transmitted to them, as an unanimous doctrine,
the message that Christ is the Lord who is to be worshipped, and that one must
think of him as the Judge of the living and the dead, that is, ὡς περὶ θεοῦ. But it
certainly could not fail to be of importance for the result that already many of
the earliest Christian writers, and therefore even Paul, perceived in Jesus a spiritual
being come down from heaven (πνεῦμα) who was ἐν μορφῇ θεοῦ, and whose real
act of love consisted in his very descent.

and the prevailing methods of speculation, does not suffice
to explain all the elements which are found in the different
types of Christian preaching. We must rather bear in mind
here that the earliest communities were enthusiastic, and had
yet among them prophets and ecstatic persons. Such circumstances will always directly produce facts in the history. But,
in the majority of cases, it is absolutely impossible to account
subsequently for the causes of such productions, because their
formation is subject to no law accessible to the understanding.
It is therefore inadmissible to regard as proved the reality of
what is recorded and believed to be a fact, when the motive and
interest which led to its acceptance can no longer be ascertained.[1]

Moreover, if we consider the conditions, outer and inner,
in which the preaching of Christ in the first decades was
placed, conditions which in every way threatened the Gospel
with extravagance, we shall only see cause to wonder that it

[1] The creation of the New Testament canon first paved the way for putting an
end, though only in part, to the production of Evangelic "facts" within the
Church. For Hermas (Sim. IX. 16) can relate that the Apostles also descended
to the under world and there preached. Others report the same of John the Baptist.
Origen in his homily on 1. Kings XXVII. says that Moses, Samuel and all the
Prophets descended to Hades and there preached. A series of facts of Evangelic
history which have no parallel in the accounts of our Synoptists, and are certainly
legendary, may be but together from the epistle of Barnabas, Justin, the second
epistle of Clement, Papias, the Gospel to the Hebrews, and the Gospel to the
Egyptians. But the synoptic reports themselves, especially in the articles for which
we have only a solitary witness, shew an extensive legendary material, and even
in the Gospel of John, the free production of facts cannot be mistaken. Of what
a curious nature some of these were, and that they are by no means to be entirely
explained from the Old Testament, as for example, Justin's account of the ass on
which Christ rode into Jerusalem, having been bound to a vine, is shewn by the
very old fragment in one source of the Apostolic constitutions (Texte u. Unters.
II. 5. p. 28 ff.); ὅτε ᾔτωσεν ὁ διδάσκαλος τὸν ἄρτον καὶ τὸ ποτήριον καὶ ηὐλόγησεν
αὐτὰ λέγων· τοῦτο ἐστι τὸ σῶμά μου καὶ τὸ αἷμα, οὐκ ἐπέτρεψε ταύταις the
women) συστῆναι ἡμῖν.... Μάρθα εἶπεν διὰ Μαριάμ, ὅτι εἶδεν αὐτὴν μειδιῶσαν.
Μαρία εἶπεν οὐκέτι ἐγέλασα. Narratives such as those of Christ's descent to Hell
and ascent to heaven, which arose comparatively late, though still at the close of
the first century (see Book I. Chap. 3) sprang out of short formulæ containing an
antithesis (death and resurrection, first advent in lowliness, second advent in glory :
descensus de cœlo, ascensus in cœlum ; ascensus in cœlum, descensus ad inferna)
which appeared to be required by Old Testament predictions, and were commended
by their naturalness. Just as it is still, in the same way naively inferred : if Christ
rose bodily he must also have ascended bodily (visibly ?) into heaven.

continued to shine forth amid all its wrappings. We can still, out of the strangest "fulfilments", legends and mythological ideas, read the religious conviction that the aim and goal of history is disclosed in the history of Christ, and that the Divine has now entered into history in a pure form.

Literature.—The Apocalypses of Daniel, Enoch, Moses, Baruch, Ezra; Schürer, History of the Jewish People in the time of Christ; Baldensperger, in the work already mentioned. Weber, System der Altsynagogalen palästinischen Theologie, 1880, Kuenen, Hibbert Lectures, 1883. Hilgenfeld, Die jüdische Apokalyptik, 1857. Wellhausen, Sketch of the History of Israel and Judah, 1887. Diestel, Gesch. des A. T. in der Christl. Kirche, 1869. Other literature in Schürer. The essay of Hellwag in the Theol. Jahrb. von Baur and Zeller, 1848, "Die Vorstellung von der Präexistenz Christi in der ältesten Kirche", is worth noting; also Joël; Blicke in die Religionsgeschichte zu Anfang des 2 Christl. Jahrhunderts, 1880—1883.

§ 5. *The Religious Conceptions and the Religious Philosophy of the Hellenistic Jews, in their significance for the later formulation of the Gospel.*

1. From the remains of the Jewish Alexandrian literature and the Jewish Sibylline writings, also from the work of Josephus, and especially from the great propaganda of Judaism in the Græco-Roman world, we may gather that there was a Judaism in the Diaspora, for the consciousness of which the cultus and ceremonial law were of comparatively subordinate importance; while the monotheistic worship of God, apart from images, the doctrines of virtue and belief in a future reward beyond the grave, stood in the foreground as its really essential marks. Converted Gentiles were no longer everywhere required to be even circumcised; the bath of purification was deemed sufficient. The Jewish religion here appears transformed into a universal human ethic and a monotheistic cosmology. For that reason, the idea of the Theocracy as well as the Messianic hopes of the future faded away or were uprooted. The latter, indeed, did not altogether pass away; but as the oracles

of the Prophets were made use of mainly for the purpose of
proving the antiquity and certainty of monotheistic belief, the
thought of the future was essentially exhausted in the expectation of the dissolution of the Roman empire, the burning
of the world, and the eternal recompense. The specific Jewish
element, however, stood out plainly in the assertion that the
Old Testament, and especially the books of Moses, were the
source of all true knowledge of God, and the sum total of all
doctrines of virtue for the nations, as well as in the connected
assertion that the religious and moral culture of the Greeks
was derived from the Old Testament, as the source from which
the Greek Poets and Philosophers had drawn their inspiration. [1]

These Jews and the Greeks converted by them formed, as
it were, a Judaism of a second order without law, *i.e.*, ceremonial law, and with a minimum of statutory regulations.
This Judaism prepared the soil for the Christianising of the
Greeks, as well as for the genesis of a great Gentile Church
in the empire, free from the law; and this the more that, as
it seems, after the second destruction of Jerusalem, the punctilious observance of the law [2] was imposed more strictly than
before on all who worshipped the God of the Jews. [3]

[1] The Sibylline Oracles, composed by Jews, from 160 B.C. to 189 A.D. are
specially instructive here: see the Editions of Friedlieb. 1852; Alexandre, 1869;
Rzach. 1891. Delaunay, Moines et Sibylles dans l'antiquité judéo-grecque, 1874.
Schürer in the work mentioned above. The writings of Josephus also yield rich
booty, especially his apology for Judaism in the two books against Apion. But it
must be noted that there were Jews enlightened by Hellenism, who were still very
zealous in their observance of the law. "Philo urges most earnestly to the observance of the law in opposition to that party which drew the extreme inferences
of the allegoristic method, and put aside the outer legality as something not essential
for the spiritual life. Philo thinks that by exact observance of these ceremonies
on their material side, one will also come to know better their symbolical meaning"
(Siegfried, Philo, p. 157).

[2] Direct evidence is certainly almost entirely wanting here, but the indirect
speaks all the more emphatically: see § 3, Supplement 1. 2.

[3] The Jewish propaganda, though by no means effaced, gave way very distinctly
to the Christian from the middle of the second century. But from this time we
find few more traces of an enlightened Hellenistic Judaism. Moreover, the Messianic expectation also seems to have somewhat given way to occupation with the
law. But the God of Abraham, Isaac and Jacob, as well as other Jewish terms
certainly played a great rôle in Gentile and Gnostic magical formulæ of the third
century, as may be seen *e.g.*, from many passages in Origen c. Celtum.

The Judaism just portrayed, developed itself, under the influence of the Greek culture with which it came in contact, into a kind of Cosmopolitanism. It divested itself, as religion, of all national forms, and exhibited itself as the most perfect expression of that "natural" religion which the stoics had disclosed. But in proportion as it was enlarged and spiritualised to a universal religion for humanity, it abandoned what was most peculiar to it, and could not compensate for that loss by the assertion of the thesis that the Old Testament is the oldest and most reliable source of that natural religion, which in the traditions of the Greeks had only witnesses of the second rank. The vigour and immediateness of the religious feeling was flattened down to a moralism, the barrenness of which drove some Jews even into Gnosis, mysticism and asceticism. [1]

2. The Jewish Alexandrian philosophy of religion, of which Philo gives us the clearest conception, [2] is the scientific theory which corresponded to this religious conception. The theological system which Philo, in accordance with the example of

---

[1] The prerogative of Israel was, for all that, clung to: Israel remains the chosen people.

[2] The brilliant investigations of Bernays, however, have shewn how many-sided that philosophy of religion was. The proofs of asceticism in this Hellenistic Judaism are especially of great interest for the history of dogma (see Theophrastus' treatise on piety). In the eighth Epistle of Heraclitus, composed by a Hellenistic Jew in the first century, it is said (Bernays, p. 182). "So long a time before, O Hermodorus, saw thee that Sibyl, and even then thou wert" (εἶδε σε πρὸ τοσούτου αἰῶνος, Ἑρμόδωρε, ἡ Σίβυλλα ἐκείνη, καὶ τότε ἦσθα). Even here then the notion is expressed that foreknowledge and predestination invest the known and the determined with a kind of existence. Of great importance is the fact that even before Philo, the idea of the wisdom of God creating the world and passing over to men had been hypostatised in Alexandrian Judaism (see Sirach, Baruch, the wisdom of Solomon, Enoch, nay, even the book of Proverbs). But so long as the deutero-canonical Old Testament, and also the Alexandrine and Apocalyptic literature continue in the sad condition in which they are at present, we can form no certain judgment and draw no decided conclusions on the subject. When will the scholar appear who will at length throw light on these writings, and therewith on the section of inner Jewish history most interesting to the Christian theologian? As yet we have only a most thankworthy preliminary study in Schürer's great work, and beside it particular or dilettante attempts which hardly shew what the problem really is, far less solve it. What disclosures even the fourth book of the Maccabees alone yields for the connection of the Old Testament with Hellenism!

others, gave out as the Mosaic system revealed by God, and
proved from the Old Testament by means of the allegoric
exegetic method, is essentially identical with the system of
Stoicism, which had been mixed with Platonic elements and
had lost its Pantheistic materialistic impress. The fundamental
idea from which Philo starts is a Platonic one; the dualism
of God and the world, spirit and matter. The idea of God
itself is therefore abstractly and negatively conceived (God,
the real substance which is not finite), and has nothing more
in common with the Old Testament conception. The possibility, however, of being able to represent God as acting on
matter, which as the finite is the non-existent, and therefore
the evil, is reached, with the help of the Stoic λόγοι as working
powers and of the Platonic doctrine of archetypal ideas, and
in outward connection with the Jewish doctrine of angels and
the Greek doctrine of demons, by the introduction of intermediate spiritual beings which, as personal and impersonal
powers proceeding from God, are to be thought of as operative causes and as Archetypes. All these beings are, as it
were, comprehended in the Logos. By the Logos Philo understands the operative reason of God, and consequently also the
power of God. The Logos is to him the thought of God and
at the same time the product of his thought, therefore both
idea and power. But further, the Logos is God himself on
that side of him which is turned to the world, as also the
ideal of the world and the unity of the spiritual forces which
produce the world and rule in it. He can therefore be put
beside God and in opposition to the world; but he can also,
so far as the spiritual contents of the world are comprehended
in him, be put with the world in contrast with God. The
Logos accordingly appears as the Son of God, the foremost
creature, the representative, Viceroy, High Priest, and Messenger of God; and again as principle of the world, spirit of
the world, nay, as the world itself. He appears as a power
and as a person, as a function of God and as an active divine being. Had Philo cancelled the contradiction which lies
in this whole conception of the Logos, his system would have
been demolished; for that system with its hard antithesis of

God and the world, needed a mediator who was, and yet was
not God, as well as world. From this contrast, however, it
further followed that we can only think of a world-formation
by the Logos, not of a world-creation.[1] Within this world
man is regarded as a microcosm, that is, as a being of Divine
nature according to his spirit, who belongs to the heavenly
world, while the adhering body is a prison which holds men
captive in the fetters of sense, that is, of sin.

The Stoic and Platonic ideals and rules of conduct (also
the Neo-pythagorean) were united by Philo in the religious
Ethic as well as in the Cosmology. Rationalistic moralism is
surmounted by the injunction to strive after a higher good
lying above virtue. But here, at the same time, is the point
at which Philo decidedly goes beyond Platonism, and introduces
a new thought into Greek Ethics, and also in correspondence
therewith into theoretic philosophy. This thought, which
indeed lay altogether in the line of the development of Greek
philosophy, was not, however, pursued by Philo into all its
consequences, though it was the expression of a new frame
of mind. While the highest good is resolved by Plato and
his successors into knowledge of truth, which truth, together
with the idea of God, lies in a sphere really accessible to the
intellectual powers of the human spirit, the highest good, the
Divine original being, is considered by Philo, though not
invariably, to be above reason, and the power of comprehending it is denied to the human intellect. This assumption,
a concession which Greek speculation was compelled to make
to positive religion for the supremacy which was yielded to
it, was to have far-reaching consequences in the future. *A
place was now for the first time provided in philosophy for a*

---

[1] "So far as the sensible world is a work of the Logos, it is called νεώτερος
υἱός (quod deus immut. 6. I. 277), or according to Prov. VIII. 22, an offspring of
God and wisdom: ἡ δὲ παραδεξαμένη τὸ τοῦ θεοῦ σπέρμα τελεσφόροις ὠδῖσι τὸν
μόνον καὶ ἀγαπητὸν αἰσθητὸν υἱὸν ἀπεκύησε τόνδε τὸν κόσμον (de ebriet. 8. I. 361 f.).
So far as the Logos is High Priest his relation to the world is symbolically expressed by the garment of the High Priest, to which exegesis the play on the word
κόσμος, as meaning both ornament and world, lent its aid." This speculation (see
Siegfried. Philo. 235) is of special importance, for it shews how closely the ideas
κόσμος and λόγος were connected.

mythology to be regarded as revelation. The highest truths which could not otherwise be reached, might be sought for in the oracles of the Deity; for knowledge resting on itself had learnt by experience its inability to attain to the truth in which blessedness consists. *In this very experience the intellectualism of Greek Ethics was, not indeed cancelled, but surmounted.* The injunction to free oneself from sense and strive upwards by means of knowledge, remained; but the wings of the thinking mind bore it only to the entrance of the sanctuary. Only ecstasy produced by God himself was able to lead to the reality above reason. The great novelties in the system of Philo, though in a certain sense the way had already been prepared for them, are the introduction of the idea of a philosophy of revelation and the advance beyond the absolute intellectualism of Greek philosophy, an advance based on scepticism, but also on the deep-felt needs of life. Only the germs of these are found in Philo, but they are already operative. They are innovations of world-wide importance : for in them the covenant between the thoughts of reason on the one hand, and the belief in revelation and mysticism on the other, is already so completed that neither by itself could permanently maintain the supremacy. Thought about the world was henceforth dependent, not only on practical motives, it is always that, but on the need of a blessedness and peace which is higher than all reason. It might, perhaps, be allowable to say that Philo was the first who, as a philosopher, plainly expressed that need, just because he was not only a Greek, but also a Jew. [1]

Apart from the extremes into which the ethical counsels of Philo run, they contain nothing that had not been demanded by philosophers before him. The purifying of the affections, the renunciation of sensuality, the acquisition of the four cardinal virtues, the greatest possible simplicity of life, as well

---

[1] Of all the Greek Philosophers of the second century, Plutarch of Chäronea, died c. 125 A.D., and Numenius of Apamea, second half of the second century, approach nearest to Philo; but the latter of the two was undoubtedly familiar with Jewish philosophy, specially with Philo, and probably also with Christian writings.

as a cosmopolitan disposition are enjoined.[1] But the attainment
of the highest morality by our own strength is despaired of,
and man is directed beyond himself to God's assistance. Redemption begins with the spirit reflecting on its own condition; it advances by a knowledge of the world and of the
Logos, and it is perfected, after complete asceticism, by mystic
ecstatic contemplation in which a man loses himself, but in
return is entirely filled and moved by God.[2] In this condition
man has a foretaste of the blessedness which shall be given
him when the soul, freed from the body, will be restored to
its true existence as a heavenly being.

This system, notwithstanding its appeal to revelation, has,
in the strict sense of the word, no place for Messianic hopes,
of which nothing but very insignificant rudiments are found
in Philo. But he was really animated by the hope of a glorious time to come for Judaism. The synthesis of the Messiah
and the Logos did not lie within his horizon.[3]

3. Neither Philo's philosophy of religion, nor the mode of
thought from which it springs, exercised any appreciable influence on the first generation of believers in Christ.[4] But
its practical ground-thoughts, though in different degrees,
must have found admission very early into the Jewish Christian circles of the Diaspora, and through them to Gentile
Christian circles also. Philo's philosophy of religion became

---

[1] As to the way in which Philo (see also 4 Maccab. V. 24) learned to connect
the Stoic ethics with the authority of the Torah, as was also done by the Palestinian Midrash, and represented the Torah as the foundation of the world, and
therewith as the law of nature: see Siegfried, Philo, p. 156.

[2] Philo by his exhortations to seek the blessed life, has by no means broken
with the intellectualism of the Greek philosophy, he has only gone beyond it. The
way of knowledge and speculation is to him also the way of religion and morality.
But his formal principle is supernatural and leads to a supernatural knowledge
which finally passes over into sight.

[3] But everything was now ready for this synthesis, so that it could be, and
immediately was, completed by Christian philosophers.

[4] We cannot discover Philo's influence in the writings of Paul. But here again
we must remember that the scripture learning of Palestinian teachers developed
speculations which appear closely related to the Alexandrian, and partly are so, but
yet cannot be deduced from them. The element common to them must, for the present
at least, be deduced from the harmony of conditions in which the different nations
of the East were at that time placed, a harmony which we cannot exactly measure.

operative among Christian teachers from the beginning of the second century,[1] and at a later period actually obtained the significance of a standard of Christian theology, Philo gaining a place among Christian writers. The systems of Valentinus and Origen presuppose that of Philo. It can no longer, however, be shewn with certainty how far the direct influence of Philo reached, as the development of religious ideas in the second century took a direction which necessarily led to views similar to those which Philo had anticipated (see § 6, and the whole following account).

Supplement. — The hermeneutic principles (the "Biblical-alchemy"), above all, became of the utmost importance for the following period. These were partly invented by Philo himself, partly traditional,—the Haggadic rules of exposition and the hermeneutic principles of the Stoics having already at an earlier period been united in Alexandria. They fall into two main classes: "first, those according to which the literal sense is excluded, and the allegoric proved to be the only possible one; and then, those according to which the allegoric sense is discovered as standing beside and above the literal sense."[2] That these rules permitted the discovery of a new sense by minute changes within a word, was a point of special importance.[3] Christian teachers went still further in this direction, and, as can be proved, altered the text of the Septuagint in order to make more definite what suggested itself to them as the meaning of a passage, or in order to give a satisfactory meaning to a sentence which appeared to them unmeaning or offensive.[4] Nay, attempts were not want-

[1] The conception of God's relation to the world as given in the fourth Gospel is not Philonic. The Logos doctrine there is therefore essentially not that of Philo. (Against Kuenen and others, see p. 93.)

[2] Siegfried (Philo. pp. 160-197) has presented in detail Philo's allegorical interpretation of scripture, his hermeneutic principles and their application. Without an exact knowledge of these principles we cannot understand the Scripture expositions of the Fathers, and therefore also cannot do them justice.

[3] See Siegfried, Philo, p. 176. Yet, as a rule, the method of isolating and adapting passages of scripture, and the method of unlimited combination were sufficient.

[4] Numerous examples of this may be found in the epistle of Barnabas (see cc. 4-9), and in the dialogue of Justin with Trypho (here they are objects of controversy, see cc. 71-73, 120), but also in many other Christian writings, (*e.g.* 1 Clem. ad Cor. VIII. 3 : XVII. 6 : XXIII. 3, 4 : XXVI. 5 : XLVI. 2 : 2 Clem.

ing among Christians in the second century—they were
aided by the uncertainty that existed about the extent of
the Septuagint, and by the want of plain predictions about
the death upon the cross—to determine the Old Testament
canon in accordance with new principles; that is, to alter
the text on the plea that the Jews had corrupted it, and to
insert new books into the Old Testament, above all, Jewish
Apocalypses revised in a Christian sense. Tertullian (de cultu
fem. 1. 3,) furnishes a good example of the latter. "Scio
scripturam Enoch, quæ hunc ordinem angelis dedit, non recipi
a quibusdam, quia nec in armorium Judaicum admittitur . . .
sed cum Enoch eadem scriptura etiam de domino prædicarit,
a nobis quidem nihil omnino reiciendum est quod pertinet ad
nos. Et legimus omnem scripturam ædificationi habilem
divinitus inspirari. A Judæis potest jam videri propterea
reiecta, sicut et cetera fera quæ Christum sonant. . . . . Eo
accedit quod Enoch apud Judam apostolum testimonium pos-
sidet." Compare also the history of the Apocalypse of Ezra in
the Latin Bible (Old Testament). Not only the genuine Greek
portions of the Septuagint, but also many Apocalypses were
quoted by Christians in the second century as of equal value
with the Old Testament. It was the New Testament that
slowly put an end to these tendencies towards the formation
of a Christian Old Testament.

XIII. 2). These Christian additions were long retained in the Latin Bible, (see
also Lactantius and other Latins : Pseudo-Cyprian de aleat. 2 etc), the most celebrated
of them is the addition "a ligno" to "dominus regnavit" in Psalm XCVI., see
Credner, Beiträge II. The treatment of the Old Testament in the epistle of
Barnabas is specially instructive, and exhibits the greatest formal agreement with
that of Philo. We may close here with the words in which Siegfried sums up
his judgment on Philo: "No Jewish writer has contributed so much as Philo to
the breaking up of particularism and the dissolution of Judaism. The history of
his people, though he believed in it literally, was in its main points a didactic
allegoric poem for enabling him to inculcate the doctrine that man attains the
vision of God by mortification of the flesh. The law was regarded by him as the
best guide to this, but it had lost its exclusive value, as it was admitted to be
possible to reach the goal without it, and it had, besides, its aim outside itself.
The God of Philo was no longer the old living God of Israel, but an imaginary
being who, to obtain power over the world, needed a Logos by whom the palladium of Israel, the unity of God, was taken a prey. So Israel lost everything which
had hitherto characterised her."

To find the spiritual meaning of the sacred text, partly beside the literal, partly by excluding it, became the watchword for the "scientific" Christian theology which was possible only on this basis, as it endeavoured to reduce the immense and dissimilar material of the Old Testament to unity with the Gospel, and both with the religious and scientific culture of the Greeks,—yet without knowing a relative standard, the application of which would alone have rendered possible in a loyal way the solution of the task. Here, Philo was the master; for he first to a great extent poured the new wine into old bottles. Such a procedure is warranted by its final purpose; for history is a unity. But applied in a pedantic and stringently dogmatic way it is a source of deception, of untruthfulness, and finally of total blindness.

Literature.—Gefrörer, Das Jahr des Heils, 1838. Parthey, Das Alexandr. Museum, 1838. Matter, Hist. de l'école d'Alex. 1840. Dähne, Gesch. Darstellung der jüd.-alex. Religionsphilos. 1834. Zeller, Die Philosophie der Griechen, III. 2. 3rd Edition. Mommsen, History of Rome, Vol. V. Siegfried, Philo van Alex. 1875. Massebieau, Le Classement des Œuvres de Philon. 1889. Hatch, Essays in Biblical Greek, 1889. Drummond, Philo Judæus, 1888. Bigg, The Christian Platonists of Alexandria, 1886. Schürer, History of the Jewish People. The investigations of Freudenthal (Hellenistische Studien), and Bernays (Ueber das phokylideische Gedicht; Theophrastos' Schrift über Frömmigkeit; Die heraklitischen Briefe). Kuenen, Hibbert Lectures: "Christian Theology could have made and has made much use of Hellenism. But the Christian religion cannot have sprung from this source." Havet thinks otherwise, though in the fourth volume of his "Origines" he has made unexpected admissions.

§ 6. *The Religious Dispositions of the Greeks and Romans in the first two centuries, and the current Græco-Roman Philosophy of Religion.*

1. After the national religion and the religious sense generally in cultured circles had been all but lost in the age of

Cicero and Augustus, there is noticeable in the Græco-Roman world from the beginning of the second century a revival of religious feeling which embraced all classes of society, and appears, especially from the middle of that century, to have increased from decennium to decennium.[1] Parallel with it went the not altogether unsuccessful attempt to restore the old national worship, religious usages, oracles, etc. In these attempts, however, which were partly superficial and artificial, the new religious needs found neither vigorous nor clear expression. These needs rather sought new forms of satisfaction corresponding to the wholly changed conditions of the time, including intercourse and mixing of the nations; decay of the old republican orders, divisions and ranks; monarchy and absolutism and social crises; pauperism; influence of philosophy on the domain of public morality and law; cosmopolitanism and the rights of man; influx of Oriental cults into the West; knowledge of the world and disgust with it. The decay of the old political cults and syncretism produced a disposition in favour of monotheism both among the cultured classes who had been prepared for it by philosophy, and also gradually among the masses. Religion and individual morality became more closely connected. There was developed a corresponding attempt at spiritualising the worship alongside of and within the ceremonial forms, and at giving it a direction towards the moral elevation of man through the ideas of moral personality, conscience, and purity, The ideas of repentance and of expiation and healing of the soul became of special importance, and consequently such Oriental cults came to the front as required the former and guaranteed the latter. But what was sought above all, was to enter into an inner union with the Deity, to be saved by him and become a partaker in the possession and enjoyment of his life. The worshipper consequently longed to find a "præsens numen" and the revelation of him in the cultus, and hoped to put himself in possession of the Deity by asceticism and mysterious rites. This new piety longed for health and purity of soul, and elevation above earthly things, and in connection with these a divine, that

---

[1] Proofs in Friedländer, Sittengeschichte, vol. 3.

is a painless and eternal, life beyond the grave ("renatus in æternum taurobolio"). A world beyond was desired, sought for, and viewed with an uncertain eye. By detachment from earthly things and the healing of its diseases (the passions) the freed, new born soul should return to its divine nature and existence. It is not a hope of immortality such as the ancients had dreamed of for their heroes, where they continue, as it were, their earthly existence in blessed enjoyment. To the more highly pitched self-consciousness this life had become a burden, and in the miseries of the present, one hoped for a future life in which the pain and vulgarity of the unreal life of earth would be completely laid aside ('Εγκράτεια and ἀνάστασις). If the new moralistic feature stood out still more emphatically in the piety of the second century, it vanished more and more behind the religious feature, the longing after life [1] and after a Redeemer God. No one could any longer be a God who was not also a saviour. [2]

With all this Polytheism was not suppressed, but only put into a subordinate place. On the contrary, it was as lively and active as ever. For the idea of a *numen supremum* did not exclude belief in the existence and manifestation of subordinate deities. Apotheosis came into currency. The old state religion first attained its highest and most powerful expression in the worship of the emperor, (the emperor glorified as "dominus ac deus noster", [3] as "præsens et corporalis deus",

---

[1] See the chapter on belief in immortality in Friedländer, Sittengesch. Roms Bde. 3. Among the numerous mysteries known to us, that of Mythras deserves special consideration. From the middle of the second century the Church Fathers saw in it, above all, the caricature of the Church. The worship of Mithras had its redeemer, its mediator, hierarchy, sacrifice, baptism and sacred meal. The ideas of expiation, immortality, and the Redeemer God, were very vividly present in this cult, which of course, in later times, borrowed from Christianity: see the accounts of Marquardt, Réville, and the Essay of Sayous, Le Taurobole in the Rev. de l'Hist. des Religions, 1887, where the earliest literature is also utilised. The worship of Mithras in the third century became the most powerful rival of Christianity. In connection with this should be specially noted the cult of Æsculapius, the God who helps the body and the soul; see my essay "Medicinisches aus der ältesten Kirchengeschichte," 1892. p. 93 ff.

[2] Hence the wide prevalence of the cult of Æsculapius.

[3] Dominus in certain circumstances means more than deus; see Tertull. Apol. It signifies more than Soter: see Irenæus I. 1. 3; ..... τὸν σωτῆρα λέγουσιν, οὐδὲ

the Antinous cult, etc.), and in many circles an incarnate ideal in the present or the past was sought, which might be worshipped as revealer of God and as God, and which might be an example of life and an assurance of religious hope. Apotheosis became less offensive in proportion as, in connection with the fuller recognition of the spiritual dignity of man, the estimate of the soul, the spirit, as of supramundane nature, and the hope of its eternal continuance in a form of existence befitting it, became more general. That was the import of the message preached by the Cynics and the Stoics, that the truly wise man is Lord, Messenger of God, and God upon the earth. On the other hand, the popular belief clung to the idea that the gods could appear and be visible in human form, and this faith, though mocked by the cultured, gained numerous adherents, even among them, in the age of the Antonines. [1]

γὰρ κύριον ὀνομάζειν αὐτὸν θέλουσιν—κύριος and δεσπότης are almost synonymous. See Philo. Quis. rer. div. heres. 6 : συνώνυμα ταῦτα εἶναι λέγεται.

[1] We must give special attention here to the variability and elasticity of the concept " θεός ", and indeed among the cultured as well as the uncultured (Orig. prolegg. in Psalm. in Pitra, Anal. T. II. p. 437, according to a Stoic source; κατ' ἄλλον δέ τρόπον λέγεσθαι θεὸν ζῷον ἀθάνατον λογικὸν σπουδαῖον, ὥστε πᾶσαν ἀστείαν ψυχήν θεὸν ὑπάρχειν, κἂν περιέχηται, ἄλλως δὲ λέγεσθαι θεὸν τὸ καθ' αὑτὸ ὂν ζῷον ἀθάνατον ὡς τὰ ἐν ἀνθρώποις σοφοῖς περιεχομένας ψυχὰς μὴ ὑπάρχειν θεούς). They still regarded the Gods as passionless, blessed men living for ever. The idea therefore of a θεοποίησις, and on the other hand, the idea of the appearance of the Gods in human form presented no difficulty (see Acts XIV. 11 : XXVIII. 6). But philosophic speculation—the Platonic, as well as in yet greater measure the Stoic, and in the greatest measure of all the Cynic—had led to the recognition of something divine in man's spirit (πνεῦμα, νοῦς). Marcus Aurelius in his Meditations frequently speaks of the God who dwells in us. Clement of Alexandria (Strom. VI. 14. 113) says: οὕτως δύναμιν λαβοῦσα κυριακὴν ἡ ψυχὴ μελετᾷ εἶναι θεός, κακὸν μὲν οὐδὲν ἄλλο πλὴν ἀγνοίας εἶναι νομίζουσα. In Bernays' Heraclitian Epistles, pp. 37 f. 135 f., will be found a valuable exposition of the Stoic [Heraclitian] thesis and its history, that men are Gods. See Norden, Beiträge zur Gesch. d. griech. Philos. Jahrb. f. klass. Philol. XIX. Suppl. Bd. p. 373 ff., about the Cynic Philosopher who, contemplating the life and activity of man [κατάσκοπος], becomes its ἐπίσκοπος, and further κύριός, ἄγγελος θεοῦ, θεὸς ἐν ἀνθρώποις. The passages which he adduces are of importance for the history of dogma in a twofold respect. (1) They present remarkable parallels to Christology [one even finds the designations, κύριος, ἄγγελος, κατάσκοπος, ἐπίσκοπος, θεὸς associated with the philosophers as with Christ, e.g., in Justin; nay, the Cynics and Neoplatonics speak of ἐπίσκοποι δαίμονες; cf. also the remarkable narrative in Laertius VI. 102, concerning the

The new thing which was here developed, continued to be greatly obscured by the old forms of worship which reasons of state and pious custom maintained. And the new piety, dispensing with a fixed foundation, groped uncertainly around, adapting the old rather than rejecting it. The old religious practices of the Fathers asserted themselves in public life generally, and the reception of new cults by the state, which was certainly effected, though with many checks, did not disturb them. The old religious customs stood out especially on state holidays, in the games in honour of the Gods, frequently degenerating into shameless immorality, but yet protecting the institutions of the state. The patriot, the wise man, the sceptic, and the pious man compounded with them, for they had not really at bottom outgrown them, and they

---

Cynic Menedemus; οὗτὸς, καθά φησιν Ἱππόβοτος, εἰς τοσος τον τερατείας ἤλασεν, ὥστε Ἐρινύος ἀναλαβὼν σχῆμα περιήει, λέγων ἐπίσκοπος ἀφῖχθαι ἐξ Ἅιδου τῶν ἁμαρτομένων, ὅπως πάλιν κατιὼν τᾳτα ἀπαγγέλλοι τοῖς ἐκεῖ, δαίμοσιν]. (2) They also explain how the ecclesiastical ἐπίσκοποι came to be so highly prized, inasmuch as these also were from a very early period regarded as mediators between God and man, and considered as ἐν ἀνθρώποις θεοί). There where not a few who in the first and second centuries, appeared with the claim to be regarded as a God or an organ inspired and chosen by God (Simon Magus [cf. the manner of his treatment in Hippol. Philos. VI. 8: see also Clem. Hom. II. 27], Apollonius of Tyana (?), see further Tacitus Hist. II. 51: "Mariccus .... iamque adsertor Galliarum et deus, nomen id sibi indiderat,"; here belongs also the gradually developing worship of the Emperor: "dominus ac deus noster." Cf. Augustus, Inscription of the year 25/24 B.C. in Egypt, [where the Ptolemies were for long described as Gods]: Ὑπὲρ Καίσαρος Αὐτοκράττορος θεοῦ (Zeitschrift für Ægypt. Sprache. XXXI. Bd. p. 3). Domitian: θεὸς Ἀδριανός, Kaibel Inscr. Gr. 829. 1053. θεός Σεουῆρος Εὐσεβής, 1061—the Antinous cult with its prophets. See also Josephus on Herod Agrippa. Antiq. XIX. 8. 2. (Euseb. H. E. II. 10). The flatterers said to him, θεὸν προσαγορεύοντες· εἰ καὶ μέχρι νῦν ὡς ἄνθρωπον ἐφοβήθημεν, ἀλλὰ τούντεῦθεν κρείττονα σε θνητῆς τῆς φύσεως ὁμολογοῦμεν. Herod himself, § 7, says to his friends in his sickness; ὁ θεὸς ὑμῖν ἐγὼ ἤδη καταστρέφειν ἐπιτάττομαι τὸν βίον..... ὁ κληθεις ἀθάνατος ὑφ' ἡμῶν ἤδη θανεῖν ἀπάγομαι). On the other hand, we must mention the worship of the founder in some philosophic schools, especially among the Epicureans. Epictetus says (Moral. 15), Diogenes and Heraclitus and those like them are justly called Gods. Very instructive in this connection are the reproaches of the heathen against the Christians, and of Christian partisans against one another with regard to the almost divine veneration of their teachers. Lucian (Peregr. 11) reproaches the Christians in Syria for having regarded Peregrinus as a God and a new Socrates. The heathen in Smyrna, after the burning of Polycarp, feared that the Christians would begin to pay him divine honours (Euseb. H. E. IV. 15. 41). Cæcilius in Minucius Felix speaks of divine honours being paid by

knew of nothing better to substitute for the services they still rendered to society (see the λόγος ἀληθής of Celsus).

2. The system of associations, naturalised centuries before among the Greeks, was developed under the social and political pressure of the empire, and was greatly extended by the change of moral and religious ideas. The free unions, which, as a rule, had a religious element and were established for mutual help, support, or edification, balanced to some extent the prevailing social cleavage, by a free democratic organisation. They gave to many individuals in their small circle the rights which they did not possess in the great world, and were frequently of service in obtaining admission for new cults. Even the new piety and cosmopolitan disposition seem to have turned to them in order to find within them forms of expression. But the time had not come for the greater corporate unions, and of an organised connection of societies in one city with those of another we know nothing. The state kept these

Christians to priests. (Octav. IX. 10.) The Antimontanist (Euseb. H. E. V. 18. 6) asserts that the Montanists worship their prophet and Alexander the Confessor as divine. The opponents of the Roman Adoptians (Euseb. H. E. V. 28) reproach them with praying to Galen. There are many passages in which the Gnostics are reproached with paying Divine honours to the heads of their schools, and for many Gnostic schools (the Carpocratians, for example) the reproach seems to have been just. All this is extremely instructive. The genius, the hero, the founder of a new school who promises to shew the certain way to the *vita beata*, the emperor, the philosopher, (numerous Stoic passages might be noted here) finally man, in so far as he is inhabited by νοῦς—could all somehow be considered as θεοί, so elastic was the concept. All these instances of Apotheosis in no way endangered the Monotheism which had been developed from the mixture of Gods and from philosophy; for the one supreme Godhead can unfold his inexhaustible essence in a variety of existences, which, while his creatures as to their origin, are parts of his essence as to their contents. This Monotheism does not yet exactly disclaim its Polytheistic origin. The Christian, Hermas, says to his Mistress (Vis. I. 1. 7) οὐ πάντοτέ σε ὡς θεάν ἡγησάμην, and the author of the Epistle of Diognetus writes (X. 6) ταῦτα τοῖς ἐπιδεομένοις χορηγῶν (*i.e.*, the rich man) θεὸς γίνεται τῶν λαμβανόντων. That the concept θεὸς was again used only of one God, was due to the fact that one now started from the definition "qui vitam æternam habet," and again from the definition "qui est super omnia et originem nescit." From the latter followed the absolute unity of God, from the former a plurality of Gods. Both could be so harmonised (see Tertull. adv. Prax. and Novat. de Trinit.) that one could assume that the God *qui est super omnia*, might allow his monarchy to be administered by several persons, and might dispense the gift of immortality and with it a relative divinity.

associations under strict control. It granted them only to the poorest classes *(collegia tenuiorum)* and had the strictest laws in readiness for them. These free unions, however, did not in their historical importance approach the fabric of the Roman state in which they stood. That represented the union of the greater part of humanity under one head, and also more and more under one law. Its capital was the capital of the world, and also, from the beginning of the third century, of religious syncretism. Hither migrated all who desired to exercise an influence on the great scale: Jew, Chaldean, Syrian priest, and Neoplatonic teacher. Law and Justice radiated from Rome to the provinces, and in their light nationalities faded away, and a cosmopolitanism was developed which pointed beyond itself, because the moral spirit can never find its satisfaction in that which is realised. When that spirit finally turned away from all political life, and after having laboured for the ennobling of the empire, applied itself, in Neoplatonism, to the idea of a new and free union of men, this certainly was the result of the felt failure of the great creation, but it nevertheless had that creation for its presupposition. The Church appropriated piecemeal the great apparatus of the Roman state, and gave new powers, new significance and respect to every article that had been depreciated. But what is of greatest importance is that the Church by her preaching would never have gained whole circles, but only individuals, had not the universal state already produced a neutralising of nationalities and brought men nearer each other in temper and disposition.

3. Perhaps the most decisive factor in bringing about the revolution of religious and moral convictions and moods, was philosophy, which in almost all its schools and representatives, had deepened ethics, and set it more and more in the foreground. After Possidonius, Seneca, Epictetus, and Marcus Aurelius of the Stoical school, and men like Plutarch of the Platonic, attained to an ethical view, which, though not very clear in principle (knowledge, resignation, trust in God), is hardly capable of improvement in details. Common to them all, as distinguished from the early Stoics, is the value put upon the soul, (not the entire human nature), while in some

of them there comes clearly to the front a religious mood, a longing for divine help, for redemption and a blessed life beyond the grave, the effort to obtain and communicate a religious philosophical therapeutic of the soul.[1] From the beginning of the second century, however, already announced itself that eclectic philosophy based on Platonism, which after two or three generations appeared in the form of a school, and after three generations more was to triumph over all other schools. The several elements of the Neoplatonic philosophy, as they were already foreshadowed in Philo, are clearly seen in the second century, viz., the dualistic opposition of the divine and the earthly, the abstract conception of God, the assertion of the unknowableness of God, scepticism with regard to sensuous experience, and distrust with regard to the powers of the understanding, with a greater readiness to examine things and turn to account the result of former scientific labour; further, the demand of emancipation from sensuality by means of asceticism, the need of authority, belief in a higher revelation, and the fusion of science and religion. The legitimising of religious fancy in the province of philosophy was already begun. The myth was no longer merely tolerated and re-interpreted as formerly, but precisely the mythic form with the meaning imported into it was the precious element.[2] There were, however, in the second century numerous representatives of every possible philosophic view. To pass over the frivolous writers of the day, the Cynics criticised the tra-

---

[1] The longing for redemption and divine help is, for example, clearer in Seneca than in the Christian philosopher, Minucius Felix: see Kühn, Der Octavius des M. F. 1882, and Theol. Lit. Ztg. 1883. No. 6.

[2] See the so-called Neopythagorean philosophers and the so-called forerunners of Neoplatonism. (Cf. Bigg, The Platonists of Alexandria, p. 250, as to Numenius.) Unfortunately, we have as yet no sufficient investigation of the question what influence, if any, the Jewish Alexandrian Philosophy of religion had on the development of Greek philosophy in the second and third centuries. The answering of the question would be of the greatest importance. But at present it cannot even be said whether the Jewish philosophy of religion had any influence on the genesis of Neoplatonism. On the relation of Neoplatonism to Christianity and their mutual approximation, see the excellent account in Tzschirner, Fall des Heidenthums, pp. 574–618. Cf. also Réville, La Religion à Rome. 1886.

ditional mythology in the interests of morality and religion. [1]
But there were also men who opposed the "ne quid nimis"
to every form of practical scepticism, and to religion at the
same time, and were above all intent on preserving the state
and society, and on fostering the existing arrangements which
appeared to be threatened far more by an intrusive religious
than by a nihilistic philosophy. [2] Yet men whose interest
was ultimately practical and political, became ever more rare,
especially as from the death of Marcus Aurelius, the main-
tenance of the state had to be left more and more to the
sword of the Generals. The general conditions from the end
of the second century were favourable to a philosophy which
no longer in any respect took into real consideration the old
forms of the state.

The theosophic philosophy which was prepared for in the
second century, [3] was, from the stand-point of enlightenment
and knowledge of nature, a relapse; but it was the expression of a deeper religious need, and of a self-knowledge such
as had not been in existence at an earlier period. The final
consequences of that revolution in philosophy, which made
consideration of the inner life the starting-point of thought
about the world, only now began to be developed. The
ideas of a divine, gracious providence, of the relationship of
all men, of universal brotherly love, of a ready forgiveness of
wrong, of forbearing patience, of insight into one's own weak-

---

[1] The Christians, that is the Christian preachers, were most in agreement with
the Cynics (see Lucian's Peregrinus Proteus), both on the negative and on the
positive side; but for that very reason they were hard on one another (Justin and
Tatian against Crescens)—not only because the Christians gave a different basis
for the right mode of life from the Cynics, but above all, because they did not
approve of the self-conscious, contemptuous, proud disposition which Cynicism
produced in many of its adherents. Morality frequently underwent change for the
worse in the hands of Cynics, and became the morality of a "Gentleman," such
as we have also experience of in modern Cynicism.

[2] The attitude of Celsus, the opponent of the Christians, is specially instructive
here.

[3] For the knowledge of the spread of the idealistic philosophy the statement
of Origen (c. Celsum VI. 2) that Epictetus was admired not only by scholars, but
also by ordinary people who felt in themselves the impulse to be raised to
something higher, is well worthy of notice.

ness—affected no doubt with many shadows—became, for wide circles, a result of the practical philosophy of the Greeks as well as the conviction of inherent sinfulness, the need of redemption, and the eternal value and dignity of a human soul which finds rest only in God. These ideas, convictions and rules, had been picked up in the long journey from Socrates to Ammonius Saccas: at first, and for long afterwards, they crippled the interest in a rational knowledge of the world; but they deepened and enriched the inner life, and therewith the source of all knowledge. Those ideas, however, lacked as yet the certain coherence, but, above all, the authority which could have raised them above the region of wishes, presentiments, and strivings, and have given them normative authority in a community of men. There was no sure revelation, and no view of history which could be put in the place of the no longer prized political history of the nation or state to which one belonged.[1] There was, in fact, no such thing as certainty. In like manner, there was no power which might overturn idolatry and abolish the old, and therefore one did not get beyond the wavering between self-deification, fear of God, and deification of nature. The glory is all the greater of those statesmen and jurists who, in the second and third centuries, introduced human ideas of the Stoics into the legal arrangements of the empire, and raised them to standards. And we must value all the more the numerous undertakings and performances in which it appeared that the new view of life was powerful enough in individuals to beget a corresponding practice even without a sure belief in revelation.[2]

---

[1] This point was of importance for the propaganda of Christianity among the cultured. There seemed to be given here a reliable, because revealed, Cosmology and history of the world—which already contained the foundation of everything worth knowing. Both were needed and both were here set forth in closest union·

[2] The universalism as reached by the Stoics is certainly again threatened by the self-righteous and self-complacent distinction between men of virtue and men of pleasure, who, properly speaking, are not men. Aristotle had already dealt with the virtuous élite in a notable way. He says (Polit. 3. 13. p. 1284), that men who are distinguished by perfect virtue should not be put on a level with the ordinary mass, and should not be subjected to the constraints of a law adapted to the average man. "There is no law for these elect, who are a law to themselves."

Supplement.—For the correct understanding of the beginning of Christian theology, that is, for the Apologetic and Gnosis, it is important to note where they are dependent on Stoic and where on Platonic lines of thought. Platonism and Stoicism, in the second century, appeared in union with each other: but up to a certain point they may be distinguished in the common channel in which they flow. Wherever Stoicism prevailed in religious thought and feeling, as, for example, in Marcus Aurelius, religion gains currency as *natural* religion in the most comprehensive sense of the word. The idea of revelation or redemption scarcely emerges. To this rationalism the objects of knowledge are unvarying, ever the same: even cosmology attracts interest only in a very small degree. Myth and history are pageantry and masks. Moral ideas (virtues and duties) dominate even the religious sphere, which in its final basis has no independent authority. The interest in psychology and apologetic is very pronounced. On the other hand, the emphasis which, in principle, is put on the contrast of spirit and matter, God and the world, had for results: inability to rest in the actual realities of the cosmos, efforts to unriddle the history of the universe backwards and forwards, recognition of this process as the essential task of theoretic philosophy, and a deep, yearning conviction that the course of the world needs assistance. Here were given the conditions for the ideas of revelation, redemption, etc., and the restless search for powers from whom help might come, received here also a scientific justification. The rationalistic apologetic interests thereby fell into the background: contemplation and historical description predominated. [1]

The stages in the ecclesiastical history of dogma, from the middle of the first to the middle of the fifth century, correspond to the stages in the history of the ancient religion during the same period. The Apologists, Irenæus, Tertullian,

---

[1] Notions of pre-existence were readily suggested by the Platonic philosophy; yet this whole philosophy rests on the fact that one again posits the thing (after stripping it of certain marks as accidental or worthless, or ostensibly foreign to it) in order to express its value in this form, and hold fast the permanent in the change of the phenomena.

Hippolytus; the Alexandrians; Methodius, and the Cappado-
cians; Dionysius, the Areopagite, have their parallels in Seneca,
Marcus Aurelius; Plutarch, Epictetus, Numenius; Plotinus,
Porphyry; Iamblichus and Proclus.

But it is not only Greek philosophy that comes into question for the history of Christian dogma. The whole of Greek
culture must be taken into account. In his posthumous work
Hatch has shewn in a masterly way how that is to be done.
He describes the Grammar, the Rhetoric, the learned Profession, the Schools, the Exegesis, the Homilies, etc., of the Greeks,
and everywhere shews how they passed over into the Church,
thus exhibiting the Philosophy, the Ethic, the speculative Theology, the Mysteries, etc., of the Greeks, as the main factors in
the process of forming the ecclesiastical mode of thought.

But, besides the Greek, there is no mistaking the special
influence of Romish ideas and customs upon the Christian
Church. The following points specially claim attention: (1) The
conception of the contents of the Gospel and its application as "salus legitima," with the results which followed from
the naturalising of this idea. (2) The conception of the word
of Revelation, the Bible, etc., as "lex." (3) The idea of tradition in its relation to the Romish idea. (4) The Episcopal
constitution of the Church, including the idea of succession,
of the Primateship and universal Episcopate, in their dependence on Romish ideas and institutions (the Ecclesiastical organisation in its dependence on the Roman Empire). (5) The
separation of the idea of the "sacrament" from that of the
"mystery," and the development of the forensic discipline of
penance. The investigation has to proceed in a historical line,
described by the following series of chapters: Rome and Tertullian; Rome and Cyprian; Rome, Optatus and Augustine;
Rome and the Popes of the fifth century. We have to shew
how, by the power of her constitution and the earnestness
and consistency of her policy, Rome a second time, step by
step, conquered the world, but this time the Christian world. [1]

---

[1] See Tzschirn. i. d. Ztschr. f. K.-Gesch. XII. p 215 ff. "The genesis of the
Romish Church in the second century." What he presents is no doubt partly
incomplete, partly overdone and not proved: yet much of what he states is useful.

Greek philosophy exercised the greatest influence not only
on the Christian mode of thought, but also through that, on
the institutions of the Church. The Church never indeed became a philosophic school: but yet in her was realised in a
peculiar way, that which the Stoics and the Cynics had aimed
at. The Stoic (Cynic) Philosopher also belonged to the factors from which the Christian Priests or Bishops were formed.
That the old bearers of the Spirit—Apostles, Prophets, Teachers—have been changed into a class of professional moralists
and preachers, who bridle the people by counsel and reproof
(νουθετεῖν καὶ ἐλέγχειν), that this class considers itself and desires to be considered as a mediating Kingly Divine class,
that its representatives became "Lords" and let themselves
be called "Lords," all this was prefigured in the Stoic wise
man and in the Cynic Missionary. But so far as these several "Kings and Lords" are united in the idea and reality
of the Church and are subject to it, the Platonic idea of the
republic goes beyond the Stoic and Cynic ideals, and subor-
dinates them to it. But this Platonic ideal has again obtained
its political realisation in the Church through the very concrete laws of the Roman Empire, which were more and
more adopted, or taken possession of. Consequently, in the
completed Church we find again the philosophic schools and
the Roman Empire.

Literature.—Besides the older works of Tzschirner, Döllin-
ger, Burckhardt, Preller, see Friedländer, Darstellungen aus
der Sittengesch. Roms in der Zeit von August bis zum Aus-
gang der Antonine, 3 Bd. Aufl. Boissier, La Religion Romaine
d'Auguste aux Antonins, 2 Bd. 1874. Ramsay, The Church in
the Roman Empire before 170. London, 1893. Réville, La
Religion à Rome sous les Sévères, 1886. Schiller, Geschichte
der Röm Kaiserzeit, 1883. Marquardt, Römische Staatsverwal-
tung, 3 Bde. 1878. Foucart, Les Associations Relig. chez les
Grecs, 1873. Liebeman, Z. Gesch. u. Organisation d. Röm.
Vereinswesen, 1890. K. J. Neumann, Der Röm. Staat und die
allg. Kirche, Bd. I. 1890. Leopold Schmidt, Die Ethik der
alten Griechen, 2 Bd. 1882. Heinrici, Die Christengemeinde

Korinth's und die religiösen Genossenschaften der Griechen, in der Ztschr. f. wissensch. Theol. 1876-77. Hatch, The Influence of Greek Ideas and Usages upon the Christian Church. Buechner, De neocoria, 1888. Hirschfeld. Z. Gesch. d. röm. Kaisercultus. The Histories of Philosophy by Zeller, Erdmann, Ueberweg, Strümpell, Windelband, etc. Heinze, Die Lehre vom Logos in der Griech. Philosophie, 1872. By same Author, Der Eudämonismus in der Griech. Philosophie, 1883. Hirzel, Untersuchungen zu Cicero's philos. Schriften, 3 Thle. 1877-1883. These investigations are of special value for the history of dogma, because they set forth with the greatest accuracy and care, the later developments of the great Greek philosophic schools, especially on Roman soil. We must refer specially to the discussions on the influence of the Roman on the Greek Philosophy. Volkmann, Die Rhetorik der Griechen und Römer, 1872.

Supplementary.

Perhaps the most important fact for the following development of the history of Dogma, the way for which had already been prepared in the Apostolic age, is the twofold conception of the aim of Christ's appearing, or of the religious blessing of salvation. The two conceptions were indeed as yet mutually dependent on each other, and were twined together in the closest way, just as they are presented in the teaching of Jesus himself; but they began even at this early period to be differentiated. Salvation, that is to say, was conceived, on the one hand, as sharing in the glorious kingdom of Christ soon to appear, and everything else was regarded as preparatory to this sure prospect; on the other hand, however, attention was turned to the conditions and to the provisions of God wrought by Christ, which first made men capable of attaining that portion, that is, of becoming sure of it. Forgiveness of sin, righteousness, faith, knowledge, etc., are the things which come into consideration here, and these blessings themselves, so far as they have as their sure result life in the kingdom of Christ, or more accurately eternal life, may be

regarded as salvation. It is manifest that these two conceptions need not be exclusive. The first regards the final effect
as the goal and all else as a preparation, the other regards
the preparation, the facts already accomplished by Christ and
the inner transformation of men as the main thing, and all
else as the natural and necessary result. Paul, above all, as
may be seen especially from the arguments in the epistle to
the Romans, unquestionably favoured the latter conception and
gave it vigorous expression. The peculiar conflicts with which
he saw himself confronted, and, above all, the great controversy about the relation of the Gospel and the new communities to Judaism, necessarily concentrated the attention on
questions as to the arrangements on which the community of
those sanctified in Christ should rest, and the conditions of
admission to this community. But the centre of gravity of
Christian faith might also for the moment be removed from
the hope of Christ's second advent, and would then necessarily be found in the first advent, in virtue of which salvation was already prepared for man, and man for salvation
(Rom. III.—VIII.). The dual development of the conception
of Christianity which followed from this, rules the whole
history of the Gospel to the present day. The eschatological
view is certainly very severely repressed, but it always
breaks out here and there, and still guards the spiritual from
the secularisation which threatens it. But the possibility of
uniting the two conceptions in complete harmony with each
other, and on the other hand, of expressing them antithetically, has been the very circumstance that has complicated in
an extraordinary degree the progress of the development of
the history of dogma. From this follows the antithesis, that
from that conception which somehow recognises salvation itself
in a present spiritual possession, eternal life in the sense of
immortality may be postulated as final result, though not a
glorious kingdom of Christ on earth; while, conversely, the
eschatological view must logically depreciate every blessing
which can be possessed in the present life.

It is now evident that the theology, and, further, the Hellenising, of Christianity, could arise and has arisen in connection,

not with the eschatological, but only with the other conception.
Just because the matters here in question were present spiritual blessings, and because, from the nature of the case, the
ideas of forgiveness of sin, righteousness, knowledge, etc., were
not so definitely outlined in the early tradition, as the hopes
of the future, conceptions entirely new and very different,
could, as it were, be secretly naturalised. The spiritual view
left room especially for the great contrast of a religious and
a moralistic conception, as well as for a frame of mind which
was like the eschatological in so far as, according to it, faith
and knowledge were to be only preparatory blessings in contrast with the peculiar blessing of immortality, which of course
was contained in them. In this frame of mind the illusion
might easily arise that this hope of immortality was the very
kernel of those hopes of the future for which old concrete forms
of expression were only a temporary shell. But it might
further be assumed that contempt for the transitory and finite
as such, was identical with contempt for the kingdom of the
world which the returning Christ would destroy.

The history of dogma has to shew how the old eschatological view was gradually repressed and transformed in the Gentile Christian communities, and how there was finally developed and carried out a spiritual conception in which a strict
moralism counterbalanced a luxurious mysticism, and wherein
the results of Greek practical philosophy could find a place.
But we must here refer to the fact, which is already taught
by the development in the Apostolic age, that Christian
dogmatic did not spring from the eschatological, but from the
spiritual mode of thought. The former had nothing but sure
hopes and the guarantee of these hopes by the Spirit, by the
words of prophecy and by the apocalyptic writings. One does
not think, he lives and dreams, in the eschatological mode of
thought; and such a life was vigorous and powerful till beyond
the middle of the second century. There can be no external
authorities here; for one has at every moment the highest
authority in living operation in the Spirit. On the other hand,
not only does the ecclesiastical christology essentially spring
from the spiritual way of thinking, but very specially also the

system of dogmatic guarantees. The co-ordination of λόγος θεοῦ, διδαχή κυρίου, κήρυγμα τῶν δώδεκα ἀποστόλων [word of God, teaching of the Lord, preaching of the twelve Apostles], which lay at the basis of all Gentile Christian speculation almost from the very beginning, and which was soon directed against the enthusiasts, originated in a conception which regarded as the essential thing in Christianity, the sure knowledge which is the condition of immortality. If, however, in the following sections of this historical presentation, the pervading and continuous opposition of the two conceptions is not everywhere clearly and definitely brought into prominence, that is due to the conviction that the historian has no right to place the factors and impelling ideas of a development in a clearer light than they appear in the development itself. He must respect the obscurities and complications as they come in his way. A clear discernment of the difference of the two conceptions was very seldom attained to in ecclesiastical antiquity, because they did not look beyond their points of contact, and because certain articles of the eschatological conception could never be suppressed or remodelled in the Church. Goethe (Dichtung und Wahrheit, II. 8,) has seen this very clearly. "The Christian religion wavers between its own historic positive element and a pure Deism, which, based on morality, in its turn offers itself as the foundation of morality. The difference of character and mode of thought shew themselves here in infinite gradations, especially as another main distinction co-operates with them, since the question arises, what share the reason, and what the feelings, can and should have in such convictions." See, also, what immediately follows.

2. The origin of a series of the most important Christian customs and ideas is involved in an obscurity which in all probability will never be cleared up. Though one part of those ideas may be pointed out in the epistles of Paul, yet the question must frequently remain unanswered, whether he found them in existence or formed them independently, and accordingly the other question, whether they are exclusively indebted to the activity of Paul for their spread and naturalisation in Christendom. What was the original conception of

baptism? Did Paul develop independently his own conception? What significance had it in the following period? When
and where did baptism in the name of the Father, Son and
Holy Spirit arise, and how did it make its way in Christendom? In what way were views about the saving value of
Christ's death developed alongside of Paul's system? When
and how did belief in the birth of Jesus from a Virgin gain
acceptance in Christendom? Who first distinguished Christendom, as ἐκκλησία τοῦ θεοῦ, from Judaism, and how did the concept ἐκκλησία become current? How old is the triad: Apostles, Prophets and Teachers? When were Baptism and the
Lord's Supper grouped together? How old are our first three
Gospels? To all these questions and many more of equal
importance there is no sure answer. But the greatest problem
is presented by Christology, not indeed in its particular features doctrinally expressed, these almost everywhere may be
explained historically, but in its deepest roots as it was preached by Paul as the principle of a new life (2 Cor. V. 17),
and as it was to many besides him the expression of a personal union with the exalted Christ (Rev. II. 3). But this
problem exists only for the historian who considers things
only from the outside, or seeks for objective proofs. Behind
and in the Gospel stands the Person of Jesus Christ who mastered
men's hearts, and constrained them to yield themselves to him
as his own, and in whom they found their God. Theology
attempted to describe in very uncertain and feeble outline
what the mind and heart had grasped. Yet it testifies of a
new life which, like all higher life, was kindled by a Person,
and could only be maintained by connection with that Person.
"I can do all things through Christ who strengtheneth me."
"I live, yet not I, but Christ liveth in me." These convictions
are not dogmas and have no history, and they can only be
propagated in the manner described by Paul, Gal. I. 15, 16.

3. It was of the utmost importance for the legitimising
of the later development of Christianity as a system of doctrine.
that early Christianity had an Apostle who was a theologian,
and that his Epistles were received into the canon. That the
doctrine about Christ has become the main article in Christi-

anity is not of course the result of Paul's preaching, but is
based on the confession that Jesus is the Christ. The theology
of Paul was not even the most prominent ruling factor in the
transformation of the Gospel to the Catholic doctrine of faith,
although an earnest study of the Pauline Epistles by the
earliest Gentile Christian theologians, the Gnostics, and their
later opponents, is unmistakable. But the decisive importance
of this theology lies in the fact that, as a rule, it formed the
boundary and the foundation — just as the words of the
Lord himself — for those who in the following period endeavoured to ascertain original Christianity, because the Epistles
attesting it stood in the canon of the New Testament. Now,
as this theology comprised both speculative and apologetic
elements, as it can be thought of as a system, as it contained
a theory of history and a definite conception of the Old Testament,—finally, as it was composed of objective and subjective
ethical considerations and included the realistic elements of a
national religion (wrath of God, sacrifice, reconciliation, Kingdom of glory), as well as profound psychological perceptions
and the highest appreciation of spiritual blessings, the Catholic
doctrine of faith as it was formed in the course of time,
seemed, at least in its leading features, to be related to it,
nay, demanded by it. For the ascertaining of the deep-lying
distinctions, above all for the perception that the question in
the two cases is about elements quite differently conditioned,
that even the method is different,—in short, that the Pauline
Gospel is not identical with the original Gospel and much
less with any later doctrine of faith, there is required such
historical judgment and such honesty of purpose not to be
led astray in the investigation by the canon of the New
Testament, [1] that no change in the prevailing ideas can be
hoped for for long years to come. Besides, critical theology

[1] What is meant here is the imminent danger of taking the several constituent
parts of the canon, even for historical investigation, as constituent parts, that is,
of explaining one writing by the standard of another and so creating an artificial
unity. The contents of any of Paul's epistles, for example, will be presented
very differently if it is considered by itself and in the circumstances in which it
was written, or if attention is fixed on it as part of a collection whose unity is
presupposed.

has made it difficult to gain an insight into the great difference that lies between the Pauline and the Catholic theology, by the one-sided prominence it has hitherto given to the
antagonism between Paulinism and Judaistic Christianity. In contrast with this view the remark of Havet, though also very
one-sided, is instructive, "Quand on vient de relire Paul, on ne
peut méconnaître le caractère élevé de son œuvre. Je dirai en
un mot, qu'il a agrandi dans une proportion extraordinaire
l'attrait que le judaïsme exerçait sur le monde ancien" (Le
Christianisme, T. IV. p. 216). That, however, was only very
gradually the case and within narrow limits. The deepest and
most important writings of the New Testament are incontest-
ably those in which Judaism is understood as religion, but
spiritually overcome and subordinated to the Gospel as a new
religion,—the Pauline Epistles, the Epistle to the Hebrews,
and the Gospel and Epistle of John. There is set forth in
these writings a new and exalted world of religious feelings,
views and judgments, into which the Christians of succeeding
centuries got only meagre glimpses. Strictly speaking, the
opinion that the New Testament in its whole extent comprehends a unique literature is not tenable; but it is correct
to say that between its most important constituent parts and
the literature of the period immediately following there is a
great gulf fixed.

But Paulinism especially has had an immeasurable and
blessed influence on the whole course of the history of dogma,
an influence it could not have had if the Pauline Epistles
had not been received into the canon. Paulinism is a religious
and Christocentric doctrine, more inward and more powerful
than any other which has ever appeared in the Church. It
stands in the clearest opposition to all merely natural moralism,
all righteousness of works, all religious ceremonialism, all
Christianity without Christ. It has therefore become the conscience of the Church, until the Catholic Church in Jansenism
killed this her conscience. "The Pauline reactions describe
the critical epochs of theology and the Church." [1] One might

---

[1] See Bigg, The Christian Platonist of Alexandria, pp. 53, 283 ff.

write a history of dogma as a history of the Pauline reactions
in the Church, and in doing so would touch on all the turn-
ing-points of the history.   Marcion after the Apostolic Fathers;
Irenæus, Clement and Origen after the Apologists; Augustine
after the Fathers of the Greek Church; [1] the great Reformers
of the middle ages from Agobard to Wessel in the bosom
of the mediæval Church; Luther after the Scholastics; Jansenism after the council of Trent:—everywhere it has been
Paul, in these men, who produced the Reformation.   Paulinism
has proved to be a ferment in the history of dogma, a basis
it has never been. [2]   Just as it had that significance in Paul
himself, with reference to Jewish Christianity, so it has continued to work through the history of the Church.

[1] Reuter (August. Studien, p. 492) has drawn a valuable parallel between Marcion and Augustine with regard to Paul.

[2] Marcion of course wished to raise it to the exclusive basis, but he entirely
misunderstood it.

DIVISION I.

THE GENESIS OF THE ECCLESIASTICAL DOGMA,

OR

THE GENESIS OF

THE CATHOLIC APOSTOLIC DOGMATIC THEOLOGY,

AND

THE FIRST SCIENTIFIC ECCLESIASTICAL

SYSTEM OF DOCTRINE.

BOOK I.

THE PREPARATION.

'Εάν μυρίους παιδαγωγοὺς ἔχητε ἐν χριστῷ ἀλλ' οὐ
πολλοὺς πατέρας.

1 Cor. IV. 15.

Eine jede Idee tritt als ein fremder Gast in die
Erscheinung, und wie sie sich zu realisiren be-
ginnt, ist sie kaum von Phantasie und Phantasterei
zu unterscheiden.

GOETHE, Sprüche in Prosa, 566.

BOOK I

THE PREPARATION

CHAPTER I

HISTORICAL SURVEY

THE first century of the existence of Gentile Christian communities is particularly characterised by the following features:

I. The rapid disappearance of Jewish Christianity. [1]

II. The enthusiastic character of the religious temper: the Charismatic teachers and the appeal to the Spirit. [2]

III. The strength of the hopes for the future, Chiliasm. [3]

IV. The rigorous endeavour to fulfil the moral precepts of Christ, and truly represent the holy and heavenly community of God in abstinence from everything unclean, and in love to God and the brethren here on earth "in these last days." [4]

[1] This fact must have been apparent as early as the year 100. The first direct evidence of it is in Justin (Apol. I. 53).

[2] Every individual was, or at least should have been conscious, as a Christian, of having received the πνεῦμα θεοῦ, though that does not exclude spiritual grades. A special peculiarity of the enthusiastic nature of the religious temper is that it does not allow reflection as to the authenticity of the faith in which a man lives. As to the Charismatic teaching, see my edition of the Didache (Texte u. Unters. II. 1. 2. p. 93 ff.).

[3] The hope of the approaching end of the world and the glorious kingdom of Christ still determined men's heart; though exhortations against theoretical and practical scepticism became more and more necessary. On the other hand, after the Epistles to the Thessalonians, there were not wanting exhortations to continue sober and diligent.

[4] There was a strong consciousness that the Christian Church is, above all, a union for a holy life, as well as a consciousness of the obligation to help one

V. The want of a fixed doctrinal form in relation to the
abstract statement of the faith, and the corresponding variety
and freedom of Christian preaching on the basis of clear formulæ and an increasingly rich tradition.

VI. The want of a clearly defined external authority in
the communities, sure in its application, and the corresponding
independence and freedom of the individual Christian in relation to the expression of the ideas, beliefs and hopes of faith. [1]

VII. The want of a fixed political union of the several communities with each other—every *ecclesia* is an image complete
in itself, and an embodiment of the whole heavenly Church—
while the consciousness of the unity of the holy Church of Christ
which has the spirit in its midst, found strong expression. [2]

VIII. A quite unique literature in which were manufactured
facts for the past and for the future, and which did not submit
to the usual literary rules and forms, but came forward with
the loftiest pretensions. [3]

another, and use all the blessings bestowed by God in the service of our neigh-
bours. Justin (2 Apol. in Euseb. H. E. IV. 17. 10) calls Christianity τὸ διδασκάλιον
τῆς θείας ἀρετῆς.

[1] The existing authorities (Old Testament, sayings of the Lord, words of
Apostles) did not necessarily require to be taken into account; for the living acting
Spirit, partly attesting himself also to the senses, gave new revelations. The validity
of these authorities therefore held good only in theory, and might in practice be
completely set aside. (Cf., above all, the Shepherd of Hermas.)

[2] Zahn remarks (Ignatius. v. A. p. VII.): "I do not believe it to be the business
of that province of historical investigation which is dependent on the writings of
the so-called Apostolic Fathers as main sources, to explain the origin of the
universal Church in any sense of the term; for that Church existed before Clement
and Hermas, before Ignatius and Polycarp. But an explanatory answer is needed
for the question: By what means did the consciousness of the "universal Church,"
so little favoured by our circumstances, maintain itself unbroken in the post-Apostolic
communities? This way of stating it obscures, at least, the problem which here
lies before us, for it does not take account of the changes which the idea "universal Church" underwent up to the middle of the third century—besides, we do
not find the title before Ignatius. In so far as the "universal Church" is set forth
as an earthly power recognisable in a doctrine or in political forms, the question
as to the origin of the idea is not only allowable, but must be regarded as one
of the most important. On the earliest conception of the "Ecclesia" and its
realisation, see the fine investigations of Sohm "Kirchenrecht," I. p. 1 ff., which,
however, suffer from being a little overdriven.

[3] See the important essay of Overbeck: Ueber die Anfänge d. patrist. Litteratur (Hist. Ztschr. N. F. Bd. XII. pp. 417–472). Early Christian literature, as a

IX. The reproduction of particular sayings and arguments of Apostolic Teachers with an uncertain understanding of them. [1]

X. The rise of tendencies which endeavoured to hasten in every respect the inevitable process of fusing the Gospel with the spiritual and religious interests of the time, viz., the Hellenic, as well as attempts to separate the Gospel from its origins and provide for it quite foreign presuppositions. To the latter belongs, above all, the Hellenic idea that knowledge is not a charismatic supplement to the faith, or an outgrowth of faith alongside of others, but that it coincides with the essence of faith itself. [2]

The sources for this period are few, as there was not much written, and the following period did not lay itself out for preserving a great part of the literary monuments of that epoch. Still we do possess a considerable number of writings and important fragments, [3] and further important inferences here are rendered possible by the monuments of the following period, since the conditions of the first century were not changed in a moment, but were partly, at least, long preserved, especially in certain national Churches and in remote communities. [4]

---

rule, claims to be inspired writing. One can see, for example, in the history of the resurrection in the recently discovered Gospel of Peter (fragment) how facts were remodelled or created.

[1] The writings of men of the Apostolic period, and that immediately succeeding, attained in part a wide circulation, and in some portions of them, often of course incorrectly understood, very great influence. How rapidly this literature was diffused, even the letters, may be studied in the history of the Epistles of Paul, the first Epistle of Clement, and other writings.

[2] That which is here mentioned is of the greatest importance; it is not a mere reference to the so-called Gnostics. The foundations for the Hellenising of the Gospel in the Church were already laid in the first century (50-150).

[3] We should not over-estimate the extent of early Christian literature. It is very probable that we know, so far as the titles of books are concerned, nearly all that was effective, and the greater part, by very diverse means, has also been preserved to us. We except, of course, the so-called Gnostic literature of which we have only a few fragments. Only from the time of Commodus, as Eusebius H. E. V. 21. 27, has remarked, did the great Church preserve an extensive literature.

[4] It is therefore important to note the locality in which a document orginates, and the more so the earlier the document is. In the earliest period, in which the history of the Church was more uniform, and the influence from without relatively less, the differences are still in the background. Yet the spirit of Rome already announces itself in the Epistle of Clement, that of Alexandria in the Epistle of Barnabas, that of the East in the Epistles of Ignatius.

Supplement. —The main features of the message concerning Christ, of the matter of the Evangelic history, were fixed in the first and second generations of believers, and on Palestinian soil. But yet, up to the middle of the second century, this matter was in many ways increased in Gentile Christian regions, revised from new points of view, handed down in very diverse forms, and systematically allegorised by individual teachers. As a whole, the Evangelic history certainly appears to have been completed at the beginning of the second century. But in detail, much that was new was produced at a later period—and not only in Gnostic circles—and the old tradition was recast or rejected. [1]

[1] The history of the genesis of the four Canonical Gospels, or the comparison of them, is instructive on this point. Then we must bear in mind the old Apocryphal Gospels, and the way in which the so-called Apostolic Fathers and Justin attest the Evangelic history, and in part reproduce it independently; the Gospels of Peter, of the Egyptians, and of Marcion; the Diatesseron of Tatian; the Gnostic Gospels and Acts of the Apostles, etc. The greatest gap in our knowledge consists in the fact, that we know so little about the course of things from about the year 61 to the beginning of the reign of Trajan. The consolidating and remodelling process must, for the most part, have taken place in this period. We possess probably not a few writings which belong to that period; but how are we to prove this? how are they to be arranged? Here lies the cause of most of the differences, combinations and uncertainties; many scholars, therefore, actually leave these 40 years out of account, and seek to place everything in the first three decennia of the second century.

CHAPTER II.

THE ELEMENT COMMON TO ALL CHRISTIANS AND THE BREACH WITH JUDAISM

On account of the great differences among those who, in the first century, reckoned themselves in the Church of God, and called themselves by the name of Christ, [1] it seems at first sight scarcely possible to set up marks which would hold good for all, or even for nearly all, the groups. Yet the great majority had one thing in common, as is proved, among other things, by the gradual expulsion of Gnosticism. The conviction that they knew the supreme God, the consciousness of being responsible to him (Heaven and Hell), reliance on Jesus Christ, the hope of an eternal life, the vigorous elevation above the world—these are the elements that formed the fundamental mood. The author of the Acts of Thecla expresses the general view when he (c. 5.7) co-ordinates τὸν τοῦ χριστοῦ λόγον, with λόγος θεοῦ περὶ ἐγκατείας, καὶ ἀναστάσεως. The following particulars may here be specified. [2]

I. The Gospel, because it rests on revelation, is the sure manifestation of the supreme God, and its believing acceptance guarantees salvation (σωτερία).

II. The essential content of this manifestation (besides the revelation and the verification of the oneness and spirituality of God), [3] is, first of all, the message of the resurrection and eternal life (ἀνάστασις, ζωὴ αἰώνιος), then the preaching of moral purity and continence (ἐγκράτεια), on the basis of repentance

---

[1] See, as to this, Celsus in Orig. III. 10 ff. and V. 59 ff.

[2] The marks adduced in the text do not certainly hold good for some comparatively unimportant Gnostic groups, but they do apply to the great majority of them, and in the main to Marcion also.

[3] Most of the Gnostic schools know only one God, and put all emphasis on he knowledge of the oneness, supramundaneness, and spirituality of this God.

toward God (μετάνοια), and of an expiation once assured by baptism, with eye ever fixed on the requital of good and evil. [1]

III. This manifestation is mediated by Jesus Christ, who is the Saviour (σωτήρ) sent by God "in these last days," and who stands with God himself in a union special and unique, (cf. the ambiguous παῖς θεοῦ, which was much used in the earliest period). He has brought the true and full knowledge of God, as well as the gift of immortality (γνῶσις καὶ ζωή, or γνῶσις τῆς ζωῆς, as an expression for the sum of the Gospel. See the supper prayer in the Didache, c. IX. and X.; εὐχαριστοῦμέν σοι, πάτερ ἡμῶν ὑπερ τῆς ζωῆς καὶ γνώσεως ἧς ἐγνώρισας ἡμῖν διὰ Ἰησοῦ τοῦ παιδός σου), and is for that very reason the redeemer (σώτηρ and victor over the demons) on whom we are to place believing trust. But he is, further, in word and walk the highest example of all moral virtue, and therefore in his own person the law for the perfect life, and at the same time the God-appointed lawgiver and judge. [2]

IV. Virtue, as continence, embraces as its highest task, renunciation of temporal goods and separation from the common world; for the Christian is not a citizen, but a stranger on the earth, and expects its approaching destruction. [3]

The Æons, the Demiurgus, the God of matter, do not come near this God though they are called Gods. See the testimony of Hippolytus c. Noet. 11; καὶ γὰρ πάντες ἀπεκλείσθησαν εἰς τοῦτο ἄκοντες εἰπεῖν, ὅτι τὸ πᾶν εἰς ἕνα ἀνατρέχει. εἰ οὖν τὰ πάντα εἰς ἕνα ἀνατρέχει καὶ κατὰ Οὐαλεντῖνον καί κατὰ Μαρκίωνα. Κήρινθόν τὲ καὶ πᾶσαν τὴν ἐκείνων φλυαρίαν, καὶ ἄκοντες εἰς τοῦτο περιέπεσαν, ἵνα τὸν ἕνα ὁμολογήσωσιν αἴτιον τῶν πάντων οὕτως οὖν συντρέχουσιν καὶ αὐτοὶ μὴ θέλοντες τῇ ἀληθείᾳ ἕνα θεὸν λέγειν ποιήσαντα ὡς ἠθέλησεν.

[1] Continence was regarded as the condition laid down by God for the resurrection and eternal life. The sure hope of this was for many, if not for the majority, the whole sum of religion, in connection with the idea of the requital of good and evil which was now firmly established. See the testimony of the heathen Lucian, in Peregrinus Proteus.

[2] Even where the judicial attributes were separated from God (Christ) as not suitable, Christ was still comprehended as the critical appearance by which every man is placed in the condition which belongs to him. The Apocalypse of Peter expects that God himself will come as Judge. See the Messianic expectations of Judaism, in which it was always uncertain whether God or the Messiah would hold the judgment.

[3] Celsus (Orig. c. Celsum, V. 59) after referring to the many Christian parties mutually provoking and fighting with each other, remarks (V. 64) that though

V. Christ has committed to chosen men, the Apostles (or
to one Apostle), the proclamation of the message he received
from God; consequently, their preaching represents that of
Christ himself. But, besides, the Spirit of God rules in Christians, "the Saints." He bestows upon them special gifts, and,
above all, continually raises up among them Prophets and spiritual Teachers who receive revelations and communications
for the edification of others, and whose injunctions are to be
obeyed.

VI. Christian Worship is a service of God in spirit and in
truth (a spiritual sacrifice), and therefore has no legal ceremonial and statutory rules. The value of the sacred acts and
consecrations which are connected with the cultus, consists in
the communication of spiritual blessings. (Didache X., ἡμῖν δὲ
ἐχαρίσω, δέσποτα, πνευματικὴν τροφὴν καὶ ποτὸν καὶ ζωὴν αἰώνιον
διὰ τοῦ παιδός σου).

VII. Everything that Jesus Christ brought with him, may
be summed up in γνῶσις καὶ ζωή, or in the knowledge of im-
mortal life. [1] To possess the perfect knowledge was, in wide
circles, an expression for the sum total of the Gospel. [2]

---

they differ much from each other, and quarrel with each other, you can yet hear
from them all the protestation, "The world is crucified to me and I to the
world." In the earliest Gentile Christian communities brotherly love for reflective
thought falls into the background behind ascetic exercises of virtue, in unquestionable deviation from the sayings of Christ, but in fact it was powerful. See the
testimony of Pliny and Lucian, Aristides, Apol. 15, Tertull. Apol. 39.

[1] The word "life" comes into consideration in a double sense, viz., as sound-
ness of the soul and as immortality. Neither, of course, is to be separated from
the other. But I have attempted to shew in my essay, "Medicinisches aus der
ältesten Kirchengesch." (1892), the extent to which the Gospel in the earliest
Christendom was preached as medicine and Jesus as a Physician, and how the
Christian Message was really comprehended by the Gentiles as a medicinal religion.
Even the Stoic philosophy gave itself out as a soul therapeutic, and Æsculapius
was worshipped as a Saviour-God; but Christianity alone was a religion of healing.

[2] Heinrici, in his commentary on the epistles to the Corinthians, has dealt
very clearly with this matter; see especially (Bd. II. p. 557 ff.) the description of
the Christianity of the Corinthians: "On what did the community base its Christian
character? It believed in one God who had revealed himself to it through Christ,
without denying the reality of the hosts of gods in the heathen world (1. VIII. 6).
It hoped in immortality without being clear as to the nature of the Christian belief
in the resurrection (I. XV.) It had no doubt as to the requital of good and evil

VIII. Christians, as such, no longer take into account the
distinctions of race, age, rank, nationality and worldly culture,
but the Christian community must be conceived as a communion resting on a divine election. Opinions were divided
about the ground of that election.

IX. As Christianity is the only true religion, and as it is
no national religion, but somehow concerns the whole of humanity, or its best part, it follows that it can have nothing
in common with the Jewish nation and its contemporary
cultus. The Jewish nation in which Jesus Christ appeared,
has, for the time at least, no special relation to the God
whom Jesus revealed. Whether it had such a relation at
an earlier period is doubtful (cf. here, *e. g.*, the attitude of
Marcion, Ptolemæus the disciple of Valentinus, the author
of the Epistle of Barnabas, Aristides and Justin); but certain
it is that God has now cast it off, and that all revelations of
God, so far as they took place at all before Christ, (the majority assumed that there had been such revelations and considered the Old Testament as a holy record), must have
aimed solely at the call of the " new people ", and in some
way prepared for the revelation of God through his Son. [1]

(I. IV. 5: 2 V. 10: XI. 15: Rom. II. 4), without understanding the value of self-
denial, claiming no merit, for the sake of important ends. It was striving to
make use of the Gospel as a new doctrine of wisdom about earthly and superearthly things, which led to the perfect and best established knowledge (1 I. 21:
VIII. 1). It boasted of special operations of the Divine Spirit, which in themselves remained obscure and non-transparent, and therefore unfruitful (1. XIV),
while it was prompt to put aside as obscure, the word of the Cross as preached
by Paul (2. IV. 1 f.). The hope of the near Parousia, however, and the completion
of all things, evinced no power to effect a moral transformation of society. We
herewith obtain the outline of a conviction that was spread over the widest circles
of the Roman Empire." Naturam si expellas furca, tamen usque recurret.

[1] Nearly all Gentile Christian groups that we know, are at one in the detachment of Christianity from empiric Judaism; the "Gnostics," however, included the
Old Testament in Judaism, while the greater part of Christians did not. That
detachment seemed to be demanded by the claims of Christianity to be the one,
true, absolute and therefore oldest religion, foreseen from the beginning. The
different estimates of the Old Testament in Gnostic circles have their exact
parallels in the different estimates of Judaism among the other Christians; cf. for
example, in this respect, the conception stated in the Epistle of Barnabas with
the views of Marcion, and Justin with Valentinus. The particulars about the
detachment of the Gentile Christians from the Synagogue, which was prepared

for by the inner development of Judaism itself, and was required by the fundamental fact that the Messiah, crucified and rejected by his own people, was
recognised as Saviour by those who were not Jews, cannot be given in the
frame-work of a history of dogma; though, see Chaps. III. IV. VI. On the other
hand, the turning away from Judaism is also the result of the mass of things
which were held in common with it, even in Gnostic circles. Christianity made
its appearance in the Empire in the Jewish propaganda. By the preaching of
Jesus Christ who brought the gift of eternal life, mediated the full knowledge of
God, and assembled round him in these last days a community, the imperfect
and hybrid creations of the Jewish propaganda in the empire were converted into
independent formations. These formations were far superior to the synagogue in
power of attraction, and from the nature of the case would very soon be directed
with the utmost vigour against the synagogue.

CHAPTER III.

THE COMMON FAITH AND THE BEGINNINGS OF KNOWLEDGE IN GENTILE CHRISTIANITY AS IT WAS BEING DEVELOPED INTO CATHOLICISM [1]

§ 1. *The Communities and the Church.*

THE confessors of the Gospels, belonging to organised communities who recognised the Old Testament as the Divine record of revelation, and prized the Evangelic tradition as a public message for all, to which, in its undiluted form, they wished to adhere truly and sincerely, formed the stem of

---

[1] The statements made in this chapter need special forbearance, especially as the selection from the rich and motley material—cf. only the so-called Apostolic Fathers—the emphasising of this, the throwing into the background of that element, cannot here be vindicated. It is not possible, in the compass of a brief account, to give expression to that elasticity and those oscillations of ideas and thoughts which were peculiar to the Christians of the earliest period. There was indeed, as will be shewn, a complex of tradition in many respects fixed, but this complex was still under the dominance of an enthusiastic fancy, so that what at one moment seemed fixed, in the next had disappeared. Finally, attention must be given to the fact that when we speak of the beginnings of knowledge, the members of the Christian community in their totality are no longer in question, but only individuals who of course were the leaders of the others. If we had no other writings from the times of the Apostolic Fathers than the first Epistle of Clement and the Epistle of Polycarp, it would be comparatively easy to sketch a clear history of the development connecting Paulinism with the Old-Catholic Theology as represented by Iræneus, and so to justify the traditional ideas. But besides these two Epistles which are the classic monuments of the mediating tradition, we have a great number of documents which shew us how manifold and complicated the development was. They also teach us how careful we should be in the interpretation of the post-Apostolic documents that immediately followed the Pauline Epistles, and that we must give special heed to the paragraphs and ideas in them, which distinguish them from Paulinism. Besides, it is of the greatest importance that those two Epistles originated in Rome and Asia Minor, as these are the places where we must seek the embryonic stage of old-Catholic doctrine. Numerous fine threads, in the form of fundamental ideas and particular views, pass over from the Asia Minor theology of the post-Apostolic period into the old-Catholic theology.

Christendom both as to extent and importance. [1] The communities stood to each other in an outwardly loose, but inwardly firm connection, and every community by the vigour of its faith, the certainty of its hope, the holy character of its life, as well as by unfeigned love, unity and peace, was to be an image of the holy Church of God which is in heaven, and whose members are scattered over the earth. They were, further, by the purity of their walk and an active brotherly disposition, to prove to those without, that is to the world, the excellence and truth of the Christian faith. [2] The hope

[1] The Epistle to the Hebrews (X. 25), the Epistle of Barnabas (IV. 10), the Shepherd of Hermas (Sim. IX. 26. 3), but especially the Epistle of Ignatius and still later documents, shew that up to the middle of the second century, and even later, there were Christians who, for various reasons, stood outside the union of communities, or wished to have only a loose and temporary relation to them. The exhortation: ἐπὶ τὸ αὐτὸ συνερχόμενοι συνζητεῖτε περὶ τοῦ κοινῇ συμφέροντος (see my note on Didache XVI. 2, and cf. for the expression the interesting State Inscription which was found at Magnesia on the Meander. Bull, Corresp. Hellén. 1883 p. 506: ἀπαγορεύω μήτε συνέρχεσθαι τοὺς ἀρτοκόκους κατ᾽ ἑταιρίαν μήτε παρεστηκότας θρασύνεσθαι, πειθάρχειν δὲ πάντως τοῖς ὑπὲρ τοῦ κοινῇ συμφέροντος ἐπιτατττομένοις κ.τ.λ. or the exhortation: κολλᾶσθε τοῖς ἁγίοις, ὅτι οἱ κολλώμενοι αὐτοῖς ἁγιασθήσονται (1 Clem. 46. 2, introduced as γραφὴ) runs through most of the writings of the post-Apostolic and pre-catholic period. New doctrines were imported by wandering Christians who, in many cases, may not themselves have belonged to a community, and did not respect the arrangements of those they found in existence, but sought to form conventicles. If we remember how the Greeks and Romans were wont to get themselves initiated into a mystery cult, and took part for a long time in the religious exercises, and then, when they thought they had got the good of it, for the most part or wholly to give up attending, we shall not wonder that the demand to become a permanent member of a Christian community was opposed by many. The statements of Hermas are specially instructive here.

[2] "Corpus sumus," says Tertullian, at a time when this description had already become an anachronism, "de conscientia religionis et disciplinæ unitate et spei foedere." (Apol. 39: cf. Ep. Petri ad Jacob. I.; εἷς θεὸς, εἷς νόμος, μία ἐλπίς). The description was applicable to the earlier period, when there was no such thing as a federation with political forms, but when the consciousness of belonging to a community and of forming a brotherhood (ἀδελφότης) was all the more deeply felt: See, above all, 1 Clem. and Corinth., the Didache (9–15), Aristides, Apol 15 : "and when they have become Christians they call them (the slaves) brethren without hesitation . . . . . for they do not call them brethren according to the flesh, but according to the spirit and in God;" cf. also the statements on brotherhood in Tertullian and Minucius Felix (also Lucian). We have in 1 Clem. 1. 2. the delineation of a perfect Christian Church. The Epistles of Ignatius are specially instructive as to the independence of each individual community : 1 Clem. and Didache, as to the obligation to assist stranger communities by counsel and action, and to support the travelling brethren. As every Christian is a πάροικος, so every community is

that the Lord would speedily appear to gather into his Kingdom the believers who were scattered abroad, punishing the
evil and rewarding the good, guided these communities in
faith and life. In the recently discovered "Teaching of the
Apostles" we are confronted very distinctly with ideas and
aspirations of communities that are not influenced by Philosophy.

The Church, that is the totality of all believers destined to
be received into the kingdom of God (Didache, 9. 10), is the
holy Church, (Hermas) because it is brought together and preserved by the Holy Spirit. It is the one Church, not because
it presents this unity outwardly, on earth the members of the
Church are rather scattered abroad, but because it will be
brought to unity in the kingdom of Christ, because it is ruled
by the same spirit and inwardly united in a common relation
to a common hope and ideal. The Church, considered in its
origin, is the number of those chosen by God, [1] the true Israel, [2] nay, still more, the final purpose of God, for the world
was created for its sake. [3] There were in connection with
these doctrines in the earliest period, various speculations about
the Church: it is a heavenly Æon, is older than the world,
was created by God at the beginning of things as a companion of the heavenly Christ; [4] its members form the new na-

---

a παροικοῦσα τὴν πόλιν, but it is under obligation to give an example to the world,
and must watch that "the name be not blasphemed." The importance of the social
element in the oldest Christian communities, has been very justly brought into
prominence in the latest works on the subject (Renan, Heinrici, Hatch). The
historian of dogma must also emphasise it, and put the fluid notions of the faith
in contrast with the definite consciousness of moral tasks. See 1. Clem. 47–50;
Polyc. Ep. 3; Didache 1 ff.; Ignat. ad Eph. 14, on ἀγάπη as the main requirement.
Love demands that everyone: "ζητεῖ τὸ κοινωφελὲς πᾶσιν καὶ μὴ τὸ ἑαυτοῦ"
(1. Clem. 48. 6. with parallels; Didache 16. 3; Barn. 4. 10; Ignatius).

[1] 1 Clem. 59. 2, in the church prayer; ὅπως τὸν ἀριθμὸν τὸν κατηριθμημένον
τῶν ἐκλεκτῶν αὐτοῦ ἐν ὅλῳ τῷ κόσμῳ διαφυλάξῃ ἄθραυστον ὁ δημιουργὸς τῶν ἀπάν-
των διὰ τοῦ ἠγαπημένου παιδὸς αὐτοῦ Ἰησοῦ Χριστοῦ.

[2] See 1 Clem., 2 Clem., Ignatius (on the basis of the Pauline view; but see
also Rev. II. 9).

[3] See Hermas (the passage is given above, p. 103, note.)

[4] See Hermas. Vis. I.–III. Papias. Fragm. VI. and VII. of my edition, 2 Clem.
14: ποιοῦντες τὸ θέλημα τοῦ πατρὸς ἡμῶν ἐσόμεθα ἐκ τῆς ἐκκλησίας τῆς πρώτης τῆς
πνευματικῆς, τῆς πρὸ ἡλίου καὶ σελήνης ἐκτισμένης.... ἐκκλησία ζῶσα σῶμά ἐστι
Χριστοῦ· λέγει γάρ ἡ γραφή· ἐποίησεν ὁ θεὸς τὸν ἄνθρωπον ἄρσεν καὶ θῆλυ. τὸ ἄρσεν
ἐστὶν ὁ Χριστός, τὸ θῆλυ ἡ ἐκκλησία.

tion which is really the oldest nation, [1] it is the λαὸς ὁ τοῦ
ἠγαπημένου ὁ Φιλούμενος καὶ Φιλῶν αὐτόν, [2] the people whom God
has prepared "in the Beloved", [3] etc.   The creation of God,
the Church, as it is of an antemundane and heavenly nature,
will also attain its true existence only in the Æon of the
future, the Æon of the Kingdom of Christ.   The idea of a
heavenly origin, and of a heavenly goal of the Church, was
therefore an essential one, various and fluctuating as these
speculations were.   Accordingly, the exhortations, so far as
they have in view the Church, are always dominated by the
idea of the contrast of the kingdom of Christ with the kingdom of the world.   On the other hand, he who communicated
knowledge for the present time, prescribed rules of life, endeavoured to remove conflicts, did not appeal to the peculiar
character of the Church.   The mere fact, however, that from
nearly the beginning of Christendom, there were reflections
and speculations not only about God and Christ, but also
about the Church, teaches us how profoundly the Christian
consciousness was impressed with being a new people, viz.,
the people of God. [4]   These speculations of the earliest Gentile
Christian time about Christ and the Church, as inseparable
correlative ideas, are of the greatest importance, for they
have absolutely nothing Hellenic in them, but rather have
their origin in the Apostolic tradition.   But for that very reason the combination very soon, comparatively speaking, became obsolete or lost its power to influence.   Even the Apologists made no use of it, though Clement of Alexandria and
other Greeks held it fast, and the Gnostics by their Æon
"Church" brought it into discredit.   Augustine was the first to
return to it.

The importance attached to morality is shewn in *Didache*

---

[1]   See Barn. 13 (2 Clem. 2).

[2]   See Valentinus in Clem. Strom. VI. 6. 52. "Holy Church", perhaps also in
Marcion, if his text (Zahn. Gesch. des N. T. lichen Kanons, II p. 502) in Gal. IV.
21, read; ἥτις ἐστὶν μήτηρ ἡμῶν, γεννῶσα εἰς ἣν ἐπηγγειλάμεθα ἁγίαν ἐκκλησίαν.

[3]   Barn. 3. 6.

[4]   We are also reminded here of the "tertium genus." The nickname of the
heathen corresponded to the self-consciousness of the Christians, (see Aristides, Apol.).

cc. 1-6, with parallels. [1] But this section and the statements so closely related to it in the pseudo-phocylidean poem which is probably of Christian origin, as well as in Sibyl, II. v. 56-148, which is likewise to be regarded as Christian, and in many other Gnomic paragraphs, shews at the same time, that in the memorable expression and summary statement of higher moral commandments, the Christian propaganda had been preceded by the Judaism of the Diaspora, and had entered into its labours. These statements are throughout dependent on the Old Testament wisdom, and have the closest relationship with the genuine Greek parts of the Alexandrian Canon, as well as with Philonic exhortations. Consequently, these moral rules, "the two ways," so aptly compiled and filled with such an elevated spirit, represent the ripest fruit of Jewish as well as of Greek development. The Christian spirit found here a disposition which it could recognise as its own. It was of the utmost importance, however, that this disposition was already expressed in fixed forms suitable for didactic purposes. The young Christianity therewith received a gift of first importance. It was spared a labour in a region, the moral, which experience shews can only be performed in generations, viz., the creation of simple fixed impressive rules, the labour of the Catechist. The sayings of the Sermon on the Mount were not of themselves sufficient here. Those who in the second century attempted to rest in these alone, and turned aside from the Judæo-Greek inheritance, landed in Marcionite or Encratite doctrines. [2] We can see, especially

---

[1] See also the letter of Pliny, the paragraphs about Christian morality in the first third-part of Justin's apology, and especially the apology of Aristides, c. 15. Aristides portrays Christianity by portraying Christian morality. "The Christians know and believe in God, the creator of heaven and of earth, the God by whom all things consist, *i.e.*, in him from whom they have received the commandments which they have written in their hearts, commandments which they observe in faith and in the expectation of the world to come. For this reason they do not commit adultery, nor practise unchastity, nor bear false witness, nor covet that with which they are entrusted, or what does not belong to them, etc." Compare how in the Apocalypse of Peter definite penalties in hell are portrayed for the several forms of immorality.

[2] An investigation of the Græco-Jewish, Christian literature of gnomes and moral rules, commencing with the Old Testament doctrine of wisdom on the one

from the Apologies of Aristides (c. 15), Justin and Tatian (see also Lucian), that the earnest men of the Græco-Roman world were won by the morality and active love of the Christians.

§ 2. *The Foundations of the Faith.*

The foundations of the faith—whose abridged form was, on the one hand, the confession of the one true God, μόνος ἀληθινὸς θεός, [1] and of Jesus, the Lord, the Son of God, the Saviour, [2] and also of the Holy Spirit; and on the other hand, the confident hope of Christ's kingdom and the resurrection—were laid on the Old Testament interpreted in a Christian sense together with the Apocalypses, [3] and the progressively enriched traditions about Jesus Christ. (ἡ παράδοσις — ὁ παραδοθεὶς λόγος — ὁ κανὼν τῆς ἀληθείας or τῆς παραδόσεως — ἡ πίστις — ὁ κανών τῆς πίστεως —

hand, and the Stoic collections on the other, then passing beyond the Alexandrian and Evangelic gnomes up to the Didache, the Pauline tables of domestic duties, the Sibylline sayings, Phocylides, the Neopythagorean rules, and to the gnomes of the enigmatic Sextus, is still an unfulfilled task. The moral rules of the Pharisaic Rabbis should also be included.

[1] Herm. Mand. I. has merely fixed the Monotheistic confession: πρῶτον πάντων πίστευσον, ὅτι εἷς ἐστὶν ὁ θεὸς, ὁ τὰ πάντα κτίσας καὶ καταρτίσας, κ.τ.λ. See Praed. Petri in Clem. Strom. VI. 6. 48: VI. 5. 39: Aristides gives in c. 2. of his Apology the preaching of Jesus Christ: but where he wishes to give a short expression of Christianity he is satisfied with saying that Christians are those who have found the one true God. See, *e. g.*, c. 15 "Christians have .... found the truth .... They know and believe in God, the creator of heaven and of earth, by whom all things consist, and from whom all things come, who has no other god beside him, and from whom they have received commandments which they have written in their hearts, commandments which they observe in faith and in expectation of the world to come." It is interesting to note how Origen, Comm. in Joh. XXXII 9, has brought the Christological Confession into approximate harmony with that of Hermas First, Mand. I. is verbally repeated and then it is said: χρὴ δὲ καὶ πιστεύειν, ὅτι κύριος Ἰησοῦς Χριστὸς καὶ πασῃ τῇ περὶ αὐτοῦ κατὰ τὴν θεότητα καὶ τὴν ἀνθρωπότητα· ἀληθείᾳ δεῖ δὲ καὶ εἰς τὸ ἅγιον πιστεύειν πνεῦμα, καὶ ὅτι αὐτεξούσιοι ὄντες κολαζόμεθα μὲν ἐφ᾽ οἷς ἁμαρτάνομεν, τιμώμεθα δὲ ἐφ᾽ οἷς εὖ πράττομεν.

[2] Very instructive here is 2 Clem. ad Corinth. 20. 5: τῷ μόνῳ θεῷ ἀοράτῳ, πατρὶ τῆς ἀληθείας, τῷ ἐξαποστείλαντι ἡμῖν τὸν σωτῆρα καὶ ἀρχηγὸν τῆς ἀφθαρσίας, δι᾽ οὗ καὶ ἐφανέρωσεν ἡμῖν τὴν ἀλήθειαν καὶ τὴν ἐπουράνιον ζωήν, αὐτῷ ἡ δόξα. On the Holy Spirit see previous note.

[3] They were quoted as ἡ γραφὴ, τὰ βιβλία, or with the formula ὁ θεὸς (κύριος) λέγει, γέγραπται. Also "Law and Prophets," "Law Prophets and Psalms." See the original of the first six books of the Apostolic Constitutions.

ὁ δοθεῖσα πίστις — τὸ κήρυγμα — τὰ διδάγματα τοῦ χριστοῦ — ἡ διδαχὴ — τὰ μαθήματα, or τὸ μάθημα).[1] The Old Testament revelations and oracles were regarded as pointing to Christ; the Old Testament itself, the words of God spoken by the Prophets, as the primitive Gospel of salvation, having in view the new people, which is, however, the oldest, and belonging to it alone.[2] The exposition of the Old Testament, which, as a rule, was of course read in the Alexandrian Canon of the Bible, turned it into a Christian book. A historical view of it, which no born Jew could in some measure fail to take, did not come into fashion, and the freedom that was used in interpreting the Old Testament, — so far as there was a method, it was the Alexandrian Jewish — went the length of even correcting the letter and enriching the contents.[3]

The traditions concerning Christ on which the communities were based, were of a twofold character. First, there were words of the Lord, mostly ethical, but also of eschatological content, which were regarded as rules, though their expression was uncertain, ever changing, and only gradually assuming a fixed form. The διδάγματα τοῦ χριστοῦ are often just the moral commandments.[4] Second, the foundation of the faith, that is, the assurance of the blessing of salvation, was formed by a proclamation of the history of Jesus concisely expressed, and

[1] See the collection of passages in Patr. App. Opp. edit. Gebhardt. I. 2 p. 133, and the formula, Diogn. 11: ἀποστόλων γένομενος μαθητὴς γίνομαι διδάσκαλος εθνῶν, τὰ παραδοθέντα ἀξίως ὑπηρετῶν γινομένοις ἀληθείας μαθηταῖς. Besides the Old Testament and the traditions about Jesus (Gospels), the Apocalyptic writings of the Jews, which were regarded as writings of the Spirit, were also drawn upon. Moreover, Christian letters and manifestoes proceeding from Apostles, prophets, or teachers, were read. The Epistles of Paul were early collected and obtained wide circulation in the first half of the second century; but they were not Holy Scripture in the specific sense, and therefore their authority was not unqualified.

[2] Barn. 5. 6, οἱ προφῆται, ἀπὸ τοῦ κυρίου ἐχοντες τὴν χάριν, εἰς αὐτὸν ἐπροφήτευσαν. Ignat. ad Magn. 8. 2: cf. also Clem. Paedag. I. 7. 59: ὁ γὰρ αὐτὸς οὗτος παιδαγωγὸς τότε μὲν "φοβηθήσῃ κύριον τὸν θεὸν ἔλεγεν, ἡμῖν δὲ "ἀγαπήσεις κύριον τὸν θεὸν σου" ταρήνεσεν. διὰ τοῦτο καὶ ἐντέλλεται ἡμῖν "παύσασθε ἀπὸ τῶν ἔργων ὑμῶν" τῶν παλαιῶν ἁμαρτιῶν, "μάθετε καλὸν ποιεῖν, ἔκκλινον ἀπὸ κακοῦ καὶ ποίησον ἀγαθόν, ἠγάπησας δικαιοσύνην, ἐμίσησας ἀνομίαν" αὕτη μου ἡ νέα διαθήκη παλαιῷ κεχαραγμένη γράμματι.

[3] See above § 5, p. 114 f.

[4] See my edition of the Didache, Prolegg. p. 32 ff.; Rothe, "De disciplina arcani origine," 1841.

composed with reference to prophecy. [1] The confession of God the Father Almighty, of Christ as the Lord and Son of God, and of the Holy Spirit, [2] was, at a very early period in the communities, united with the short proclamation of the history of Jesus, and at the same time, in certain cases, referred expressly to the revelation of God (the Spirit) through the prophets. [3] The confession thus conceived had not everywhere obtained a fixed definite expression in the first century (cc. 50-150). It would rather seem that, in most of the communities, there was no exact formulation beyond a confession of Father, Son and Spirit, accompanied in a free way by the historical proclamation. [4] It is highly probable, however, that a short confession was strictly formulated in the Roman community before the middle of the second century, [5] expressing belief in the Father, Son and Spirit, embracing also the most important facts in the history of Jesus, and mentioning the Holy Church, as well as the two great blessings of Christianity, the forgiveness of sin, and the resurrection of the dead (ἄφεσις ἁμαρτιῶν, σαρκὸς ἀνάστασις [6]). But, however the proclamation might be handed

---

[1] The earliest example is 1. Cor. XI. 1 f. It is different in 1 Tim. III. 16 where already the question is about τὸ τῆς εὐσεβείας μυστήριον: See Patr. App. Opp. I. 2. p. 134.

[2] Father, son, and spirit: Paul; Matt. XXVIII. 19; 1 Clem. ad. Cor. 58. 2, (see 2. 1. f.: 42. 3: 46. 6); Didache 7; Ignat. Eph. 9. 1; Magn. 13. 1. 2.; Philad. inscr.; Mart. Polyc. 14. 1. 2; Ascens. Isai. 8. 18: 9. 27: 10. 4: 11. 32 ff; Justin *passim*; Montan. ap. Didym. de trinit. 411; Excerpta ex Theodot. 80; Pseudo Clem. de virg. 1. 13. Yet the omission of the Holy Spirit is frequent, as in Paul; or the Holy Spirit is identified with the Spirit of Christ. The latter takes place even with such writers as are familiar with the baptismal formula, Ignat. ad Magn. 15; κεκτημένοι ἀδιάκριτον πνεῦμα, ὅς ἐστιν Ἰησοῦς Χριστὸς.

[3] The formulæ run: "God who has spoken through the Prophets," or the "Prophetic Spirit," etc.

[4] That should be assumed as certain in the case of the Egyptian Church, yet Caspari thinks he can shew that already Clement of Alexandria presupposes a symbol.

[5] Also in the communities of Asia Minor (Smyrna); for a combination of Polyc. Ep. c. 2 with c. 7, proves that in Smyrna the παραδοθεὶς λόγος must have been something like the Roman Symbol, see Lightfoot on the passage; it cannot be proved that it was identical with it. See, further, how in the case of Polycarp the moral element is joined on to the dogmatic. This reminds us of the Didache and has its parallel even in the first homily of Aphraates.

[6] See Caspari, Quellen z. Gesch. des Taufsymbols, III. p. 3. ff., and Patr. App. Opp. I. 2. pp. 115-142. The old Roman Symbol reads: Πιστεύω εἰς θεὸν πατέρα παντοκράτορα καὶ εἰς Χριστὸν Ἰησοῦν (τὸν) υἱὸν αὐτοῦ τὸν μονογενῆ, (on this word

down, in a form somehow fixed, or in a free form, the disciples
of Jesus, the (twelve) Apostles, were regarded as the authorities who mediated and guaranteed it.   To them was traced

see Westcott's Excursus in his commentary on 1st John) τὸν κύριον ἡμῶν τὸν
γεννηθέντα ἐκ πνεύματος ἁγίου καὶ Μαρίας τῆς παρθένου, τὸν ἐπὶ Ποντίου Πιλάτου
σταυρωθέντα καὶ ταφέντα; τῇ τρίτῃ ἡμέρᾳ ἀναστάντα ἐκ νεκρῶν, ἀναβάντα εἰς τοὺς
οὐρανούς, καθήμενον ἐν δεξιᾷ τοῦ πατρός, ὅθεν ἔρχεται κρῖναι ζῶντας καὶ νεκρούς· καὶ
εἰς πνεῦμα ἅγιον, ἁγίαν ἐκκλησίαν, ἄφεσιν ἁμαρτιῶν σαρκὸς ἀνάστασιν, ἀμήν.   To
estimate this very important article aright we must note the following: (1) It is
not a formula of doctrine, but of confession. (2) It has a liturgical form which is
shewn in the rhythm and in the disconnected succession of its several members,
and is free from everything of the nature polemic. (3) It tapers off into the three
blessings, Holy Church, forgiveness of sin, resurrection of the body, and in this
as well as in the fact that there is no mention of γνῶσις (ἀλήθεια) καὶ ζωὴ αἰώνος,
is revealed an early Christian untheological attitude.   (4) It is worthy of note, on
the other hand, that the birth from the Virgin occupies the first place, and all
reference to the baptism of Jesus, also to the Davidic Sonship, is wanting.   (5) It is
further worthy of note, that there is no express mention of the death of Jesus, and
that the Ascension already forms a special member (that is also found elsewhere,
Ascens. Isaiah, c. 3. 13. ed. Dillmann. p. 13. Murator. Fragment, etc.).   Finally,
we should consider the want of the earthly Kingdom of Christ and the mission
of the twelve Apostles, as well as, on the other hand, the purely religious attitude,
no notice being taken of the new law. Zahn (Das Apostol. Symbolum, 1893)
assumes, "That in all essential respects the identical baptismal confession which
Justin learned in Ephesus about 130, and Marcion confessed in Rome about 145,
originated at latest somewhere about 120".   In some "unpretending notes"
(p. 37 ff.) he traces this confession back to a baptismal confession of the Pauline
period ("it had already assumed a more or less stereotyped form in the earlier
Apostolic period"), which, however, was somewhat revised, so far as it contained,
for example, "of the house of David", with reference to Christ. "The original
formula, reminding us of the Jewish soil of Christianity, was thus remodelled,
perhaps about 70-120, with retention of the fundamental features so that it might
appear to answer better to the need of candidates for baptism, proceeding more
and more from the Gentiles. . . . This changed formula soon spread on all sides.
It lies at the basis of all the later baptismal confessions of the Church, even of
the East.   The first article was slightly changed in Rome about 200-220 ". While
up till then, in Rome as everywhere else, it had read πιστεύω εἰς ἕνα θεὸν παντοκράτορα, it was now changed in πιστεύω εἰς θεὸν πατέρα παντοκράτορα.   This
hypothesis, with regard to the early history of the Roman Symbol, presupposes
that the history of the formation of the baptismal confession in the Church, in
east and west, was originally a uniform one.   This cannot be proved; besides, it
is refuted by the facts of the following period. It presupposes secondly, that
there was a strictly formulated baptismal confession outside Rome before the
middle of the second century, which likewise cannot be proved; (the converse
rather is probable, that the fixed formulation proceeded from Rome).   Moreover,
Zahn himself retracts everything again by the expression "more or less stereotyped
form;" for what is of decisive interest here is the question, when and where the
fixed sacred form was produced.   Zahn here has set up the radical thesis that it

back in the same way everything that was narrated of the history of Jesus, and everything that was inculcated from his sayings. [1] Consequently, it may be said, that beside the Old can only have taken place in Rome between 200 and 220. But neither his negative nor his positive proof for a change of the Symbol in Rome at so late a period is sufficient. No sure conclusion as to the Symbol can be drawn from the wavering *regulæ fidei* of Irenæus and Tertullian, which contain the "unum"; further, the "unum" is not found in the western provincial Symbols, which, however, are in part earlier than the year 200. The Romish correction must therefore have been subsequently taken over in the provinces (Africa?). Finally, the formula θεὸν πάτερα παντοκράτορα beside the more frequent θεὸν παντοκράτορα, is attested by Irenæus, I. 10. 1, a decisive passage. With our present means we cannot attain to any direct knowledge of Symbol formation before the Romish Symbol. But the following hypotheses, which I am not able to establish here, appear to me to correspond to the facts of the case and to be fruitful: (1) There were, even in the earliest period, separate *Kerygmata* about God and Christ: see the Apostolic writings, Hermas, Ignatius, etc. (2) The *Kerygma* about God was the confession of the one God of creation, the almighty God. (3) The *Kerygma* about Christ had essentially the same historical contents everywhere, but was expressed in diverse forms: (a) in the form of the fulfilment of prophecy, (b) in the form κατὰ σάρκα, κατὰ πνεῦμα, (c) in the form of the first and second advent, (d) in the form, καταβάς·ἀναβάς; these forms were also partly combined. (4) The designations "Christ", "Son of God" and "Lord"; further, the birth from the Holy Spirit, or κατὰ πνεῦμα, the sufferings (the practice of exorcism contributed also to the fixing and naturalising of the formula "crucified under Pontius Pilate"), the death, the resurrection, the coming again to judgment, formed the stereotyped content of the *Kerygma* about Jesus. The mention of the Davidic Sonship, of the Virgin Mary, of the baptism by John, of the third day, of the descent into Hades, of the *demonstratio veræ carnis post resurrectionem*, of the ascension into heaven and the sending out of the disciples, were additional articles which appeared here and there. The σάρκα λαβών, and the like, were very early developed out of the forms (b) and (d). All this was already in existence at the transition of the first century to the second. (5) The proper contribution of the Roman community consisted in this, that it inserted the *Kerygma* about God and that about Jesus into the baptismal formula; widened the clause referring to the Holy Spirit, into one embracing Holy Church, forgiveness of sin, resurrection of the body; excluded theological theories in other respects; undertook a reduction all round, and accurately defined everything up to the last world. (6) The western *regulæ fidei* do not fall back exclusively on the old Roman Symbol, but also on the earlier freer *Kerygmata* about God and about Jesus which were common to the east and west; not otherwise can the *regulæ fidei* of Irenæus and Tertullian, for example, be explained. But the symbol became more and more the support of the *regula*. (7) The eastern confessions (baptismal symbols) do not fall back directly on the Roman Symbol, but were probably on the model of this symbol, made up from the provincial *Kerygmata*, rich in contents and growing ever richer, hardly, however, before the third century. (8) It cannot be proved, and it is not probable, that the Roman Symbol was in existence before Hermas, that is, about 135.

[1] See the fragment in Euseb. H. E. III. 39, from the work of Papias.

Testament, the chief court of appeal in the communities was formed by an aggregate of words and deeds of the Lord;—for the history and the suffering of Jesus are his deed: ὁ Ἰησοῦς ὑπέμεινεν παθεῖν, κ.τ.λ.,—fixed in certain fundamental features, though constantly enriched, and traced back to apostolic testimony. [1]

The authority which the Apostles in this way enjoyed, did not, in any great measure, rest on the remembrance of direct services which the twelve had rendered to the Gentile Churches: for, as the want of reliable concrete traditions proves, no such services had been rendered, at least not by the *twelve*,

---

[1] Διδαχὴ κύριον διὰ τῶν ιβ' ἀποστόλων (Διδ. inscr.) is the most accurate expression (similarly 2. Pet. III. 2). Instead of this might be said simply ὁ κύριος (Hegesipp.). Hegesippus (Euseb. H. E., IV. 22. 3: See also Steph. Gob.) comprehends the ultimate authorities under the formula: ὡς ὁ νομος κηρύσσει καὶ οἱ προφῆται καὶ ὁ κύριος; just as even Pseudo Clem. de Virg. I. 2: "Sicut ex lege ac prophetis et a domino nostro Jesu Christo didicimus." Polycarp (6. 3) says: καθὼς αὐτὸς ἐνετείλατο καὶ οἱ εὐαγγελισάμενοι ἡμᾶς ἀπόστολοι καὶ οἱ προφῆται οἱ προκηρύξαντες τὴν ἔλευσιν τοῦ κυρίου ἡμῶν. In the second Epistle of Clement (14. 2) we read: τὰ βιβλία (O. T.) καὶ οἱ ἀπόστολοι; τὸ εὐαγγέλιον may also stand for ὁ κύριος (Ignat., Didache. 2 Clem. etc.). The Gospel, so far as it is described, is quoted as τὰ ἀπομνημονεύματα τ. ἀποστόλων (Justin, Tatian), or on the other hand, as αἱ κυριακαὶ γραφαί, (Dionys. Cor. in Euseb. H. E. IV. 23. 12: at a later period in Tertull. and Clem. Alex.). The words of the Lord, in the same way as the words of God, are called simply τά λόγια (κυριακά). The declaration of Serapion at the beginning of the third century (Euseb., H. E. VI. 12. 3): ἡμεῖς καὶ Πέτρον καὶ τοὺς ἄλλους ἀποστόλους ἀποδεχόμεθα ὡς Χριστόν, is an innovation in so far as it puts the words of the Apostles fixed in writing and as distinct from the words of the Lord, on a level with the latter. That is, while differentiating the one from the other, Serapion ascribes to the words of the apostles and those of the Lord equal authority. But the development which led to this position, had already begun in the first century. At a very early period there were read in the communities, beside the Old Testament, Gospels, that is collections of words of the Lord, which at the same time contained the main facts of the history of Jesus. Such notes were a necessity (Luke I. 4: ἵνα ἐπιγνῶς περὶ ὧν κατηχήθης λόγων τὴν ἀσφάλειαν), and though still indefinite and in many ways unlike, they formed the germ for the genesis of the New Testament. (See Weiss. Lehrb. d. Einleit in d. N. T. p. 21 ff.) Further, there were read Epistles and Manifestoes by apostles, prophets and teachers, but, above all, Epistles of Paul. The Gospels at first stood in no connection with these Epistles, however high they might be prized. But there did exist a connection between the Gospels and the ἀπ' ἀρχῆς αὐτόπταις καὶ ὑπηρέταις τοῦ λόγου, so far as these mediated the tradition of the Evangelic material, and on their testimony rests the *Kerygma* of the Church about the Lord as the Teacher, the crucified and risen One. Here lies the germ for the genesis of a canon which will comprehend the Lord and the Apostles, and will also draw in the Pauline Epistles. Finally, Apocalypses were read as Holy Scriptures.

On the contrary, there was a theory operative here regarding the special authority which the twelve enjoyed in the Church at Jerusalem, a theory which was spread by the early missionaries, including Paul, and sprang from the *a priori* consideration that the tradition about Christ, just because it grew up so quickly, [1] must have been entrusted to eye-witnesses who were commissioned to proclaim the Gospel to the whole world, and who fulfilled that commission. The *a priori* character of this assumption is shewn by the fact that—with the exception of reminiscences of an activity of Peter and John among the ἔθνη, not sufficiently clear to us [2]—the twelve, as a rule, are regarded as a *college*, to which the mission and the tradition are traced back. [3] That such a theory, based on a dogmatic construction of history, could have at all arisen, proves that either the Gentile Churches never had a living relation to the twelve, or that they had very soon lost it in the rapid disappearance of Jewish Christianity, while they had been referred to the twelve from the beginning. But even in the communities which Paul had founded and for a long time guided, the remembrance of the controversies of the Apostolic age must have been very soon effaced, and the vacuum thus produced filled by a theory which directly traced back the *status quo* of the Gentile Christian communities to a tradition of the twelve as its foundation. This fact is extremely paradoxical, and is not altogether explained by the assumptions that the Pauline-Judaistic controversy had not made a great impression on the Gentile Christians, that the way in which Paul, while fully recognising the twelve, had insisted on his own independent importance, had long ceased to be really under-

---

[1] Read, apart from all others, the canonical Gospels, the remains of the so-called Apocryphal Gospels, and perhaps the Shepherd of Hermas: see also the statements of Papias.

[2] That Peter was in Antioch follows from Gal. II.; that he laboured in Corinth, perhaps before the composition of the first epistle to the Corinthians, is not so improbable as is usually maintained (1 Cor.; Dionys. of Corinth); that he was at Rome even is very credible. The sojourn of John in Asia Minor cannot, I think, be contested.

[3] See how in the three early " writings of Peter " (Gospel, Apocalypse, *Kerygma*) the twelve are embraced in a perfect unity. Peter is the head and spokesman for them all.

stood, and that Peter and John had also really been missionaries
to the Gentiles. The guarantee that was needed for the
"teaching of the Lord" must finally be given not by Paul,
but only by chosen eye-witnesses. The less that was known
about them, the easier it was to claim them. The conviction
as to the unanimity of the twelve, and as to their activity in
founding the Gentile Churches, appeared in these Churches as
early as the urgent need of protection against the serious consequences of unfettered religious enthusiasm and unrestrained
religious fancy. This urgency cannot be dated too far back.
In correspondence therewith, the principle of tradition in the
Church (Christ, the twelve Apostles) in the case of those who
were intent on the unity and completeness of Christendom, is
also very old. But one passed logically from the Apostles to
the disciples of the Apostles, "the Elders," without at first
claiming for them any other significance than that of reliable
hearers (Apostoli et discentes ipsorum). In coming down to
them, one here and there betook oneself again to real historical ground, disciples of Paul, of Peter, of John.[1] Yet even
here legends with a tendency speedily got mixed with facts,
and because, in consequence of this theory of tradition, the
Apostle Paul must needs fall into the background, his disciples
also were more or less forgotten. The attempt which we have
in the Pastoral Epistles remained without effect, as regards
those to whom these epistles were addressed. Timothy and
Titus obtained no authority outside these epistles. But so far
as the epistles of Paul were collected, diffused, and read, there
was created a complex of writings which at first stood beside
the "Teaching of the Lord by the twelve Apostles", without
being connected with it, and only obtained such connection by
the creation of the New Testament, that is, by the interpolation
of the Acts of the Apostles, between Gospels and Epistles.[2]

---

[1] See Papias and the Reliq. Presbyter. ap. Iren., collecta in Parr. Opp. I. 2,
p. 105: see also Zahn, Forschungen. III., p. 156 f.

[2] The Gentile-Christian conception of the significance of the twelve—a fact to
be specially noted—was all but unanimous (see above Chap. II.): the only one
who broke through it was Marcion. The writers of Asia Minor, Rome and Egypt,
coincide in this point. Beside the Acts of the Apostles, which is specially instructive
see 1 Clem. 42; Barn. 5. 9. 8. 3: Didache inscr.; Hermas. Vis. III. 5, 11; Sim.

§ 3. *The Main Articles of Christianity and the Conceptions of Salvation. Eschatology.*

1. The main articles of Christianity were (1) belief in God the δεσπότης, and in the Son in virtue of proofs from prophecy, and the teaching of the Lord as attested by the Apostles; (2) discipline according to the standard of the words of the Lord; (3) baptism;

IX. 15, 16, 17, 25; Petrusev-Petrusapok. Præd. Petr. ap. Clem. Strom. VI. 6, 48; Ignat. ad Trall. 3; ad Rom. 4; ad Philad. 5; Papias; Polyc.; Aristides; Justin *passim*; inferences from the great work of Irenæus, the works of Tertull. and Clem. Alex.; the Valentinians. The inference that follows from the eschatological hope, that the Gospel has already been preached to the world, and the growing need of having a tradition mediated by eye-witnesses co-operated here, and out of the twelve who were in great part obscure, but who had once been authoritative in Jerusalem and Palestine, and highly esteemed in the Christian Diaspora from the beginning, though unknown, created a court of appeal which presented itself as not only taking a second rank after the Lord himself, but as the medium through which alone the words of the Lord became the possession of Christendom, as he neither preached to the nations nor left writings. The importance of the twelve in the main body of the Church may at any rate be measured by the facts, that the personal activity of Jesus was confined to Palestine, that he left behind him neither a confession nor a doctrine, and that in this respect the tradition tolerated no more corrections. Attempts which were made in this direction, the fiction of a semi-Gentile origin of Christ, the denial of the Davidic Sonship, the invention of a correspondence between Jesus and Abgarus, meeting of Jesus with Greeks, and much else, belong only in part to the earliest period, and remained as really inoperative as they were uncertain (according to Clem. Alex., Jesus himself is the Apostle to the Jews; the twelve are the Apostles to the Gentiles in Euseb. H. E. VI. 14). The notion about the twelve Apostles evangelising the world in accordance with the commission of Jesus, is consequently to be considered as the means by which the Gentile Christians got rid of the inconvenient fact of the merely local activity of Jesus. (Compare how Justin expresses himself about the Apostles: their going out into all the world is to him one of the main articles predicted in the Old Testament, Apol. I. 39; compare also the Apology of Aristides, c. 2, and the passage of similar tenor in the Ascension of Isaiah, where the "adventus XII. discipulorum" is regarded as one of the fundamental facts of salvation, c. 3. 13, ed. Dillmann, p. 13, and a passage such as Iren. fragm. XXIX. in Harvey II., p. 494, where the parable about the grain of mustard seed is applied to the λόγος ἐπουράνιος, and the twelve Apostles; the Apostles are the branches ὑφ' ὧν κλάδων σκεπασθέντες οἱ πάντες ὡς ὄρνεα ὑπὸ καλιὰν συνελθόντα μετέλαβον τῆς ἐξ αὐτῶν προερχομένης ἐδωδίμου καὶ ἐπουρανίου τροφῆς Hippol., de Antichr. 61. Orig c. Cels. III. 28.) This means, as it was empty of contents, was very soon to prove the very most convenient instrument for establishing ever new historical connections, and legitimising the *status quo* in the communities. Finally, the whole catholic idea of tradition was rooted in that statement which was already, at the close of the first century, formulated by Clement of Rome (c. 42): οἱ ἀπόστολοι ἡμῖν εὐηγγελίσθησαν ἀπὸ τοῦ κυρίου Ἰησοῦ Χριστοῦ, Ἰησοῦς ὁ χριστὸς ἀπο τοῦ θεοῦ

(4) the common offering of prayer, culminating in the Lord's Supper and the holy meal; (5) the sure hope of the nearness of Christ's glorious kingdom. In these appears the unity of Christendom, that is, of the Church which possesses the Holy

ἐξεπέμφθη. ὁ χριστὸς οὖν ἀπὸ τοῦ θεοῦ, καὶ οἱ ἀπόστολοι ἀπὸ τοῦ Χριστοῦ· ἐγένοντο οὖν ἀμφότερα εὐτάκτως ἐκ θελήματος θεοῦ κ.τ.λ. Here, as in all similar statements which elevate the Apostles into the history of revelation, the unanimity of all the Apostles is always presupposed, so that the statement of Clem. Alex. (Strom. VII., 17, 108 : μία ἡ πάντων γέγονε τῶν ἀποστόλων ὥσπερ διδασκαλία οὕτως δὲ καὶ ἡ παράδοσις; see Tertull., de præscr. 32 : "Apostoli non diversa inter se docuerent," Iren alii), contains no innovation, but gives expression to an old idea. That the twelve unitedly proclaimed one and the same message, that they proclaimed it to the world, that they were chosen to this vocation by Christ, that the communities possess the witness of the Apostles as their rule of conduct (Excerp. ex Theod. 25. ὥσπερ ὑπὸ τῶν ζωδίων ἡ γένεσις διοικεῖται, οὕτως ὑπὸ τῶν ἀποστόλων ἡ ἀναγέννησις), are authoritative theses which can be traced back as far as we have any remains of Gentile-Christian literature. It was thereby presupposed that the unanimous *kerygma* of the twelve Apostles, which the communities possess as κανὼν τῆς παραδόσεως (1 Clem. 7), was public and accessible to all. Yet the idea does not seem to have been everywhere kept at a distance, that besides the *kerygma* a still deeper knowledge was transmitted by the Apostles, or by certain Apostles, to particular Christians who were specially gifted. Of course we have no direct evidence of this; but the connection in which certain Gnostic unions stood at the beginning with the communities developing themselves to Catholicism, and inferences from utterances of later writers (Clem. Alex. Tertull.), make it probable that this conception was present in the communities here and there even in the age of the so-called Apostolic Fathers. It may be definitely said that the peculiar idea of tradition (θεός—χριστος—οἱ δώδεκα ἀπόστολοι—ἐκκλησίαι) in the Gentile Churches is very old, but that it was still limited in its significance at the beginning, and was threatened (1) by a wider conception of the idea "Apostle" (besides, the fact is important, that Asia Minor and Rome were the very places where a stricter idea of "Apostle" made its appearance: See my Edition of the Didache, p. 117); (2) by free prophets and teachers moved by the Spirit, who introduced new conceptions and rules, and whose word was regarded as the word of God; (3) by the assumption, not always definitely rejected, that besides the public tradition of the *kerygma* there was a secret tradition. That Paul, as a rule, was not included in this high estimate of the Apostles is shewn by this fact, among others, that the earlier Apocryphal Acts of the Apostles are much less occupied with his person than with the rest of the Apostles. The features of the old legends which make the Apostles in their deeds, their fate, nay, even in appearance as far as possible equal to the person of Jesus himself, deserve special consideration, (see, for example, the descent of the Apostles into hell in Herm. Sim. IX. 16); for it is just here that the fact above established, that the activity of the Apostles was to make up for the want of the activity of Jesus himself among the nations, stands clearly out. (See Acta Johannis ed. Zahn, p. 246: ὁ ἐκλεξάμενος ἡμᾶς εἰς ἀποστολὴν ἐθνῶν, ὁ ἐκπέμψας ἡμας εἰς τὴν οἰκουμένην θεός, ὁ δείξας ἑαυτὸν διὰ τῶν ἀποστόλων, also the remarkable declaration of Origen about the Chronicle [Hadrian], that what

Spirit.[1] On the basis of this unity Christian knowledge was free and manifold. It was distinguished as σοφία, σύνεσις, ἐπιστήμη, γνῶσις (τῶν δικαιωμάτων), from the λόγος θεοῦ τῆς πίστεως,

holds good of Christ, is in that Chronicle transferred to Peter; finally we may recall to mind the visions in which an Apostolic suddenly appears as Christ.) Between the judgment of value: ἡμεῖς τούς ἀποστόλους ἀποδεχόμεθα ὡς Χριστὸν, and those creations of fancy in which the Apostles appear as gods and demigods, there is certainly a great interval; but it can be proved that there are stages lying between the extreme points. It is therefore permissible to call to mind here the oldest Apocryphal Acts of the Apostles, although they may have originated almost completely in Gnostic circles (see also the Pistis Sophia which brings a metaphysical theory to the establishment of the authority of the Apostles, p. 11, 14, see Texte u. Unters. VII. 2. p. 61 ff.). Gnosticism here, as frequently elsewhere, is related to common Christianity, as excess progressing to the invention of a myth with a tendency, to a historical theorem determined by the effort to maintain one's own position, (cf. the article from the *kerygma* of Peter in Clem. Strom. VI. 6, 48: Ἐξελεξάμην ὑμᾶς δώδεκα μαθητὰς, κ.τ.λ., the introduction to the basal writing of the first 6 books of the Apostolic Constitutions, and the introduction to the Egyptian ritual, κατὰ κέλευσίν τοῦ κυρίου ὑμῶν, κ.ω.λ.). Besides, it must be admitted that the origin of the idea of tradition and its connection with the twelve, is obscure: what is historically reliable here has still to be investigated; even the work of Seufert (Der Urspr. u. d. Bedeutung des Apostolats in der christl. Kirche der ersten zwei Jahrhunderte, 1887) has not cleared up the dark points. We will, perhaps, get more light by following the important hint given by Weizsäcker (Apost. Age, p. 13 ff.) that Peter was the first witness of the resurrection, and was called such in the *kerygma* of the communities (see 1 Cor. XV. 5 : Luke XXIV. 34). The twelve Apostles are also further called οἱ περὶ τὸν Πετρὸν (Mrc. fin. in L. Ign. ad Smyrn. 3; cf. Luke VIII. 45; Acts. II. 14; Gal. I. 18 f ; 1 Cor. XV. 5), and it is a correct historical reminiscence when Chrysostom says (Hom. in Joh. 88), ὁ Πέτρος ἔκκριτος ἦν τῶν ἀποστόλων καὶ στόμα τῶν μαθητῶν καὶ κορυφὴ τοῦ χόρου. Now, as Peter was really in personal relation with important Gentile-Christian communities, that which held good of him, the recognized head and spokesman of the twelve, was perhaps transferred to these. One has finally to remember that besides the appeal to the twelve there was in the Gentile Churches an appeal to Peter and Paul (but not for the evangelic *kerygma*), which has a certain historical justification; cf. Gal. II. 8; 1 Cor. I. 12 f., IX. 5; 1 Clem. Ign. ad Rom. 4, and the numerous later passages. Paul in claiming equality with Peter, though Peter was the head and mouth of the twelve and had himself been active in mission work, has perhaps contributed most towards spreading the authority of the twelve. It is notable how rarely we find any special appeal to John in the tradition of the main body of the Church. For the middle of the 2nd century, the authority of the twelve Apostles may be expressed in the following statements: (1) They were missionaries for the world; (2) They ruled the Church and established Church Offices; (3) They guaranteed the true doctrine, (a) by the tradition going back to them, (b) by writings; (4) They are the ideals of Christian life; (5) They are also directly mediators of salvation— though this point is uncertain.

[1] See Διδαχὴ, c. 1-10, with parallel passages.

the κλῆσις τῆς ἐπαγγελίας, and the ἐντολαὶ τῆς διδαχῆς (Barn.
16, 9, similarly Hermas). Perception and knowledge of Divine
things was a Charism, possessed only by individuals; but, like
all Charisms, it was to be used for the good of the whole.
In so far as every actual perception was a perception produced by the Spirit, it was regarded as important and indubi-
table truth, even though some Christians were unable to understand it. While attention was given to the firm inculcation
and observance of the moral precepts of Christ, as well as to
the awakening of sure faith in Christ, and while all waverings
and differences were excluded in respect of these, there was
absolutely no current doctrine of faith in the communities, in
the sense of a completed theory; and the theological speculations of even closely related Christian writers of this epoch,
exhibit the greatest differences. [1] The productions of fancy,
the terrible or consoling pictures of the future pass for sacred
knowledge, just as much as intelligent and sober reflections,
and edifying interpretation of Old Testament sayings. Even
that which was afterwards separated as Dogmatic and Ethics
was then in no way distinguished. [2] The communities gave
expression in the cultus, chiefly in the hymns and prayers,
to what they possessed in their God and their Christ; here
sacred formulæ were fashioned and delivered to the members. [3]
The problem of surrendering the world in the hope of a life
beyond was regarded as the practical side of the faith, and
the unity in temper and disposition resting on faith in the
saving revelation of God in Christ, permitted the highest degree

[1] Cf., for example, the first epistle of Clement to the Corinthians with the
Shepherd of Hermas. Both documents originated in Rome.

[2] Compare how dogmatic and ethical elements are inseparably united in the
Shepherd, in first and second Clement, as well as in Polycarp and Justin.

[3] Note the hymnal parts of the Revelation of John, the great prayer with which
the first epistle of Clement closes, the "carmen dicere Christo quasi deo" reported
by Pliny, the eucharist prayer in the Διδαχὴ, the hymn 1 Tim. III. 16, the fragments from the prayers which Justin quotes, and compare with these the declaration
of the anonymous writer in Euseb. H. E. V. 28. 5, that the belief of the earliest
Christians in the Deity of Christ might be proved from the old Christian hymns
and odes. In the epistles of Ignatius the theology frequently consists of an aimless
stringing together of articles manifestly originating in hymns and the cultus.

of freedom in knowledge, the results of which were absolutely
without control as soon as the preacher or the writer was
recognised as a true teacher, that is inspired by the Spirit
of God.[1]   There was also in wide circles a conviction that
the Christian faith, after the night of error, included the full
knowledge of everything worth knowing, that precisely in its
most important articles it is accessible to men of every degree
of culture, and that in it, in the now attained truth, is contained one of the most essential blessings of Christianity.   When
it is said in the Epistle of Barnabas (II. 2. 3); τῆς πίστεως ἡμῶν
εἰσὶν βοηθοὶ φόβος καὶ ὑπομονή, τὰ δὲ συμμαχοῦντα ἡμῖν μακροθυ-
μία καὶ ἐγκράτεια· τούτων μενόντων τὰ πρὸς κύριον ἁγνῶς, συνευ-
φραίνονταί αὐτοῖς σοφία, σύνεσις, ἐπιστήμη, γνῶσις, knowledge
appears in this classic formula to be an essential element in
Christianity, conditioned by faith and the practical virtues, and
dependent on them.   Faith takes the lead, knowledge follows
it: but of course in concrete cases it could not always be
decided what was λόγος τῆς πίστεως, which implicitly contained
the highest knowledge, and what the special γνῶσις; for in the
last resort the nature of the two was regarded as identical,
both being represented as produced by the Spirit of God.

2.   The conceptions of Christian salvation, or of redemption, were grouped around two ideas, which were themselves
but loosely connected with each other, and of which the one
influenced more the temper and the imagination, the other
the intellectual faculty.   On the one hand, salvation, in accordance with the earliest preaching, was regarded as the glorious
kingdom which was soon to appear on earth with the visible return
of Christ, which will bring the present course of the world
to an end, and introduce for a definite series of centuries,
before the final judgment, a new order of all things to the

---

[1] The prophet and teacher express what the Spirit of God suggest to them.
Their word is therefore God's word, and their writings, in so far as they apply
to the whole of Christendom, are inspired, holy writings. Further, not only does
Acts XV. 22 f. exhibit the formula; ἔδοξεν τῷ πνεύματι τῷ ἁγίῳ καὶ ἡμῖν (see
similar passages in the Acts), but the Roman writings also appeal to the Holy
Spirit (1 Clem. 63. 2): likewise Barnabas, Ignatius, etc. Even in the controversy
about the baptism of heretics a Bishop gave his vote with the formula "secundum
motum animi mei et spiritus sancti" (Cypr. Opp. ed. Hartel. I. p. 457).

joy and blessedness of the saints.¹ In connection with this
the hope of the resurrection of the body occupied the fore-

¹ The so-called Chiliasm—the designation is unsuitable and misleading—is found
wherever the Gospel is not yet Hellenised (see, for example, Barn. 4. 15; Hermas;
2 Clem.; Papias [Euseb. III. 39]; Διδαχή, 10. 16; Apoc. Petri; Justin, Dial. 32,
51, 80, 82, 110, 139; Cerinthus), and must be regarded as a main element of the
Christian preaching (see my article "Millenium" in the Encycl. Brit.). In it lay
not the least of the power of Christianity in the first century, and the means
whereby it entered the Jewish propaganda in the Empire and surpassed it. The
hopes springing out of Judaism were at first but little modified, that is, only so
far as the substitution of the Christian communities for the nation of Israel made
modification necessary. In all else, even the details of the Jewish hopes of the
future were retained, and the extra-canonical Jewish Apocalypses (Esra, Enoch,
Baruch, Moses, etc.) were diligently read alongside of Daniel. Their contents were
in part joined on to sayings of Jesus, and they served as models for similar productions (here, therefore, an enduring connection with the Jewish religion is very
plain). In the Christian hopes of the future, as in the Jewish eschatology, may
be distinguished essential and accidental, fixed and fluid elements To the former
belong (1) the notion of a final fearful conflict with the powers of the world which
is just about to break out τὸ τέλειον σκάνδαλον ἤγγικεν, (2) belief in the speedy
return of Christ, (3) the conviction that after conquering the secular power (this
was variously conceived, as God's Ministers, as "that which restrains"—2 Thess.
II. 6, as a pure kingdom of Satan; see the various estimates in Justin, Melito,
Irenæus and Hyppolytus), Christ will establish a glorious kingdom on the earth,
and will raise the saints to share in that kingdom, and (4) that he will finally judge
all men. To the fluid elements belong the notions of the Antichrist, or of the
secular power culminating in the Antichrist, as well as notions about the place, the
extent, and the duration of Christ's glorious kingdom. But it is worthy of special
note, that Justin regarded the belief that Christ will set up his kingdom in Jerusalem, and that it will endure for 1000 years, as a necessary element of orthodoxy,
though he confesses he knew Christians who did not share this belief, while they
did not, like the pseudo-Christians, reject also the resurrection of the body (the
promise of Montanus that Christ's kingdom would be let down at Pepuza and
Tymion is a thing by itself, and answers to the other promises and pretensions
of Montanus). The resurrection of the body is expressed in the Roman Symbol,
while, very notably, the hope of Christ's earthly kingdom is not there mentioned,
(see above, p. 157). The great inheritance which the Gentile Christian communities received from Judaism, is the eschatological hopes, along with the Monotheism
assured by revelation and belief in providence. The law as a national law was
abolished. The Old Testament became a new book in the hands of the Gentile
Christians. On the contrary, the eschatological hopes in all their details,
and with all the deep shadows which they threw on the state and public life,
were at first received, and maintained themselves in wide circles pretty much unchanged, and only succumbed in some of their details—just as in Judaism—to the
changes which resulted from the constant change of the political situation. But
these hopes were also destined in great measure to pass away after the settlement
of Christianity on Græco-Roman soil. We may set aside the fact that they did
not occupy the foreground in Paul, for we do not know whether this was of

ground.[1] On the other hand, salvation appeared to be given in the truth, that is, in the complete and certain knowledge of God, as contrasted with the error of heathendom and the night of sin, and this truth included the certainty of the gift

importance for the period that followed. But that Christ would set up the kingdom in Jerusalem, and that it would be an earthly kingdom with sensuous enjoyments—these and other notions contend, on the one hand, with the vigorous antijudaism of the communities, and on the other, with the moralistic spiritualism, in the pure carrying out of which the Gentile Christians, in the East at least, increasingly recognised the essence of Christianity. Only the vigorous world-renouncing enthusiasm which did not permit the rise of moralistic spiritualism and mysticism, and the longing for a time of joy and dominion that was born of it, protected for a long time a series of ideas which corresponded to the spiritual disposition of the great multitude of converts, only at times of special oppression. Moreover, the Christians, in opposition to Judaism, were, as a rule, instructed to obey magistrates, whose establishment directly contradicted the judgment of the state contained in the Apocalypses. In such a conflict, however, that judgment necessarily conquers at last, which makes as little change as possible in the existing forms of life. A history of the gradual attenuation and subsidence of eschatological hopes in the II.–IV. centuries can only be written in fragments. They have rarely —at best, by fits and starts—marked out the course. On the contrary, if I may say so, they only gave the smoke: for the course was pointed out by the abiding elements of the Gospel, trust in God and the Lord Christ, the resolution to a holy life, and a firm bond of brotherhood. The quiet, gradual change in which the eschatological hopes passed away, fell into the background, or lost important parts, was, on the other hand, a result of deep-reaching changes in the faith and life of Christendom. Chiliasm as a power was broken up by speculative mysticism, and on that account very much later in the West than in the East. But speculative mysticism has its centre in christology. In the earliest period, this, as a theory, belonged more to the defence of religion than to religion itself. Ignatius alone was able to reflect on that transference of power from Christ which Paul had experienced. The disguises in which the apocalyptic eschatological prophecies were set forth, belonged in part to the form of this literature, (in so far as one could easily be given the lie if he became too plain, or in so far as the prophet really saw the future only in large outline), partly it had to be chosen in order not to give political offence. See Hippol., comm. in Daniel (Georgiades, p. 49, 51 : νοεῖν ὀφείλομεν τὰ κατὰ καιρὸν συμβαίνοντα καὶ εἰδότας σιωπᾶν); but, above all, Constantine, orat. ad. s. cœtum 19, on some verses of Virgil which are interpreted in a Christian sense," but that none of the rulers in the capital might be able to accuse their author of violating the laws of the state with his poetry, or of destroying the traditional ideas of the procedure about the gods, he concealed the truth under a veil." That holds good also of the Apocalyptists and the poets of the Christian Sibylline sayings.

[1] The hope of the resurrection of the body (1 Clem. 26. 3: ἀναστήσεις τὴν σάρκα μου ταύτην. Herm. Sim. V. 7. 2: βλέπε μήποτε ἀναβῇ ἐπὶ τὴν καρδίαν σου τὴν σάρκα σου ταύτην φθαρτὴν εἶναι. Barn. 5. 6 f.: 21. 1: 2 Clem. 1: καὶ μή λεγέτω τις ὑμῶν ὅτι αὕτη ἡ σὰρξ οὐ κρίνεται οὐδὲ ἀνίσταται. Polyc. Ep. 7. 2:

of eternal life, and all conceivable spiritual blessings.[1] Of these the community, so far as it is a community of saints, that is, so far as it is ruled by the Spirit of God, already possesses forgiveness of sins and righteousness. But, as a rule, neither blessing was understood in a strictly religious sense, that is to say, the effect of their religious sense was narrowed.

Justin, Dial. 80 etc.,) finds its place originally in the hope of a share in the glorious kingdom of Christ. It therefore disappears or is modified wherever that hope itself falls into the background. But it finally asserted itself throughout and became of independent importance, in a new structure of eschatological expectations, in which it attained the significance of becoming the specific conviction of Christian faith. With the hope of the resurrection of the body was originally connected the hope of a happy life in easy blessedness, under green trees in magnificent fields with joyous feeding flocks, and flying angels clothed in white. One must read the Revelation of Peter, the Shepherd, or the Acts of Perpetua and Felicitas, in order to see how entirely the fancy of many Christians, and not merely of those who were uncultured, dwelt in a fairyland in which they caught sight now of the Ancient of Days, and now of the Youthful Shepherd, Christ. The most fearful delineations of the torments of Hell formed the reverse side to this. We now know, through the Apocalypse of Peter, how old these delineations are.

[1] The perfect knowledge of the truth and eternal life are connected in the closest way (see p. 144, note 1), because the Father of truth is also Prince of life (see Diognet. 12: οὐδὲ γάρ ζωὴ ἄνευ γνώσεως οὐδὲ γνῶσις ἀσφαλὴς ἄνευ ζωῆς ἀληθοῦς· διὸ πλησιον ἑκάτερον πεφύτευται, see also what follows). The classification is a Hellenic one, which has certainly penetrated also into Palestinian Jewish theology. It may be reckoned among the great intuitions, which in the fulness of the times, united the religious and reflective minds of all nations. The Pauline formula, "Where there is forgiveness of sin, there also is life and salvation", had for centuries no distinct history. But the formula, "Where there is truth, perfect knowledge, there also is eternal life", has had the richest history in Christendom from the beginning. Quite apart from John, it is older than the theology of the Apologists (see, for example, the Supper prayer in the Didache, 9. 10, where there is no mention of the forgiveness of sin, but thanks are given, ὑπὲρ τῆς γνώσεως καὶ πίστεως καὶ ἀθανασίας ἧς ἐγνώρισεν ἡμῖν ὁ θεὸς διὰ Ἰησοῦ, or ὑπὲρ τῆς ζωῆς καὶ γνώσεως, and 1 Clem. 36. 2: διὰ τούτο ἠθέλησεν ὁ δεσπότης τῆς ἀθανάτου γνώσεως ἡμᾶς γεύσασθαι). It is capable of a very manifold content, and has never made its way in the Church without reservations, but so far as it has we may speak of a hellenising of Christianity. This is shewn most clearly in the fact that the ἀθανασία, identical with ἀφθαρσία and ζωὴ αἰώνιος, as is proved by their being often interchanged, gradually supplanted the βασιλεία τοῦ θεοῦ (χριστοῦ) and thrust it out of the sphere of religious intuition and hope into that of religious speech. It should also be noted at the same time, that in the hope of eternal life which is bestowed with the knowledge of the truth, the resurrection of the body is by no means with certainty included. It is rather added to it (see above) from another series of ideas. Conversely, the words ζωὴν αἰώνιον were first added to the words σαρκὸς ἀνάστασιν in the western Symbols at a comparatively late period, while in the prayers they are certainly very old.

The moralistic view, in which eternal life is the wages and reward of a perfect moral life wrought out essentially by one's own power, took the place of first importance at a very early period. On this view, according to which the righteousness of God is revealed in punishment and reward alike, the forgiveness of sin only meant a single remission of sin in connection with entrance into the Church by baptism,[1] and righteousness became identical with virtue. The idea is indeed still operative, especially in the oldest Gentile-Christian writings known to us, that sinlessness rests upon a new creation (regeneration) which is effected in baptism;[2] but, so far as dissimilar eschatological hopes do not operate, it is everywhere in danger of being supplanted by the other idea, which main-

---

[1] Even the assumption of such a remission is fundamentally in contradiction with moralism; but that solitary remission of sin was not called in question, was rather regarded as distinctive of the new religion, and was established by an appeal to the omnipotence and special goodness of God, which appears just in the calling of sinners. In this calling, grace as grace is exhausted (Barn. 5. 9; 2 Clem. 2. 4-7). But this grace itself seems to be annulled, inasmuch as the sins committed before baptism were regarded as having been committed in a state of ignorance (Tertull. de bapt. I.: delicta pristinæ cæcitatis), on account of which it seemed worthy of God to forgive them, that is, to accept the repentance which followed on the ground of the new knowledge. So considered, everything, in point of fact, amounts to the gracious gift of knowledge, and the memory of the saying, "Jesus receiveth sinners", is completely obscured. But the tradition of this saying and many like it, and above all, the religious instinct, where it was more powerfully stirred, did not permit a consistent development of that moralistic conception. See for this, Hermas. Sim. V. 7. 3: περὶ τῶν προτέρων ἀγνοημάτων τῷ θεῷ μόνῳ δυνατὸν ἴασιν δοῦναι· αὐτοῦ γὰρ ἐστι πᾶσα ἐξουσία. Præd. Petri ap. Clem. Strom. VI. 6. 48: ὅσα ἐν ἀγνοίᾳ τις ὑμῶν ἐποίησεν μὴ εἰδὼς σαφῶς τὸν θεὸν, ἐὰν ἐπιγνοὺς μετανοήσῃ, πάντα αὐτῷ ἀφεθήσεται τὰ ἁμαρτήματα. Aristides, Apol. 17: "The Christians offer prayers (for the unconverted Greeks) that they may be converted from their error. But when one of them is converted he is ashamed before the Christians of the works which he has done. And he confesses to God, saying: 'I have done these things in ignorance.' And he cleanses his heart, and his sins are forgiven him, because he had done them in ignorance, in the earlier period when he mocked and jeered at the true knowledge of the Christians." Exactly the same in Tertull. de pudic. 10. init. The statement of this same writer (1. c. fin), "Cessatio delicti radix est veniæ, ut venia sit pænitentiæ fructus", is a pregnant expression of the conviction of the earliest Gentile Christians.

[2] This idea appears with special prominence in the Epistle of Barnabas (see 6. 11. 14); the new formation (ἀναπλάσσειν) results through the forgiveness of sin. In the moralistic view the forgiveness of sin is the result of the renewal that is spontaneously brought about on the ground of knowledge shewing itself in penitent feeling.

tains that there is no other blessing in the Gospel than the
perfect truth and eternal life. All else is but a sum of obligations in which the Gospel is presented as a new law. The
christianising of the Old Testament supported this conception.
There was indeed an opinion that the Gospel, even so far as
it is a law, comprehends a gift of salvation which is to be
grasped by faith (νόμος ἄνευ ζυγοῦ ἀνάγκης,[1] νόμος τ. ἐλευθερίας,[2]
Christ himself the law);[3] but this notion, as it is obscure in
itself, was also an uncertain one and was gradually lost. Further,
by the "law" was frequently meant in the first place, not the
law of love, but the commandments of ascetic holiness, or an
explanation and a turn were given to the law of love, according
to which it is to verify itself above all in asceticism.[4]

The expression of the contents of the Gospel in the concepts
ἐπαγγελία (ζωὴ αἰώνιος) γνῶσις (ἀλήθεια) νόμος (ἐγκράτεια), seemed
quite as plain as it was exhaustive, and the importance of
faith which was regarded as the basis of hope and knowledge
and obedience in a holy life, was at the same time in every
respect perceived.[5]

Supplement I. — The moralistic view of sin, forgiveness of
sin, and righteousness, in Clement, Barnabas, Polycarp and
Ignatius, gives place to Pauline formulæ; but the uncertainty
with which these are reproduced, shews that the Pauline idea

---

[1] Barn. 2. 6, and my notes on the passage.

[2] James I. 25.

[3] Hermas. Sim. VIII. 3. 2; Justin Dial. II. 43; Praed. Petri in Clem., Strom.
I. 29. 182; II. 15. 68.

[4] Didache, c I., and my notes on the passage (Prolegg. p. 45 f.).

[5] The concepts, ἐπαγγελία, γνῶσις, νόμος, form the Triad on which the later
catholic concèption of Christianity is based, though it can be proved to have been
in existence at an earlier period. That πίστις must everywhere take the lead was
undoubted, though we must not think of the Pauline idea of πίστις. When the
Apostolic Fathers reflect upon faith, which, however, happens only incidentally,
they mean a holding for true of a sum of holy traditions, and obedience to them,
along with the hope that their consoling contents will yet be fully revealed. But
Ignatius speaks like a Christian who knows what he possesses in faith in Christ,
that is, in confidence in him. In Barn. I.: Polyc. Ep. 2, we find "faith, hope
love"; in Ignatius, "faith and love". Tertullian, in an excellent exposition, has
shewn how far patience is a temper corresponding to Christian faith (see besides
the Epistle of James).

has not been clearly seen. [1]   In Hermas, however, and in the second Epistle of Clement, the consciousness of being under grace, even after baptism, almost completely disappears behind the demand to fulfil the tasks which baptism imposes. [2]   The idea that serious sins, in the case of the baptised, no longer should or can be forgiven, except under special circumstances, appears to have prevailed in wide circles, if not everywhere. [3] It reveals the earnestness of those early Christians and their elevated sense of freedom and power; but it might be united either with the highest moral intensity, or with a lax judgment on the little sins of the day.   The latter, in point of fact, threatened to become more and more the presupposition and result of that idea—for there exists here a fatal reciprocal action.

Supplement 2.—The realisation of salvation—as $\beta\alpha\sigma\iota\lambda\epsilon\iota\alpha\ \tau\sigma\tilde{\upsilon}$ $\theta\epsilon\sigma\tilde{\upsilon}$ and as $\dot{\alpha}\phi\theta\alpha\rho\sigma\iota\alpha$—being expected from the future, the whole present possession of salvation might be comprehended under the title of vocation ($\varkappa\lambda\tilde{\eta}\sigma\iota\varsigma$): see, for example, the second Epistle of Clement.   In this sense *gnosis* itself was regarded as something only preparatory.

Supplement 3.—In some circles the Pauline formula about righteousness and salvation by faith alone, must, it would appear, not infrequently (as already in the Apostolic age itself) have been partly misconstrued, and partly taken advantage of as a cloak for laxity.   Those who resisted such a disposition, and therefore also the formula in the post-Apostolic age, shew indeed by their opposition how little they have hit upon or understood the Pauline idea of faith: for they not only issued the watchword "faith and works" (though the Jewish ceremonial law was not thereby meant), but they admitted, and not only hypothetically,

[1]   See Lipsius De Clementis. R. ep ad. Cor. priore disquis. 1855.   It would be in point of method inadmissible to conclude from the fact that in 1 Clem. Pauline formulæ are relatively most faithfully produced, that Gentile Christianity generally understood Pauline theology at first, but gradually lost this understanding in the course of two generations.

[2]   Formally : $\tau\eta\rho\dot{\eta}\sigma\alpha\tau\epsilon\ \tau\dot{\eta}\nu\ \sigma\dot{\alpha}\rho\varkappa\alpha\ \dot{\alpha}\gamma\nu\dot{\eta}\nu\ \varkappa\alpha\dot{\iota}\ \tau\dot{\eta}\nu\ \sigma\phi\rho\alpha\gamma\tilde{\iota}\delta\alpha\ \ddot{\alpha}\sigma\pi\iota\lambda\sigma\nu$ (2 Clem. 8. 6.)

[3]   Hermas (Mand. IV. 3) and Justin presuppose it.   Hermas of course sought and found a way of meeting the results of that idea which were threatening the Church with decimation; but he did not question the idea itself.   Because Christendom is a community of saints which has in its midst the sure salvation, all its members—this is the necessary inference—must lead a sinless life.

that one might have the true faith even though in his case that faith remained dead or united with immorality. See, above all, the Epistle of James and the Shepherd of Hermas; though the first Epistle of John comes also into consideration (III. 7: "He that doeth righteousness is righteous"). [1]

Supplement 4.—However similar the eschatological expectations of the Jewish Apocalyptists and the Christians may seem, there is yet in one respect an important difference between them. The uncertainty about the final consummation was first set aside by the Gospel. It should be noted as highly characteristic of the Jewish hopes of the future, even of the most definite, how the beginning of the end, that is, the overthrow of the world-powers and the setting up of the earthly kingdom of God, was much more certainly expressed than the goal and the final end. Neither the general judgment, nor what we, according to Christian tradition, call heaven and hell, should be described as a sure possession of Jewish faith in the primitive Christian period. It is only in the Gospel of Christ, where everything is subordinated to the idea of a higher righteousness and the union of the individual with God, that the general judgment and the final condition after it are the clear, firmly grasped goal of all meditation. No doctrine has been more surely preserved in the convictions and preaching of believers in Christ than this. Fancy might roam ever so much and, under the direction of the tradition, thrust bright and precious images between the present condition and the final end, the main thing continued to be the great judgment of the world, and the certainty that the saints would go to God in heaven, the wicked to hell. But while the judgment, as a rule, was connected with the Person of Jesus himself (see the Romish Symbol: the words κριτὴς ζώντων καὶ νεκρῶν, were very frequently applied to Christ in the earliest writings), the moral condition of the individual, and the believing recognition of the Person of Christ were put in the closest relation. The Gentile Christians held firmly

---

[1] The formula, "righteousness by faith alone," was really repressed in the second century; but it could not be entirely destroyed: see my Essay, "Gesch. d. Seligkeit allein durch den Glauben in der alten K." Ztsch. f. Theol. u. Kirche. I. pp. 82–105.

to this. Open the Shepherd, or the second Epistle of Clement, or any other early Christian writing, and you will find that the judgment, heaven and hell, are the decisive objects. But that shews that the moral character of Christianity as a religion is seen and adhered to. The fearful idea of hell, far from signifying a backward step in the history of the religious spirit, is rather a proof of its having rejected the morally indifferent point of view, and of its having become sovereign in union with the ethical spirit.

§ 4. *The Old Testament as Source of the Knowledge of Faith.* [1]

The sayings of the Old Testament, the word of God, were believed to furnish inexhaustible material for deeper knowledge. The Christian prophets were nurtured on the Old Testament, the teachers gathered from it the revelation of the past, present and future (Barn. I. 7), and were therefore able as prophets to edify the Churches; from it was further drawn the confirmation of the answers to all emergent questions, as one could always find in the Old Testament what he was in search of. The different writers laid the holy book under contribution in very much the same way; for they were all dominated by the presupposition that this book is a Christian book, and contains the explanations that are necessary for the occasion. There were several teachers,—*e.g.*, Barnabas,—who at a very early period boasted of finding in it ideas of special profundity and value—these were always an expression of the difficulties that were being felt. The plain words of the Lord as generally known, did not seem sufficient

[1] The only thorough discussion of the use of the Old Testament by an Apostolic Father, and of its authority, that we possess, is Wrede's "Untersuchungen zum I Clementsbrief" (1891). Excellent preliminary investigations, which, however, are not everywhere quite reliable, may be found in Hatch's Essays in Biblical Greek, 1889. Hatch has taken up again the hypothesis of earlier scholars, that there were very probably in the first and second centuries systematised extracts from the Old Testament (see pp. 203-214). The hypothesis is not yet quite established (see Wrede, above work, p. 65), but yet it is hardly to be rejected. The Jewish catechetical and missionary instruction in the Diaspora needed such collections, and their existence seem to be proved by the Christian Apologies and the Sybilline books.

to satisfy the craving for knowledge, or to solve the problems that were emerging;[1] their origin and form also opposed difficulties at first to the attempt to obtain from them new disclosures by re-interpretation. But the Old Testament sayings and histories were in part unintelligible, or in their literal sense offensive; they were at the same time regarded as fundamental words of God. This furnished the conditions for turning them to account in the way we have stated. The following are the most important points of view under which the Old Testament was used. (1) The Monotheistic cosmology and view of nature were borrowed from it (see, for example, 1 Clem.). (2) It was used to prove that the appearance and entire history of Jesus had been foretold centuries, nay, thousands of years beforehand, and that the founding of a new people gathered out of all nations had been predicted and prepared for from the very beginning.[2] (3) It was used as

---

[1] It is an extremely important fact that the words of the Lord were quoted and applied in their literal sense (that is chiefly for the statement of Christian morality) by Ecclesiastical authors, almost without exception, up to and inclusive of Justin. It was different with the theologians of the age, that is the Gnostics, and the Fathers from Irenæus.

[2] Justin was not the first to do so, for it had already been done by the so-called Barnabas (see especially c. 13) and others. On the proofs from prophecy see my Texte und Unters. Bd. I. 3. pp. 56–74. The passage in the Praed. Petri (Clem. Strom. VI. 15. 128) is very complete: Ἡμεῖς ἀναπτίξαντες τὰς βίβλους ὰς εἴχομεν τῶν προφητῶν, ὰ μὲν διὰ παραβολῶν ὰ δὲ διὰ αἰνιγμάτων, ὰ δὲ αὐθεντικῶς καὶ αὐτολεξεὶ τὸν Χριστὸν Ἰησοῦν ὀνομαζόντων, εὕρομεν καὶ τὴν παρουσίαν αὐτοῦ καὶ τὸν θανατον καὶ τὸν σταυρὸν καὶ τὰς λοιπάς κολάσεις πάσας, ὅσας ἐποίησαν αὐτῷ οἱ Ἰουδαῖοι, καὶ τὴν ἔγερσιν καὶ τὴν εἰς οὐρανοὺς ἀνάληψιν πρὸ τοῦ Ἱερσόλυμα κριθῆναι, καθὼς ἐγέγραπτο ταῦτα πάντα ὰ ἔδϵι αὐτὸν παθεῖν καὶ μετ᾽ αὐτὸν ὰ ἔσται· ταῦτα οὖν ἐπιγνόντες ἐπιστεύσαμεν τῷ θεῷ διὰ τῶν γεγραμμένων εἰς αὐτόν. With the help of the Old Testament the teachers dated back the Christian religion to the beginning of the human race, and joined the preparations for the founding of the Christian community with the creation of the world. The Apologists were not the first to do so, for Barnabas and Hermas, and before these, Paul, the author of the Epistle to the Hebrews, and others had already done the same. This was undoubtedly to the cultured classes one of the most impressive articles in the missionary preaching. The Christian religion in this way got a hold which the others—with the exception of the Jewish—lacked. But for that very reason, we must guard against turning it into a formula, that the Gentile Christians had comprehended the Old Testament essentially through the scheme of prediction and fulfilment. The Old Testament is certainly the book of predictions, but for that very reason the complete revelation of God which needs no additions and excludes

a means of verifying all principles and institutions of the Christian Church, — the spiritual worship of God without images, the abolition of all ceremonial legal precepts, baptism, etc. (4) The Old Testament was used for purposes of exhortation according to the formula *a minori ad majus;* if God then punished and rewarded this or that in such a way, how much more may we expect, who now stand in the last days, and have received the κλῆσις τῆς ἐπαγγελίας. (5) It was proved from the Old Testament that the Jewish nation is in error, and either never had a covenant with God or has lost it, that it has a false apprehension of God's revelations, and therefore has, now at least, no longer any claim to their possession. But beyond all this, (6) there were in the Old Testament books, above all, in the Prophets and in the Psalms, a great number of sayings—confessions of trust in God and of help received from God, of humility and holy courage, testimonies of a world-overcoming faith and words of comfort, love and communion—which were too exalted for any cavilling, and intelligible to every spiritually awakened mind. Out of this treasure which was handed down to the Greeks and Romans, the Church edified herself, and in the perception of its riches was largely rooted the conviction that the holy book must in every line contain the highest truth.

The point mentioned under (5) needs, however, further explanation. The self-consciousness of the Christian community of being the people of God, must have been, above all, expressed in its position towards Judaism, whose mere existence —even apart from actual assaults—threatened that consciousness most seriously. A certain antipathy of the Greeks and Romans towards Judaism co-operated here with a law of self-preservation. On all hands, therefore, Judaism as it then existed was abandoned as a sect judged and rejected by God, as a

subsequent changes. The historical fulfilment only proves to the world the truth of those revelations. Even the scheme of shadow and reality is yet entirely out of sight. In such circumstances the question necessarily arises, as to what independent meaning and significance Christ's appearance could have, apart from that confirmation of the Old Testament. But, apart from the Gnostics, a surprisingly long time passed before this question was raised, that is to say, it was not raised till the time of Irenæus.

society of hypocrites, [1] as a synagogue of Satan, [2] as a people seduced by an evil angel, [3] and the Jews were declared to have no further right to the possession of the Old Testament. Opinions differed, however, as to the earlier history of the nation and its relation to the true God. While some denied that there ever had been a covenant of salvation between God and this nation, and in this respect recognised only an intention of God, [4] which was never carried out because of the idolatry of the people, others admitted in a hazy way that a relation did exist; but even they referred all the promises of the Old Testament to the Christian people. [5] While the former saw in the observance of the letter of the law, in the case of circumcision, sabbath, precepts as to food, etc., a proof of the special devilish temptation to which the Jewish people succumbed, [6] the latter saw in circumcision a sign [7] given by

[1] See Διδαχή, 8.

[2] See the Revelation of John II. 9 : III. 9; but see also the "Jews" in the Gospels of John and Peter. The latter exonerates Pilate almost completely, and makes the Jews and Herod responsible for the crucifixion.

[3] See Barn. 9. 4. In the second epistle of Clement the Jews are called: "οἱ δοκοῦντες ἔχειν θεὸν," cf. Præd. Petri in Clem. Strom. VI. 5. 41 : μηδὲ κατὰ Ἰουδαίους σέβεσθε· καὶ γὰρ ἐκεῖνοι μόνοι οἰόμενοι τὸν θεὸν γιγνώσκειν οὐκ ἐπίστανται, λατρεύοντες ἀγγέλοις καὶ ἀρχαγγέλοις, μηνὶ καὶ σελήνη, καὶ ἐὰν μὴ σελήνη φανῇ, σάββατον οὐκ ἄγουσι τὸ λεκόμενον πρῶτον, οὐδὲ νεομηνίαν ἄγουσιν, οὐδὲ ἄζυμα, οὐδὲ ἑορτήν, οὐδὲ μεγάλην ἡμέραν. (Cf. Diognet. 34.) Even Justin does not judge the Jews more favourably than the Gentiles, but less favourably; see Apol. I. 37, 39, 43, 44, 47, 53, 60. On the other hand, Aristides (Apol. c. 14, especially in the Syrian text) is much more friendly disposed to the Jews and recognises them more. The words of Pionius against and about the Jews in the "Acta Pionii," c. 4, are very instructive.

[4] Barn. 4. 6. f. : 14. 1. f. The author of Præd. Petri must have had a similar view of the matter.

[5] Justin in the Dialogue with Trypho.

[6] Barn. 9. f. It is a thorough misunderstanding of Barnabas' position towards the Old Testament to suppose it possible to pass over his expositions, c. 6-10, as oddities and caprices, and put them aside as indifferent or unmethodical. There is nothing here unmethodical, and therefore nothing arbitrary. Barnabas' strictly spiritual idea of God, and the conviction that all (Jewish) ceremonies are of the devil, compel his explanations. These are so little ingenious conceits to Barnabas that, but for them, he would have been forced to give up the Old Testament altogether. The account, for example, of Abraham having circumcised his slaves would have forced Barnabas to annul the whole authority of the Old Testament if he had not succeeded in giving it a particular interpretation. He does this by combining other passages of Genesis with the narrative, and then finding in it no longer circumcision, but a prediction of the crucified Christ.

[7] Barn 9. 6: ἀλλ᾽ ἐρεῖς· καὶ μὴν περιτέτμηται ὁ λαὸς εἰς σφραγῖδα.

God, and in virtue of certain considerations acknowledged that the literal observance of the law was for the time God's intention and command, though righteousness never came from such observance. Yet even they saw in the spiritual the alone true sense, which the Jews had denied, and were of opinion that the burden of ceremonies was a pædagogic necessity with reference to a people stiff-necked and prone to idolatry, *i.e.*, a defence of monotheism, and gave an interpretation to the sign of circumcision which made it no longer a blessing, but rather the mark for the execution of judgment on Israel. [1]

Israel was thus at all times the pseudo-Church. The older people does not in reality precede the younger people, the Christians, even in point of time; for though the Church appeared only in the last days, it was foreseen and created by God from the beginning. The younger people is therefore really the older, and the new law rather the original law. [2] The Patriarchs, Prophets, and men of God, however, who were favoured with the communication of God's words, have nothing inwardly in common with the Jewish people. They are God's elect who were distinguished by a holy walk, and must be regarded as the forerunners and fathers of the Christian people. [3] To the question how such holy men appeared exclusively, or almost exclusively, among the Jewish people, the documents preserved to us yield no answer.

---

[1] See the expositions of Justin in the Dial. (especially, 16, 18, 20, 30, 40-46); Von Engelhardt, "Christenthum Justin's," p. 429. ff. Justin has the three estimates side by side. (1) That the ceremonial law was a pædagogic measure of God with reference to a stiff-necked people prone to idolatry. (2) That it—like circumcision —was to make the people conspicuous for the execution of judgment, according to the Divine appointment. (3) That in the ceremonial legal worship of the Jews is exhibited the special depravity and wickedness of the nation. But Justin conceived the Decalogue as the natural law of reason, and therefore definitely distinguished it from the ceremonial law.

[2] See Ztschr. für K. G, I., p. 330 f.

[3] This is the unanimous opinion of all writers of the post-Apostolic age. Christians are the true Israel; and therefore all Israel's predicates of honour belong to them. They are the twelve tribes, and therefore Abraham, Isaac and Jacob, are the Fathers of the Christians. This idea, about which there was no wavering, cannot everywhere be traced back to the Apostle Paul. The Old Testament men of God were in certain measure Christians. See Ignat. Magn. 8. 2: οἱ προφῆται κατὰ Χριστὸν Ἰησοῦν ἔζησαν.

§ 5. The Knowledge of God and of the World. Estimate of the World.

The knowledge of faith was, above all, the knowledge of God as one, supramundane, spiritual, [1] and almighty (παντο-κράτωρ); God is creator and governor of the world and therefore the Lord. [2] But as he created the world a beautiful ordered whole (monotheistic view of nature) [3] for the sake of man, [4] he is at the same time the God of goodness and

[1] God was naturally conceived and represented as corporeal by uncultured Christians, though not by these alone, as the later controversies prove (e.g., Orig. contra Melito; see also Tertull. De anima). In the case of the cultured, the idea of a corporeality of God may be traced back to Stoic influences; in the case of the uncultured, popular ideas co-operated with the sayings of the Old Testament literally understood, and the impression of the Apocalyptic images.

[2] See Joh. IV. 22; ἡμεῖς προσκυνοῦμεν ὃ οἴδαμεν. 1 Clem. 59. 3. 4; Herm. Mand. I.; Præd. Petri in Clem. Strom. VI. 5. 9.: γινώσκετε ὅτι εἷς θεὸς ἐστιν, ὅς ἀρχὴν πάντων ἐποίησεν, καὶ τέλους ἐξουσίαν ἔχων. Aristides Apol. 15 (Syr.): "The Christians know and believe in God, the creator of heaven and of earth." Chap. 16: "Christians as men who know God, pray to him for things which it becomes him to give and them to receive." (Similarly Justin.) From very many old Gentile Christian writings we hear it as a cry of joy. "We know God the Almighty; the night of blindness is past" (see, e.g., 2 Clem. c. 1). God is δεσπότης, a designation which is very frequently used (it is rare in the New Testament). Still more frequently do we find κύριος. As the Lord and Creator, God is also called the Father (of the world) so 1 Clem. 19. 2: ὁ πατὴρ καὶ κτίστης τοῦ σύμπαντος κόσμου. 35. 3: δημιουργὸς καὶ πατὴρ τῶν αἰώνων. This use of the name Father for the supreme God was, as is well known, familiar to the Greeks, but the Christians alone were in earnest with the name. The creation out of nothing was made decidedly prominent by Hermas, see Vis. I. 1. 6, and my notes on the passage. In the Christian Apocrypha, in spite of the vividness of the idea of God, the angels play the same rôle as in the Jewish, and as in the current Jewish speculations. According to Hermas, e.g., all God's actions are mediated by special angels, nay, the Son of God himself is represented by a special angel, viz., Michael, and works by him. But outside the Apocalypses there seems to have been little interest in the good angels.

[3] See, for example, 1 Clem. 20.

[4] This is frequent in the Apologists; see also Diogn. 10. 2 : but Hermas, Vis. II. 4. 1 (see also Cels. ap. Orig. IV. 23) says: διὰ τὴν ἐκκλησίαν ὁ κόσμος κατηρτίσθη (cf. I. 1. 6. and my notes on the passage). Aristides (Apol. 16) declares it as his conviction that "the beautiful things," that is, the world, are maintained only for the sake of Christians; see, besides, the words (I. c.); "I have no doubt, that the earth continues to exist (only) on account of the prayers of the Christians." Even the Jewish Apocalyptists wavered between the formulæ, that the world was created for the sake of man, and for the sake of the Jewish nation. The two are not mutually exclusive. The statement in the Eucharistic prayer of Didache, 9. 3, ἔκτισας τὰ πάντα ἕνεκεν τοῦ ὀνόματός σου, is singular.

redemption (θεὸς σωτήρ), and the true faith in God and know-ledge of him as the Father, [1] is made perfect only in the knowledge of the identity of the God of creation and the God of redemption. Redemption, however, was necessary, because at the beginning humanity and the world alike fell under the dominion of evil demons, [2] of the evil one. There was no

[1] God is named the Father, (1) in relation to the Son (very frequent), (2) as Father of the world (see above), (3) as the merciful one who has proved his good-ness, declared his will, and called Christians to be his sons (1 Clem. 23. 1; 29, 1; 2 Clem. 1. 4; 8. 4; 10. 1; 14. 1; see the index to Zahn's edition of the Ignatian Epistles; Didache. 1. 5; 9. 2. 3; 10. 2.) The latter usage is not very common; it is entirely wanting, for example, in the Epistle of Barnabas. Moreover, God is also called πατὴρ τῆς ἀληθείας, as the source of all truth (2 Clem. 3. 1 : 20, 5 : θεὸς τ. ἀληθείας). The identity of the Almighty God of creation with the merciful God of redemption is the tacit presupposition of all declarations about God, in the case of both the cultured and the uncultured. It is also frequently expressed (see, above all, the Pastoral Epistles), most frequently by Hermas (Vis. I. 3. 4), so far as the declaration about the creation of the world is there united in the closest way with that about the creation of the Holy Church. As to the designation of God in the Roman Symbol, as the "Father Almighty," that threefold exposition just given may perhaps allow it.

[2] The present dominion of evil demons, or of one evil demon, was just as generally presupposed as man's need of redemption, which was regarded as a result of that dominion. The conviction that the world's course (the πολιτεία ἐν τῷ κοσμῳ : the Latins afterwards used the word Sæculum) is determined by the devil, and that the dark one (Barnabas) has dominion, comes out most prominently where eschatological hopes obtain expression. But where salvation is thought of as knowledge and immortality, it is ignorance and frailty from which men are to be delivered. We may here also assume with certainty that these, in the last instance, were traced back by the writers to the action of demons. But it makes a very great difference whether the judgment was ruled by fancy which saw a real devil everywhere active, or whether, in consequence of theoretic reflection, it based the impression of universal ignorance and mortality on the assumption of demons who have produced them. Here again we must note the two series of ideas which intertwine and struggle with each other in the creeds of the earliest period; the traditional religious series, resting on a fanciful view of history—it is essentially identical with the Jewish Apocalyptic: see, for example, Barn. 4—and the empiric moralistic (see 2 Clem. 1. 2–7, as a specially valuable discussion, or Præd. Petri in Clem. Strom. VI. 5, 39, 40), which abides by the fact that men have fallen into ignorance, weakness and death (2 Clem. 1. 6: ὁ βίος ἡμῶν ὅλος ἄλλο οὐδὲν ἦν εἰ μὴ θάνατος). But, perhaps, in no other point, with the exception of the ἀνάστασις σαρκὸς, has the religious conception remained so tenacious as in this, and it decidedly prevailed, especially in the epoch with which we are now dealing. Its tenacity may be ex-plained, among other things, by the living impression of the polytheism that surrounded the communities on every side. Even where the national gods were looked upon as dead idols—and that was perhaps the rule, see Præd. Petri, I. c.;

universally accepted theory as to the origin of this dominion;
but the sure and universal conviction was that the present
condition and course of the world is not of God, but is of
the devil. Those, however, who believed in God, the almighty creator, and were expecting the transformation of the
earth, as well as the visible dominion of Christ upon it, could
not be seduced into accepting a dualism in principle (God

2 Clem. 3. 1; Didache, 6—one could not help assuming that there were mighty
demons operative behind them, as otherwise the frightful power of idolatry could
not be explained. But, on the other hand, even a calm reflection and a temper
unfriendly to all religious excess must have welcomed the assumption of demons
who sought to rule the world and man. For by means of this assumption, which
was wide-spread even among the Greeks, humanity seemed to be unburdened, and
the presupposed capacity for redemption could therefore be justified in its widest
range. From the assumption that the need of redemption was altogether due to
ignorance and mortality, there was but one step, or little more than one step, to
the assumption that the need of redemption was grounded in a condition of man
for which he was not responsible, that is, in the flesh. But this step, which would
have led either to dualism (heretical Gnosis) or to the abolition of the distinction
between natural and moral, was not taken within the main body of the Church.
The eschatological series of ideas with its thesis that death, evil and sin entered
into humanity at a definite historical moment, when the demons took possession
of the world, drew a limit which was indeed overstepped at particular points, but
was in the end respected. We have therefore the remarkable fact that, on the
one hand, early Christian (Jewish) eschatology called forth and maintained a
disposition in which the Kingdom of God and that of the world (Kingdom of the
devil) were felt to be absolutely opposed (practical dualism), while, on the other hand,
it rejected theoretic dualism. Redemption through Christ, however, was conceived
in the eschatological Apocalyptic series of ideas as essentially something entirely
in the future, for the power of the devil was not broken, but rather increased (or
it was virtually broken in believers and increased in unbelievers) by the first
advent of Christ, and therefore the period between the first and second advent of
Christ belongs to οὗτος ὁ αἰών (see Barn. 2. 4; Herm. Sim. I; 2. Clem. 6. 3:
ἔστιν δὲ οὗτος ὁ αἰὼν καὶ ὁ μέλλων δύο ἐχθροί· οὗτος λέγει μοιχείαν καὶ φθορὰν καὶ
φιλαργυρίαν καὶ ἀπάτην, ἐκεῖνος δὲ τούτοις ἀποτάσσεται; Ignat. Magn. 5. 2).
For that very reason, the second coming of Christ must, as a matter of course, be
at hand, for only through it could the first advent get its full value. The painful
impression that nothing had been outwardly changed by Christ's first advent (the
heathen, moreover, pointed this out in mockery to the suffering Christians), must
be destroyed by the hope of his speedy coming again. But the first advent had
its independent significance in the series of ideas which regarded Christ as redeeming man from ignorance and mortality; for the knowledge was already given and
the gift of immortality could only of course be dispensed after this life was ended,
but then immediately. The hope of Christ's return was therefore a superfluity,
but was not felt or set aside as such, because there was still a lively expectation
of Christ's earthly Kingdom.

and devil: spirit and matter). Belief in God, the creator, and eschatological hopes preserved the communities from the theoretic dualism that so readily suggested itself, which they slightly touched in many particular opinions, and which threatened to dominate their feelings. The belief that the world is of God and therefore good, remained in force. A distinction was made between the present constitution of the world, which is destined for destruction, and the future order of the world which will be a glorious "restitutio in integrum". The theory of the world as an articulated whole which had already been proclaimed by the Stoics, and which was strengthened by Christian monotheism, would not, even if it had been known to the uncultured, have been vigorous enough to cope with the impression of the wickedness of the course of this world, and the vulgarity of all things material. But the firm belief in the omnipotence of God, and the hope of the world's transformation grounded on the Old Testament, conquered the mood of absolute despair of all things visible and sensuous, and did not allow a theoretic conclusion, in the sense of dualism in principle, to be drawn from the practical obligation to renounce the world, or from the deep distrust with regard to the flesh.

§ 6. *Faith in Jesus Christ.*

1. As surely as redemption was traced back to God himself, so surely was Jesus ($\acute{o}$ $\sigma\omega\tau\grave{\eta}\rho$ $\acute{\eta}\mu\tilde{\omega}\nu$) held to be the mediator of it. Faith in Jesus was therefore, even for Gentile Christians, a compendium of Christianity. Jesus is mostly designated with the same name as God,[1] $\acute{o}$ $\varkappa\acute{v}\rho\iota o\varsigma$ ($\acute{\eta}\mu\tilde{\omega}\nu$), for we must remember the ancient use of this title. All that has taken place or will take place with reference to salvation, is

---

[1] No other name adhered to Christ so firmly as that of $\varkappa\acute{v}\rho\iota o\varsigma$: see a specially clear evidence of this, Novatian de trinit. 30, who argues against the Adoptian and Modalistic heretics thus: "Et in primis illud retorquendum in istos, qui duorum nobis deorum controversiam facere præsumunt. Scriptum est, quod negare non possunt: "Quoniam unus est dominus." De Christo ergo quid sentiunt? Dominum esse, aut illum omnino non esse? Sed dominum illum omnino non dubitant. Ergo si vera est illorum ratiocinatio, jam duo sunt domini." On $\varkappa\acute{v}\rho\iota o\varsigma = \delta\varepsilon\sigma\pi o\tau\eta\varsigma$, see above, p. 119, note.

traced back to the "Lord." The carelessness of the early
Christian writers about the bearing of the word in particular
cases, [1] shews that in a religious relation, so far as there
was reflection on the gift of salvation, Jesus could directly
take the place of God. The invisible God is the author,
Jesus the revealer and mediator, of all saving blessings. The
final subject is presented in the nearest subject, and there is
frequently no occasion for expressly distinguishing them, as
the range and contents of the revelation of salvation in Jesus
coincide with the range and contents of the will of salvation
in God himself. Yet prayers, as a rule, were addressed to
God: at least, there are but few examples of direct prayers to
Jesus belonging to the first century (apart from the prayers in
the Act. Joh. of the so-called Leucius). The usual formula
rather reads: θεῷ ἐξομολογούμεθα διὰ Ἰ. Χρ.—θεῷ δόξα διά Ἰ. Χρ. [2]

2. As the Gentile Christians did not understand the significance of the idea that Jesus is the Christ (Messiah), the designation "χριστός" had either to be given up in their communities, or to subside into a mere name. [3] But even where,

---

[1] Specially instructive examples of this are found in the Epistle of Barnabas
and the second Epistle of Clement. Clement (Ep. 1) speaks only of faith in God.

[2] See 1 Clem. 59-61. Διδαχή, c. 9. 10. Yet Novatian (de trinit. 14) exactly
reproduces the old idea, "Si homo tantummodo Christus, cur homo in orationibus
mediator invocatur, cum invocatio hominis ad præstandam salutem inefficax judi-
cetur." As the Mediator, High Priest, etc., Christ is of course always and everywhere invoked by the Christians, but such invocations are one thing and formal
prayer another. The idea of the congruence of God's will of salvation with the
revelation of salvation which took place through Christ, was further continued in
the idea of the congruence of this revelation of salvation with the universal preaching of the twelve chosen Apostles (see above, p. 162 ff.), the root of the Catholic
principle of tradition. But the Apostles never became "οἱ κύριοι," though the
concepts διδαχὴ (λόγος) κύριου, διδαχὴ (κήρυγμα) τῶν ἀποστόλων were just as
interchangeable as λόγος θεοῦ and λόγος χριστοῦ. The full formula would be
λόγος θεοῦ διὰ Ἰησοῦ Χριστοῦ διὰ τῶν ἀποστόλων. But as the subjects introduced by
διὰ are chosen and perfect media, religious usage permitted the abbreviation.

[3] In the epistle of Barnabas "Jesus Christ" and "Christ" appear each once,
but "Jesus" twelve times: in the Didache "Jesus Christ" once, "Jesus" three
times. Only in the second half of the second century, if I am not mistaken, did
the designation "Jesus Christ," or "Christ," become the current one, more and
more crowding out the simple "Jesus." Yet the latter designation—and this is not
surprising—appears to have continued longest in the regular prayers. It is worthy
of note that in the Shepherd there is no mention either of the name Jesus or of Christ.
The Gospel of Peter also says ὁ κύριος where the other Gospels use these names.

through the Old Testament, one was reminded of the meaning of the word, and allowed a value to it, he was far from finding in the statement that Jesus is the Lord's anointed, a clear expression of the dignity peculiar to him. That dignity had therefore to be expressed by other means. Nevertheless the eschatological series of ideas connected the Gentile Christians very closely with the early Christian ideas of faith, and therefore also with the earliest ideas about Jesus. In the confession that God chose[1] and prepared Jesus, that Jesus is the Angel[3] and the servant of God,[4] that he will judge

---

[1] See 1 Clem. 64: ὁ θεὸς, ὁ ἐκλεξάμενος τὸν κύριον Ἰησοῦν Χριστὸν καὶ ἡμᾶς δι' αὐτοῦ εἰς λαὸν περιούσιον δῷη, κ.τ.λ. (It is instructive to note that wherever the idea of election is expressed, the community is immediately thought of, for in point of fact the election of the Messiah has no other aim than to elect or call the community; Barn. 3. 6: ὁ λαὸς ὅν ἡτοίμασεν ἐν τῷ ἠγαπημένῳ αὐτοῦ.) Herm. Sim. V. 2: ἐκλεξάμενος δοῦλόν τινα πιστὸν καὶ εὐάρεστον. V. 6. 5. Justin, Dial. 48: μὴ ἀρνεῖσθαι ὅτι οὗτός ἐστιν ὁ Χριστὸς, ἐὰν φαίνηται ὡς ἄνθρωπος ἐξ ἀνθρώπου γεννηθεὶς καὶ ἐκλογῇ γενόμενος εἰς τὸ Χριστὸν εἶναι ἀποδεικνύηται.

[2] See Barn. 14. 5: Ἰησοῦς εἰς τοῦτο ἡτοιμάσθη, ἵνα.... ἡμᾶς λυτρωσάμενος ἐκ τοῦ σκότους διάθηται ἐν ἡμῖν διαθήκην λόγῳ. The same word concerning the Church, l. c. 3. 6. and 5. 7: αὐτὸς ἑαυτῷ τὸν λαὸν τὸν καινὸν ἑτοιμάζων. 14. 6.

[3] "Angel" is a very late designation for Christ (see Justin's Dial.) which maintained itself up to the Nicean controversy, and is expressly claimed for him in Novatian's treatise "de trinit." 11. 25 ff. (the word was taken from Old Testament passages which were applied to Christ). As a rule, however, it is not to be understood as a designation of the nature, but of the office of Christ as such, though the matter was never very clear. There were Christians who used it as a designation of the nature, and from the earliest times we find this idea contradicted. (See the Apoc. Sophoniæ, ed Stern, 1886, IV. fragment, p. 10: "He appointed no Angel to come to us, nor Archangel, nor any power, but he transformed himself into a man that he might come to us for our deliverance." Cf. the remarkable parallel, ep. ad. Diagn. 7. 2:.... οὐ, καθάπερ ἄν τις εἰκάσειεν ἄνθρωπος, ὑπηρέτην τινὰ πέμψας ἢ ἄγγελον ἢ ἄρχοντα ἢ τινα τῶν διεπόντων τὰ ἐπίγεια ἢ τινα τῶν πεπιστευμένων τὰς ἐν οὐρανοῖς διοικήσεις, ἀλλ' αὐτὸν τὸν τεχνίτην καὶ δημιουργὸν τῶν ὅλων, κ.τ.λ.) Yet it never got the length of a great controversy, and as the Logos doctrine gradually made way, the designation "Angel" became harmless and then vanished.

[4] Παῖς (after Isaiah): this designation, frequently united with Ἰησοῦς and with the adjectives ἅγιος and ἠγαπημένος (see Barn. 3. 6: 4. 3: 4. 8: Valent. ap. Clem. Alex., Strom. VI. 6. 52, and the Ascensio Isaiæ), seems to have been at the beginning a usual one. It sprang undoubtedly from the Messianic circle of ideas, and at its basis lies the idea of election. It is very interesting to observe how it was gradually put into the background and finally abolished. It was kept longest in the liturgical prayers: see 1 Clem. 59. 2; Barn. 61: 9. 2; Acts iii. 13. 26; iv. 27. 30; Didache, 9. 2. 3; Mart. Polyc. 14. 20; Act. Pauli et Theclæ, 17. 24;

the living and the dead, [1] etc., expression is given to ideas about Jesus, in the Gentile Christian communities, which are borrowed from the thought that he is the Christ called of God and entrusted with an office. [2] Besides, there was a very old designation handed down from the circle of the disciples, and specially intelligible to Gentile Christians, though not frequent and gradually disappearing, viz., "the Master". [3]

3. But the earliest tradition not only spoke of Jesus as κύριος, σωτήρ, and διδάσκαλος, but as "ὁ υἱὸς τοῦ θεοῦ", and this name was firmly adhered to in the Gentile Christian communities. [4] It followed immediately from this that Jesus belongs to the sphere of God, and that, as is said in the earliest preaching known to us, [5] one must think of him "ὡς περὶ θεοῦ".

Sibyl. I. v. 324, 331, 364; Diogn. 8, 9, 10: ὁ ἀγαπητὸς παῖς, 9. 1; also Ep. Orig. ad Afric. init; Clem. Strom. VII. I. 4: ὁ μονογενὴς παῖς, and my note on Barn. 6. 1. In the Didache (9. 2) Jesus as well as David is in one statement called "Servant of God." Barnabas, who calls Christ the "Beloved," uses the same expression for the Church (4. 1. 9); see also Ignat. ad Smyrn. inscr.

[1] See the old Roman Symbol and Acts X. 42; 2 Tim. IV. 1; Barn. 7. 2; Polyc. Ep. 2. 1; 2 Clem. 2. 1; Hegesipp. in Euseb., H. E. III. 20 6: Justin Dial. 118.

[2] There could of course be no doubt that Christ meant the "anointed" (even Aristides Apol. 2 fin., if Nestle's correction is right, Justin's Apol. I. 4 and similar passages do not justify doubt on that point). But the meaning and the effect of this anointing was very obscure. Justin says (Apol. II. 6): Χριστὸς μὲν κατὰ τὸ κεχρῖσθαι καὶ κοσμῆσαι τα πάντα δι' αὐτοῦ τὸν θεὸν λέγεται, and therefore (see Dial. 76 fin.) finds in this designation an expression of the cosmic significance of Christ.

[3] See the Apologists Apost. K. O. (Texte v. Unters. II. 5. p. 25), προορῶντας τοὺς λόγους τοῦ διδασκάλου ἡμῶν, ibid., p. 28: ὅτε ἤτησεν ὁ διδάσκαλος τὸν ἄρτον, ibid. p. 30: προέλεγεν, ὅτε ἐδίδασκεν. Apost. Constit. (original writing) III. 6: αὐτὸς ὁ διδάσκαλος ἡμῶν καὶ κύριος. III. 7: ὁ κύριος καὶ διδάσκαλος ἡμῶν εἶπεν. III. 19: III. 20: V. 12: I Clem. 13. 1 .... τῶν λόγων τοῦ κύριου Ἰησοῦ, οὓς ἐλάλησεν διδάσκων. Polyc. Ep. 2: μνημονεύοντες ὧν εἶπεν ὁ κυρίος διδάσκων. Ptolem. ad Floram. 5: ἡ διδασκαλια τοῦ σωτῆρος.

[4] The baptismal formula, which had been naturalised everywhere in the communities at this period, preserved it above all. The addition of ίδιος, πρωτότοκος is worthy of notice. Μονογενής (= the only begotten and also the beloved) is not common; it is found only in John, in Justin, in the Symbol of the Romish Church, and in Mart. Polyc. (Diogn. 10. 3).

[5] The so-called second Epistle of Clement begins with the words: Ἀδελφοί, οὕτως δεῖ ἡμᾶς φρονεῖν περὶ Ἰησοῦ, ὡς περὶ θεοῦ, ὡς περὶ κριτοῦ ζώντων καὶ νεκρῶν, (this order in which the Judge appears as the higher is also found in Barn. 7. 2), καὶ οὐ δεῖ ἡμᾶς μικρὰ φρονεῖν περὶ τῆς σωτηρίας ἡμῶν· ἐν τῷ γὰρ φρονεῖν ἡμᾶς μικρὰ περὶ αὐτοῦ, μικρὰ καὶ ἐλπίζομεν λαβεῖν. This argumentation (see also the following verses up to II. 7) is very instructive; for it shews the grounds on which

This formula describes in a classic manner the indirect "theologia Christi" which we find unanimously expressed in all witnesses of the earliest epoch. [1] We must think about Christ as we think about God, because, on the one hand, God had exalted him, and committed to him as Lord, judgment over

the φρονεῖν περὶ αὐτοῦ ὡς περὶ θεοῦ was based. H. Schultz, (L. v. d. Gottheit Christi, p. 25 f.) very correctly remarks: "In the second Epistle of Clement, and in the Shepherd, the Christological interest of the writer ends ' in obtaining the assurance, through faith in Christ as the world-ruling King and Judge, that the community of Christ will receive a glory corresponding to its moral and ascetic works.

[1] Pliny in his celebrated letter (96), speaks of a "Carmen dicere Christo quasi deo" on the part of the Christians. Hermas has no doubt that the Chosen Servant, after finishing his work, will be adopted as God's Son, and therefore has been destined from the beginning, εἰς ἐξουσίαν μεγάλην καὶ κυριότητα (Sim. V. 6. 1). But that simply means that he is now in a Divine sphere, and that one must think of him as of God. But there was no unanimity beyond that. The formula says nothing about the nature or constitution of Jesus. It might indeed appear from Justin's dialogue that the direct designation of Jesus as θεός (not as ὁ θεός) was common in the communities; but not only are there some passages in Justin himself to be urged against this, but also the testimony of other writers. Θεός, even without the article, was in no case a usual designation for Jesus. On the contrary, it was always quite definite occasions which led them to speak of Christ as of a God. In the first place there were Old Testament passages such as Ps. XLV. 8: CX. 1 f., etc., which, as soon as they were interpreted in relation to Christ, led to his getting the predicate θεός. These passages, with many others taken from the Old Testament, were used in this way by Justin. Yet it is very well worth noting, that the author of the Epistle of Barnabas avoided this expression, in a passage which must have suggested it. (12, 10, 11 on Ps. CX. 4.) The author of the Didache calls him "ὁ θεὸς Δάβιδ" on the basis of the above psalm. It is manifestly therefore in liturgical formulæ of exalted paradox, or living utterances of religious feeling that Christ is called God. See Ignat. ad Rom. 6. 3; ἐπιτρέψατέ μοι μιμητὴν εἶναι τοῦ παθους τοῦ θεοῦ μου (the μου here should be observed); ad Eph. 1. 1: ἀναζωπυρήσαντες ἐν αἵματι θεοῦ: Tatian Orat. 13: διάκονος τοῦ πεπονθότος θεοῦ. As to the celebrated passage 1 Clem. ad Cor. 2, 10: τὰ παθήματα αὐτοῦ, (the αὐτοῦ refers to θεός) we may perhaps observe that that ὁ θεὸς stands far apart. However, such a consideration is hardly in place. The passages just adduced shew that precisely the union of suffering (blood, death) with the concept "God" —and only this union—must have been in Christendom from a very early period; see Acts XX. 28 ... τὴν ἐκκλησίαν τοῦ θεοῦ ἣν περιεποιήσατο διὰ τοῦ αἵματος τοῦ ἰδίου, and from a later period, Melito, Fragm. (in Routh Rel. Sacra I. 122): ὁ θεὸς πέπονθεν ὑπὸ δεξιᾶς Ἰσραηλιτίδος; Anonym. ap. Euseb. H. E. V. 28. 11; ὁ εὔσπλαγχνος θεὸς καὶ κυριός ἡμῶν Ἰησοῦς Χριστὸς οὐκ ἐβούλετο ἀπολέσθαι μάρτυρα τῶν ἰδίων παθημάτων; Test. XII. Patriarch. (Levi 4): ἐπὶ τῷ πάθει τοῦ ὑψίστου; Tertull. de carne 5; "passiones dei," ad Uxor II. 3: "sanguine dei." Tertullian also speaks frequently of the crucifying of God, the flesh of God, the death of God. (See Lightfoot, Clem. of Rome, p. 400 sq.) These formulæ were first subjected to examina-

the living and the dead, and because, on the other hand, he
has brought the knowledge of the truth, called sinful men,
delivered them from the dominion of demons, and hath led,
or will lead them, out of the night of death and corruption
to eternal life. Jesus Christ is "our faith", "our hope", "our

tion in the Patripassian controversy. They were rejected by Athanasius, for example,
in the fourth century (cf. Apollin. II. 13. 14. Opp. I. p. 758); πῶς οὖν γεγράφατε
ὅτι θεός ὁ διὰ σάρκος παθὼν καὶ ἀναστάς, ... οὐδαμοῦ δὲ αἷμα θεοῦ δίχα σαρκὸς
παραδεδώκασιν αἱ γραφαὶ ἢ θεὸν διὰ σαρκὸς παθόντα καὶ ἀναστάντα. They continued in use in the west and became of the utmost significance in the christological
controversies of the fifth century. It is not quite certain whether there is a
"theologia Christi" in such passages as Tit. II. 13 : 2 Pet. I. 1 (see the controversies on Rom. IX. 5). Finally, θεός and Christus were often interchanged in
religious discourse (see above). In the so-called second Epistle of Clement (c. 1. 4)
the dispensing of light, knowledge, is traced back to Christ. It is said of him
that, like a Father, he has called us children, he has delivered us, he has called us
into existence out of non-existence, and in this God himself is not thought of. Indeed
he is called (2. 2. 3) the hearer of prayer and controller of history; but immediately
thereon a saying of the Lord is introduced as a saying of God (Matt. IX. 13). On
the contrary, Isaiah XXIX. 13, is quoted 3. 5) as a declaration of Jesus, and again
(13. 4) a saying of the Lord with the formula: λέγει ὁ θεός. It is Christ who pitied
us (3. 1 : 16. 2); he is described simply as the Lord who hath called and redeemed
us (5. 1 : 8. 2 : 9. 5 : etc.). Not only is there frequent mention of the ἐντολαι (ἐντάλματα)
of Christ, but 6, 7 (see 14. 1) speak directly of a ποιεῖν τὸ θέλημα τοῦ Χριστοῦ.
Above all, in the entire first division (up to 9. 5) the religious situation is for the
most part treated as if it were something essentially between the believer and Christ.
On the other hand, (10. 1) the Father is he who calls (see also 16. 1), who brings
salvation (9. 7), who accepts us as sons (9. 10 : 16. 1); he has given us promises
(11. 1. 6. 7); we expect his kingdom, nay, the day of his appearing (12. 1 f : 6. 9 :
9. 6 : 11. 7 : 12. 1). He will judge the world, etc.; while in 17. 4 we read of
the day of Christ's appearing, of his kingdom and of his function of Judge, etc.
Where the preacher treats of the relation of the community to God, where he
describes the religious situation according to its establishment or its consummation,
where he desires to rule the religious and moral conduct, he introduces, without
any apparent distinction, now God himself, and now Christ. But this religious
view, in which acts of God coincide with acts of Christ, did not, as will be shewn
later on, influence the theological speculations of the preacher. We have also to
observe that the interchanging of God and Christ is not always an expression of
the high dignity of Christ, but, on the contrary, frequently proves that the personal
significance of Christ is misunderstood, and that he is regarded only as the dependent
revealer of God. All this shews that there cannot have been many passages in
the earliest literature where Christ was roundly designated θεός. It is one thing
to speak of the blood (death, suffering) of God, and to describe the gifts of salvation brought by Christ as gifts of God, and another thing to set up the proposition
that Christ is a God (or God). When, from the end of the second century, one
began to look about in the earlier writings for passages ἐν οἷς θεολογεῖται ὁ χριστός,
because the matter had become a subject of controversy, one could, besides the

life", and in this sense "our God". The religious assurance that he is this, for we find no wavering on this point, is the root of the "theologia Christi"; but we must also remember that the formula "θεός" was inserted beside "κύριος," that the "dominus ac deus" was very common at that time, [1] and that a Saviour (σωτήρ) could only be represented somehow as

Old Testament, point only to the writings of authors from the time of Justin, (to apologists and controversialists) as well as to Psalms and odes (see the Anonymn. in Euseb. H. E. V. 28. 4-6). In the following passages of the Ignatian Epistles "θεός" appears as a designation of Christ; he is called ὁ θεὸς ἡμῶν in Ephes. inscript ; Rom. inscr. bis 3. 2; Polyc. 8. 3; Eph. I. 1, αἵμα θεοῦ; Rom. 6. 3, τὸ πάθος τοῦ θεοῦ μου; Eph. 7. 2, ἐν σαρκὶ γενόμενος θεός, in another reading, ἐν ἀνθρώπω θεός, Smyrn. I. 1., 'I. Χρ. ὁ θεός ὁ οὕτως ὑμᾶς σοφίσας. The latter passage, in which the relative clause must he closely united with "θεός," seems to form the transition to the three passages (Trall. 7. 1; Smyrn. 6. 1; 10. 1), in which Jesus is called θεός without addition. But these passages are critically suspicious, see Lightfoot *in loco*. In the same way the "deus Jesus Christus" in Polyc. Ep. 12. 2, is suspicious, and indeed in both parts of the verse. In the first, all Latin codd. have "dei filius," and in the Greek codd. of the Epistle, Christ is nowhere called θεός. We have a keen polemic against the designation of Christ as θεός in Clem. Rom. Homil. XVI. 15 sq.; Ὁ Πέτρος ἀπεκρίθη· ὁ κύριος ἡμῶν οὔτε θεοὺς εἶναι ἐφθέγξατο παρὰ τὸν κτίσαντα τὰ πάντα οὔτε ἑαυτὸν θεὸν εἶναι ἀνηγόρευσεν, υἱὸν δὲ θεοῦ τοῦ τὰ πάντα διακοσμήσαντος τὸν εἰπόντα αὐτὸν εὐλόγως ἐμακάρισεν καὶ ὁ Σίμων ἀπεκρίνατο· οὐ δοκεῖ σοι οὖν τὸν ἀπὸ θεοῦ θεὸν εἶναι; καὶ ὁ Πέτρος ἔφη· πῶς τοῦτο εἶναι δύναται, φράσον ἡμῖν, τοῦτο γὰρ ἡμεῖς εἰπεῖν σοι οὐ δυνάμεθα ὅτι μὴ ἠκούσαμεν παρ' αὐτοῦ.

[1] On the further use of the word θεός in antiquity, see above, § 8, p. 120 f.; the formula "θεός ἐκ θεοῦ" for Augustus, even 24 years before Christ's birth; on the formula "dominus ac deus," see John XX. 28; the interchange of these concepts in many passages beside one another in the anonymous writer (Euseb. H. E. V. 28. 11.) Domitian first allowed himself to be called "dominus ac deus." Tertullian Apol. 10. 11, is very instructive as to the general situation in the second century. Here are brought forward the different causes which then moved men, the cultured and the uncultured, to give to this or that personality the predicate of Divinity. In the third century the designation of "domus ac deus noster" for Christ was very common, especially in the west. (See Cyprian, Pseudo-Cyprian, Novatian; in the Latin Martyrology a Greek ὁ κύριος is also frequently so translated.) But only at this time had the designation come to be in actual use even for the Emperor. It seems at first sight to follow from the statements of Celsus (in Orig. c. Cels. III. 22-43) that this Greek had and required a very strict conception of the Godhead; but his whole work shews how little that was really the case. The reference to these facts of the history of the time is not made with the view of discovering the "theologia Christi" itself in its ultimate roots—these roots lie elsewhere, in the person of Christ and Christian experience; but that this experience, before any technical reflection, had so easily and so surely substituted the new formula instead of the idea of Messiah, can hardly be explained without reference to the general religious ideas of the time.

a Divine being.[1] Yet Christ never was, as "θεός", placed
on an equality with the Father,[2]—monotheism guarded against
that. Whether he was intentionally and deliberately identified
with Him the following paragraph will shew.

4. The common confession did not go beyond the statements
that Jesus is the Lord, the Saviour, the Son of God, that
one must think of him as of God, that dwelling now with
God in heaven, he is to be adored as προστάτης καὶ βοηθὸς τῆς
ἀσθενείας, and as ἀρχιερεὺς τῶν προσφορῶν ἡμῶν [as guardian and
helper of the weak and as High Priest of our oblations], to
be feared as the future Judge, to be esteemed most highly
as the bestower of immortality, that he is our hope and our
faith. There are found rather, on the basis of that confession,
very diverse conceptions of the Person, that is, of the nature
of Jesus, beside each other,[3] which collectively exhibit a
certain analogy with the Greek theologies, the naive and the
philosophic.[4] There was as yet no such thing here as ecclesiastical "doctrines" in the strict sense of the word, but rather
conceptions more or less fluid, which were not seldom fashi-

---

[1] The combination of θεὸς and σωτήρ in the Pastoral Epistles is very important.
The two passages in the New Testament in which perhaps a direct "theologia
Christi" may be recognised, contain likewise the concept σωτήρ; see Tit. II. 13;
προσδεχόμενοι τὴν μακαρίαν ἐλπίδα καὶ ἐπιφάνειαν τῆς δόξης τοῦ μεγάλου θεοῦ καὶ
σωτῆρος ἡμῶν Χριστοῦ ᾿Ιησοῦ (cf. Abbot, Journal of the Society of Bibl. Lit., and
Exeg. 1881. June. p. 3 sq.): 2 Pet. I. 1 : ἐν δικαιοσυνῃ τοῦ θεοῦ ἡμῶν καὶ σωτῆρος.
᾿Ι. Χρ. In both cases the ἡμῶν should be specially noted. Besides, θεὸς σωτήρ is
also an ancient formula.

[2] A very ancient formula ran "θεὸς καὶ θεὸς υἱός," see Cels. ap. Orig II. 30;
Justin, frequently: Alterc. Sim. et Theoph. 4, etc. The formula is equivalent to
θεὸς μονογενής (see Joh. I. 18).

[3] Such conceptions are found side by side in the same writer. See, for example,
the second Epistle of Clement, and even the first.

[4] See § 6, p. 120. The idea of a θεοποίησις was as common as that of the
appearances of the gods. In wide circles, however, philosophy had long ago
naturalised the idea of the λόγος τοῦ θεοῦ. But now there is no mistaking a new
element everywhere. In the case of the Christologies which include a kind of
θεοποίησις, it is found in the fact that the deified Jesus was to be recognised not
as a Demigod or Hero, but as Lord of the world, equal in power and honour to
the Deity. In the case of those Christologies which start with Christ as the
heavenly spiritual being, it is found in the belief in an actual incarnation. These
two articles, as was to be expected, presented difficulties to the Gentile Christians
and the latter more than the former.

oned *ad hoc*[1] These may be reduced collectively to two.[2]
Jesus was either regarded as the man whom God hath chosen,
in whom the Deity or the Spirit of God dwelt, and who,
after being tested, was adopted by God and invested with
dominion, (Adoptian Christology);[3] or Jesus was regarded as
a heavenly spiritual being (the highest after God) who took

[1] This is usually overlooked. Christological doctrinal conceptions are frequently
constructed by a combination of particular passages, the nature of which does not
permit of combination. But the fact that there was no universally recognised
theory about the nature of Jesus till beyond the middle of the second century,
should not lead us to suppose that the different theories were anywhere declared
to be of equal value, etc., therefore more or less equally valid; on the contrary,
everyone, so far as he had a theory at all, included his own in the revealed truth.
That they had not yet come into conflict is accounted for, on the one hand, by
the fact that the different theories ran up into like formulæ, and could even frequently be directly carried over into one another; and on the other hand, by the
fact that their representatives appealed to the same authorities. But we must,
above all, remember that conflict could only arise after the enthusiastic element,
which also had a share in the formation of Christology, had been suppressed,
and problems were felt to be such, that is, after the struggle with Gnosticism, or
even during that struggle.

[2] Both were clearly in existence in the Apostolic age.

[3] Only one work has been preserved entire which gives clear expression to the
Adoptian Christology, viz., the Shepherd of Hermas (see Sim. V. and IX. 1. 12).
According to it, the Holy Spirit—it is not certain whether he is identified with
the chief Archangel—is regarded as the pre-existent Son of God, who is older than
creation, nay, was God's counsellor at creation. The Redeemer is the virtuous man
(σάρξ) chosen by God, with whom that Spirit of God was united. As he did not
defile the Spirit, but kept him constantly as his companion, and carried out the
work to which the Deity had called him, nay, did more than he was commanded,
he was in virtue of a Divine decree adopted as a son and exalted to μεγάλη ἐξουσία
καὶ κυριότης. That this Christology is set forth in a book which enjoyed the
highest honour and sprang from the Romish community, is of great significance.
The representatives of this Christology, who in the third century were declared
to be heretics, expressly maintained that it was at one time the ruling Christology
at Rome and had been handed down by the Apostles. (Anonym. H. E. V. 28. 3,
concerning the Artemonites: φασὶ τοὺς μὲν προτέρους ἅπαντας καὶ αὐτοὺς τοὺς
ἀποστόλους παρειληφέναι τε καὶ δεδιδαχέναι ταῦτα, ἃ νῦν οὗτοι λέγουσι, καὶ τετη-
ρῆσθαι τὴν ἀλήθειαν τοῦ κηρύγματος μέχρι τῶν χρόνων τοῦ Βίκτορος ... ἀπὸ δὲ τοῦ
διαδόχου αὐτοῦ Ζεφυρίνου παρακεχαράχθαι τὴν ἀλήθειαν.) This assertion, though
exaggerated, is not incredible after what we find in Hermas. It cannot, certainly,
be verified by a superficial examination of the literary monuments preserved to
us, but a closer investigation shews that the Adoptian Christology must at one
time have been very widespread, that it continued here and there undisturbed up
to the middle of the third century (see the Christology in the Acta Archelai. 49.
50), and that it continued to exercise great influence even in the fourth and fifth

flesh, and again returned to heaven after the completion of
his work on earth (pneumatic Christology). [1] These two

centuries (see Book II. c. 7). Something similar is found even in some Gnostics,
e.g.. Valentinus himself (see Iren. I. 11. 1: καὶ τὸν Χριστὸν δὲ οὐκ ἀπὸ τῶν ἐν τῷ
πληρώματι αἰώνων προβεβλῆσθαι, ἀλλὰ ὑπὸ τῆς μητρὸς, ἔξω δὲ γενομένης, κατὰ τὴν
γνώμην τῶν κρειττόνων ἀποκεκυῆσθαι μετὰ σκιᾶς τινός. Καὶ τοῦτον μέν, ἅτε ἄρρενα
ὑπάρχοντα, ἀποκόψαντα ὑφ᾽ ἑαυτοῦ τὴν σκιὰν, ἀναδραμεῖν εἰς τὸ πλήρωμα. The
same in the Exc. ex Theodot §§ 22, 23, 32, 33), and the Christology of Basilides
presupposes that of the Adoptians. Here also belongs the conception which traces
back the genealogy of Jesus to Joseph. The way in which Justin (Dialogues 48,
49, 87 ff.) treats the history of the baptism of Jesus, against the objection of Trypho
that a pre-existent Christ would not have needed to be filled with the Spirit of
God, is instructive. It is here evident that Justin deals with objections which were
raised within the communities themselves to the pre-existence of Christ, on the
ground of the account of the baptism In point of fact, this account (it had,
according to very old witnesses, see Resch, Agrapha Christi, p. 307, according to
Justin, for example, Dial. 88, 103, the wording: ἅμα τῷ ἀναβῆναι αὐτὸν ἀπὸ τοῦ
ποταμοῦ τοῦ Ἰορδάνου, τῆς φωνῆς αὐτοῦ λεχθείσης υἱός μου εἶ σύ, ἐγὼ σήμερον
γεγέννηκά σε; see the Cod. D. of Luke. Clem. Alex. etc.) forms the strongest foundation of the Adoptian Christology, and hence it is exceedingly interesting to see
how one compounds with it from the second to the fifth century, an investigation
which deserves a special monograph. But, of course, the edge was taken off the
report by the assumption of the miraculous birth of Jesus from the Holy Spirit, so
that the Adoptians in recognising this, already stood with one foot in the camp
of their opponents. It is now instructive to see here how the history of the baptism, which originally formed the beginning of the proclamation of Jesus' history,
is suppressed in the earliest formulæ, and therefore also in the Romish Symbol,
while the birth from the Holy Spirit is expressly stated. Only in Ignatius (ad
Smyrn. I; cf. ad Eph. 18. 2) is the baptism taken into account in the confession;
but even he has given the event a turn by which it has no longer any significance
for Jesus himself (just as in the case of Justin, who concludes from the *resting*
of the Spirit in his fulness upon Jesus, that there will be no more prophets among
the Jews, spiritual gifts being rather communicated to Christians; compare also the
way in which the baptism of Jesus is treated in John I.). Finally, we must point
out that in the Adoptian Christology the parallel between Jesus and all believers
who have the Spirit and are Sons of God, stands out very clearly. (Cf. Herm. Sim. V.
with Maud. III. V. 1 : X. 2 : most important is Sim. V. 6. 7.) But this was the
very thing that endangered the whole view. Celsus, I. 57, addressing Jesus, asks;
"If thou sayest that every man whom Divine Providence allows to be born (this
is of course a formulation for which Celsus alone is responsible) is a son of God,
what advantage hast thou then over others?" We can see already in the Dialogue
of Justin the approach of the later great controversy, whether Christ is Son of
God κατὰ γνώμην or κατὰ φύσιν, that is, had a pre-existence: "καὶ γὰρ εἰσί τινες,
he says, ἀπὸ τοῦ ὑμετέρου γένους ὁμολογοῦντες αὐτὸν Χριστὸν εἶναι, ἄνθρωπον δὲ ἐξ
ἀνθρώπων γενόμενον ἀποφαινόμενοι, οἷς οὐ συντίθεμαι" (c. 48).

[1] This Christology, which may be traced back to the Pauline, but which can
hardly have its point of departure in Paul alone, is found also in the Epistle to

Christologies which are, strictly speaking, mutually exclusive—
the man who has become a God, and the Divine being who
has appeared in human form—yet came very near each other
when the Spirit of God implanted in the man Jesus was con-

the Hebrews and in the writings of John, including the Apocalypse, and is represented by Barnabas, 1 and 2 Clem., Ignatius, Polycarp, the author of the Pastoral
Epistles, the Authors of Præd. Petri, and the Altercatio Jasonis et Papisci, etc. The
Classic formulation is in 2 Clem. 9. 5: Χριστὸς ὁ κύριος ὁ σώσας ἡμᾶς ὢν μὲν τὸ
πρῶτον πνεῦμα ἐγένετο σὰρξ καὶ οὕτως ἡμᾶς ἐκάλεσεν. According to Barnabas
(5. 3), the pre-existent Christ is παντὸς τοῦ κοσμου κύριος; to him God said, ἀπὸ
καταβολῆς κόσμου, "Let us make man, etc." He is (5. 6) the subject and goal of
all Old Testament revelation. He is οὐχὶ υἱὸς ἀνθρώπου ἀλλ: υἱὸς τοῦ θεοῦ, τυπῶ
δὲ ἐν σαρκὶ φανερωθείς (12. 10); the flesh is merely the veil of the Godhead,
without which man could not have endured the light (5. 10). According to 1
Clement, Christ is τὸ σκῆπτρον τῆς μελαγοσύνης τοῦ θεοῦ (16. 2), who, if he had
wished, could have appeared on earth ἐν κόμπῳ ἀλαζονείας; he is exalted far above
the angels (32), as he is the Son of God (παθήματα τοῦ θεοῦ, 2. 1); he hath
spoken through the Holy Spirit in the Old Testament (22. 1). It is not certain
whether Clement understood Christ under the λόγος μεγαλοσύνης τοῦ θεοῦ (27. 4).
According to 2 Clem., Christ and the Church are heavenly spiritual existences
which have appeared in the last times. Gen. 1. 27 refers to their creation (c. 14;
see my note on the passage: We learn from Origen that a very old Theologoumenon identified Jesus with the ideal of Adam, the Church with that of Eve.
Similar ideas about Christ are found in Gnostic Jewish Christians); one must think
about Christ as about God (I. 1). Ignatius writes (Eph. 7. 2): Εἰς, ἰατρός ἐστιν
σαρκικός τε καὶ πνευματικός, γεννητὸς καὶ ἀγέννητος, ἐν σαρκὶ γενόμενος θεὸς, ἐν
θανάτῳ ζωὴ ἀληθινή, καὶ ἐκ Μαρίας καὶ ἐκ θεοῦ, πρῶτον παθητὸς καὶ τότε ἀπαθής
Ἰησοῦς Χριστὸς ὁ κύριος ἡμῶν. As the human predicates stand here first, it might
appear as though, according to Ignatius, the man Jesus became God (ὁ θεὸς ἡμῶν,
Cf. Eph. inscr.: 18. 2). In point of fact, he regards Jesus as Son of God only
by his birth from the Spirit; but on the other hand, Jesus is ἀφ' ἑνὸς πατρός
προελθών (Magn. 7. 2), is λόγος θεοῦ (Magn. 8. 2), and when Ignatius so often
emphasises the truth of Jesus' history against Docetism (Trall. 9. for example), we
must assume that he shares the thesis with the Gnostics that Jesus is by nature a
spiritual being. But it is well worthy of notice that Ignatius, as distinguished
from Barnabas and Clement, really gives the central place to the historical Jesus
Christ, the Son of God and the Son of Mary, and his work. The like is found
only in Irenæus. The pre-existence of Christ is presupposed by Polycarp. (Ep. 7. 1);
but, like Paul, he strongly emphasises a real exaltation of Christ (2. 1). The
author of Præd. Petri calls Christ the λόγος (Clem. Strom. I. 29, 182). As Ignatius
calls him this also, as the same designation is found in the Gospel, Epistles, and
Apocalypse of John (the latter a Christian adaptation of a Jewish writing), in the
Act. Joh. (see Zahn, Acta Joh. p. 220), finally, as Celsus (II. 31) says quite generally,
"The Christians maintain that the Son of God is at the same time his incarnate
Word," we plainly perceive that this designation for Christ was not first started
by professional philosophers (see the Apologists, for example, Tatian, Orat. 5, and
Melito Apolog. fragm. in the Chron. pasch. p. 483, ed. Dindorf: Χριστὸς ὢν θεοῦ

ceived as the pre-existent Son of God,[1] and when, on the other hand, the title, Son of God, for that pneumatic being was derived only from the miraculous generation in the flesh; yet both these seem to have been the rule.[2] Yet, in spite of all transitional forms, the two Christologies may be clearly distinguished. Characteristic of the one is the development through which Jesus is first to become a Godlike Ruler,[3]

λόγος πρὸ αἰώνων). We do not find in the Johannine writings such a Logos spe-culation as in the Apologists, but the current expression is taken up in order to shew that it has its truth in the appearing of Jesus Christ. The ideas about the existence of a Divine Logos were very widely spread; they were driven out of philosophy into wide circles. The Author of the Alterc. Jas. et Papisci conceived the phrase in Gen. I. I, ἐνάρχῃ, as equivalent to ἐν υἱῷ (χριστῷ) Jerome, Quæst. hebr. in Gen. p. 3; see Tatian Orat. 5: θεὸς ἦν ἐν ἀρχῇ τὴν δὲ ἀρχὴν λόγου δύναμιν παρειλήφαμεν. Ignatius (Eph. 3) also called Christ ἡ γνώμη τοῦ πατρός (Eph. 17: ἡ γνῶσις τοῦ θεοῦ); that is a more fitting expression than λόγος. The subordina-tion of Christ as a heavenly being to the Godhead is seldom or never carefully emphasised, though it frequently comes plainly into prominence. Yet the author of the second Epistle of Clement does not hesitate to place the pre-existent Christ and the pre-existent Church on one level, and to declare of both that God created them (c. 14). The formulæ φανεροῦσθαι ἐν σαρκί, or γίγνεσθαι σάρξ, are characteristic of this Christology. It is worthy of special notice that the latter is found in all those New Testament writers who have put Christianity in contrast with the Old Testament religions, and proclaimed the conquest of that religion by the Christian, viz., Paul, John, and the author of the Epistle to the Hebrews.

[1] Hermas, for example, does this (therefore Link; Christologie des Hermas, and Weizsäcker, Gott. Gel. Anz. 1886, p. 830, declare his Christology to be directly pneumatic): Christ is then identified with this Holy Spirit (see Acta Archel. 50), similarly Ignatius (ad Magn. 15): κεκτημένοι ἀδιάκριτον πνεῦμα, ὅς ἐστιν Ἰησοῦς Χριστός, This formed the transition to Gnostic conceptions on the one hand, to pneumatic Christology on the other. But in Hermas the real substantial thing in Jesus is the σάρξ.

[2] Passages may indeed be found in the earliest Gentile Christian literature in which Jesus is designated Son of God, independently of his human birth and before it (so in Barnabas, against Zahn), but they are not numerous. Ignatius very clearly deduces the predicate "Son" from the birth in the flesh. Zahn, Marcellus, p. 216 ff.

[3] The distinct designation "θεοποίησις" is not found, though that may be an accident. Hermas has the thing itself quite distinctly, (see Epiph. c. Alog. H. 51. 18: νομίζοντες ἀπὸ Μαρίας καὶ δεῦρο Χριστὸν αὐτὸν καλεῖσθαι καὶ υἱὸν θεοῦ, καὶ εἶναι μὲν πρότερον ψιλὸν ἄνθρωπον, κατὰ προκοπὴν δὲ εἰληφέναι τὴν τοῦ υἱοῦ τοῦ θεοῦ προσηγορίαν). The stages of the προκοπή were undoubtedly the birth, baptism and resurrection. Even the adherents of the pneumatic Christology could not at first help recognising that Jesus, through his exaltation, got more than he originally possessed. Yet in their case this conception was bound to become rudimentary, and it really did so.

and connected therewith, the value put on the miraculous event at the baptism; of the other, a naive docetism. [1] For no one as yet thought of affirming two natures in Jesus: [2] the Divine dignity appeared rather, either as a gift, [3] or the human nature (σάρξ) as a veil assumed for a time, or as the metamorphosis of the Spirit. [4] The formula that Jesus

[1] The settlement with Gnosticism prepared a still always uncertain end for this naive Docetism. Apart from Barn 5. 12, where it plainly appears, we have to collect laboriously the evidences of it which have not accidentally either perished or been concealed. In the communities of the second century there was frequently no offence taken at Gnostic docetism (see the Gospel of Peter, Clem. Alex., Adumbrat. in Joh. Ep. I. c. 1. [Zahn, Forsch. z. Gesch. des N. T.-lichen Kanons, III p. 87]; " Fertur ergo in traditionibus, quoniam Johannes ipsum corpus, quod erat extrinsecus, tangens manum suam in profunda misisse et duritiam carnis nullo modo reluctatam esse, sed locum manui præbuisse discipuli." Also Acta Joh. p. 209, ed. Zahn). In spite of all his polemic against "δόκησις" proper, one can still perceive a "moderate docetism" in Clem. Alex., to which indeed certain narratives in the Canonical Gospels could not but lead. The so-called Apocryphal literature (Apocryphal Gospels and Acts of Apostles), lying on the boundary between heretical and common Christianity, and preserved only in scanty fragments and extensive alterations, was, it appears, throughout favourable to Docetism. But the later recensions attest that it was read in wide circles.

[2] Even such a formulation as we find in Paul (e.g., Rom. I. 3 f. κατὰ σάρκα— κατὰ πνεῦμα) does not seem to have been often repeated (yet see 1 Clem. 32. 2). It is of value to Ignatius only, who has before his mind the full Gnostic contrast. But even to him we cannot ascribe any doctrine of two natures: for this requires as its presupposition, the perception that the divinity and humanity are equally essential and important for the personality of the Redeemer Christ. Such insight, however, presupposes a measure and a direction of reflection which the earliest period did not possess. The expression "δύο οὐσίαι Χριστοῦ" first appears in a fragment of Melito, whose genuineness is not, however, generally recognised (see my Texte u. Unters. I. 1. 2. p. 257). Even the definite expression for Christ, θεὸς ὢν ὁμοῦ τε καὶ ἄνθρωπος, was fixed only in consequence of the Gnostic controversy.

[3] Hermas (Sim. V. 6. 7) describes the exaltation of Jesus thus: ἵνα καὶ ἡ σάρξ αὕτη, δουλεύσασα τῷ πνεύματι ἀμέμπτως, σχῇ τόπον τινὰ κατασκηνώσεως, καὶ μὴ δόξῃ τὸν μισθὸν τῆς δουλείας αὐτῆς ἀπολωλεκέναι. The point in question is a reward of grace which consists in a position of rank (see Sim. V. 6. 1). The same thing is manifest from the statements of the later Adoptians. (Cf. the teaching of Paul Samosata.)

[4] Barnabas, e.g., conceives it as a veil (5. 10: εἰ γὰρ μὴ ἦλθεν εν σαρκί, οὐδ' ἄν πως οἱ ἄνθρωποι ἐσώθησαν βλέποντες αὐτόν· ὅτε τὸν μέλλοντα μὴ εἶναι ἥλιον ἐμβλέποντες οὐκ ἰσχύσουσιν εἰς τὰς ἀκτῖνας αὐτοῦ ἀντοφθαλμῆσαι). The formulation of the Christian idea in Celsus is instructive (c. Cels. VI. 69): "Since God is great and not easily accessible to the view, he put his spirit in a body which is like our own, and sent it down in order that we might be instructed by it." To this conception corresponds the formula: ἔρχεσθαι (φανεροῦσθαι) εν σαρκί (Barnabas,

was a mere man (ψιλὸς ἄνθρωπος), was undoubtedly always and from the first regarded as offensive.¹ But the converse formulæ, which identified the person of Jesus in its essence with the Godhead itself, do not seem to have been rejected with the same decision.² Yet such formulæ may have been

---

frequently; Polyc. Ep. 7. 1). But some kind of transformation must also have been thought of (see 2 Clem. 9. 5, and Celsus IV. 18: "Either God, as these suppose, is really transformed into a mortal body . . ." Apoc. Sophon. ed Stern. 4 fragm. p. 10; "He has transformed himself into a man who comes to us to redeem us"). This conception might grow out of the formula σάρξ ἐγένετο (Ignat. ad Eph. 7. 2 is of special importance here). One is almost throughout here satisfied with the σάρξ of Christ, that is the ἀλήθεια τῆς σαρκός, against the Heretics (so Ignatius, who was already antignostic in his attitude). There is very seldom any mention of the humanity of Jesus. Barnabas (12), the author of the Didache (c. 10. 6. See my note on the passage), and Tatian questioned the Davidic Sonship of Jesus, which was strongly emphasised by Ignatius; nay, Barnabas even expressly rejects the designation "Son of Man" (12. 10; ἴδε πάλιν Ἰησοῦς, οὐχὶ υἱὸς ἀνθρώπου ἀλλὰ υἱὸς τοῦ θεοῦ, τύπῳ δὲ ἐν σαρκὶ φανερωθείς). A docetic thought, however, lies in the assertion that the spiritual being Christ only assumed human flesh, however, much the reality of the flesh may be emphasised. The passage 1 Clem. 49. 6, is quite unique: τὸ αἷμα αὐτοῦ ἔδωκεν ὑπὲρ ἡμῶν Ἰησοῦς Χριστὸς . . . καὶ τὴν σάρκα ὑπὲρ τῆς σαρκὸς ἡμῶν καὶ τὴν ψυχὴν ὑπὲρ τῶν ψυχῶν ἡμῶν. One would fain believe this an interpolation; the same idea is first found in Irenæus. (V. 1. 1).

¹ Even Hermas does not speak of Jesus as ἄνθρωπος (see Link). This designation was used by the representatives of the Adoptian Christology only after they had expressed their doctrine antithetically and developed it to a theory, and always with a certain reservation. The "ἄνθρωπος Χριστὸς Ἰησοῦς" in 1 Tim. II. 5 is used in a special sense. The expression ἄνθρωπος for Christ appears twice in the Ignatian Epistles (the third passage Smyrn. 4. 2: αὐτοῦ με ἐνδυναμοῦντος τοῦ τελείου ἀνθρωπου γενομένου, apart from the γενομένου, is critically suspicious, as well as the fourth, Eph. 7, 2; see above), in both passages, however, in connections which seem to modify the humanity; see Eph. 20. 1: οἰκονομία εἰς τὸν καινὸν ἄνθρωπον Ἰησοῦν Χριστόν; Eph. 20. 2: τῷ υἱῷ ἀνθρώπου καὶ υἱῷ θεοῦ.

² See above p. 185, note; p. 189, note. We have no sure evidence that the later so-called Modalism (Monarchianism) had representatives before the last third of the second century; yet the polemic of Justin, Dial. 128. seems to favour the idea, (the passage already presupposes controversies about the personal independence of the pre-existent pneumatic being of Christ beside God; but one need not necessarily think of such controversies within the communities; Jewish notions might be meant, and this, according to Apol. 1. 63, is the more probable). The judgment is therefore so difficult, because there were numerous formulæ in practical use which could be so understood, as if Christ was to be completely identified with the Godhead itself (see Ignat. ad Eph. 7. 2, besides Melito in Otto. Corp. Apol. IX. p. 419, and Noëtus in the Philos. IX. 10, p. 448). These formulæ may, in point of fact, have been so understood, here and there, by the rude and uncultivated. The strongest again is presented in writings whose authority was always doubtful: see

very rare, and even objects of suspicion, in the leading ecclesiastical circles, at least until after the middle of the second
century we can point to them only in documents which hardly
found approbation in wide circles. The assumption of the
existence of at least one heavenly and eternal spiritual being
beside God was plainly demanded by the Old Testament
writings, as they were understood; so that even those whose
Christology did not require them to reflect on that heavenly
being were forced to recognise it.[1]   The pneumatic Christo-

---

the Gospel of the Egyptians (Epiph. H. 62. 2), in which must have stood a statement somewhat to this effect: τὸν αὐτὸν εἶναι πατέρα, τὸν αὐτὸν εἶναι υἱὸν, τὸν
αὐτὸν εἶναι ἅγιον πνεῦμα, and the Acta Joh. (ed. Zahn, p. 220 f., 240 f.: ὁ
ἀγαθὸς ἡμῶν θεὸς ὁ εὔσπλαγχνος, ὁ ἐλεήμων, ὁ ἅγιος, ὁ καθαρός, ὁ ἀμίαντος, ὁ μόνος,
ὁ εἷς, ὁ ἀμετάβλητος, ὁ εἰλικρινής, ὁ ἄδολος, ὁ μὴ ὀργιζόμενος, ὁ πᾶσης ἡμῖν λεγο-
μένης ἢ νοουμένης προσηγορίας ἀνώτερος καὶ ὑψηλότερος ἡμῶν θεὸς 'Ιησοῦς). In the
Act. Joh. are found also prayers with the address θεὲ 'Ιησοῦ Χριστέ (pp. 242, 247).
Even Marcion and in part the Montanists—both bear witness to old traditions—put
no value on the distinction between God and Christ; cf. the Apoc. Sophon. A
witness to a naive Modalism is found also in the Acta Pionii 9: "Quem deum
colis? Respondit: Christum. Polemon (judex): Quid ergo? iste alter est? [the
co-defendant Christians had immediately before confessed God the Creator]. Respondit: Non; sed ipse quem et ipsi paullo ante confessi sunt; cf. c. 16. Yet a reasoned
Modalism may perhaps be assumed here. See also the Martyr Acts; e.g., Acta
Petri, Andræ, Pauli et Dionysiæ 1 (Ruinart, p. 205): ἡμεῖς οἱ Χριστὸν τὸν βασιλέα
ἔχομεν, ὅτι ἀληθινὸς θεός ἐστιν καὶ ποιητὴς οὐρανοῦ καὶ γῆς καὶ θαλάσσης. "Oportet
me magis deo vivo et vero, regi sæculorum omnium Christo, sacrificium offerre."
Act. Nicephor. 3 (p. 285). I take no note of the Testament of the twelve Patriarchs,
out of which one can, of course, beautifully verify the strict Modalistic, and even the
Adoptian Christology. But the Testamenta are not a primitive or Jewish Christian
writing which Gentile Christians have revised, but a Jewish writing christianised
at the end of the second century by a Catholic of Modalistic views. But he has
given us a very imperfect work, the Christology of which exhibits many contradictions. It is instructive to find Modalism in the theology of the Simonians, which
was partly formed according to Christian ideas; see Irenæus I. 23, 1: "hic igitur
a multis quasi deus glorificatus est, et docuit semetipsum esse qui inter Judæos
quidem quasi filius apparuerit, in Samaria autem quasi pater descenderit in reliquis
vero gentibus quasi Spiritus Sanctus adventaverit.

[1] That is a very important fact which clearly follows from the Shepherd.
Even the later school of the Adoptians in Rome, and the later Adoptians in
general, were forced to assume a divine hypostasis beside the Godhead, which of
course sensibly threatened their Christology. The adherents of the pneumatic
Christology partly made a definite distinction between the pre-existent Christ and
the Holy Spirit (see, e.g., 1 Clem. 22. 1), and partly made use of formulæ from
which one could infer an identity of the two. The conceptions about the Holy
Spirit were still quite fluctuating: whether he is a power of God, or personal;

logy accordingly meets us wherever there is an earnest occupation with the Old Testament, and wherever faith in Christ
as the perfect revealer of God occupies the foreground, therefore not in Hermas, but certainly in Barnabas, Clement, etc.
The future belonged to this Christology because the current
exposition of the Old Testament seemed directly to require
it, because it alone permitted the close connection between
creation and redemption, because it furnished the proof that
the world and religion rest upon the same Divine basis,
because it was represented in the most valuable writings of
the early period of Christianity, and finally, because it had
room for the speculations about the Logos. On the other
hand, no direct and natural relation to the world and to
universal history could be given to the Adoptian Christology,
which was originally determined eschatologically. If such a
relation, however, were added to it, there resulted formulæ
such as that of two Sons of God, one natural and eternal,
and one adopted, which corresponded neither to the letter of
the Holy Scriptures, nor to the Christian preaching. Moreover, the revelations of God in the Old Testament made by
Theophanies must have seemed, because of this their form,
much more exalted than the revelations made through a
man raised to power and glory, which Jesus constantly seemed

whether he is identical with the pre-existent Christ, or is to be distinguished from
him; whether he is the servant of Christ (Tatian Orat. 13); whether he is only a
gift of God to believers, or the eternal Son of God, was quite uncertain. Hermas
assumed the latter, and even Origen (de princip. præf. c. 4) acknowledges that it
is not yet decided whether or not the Holy Spirit is likewise to be regarded as
God's Son. The baptismal formula prevented the identification of the Holy Spirit
with the pre-existent Christ, which so readily suggested itself. But so far as
Christ was regarded as a πνεῦμα, his further demarcation from the angel powers
was quite uncertain, as the Shepherd of Hermas proves (though see 1 Clem. 36).
For even Justin, in a passage, no doubt, in which his sole purpose was to shew
that the Christians were not ἄθεοι, could venture to thrust in between God, the
Son and the Spirit, the good angels as beings who were worshipped and adored
by the Christians (Apol 1. 6 [if the text be genuine and not an interpolation];
see also the Suppl. of Athanagoras). Justin, and certainly most of those who
accepted a pre-existence of Christ, conceived of it as a real pre-existence. Justin
was quite well acquainted with the controversy about the independent quality of
the power which proceeded from God. To him it is not merely, " Sensus, motus,
affectus dei," but a " personalis substantia" (Dial. 128).

to be in the Adoptian Christology. Nay, even the mysterious personality of Melchisedec, without father or mother, might appear more impressive than the Chosen Servant, Jesus, who was born of Mary, to a mode of thought which, in order to make no mistake, desired to verify the Divine by outer marks. The Adoptian Christology, that is the Christology which is most in keeping with the self-witness of Jesus (the Son as the chosen Servant of God), is here shewn to be unable to assure to the Gentile Christians those conceptions of Christianity which they regarded as of highest value. It proved itself insufficient when confronted by any reflection on the relation of religion to the cosmos, to humanity, and to its history. It might, perhaps, still have seemed doubtful about the middle of the second century as to which of the two opposing formulæ, "Jesus is a man exalted to a Godlike dignity" and "Jesus is a divine spiritual being incarnate", would succeed in the Church. But one only needs to read the pieces of writing which represent the latter thesis, and to compare them, say, with the Shepherd of Hermas, in order to see to which view the future must belong. In saying this, however, we are anticipating; for the Christological reflections were not yet vigorous enough to overcome enthusiasm and the expectation of the speedy end of all things; and the mighty practical tendency of the new religion to a holy life did not allow any theory to become the central object of attention. But, still, it is necessary to refer here to the controversies which broke out at a later period; for the pneumatic Christology forms an essential article which cannot be dispensed with, in the expositions of Barnabas, Clement and Ignatius; and Justin shews that he cannot conceive of a Christianity without the belief in a real pre-existence of Christ. On the other hand, the liturgical formulæ, the prayers, etc., which have been preserved, scarcely ever take notice of the pre-existence of Christ; they either comprise statements which are borrowed from the Adoptian Christology, or they testify in an unreflective way to the Dominion and Deity of Christ.

5. The ideas of Christ's work which were influential in the communities—Christ as Teacher: creation of knowledge, set-

ting up of the new law; Christ as Saviour: creation of life,
overcoming of the demons, forgiveness of sins committed in the
time of error,—were by some, in conformity with Apostolic
tradition and following the Pauline Epistles, positively connected with the death and resurrection of Christ, while others
maintained them without any connection with these events.
But one nowhere finds independent thorough reflections on
the connection of Christ's saving work with the facts proclaimed in the preaching, above all, with the death on the cross
and the resurrection as presented by Paul. The reason of
this undoubtedly is that in the conception of the work of
salvation, the procuring of forgiveness fell into the background,
as this could only be connected by means of the notion of
sacrifice, with a definite act of Jesus, viz., with the surrender
of his life. Consequently, the facts of the destiny of Jesus
combined in the preaching formed only for the religious
fancy, not for reflection, the basis of the conception of the
work of Christ, and were therefore by many writers, Hermas,
for example, taken no notice of. Yet the idea of suffering
freely accepted, of the cross and of the blood of Christ, operated in wide circles as a holy mystery in which the deepest
wisdom and power of the Gospel must somehow lie concealed. [1] The peculiarity and uniqueness of the work of the
historical Christ seemed, however, to be prejudiced by the
assumption that Christ, essentially as the same person, was
already in the Old Testament the Revealer of God. All
emphasis must therefore fall on this—without a technical reflection which cannot be proved—that the Divine revelation
has now, through the historical Christ, become accessible and
intelligible to all, and that the life which was promised will
shortly be made manifest. [2]

[1] See the remarkable narrative about the cross in the fragment of the Gospel
of Peter, and in Justin, Apol. I. 55.

[2] We must, above all things, be on our guard here against attributing dogmas
to the churches, that is to say, to the writers of this period. The difference in
the answers to the question, How far and by what means Jesus procured salvation?
was very great, and the majority undoubtedly never at all raised the question,
being satisfied with recognising Jesus as the revealer of God's saving will (Didache,
10. 2: εὐχαριστοῦμέν σοι, πάτερ ἅγιε, ὑπερ τοῦ ἁγίου ὀνόματός σου, οὗ κατεσκή-

As to the facts of the history of Jesus, the real and the supposed, the circumstance that they formed the ever repeated proclamation about Christ gave them an extraordinary significance. In addition to the birth from the Holy Spirit and the Virgin, the death, the resurrection, the exaltation to the right hand of God, and the coming again, there now appeared more definitely the ascension to heaven, and also, though more uncertainly, the descent into the kingdom of the dead. The belief that Jesus ascended into heaven forty days after the resurrection, gradually made way against the older conception, according to which resurrection and ascension really coincided, and against other ideas which maintained a long-

νωσας ἐν ταῖς καρδίαις ἡμῶν καὶ ὑπὲρ τῆς γνώσεως καὶ πίστεως αἰ ἀθανατίας, ἧς ἐγνώρισας ἡμῖν διὰ Ἰησοῦ τοῦ παιδὸς σου), without reflecting on the fact that this saving will was already revealed in the Old Testament. There is nowhere any mention of saving work of Christ in the whole Didache—nay, even the *Kerygma* about him is not taken notice of. The extensive writing of Hermas shews that this is not an accident. There is absolutely no mention here of the birth, death, resurrection, etc., of Jesus, although the author in Sim. V. had an occasion for mentioning them. He describes the work of Jesus as (1) preserving the people whom God had chosen, (2) purifying the people from sin, (3) pointing out the path of life and promulgating the Divine law (cc. 5. 6). This work however, seems to have been performed by the whole life and activity of Jesus; even to the purifyng of sin the author has only added the words; (καὶ αὐτὸς τὰς ἁμαρτίας αὐτῶν ἐκαθάρισε) πολλὰ κοπιάσας καὶ πολλοὺς κόπους ἠντληκώς (Sim. V. 6. 2). But we must further note that Hermas held the proper and obligatory work of Jesus to be only the preservation of the chosen people (from demons in the last days, and at the end), while in the other two articles he saw a performance in excess of his duty, and wished undoubtedly to declare therewith, that the purifying from sin and the giving of the law are not, strictly speaking, integral parts of the Divine plan of salvation, but are due to the special goodness of Jesus (this idea is explained by Moralism). Now, as Hermas and others saw the saving activity of Jesus in his whole labours, others saw salvation given and assured in the moment of Jesus' entrance into the world, and in his personality as a spiritual being become flesh. This mystic conception, which attained such wide-spread recognition later on, has a representative in Ignatius, if one can at all attribute clearly conceived doctrines to this emotional confessor. That something can be declared of Jesus, κατὰ πνεῦμα and κατὰ σάρκα—this is the mystery on which the significance of Jesus seems to Ignatius essentially to rest, but how far is not made clear. But the πάθος (αἷμα, σταυρός) and ἀνάστασις of Jesus are to the same writer of great significance, and by forming paradoxical formulæ of worship, and turning to account reminiscences of Apostolic sayings, he seems to wish to base the whole salvation brought by Christ on his suffering and resurrection (see Lightfoot on Eph. inscr. Vol. II. p. 25). In this connection also, he here and there regards all articles of the *Kerygma* as of fundamental significance. At all events, we have in

er period between the two events. That probably is the result of a reflection which sought to distinguish the first from the later manifestations of the exalted Christ, and it is of the utmost importance as the beginning of a demarcation of the times. It is also very probable that the acceptance of an actual *ascensus in cœlum*, not a mere *assumptio*, was favourable to the idea of an actual descent of Christ *de cœlo*, therefore to the pneumatic Christology and vice versa. But there is also closely connected with the *ascensus in cœlum*, the notion of a *descensus ad inferna*, which commended itself on the ground of Old Testament prediction. In the first century, however, it still remained uncertain, lying on the borders of those pro-

the Ignatian Epistles the first attempt in the post-Apostolic literature to connect all the theses of the *Kerygma* about Jesus as closely as possible with the benefits which he brought. But only the will of the writer is plain here, all else is confused, and what is mainly felt is that the attempt to conceive the blessings of salvation as the fruit of the sufferings and resurrection, has deprived them of their definiteness and clearness. In proof we may adduce the following: If we leave out of account the passages in which Ignatius speaks of the necessity of repentance for the Heretics, or the Heathen, and the possibility that their sins may be forgiven (Philad. 3. 2: 8. 1; Smyrn. 4. 1: 5. 3; Eph. 10. 1), there remains only one passage in which the forgiveness of sin is mentioned, and that only contains a traditional formula (Smyrn. 7. 1: σάρξ Ἰησοῦ Χριστοῦ, ἡ ὑπὲρ τῶν ἁμαρτιῶν ἡμῶν παθοῦσα). The same writer, who is constantly speaking of the πάθος and ἀνάστασις of Christ, has nothing to say to the communities to which he writes, about the forgiveness of sin. Even the concept "sin," apart from the passages just quoted, appears only once, viz., Eph 14. 2: οὐδεὶς πίστιν ἐπαγγελλόμενος ἁμαρτάνει. Ignatius has only once spoken to a community about repentance (Smyrn. 9. 1). It is characteristic that the summons to repentance runs exactly as in Hermas and 2 Clem., the conclusion only being peculiarly Ignatian. It is different with Barnabas, Clement and Polycarp. They (see 1 Clem. 7. 4: 12. 7: 21. 6: 49. 6: Barn. 5. 1 ff.) place the forgiveness of sin procured by Jesus in the foreground, connect it most definitely with the death of Christ, and in some passages seem to have a conception of that connection, which reminds us of Paul. But this just shews that they are dependent here on Paul (or on 1st Peter), and on a closer examination we perceive that they very imperfectly understand Paul, and have no independent insight into the series of ideas which they reproduce. That is specially plain in Clement. For, in the first place, he everywhere passes over the resurrection (he mentions it only twice, once as a guarantee of our own resurrection, along with the Phœnix and other guarantees, 24. 1; and then as a means whereby the Apostles were convinced that the kingdom of God will come, 42. 3). In the second place, he in one passage declares that the χάρις μετανοίας was communicated to the world through the shedding of Christ's blood (7. 4.). But this transformation of the ἄφεσις ἁμαρτιῶν into χάρις μετανοίας plainly shews

ductions of religious fancy which were not able at once to acquire a right of citizenship in the communities. [1]

One can plainly see that the articles contained in the *Kerygma* were guarded and defended in their reality (κατ' ἀληθείαν) by the professional teachers of the Church, against sweeping at-

that Clement had merely taken over from tradition the special estimate of the death of Christ as procuring salvation; for it is meaningless to deduce the χάρις μετανοίας from the blood of Christ. Barnabas testifies more plainly that Christ behoved to offer the vessel of his spirit as a sacrifice for our sins (4. 3 : 5. 1), nay, the chief aim of his letter is to harmonise the correct understanding of the cross, the blood, and death of Christ in connection with baptism, the forgiveness of sin, and sanctification (application of the idea of sacrifice). He also unites the death and resurrection of Jesus (5. 6 : αὐτὸς δὲ ἵνα καταργήσῃ τὸν θάνατον καὶ τὴν ἐκ νεκρῶν ἀνάστασιν δείξῃ, ὅτι ἐν σαρκὶ ἔδει αὐτὸν φανερωθῆναι, ὑπέμεινεν, ἵνα καὶ τοῖς πατράσιν τὴν ἐπαγγελίαν ἀποδῷ καὶ αὐτὸς ἑαυτῷ τὸν λαὸν τὸν καινὸν ἑτοιμάζων, ἐπιδείξῃ, τῆς γῆς ὤν, ὅτι τὴν ὠνάστασιν αὐτὸς ποιήσας κρινεῖ): but the significance of the death of Christ is for him, at bottom, the fact that it is the fulfilment of prophecy. But the prophecy is related, above all, to the significance of the tree, and so Barnabas on one occasion says with admirable clearness (5, 13); αὐτὸς δὲ ἠθέλησεν οὕτω παθεῖν· ἔδει γὰρ ἵνα ἐπὶ ξύλου πάθῃ. The notion which Barnabas entertains of the σάρξ of Christ suggests the supposition that he could have given up all reference to the death of Christ, if it had not been transmitted as a fact and predicted in the Old Testament. Justin shews still less certainty. To him also, as to Ignatius, the cross (the death) of Christ is a great—nay, the greatest mystery, and he sees all things possible in it (see Apol. 1. 35, 55). He knows, further, as a man acquainted with the Old Testament, how to borrow from it very many points of view for the significance of Christ's death, (Christ the sacrifice, the Paschal lamb; the death of Christ the means of redeeming men; death as the enduring of the curse for us; death as the victory over the devil; see Dial. 44, 90, 91, 111, 134). But in the discussions which set forth in a more intelligible way the significance of Christ, definite facts from the history have no place at all, and Justin nowhere gives any indication of seeing in the death of Christ more than the mystery of the Old Testament, and the confirmation of its trustworthiness. On the other hand, it cannot be mistaken that the idea of an individual righteous man being able effectively to sacrifice himself for the whole, in order through his voluntary death to deliver them from evil, was not unknown to antiquity. Origen (c. Celsum 1. 31) has expressed himself on this point in a very instructive way. The purity and voluntariness of him who sacrifices himself are here the main things. Finally, we must be on our guard against supposing that the expressions σωτηρία, ἀπολύτρωσις and the like, were as a rule related to the deliverance from sin. In the superscription of the Epistle from Lyons, for example, (Euseb. H E. V. 1. 3 : οἱ αὐτὴν τῆς ἀπολυτρώσεως ἡμῖν πίστιν καὶ ἐλπίδα ἔχοντες) the future redemption is manifestly to be understood by ἀπολύτρωσις.

[1] On the Ascension, see my edition of the Apost. Fathers I. 2, p. 138. Paul knows nothing of an Ascension, nor is it mentioned by Clement, Ignatius, Hermas, or Polycarp. In no case did it belong to the earliest preaching. Resurrection and

tempts at explaining them away, or open attacks on them.[1]
But they did not yet possess the value of dogmas, for they
were neither put in an indissoluble union with the idea of
salvation, nor were they stereotyped in their extent, nor were
fixed limits set to the imagination in the concrete delineation
and conception of them.[2]

§ 7. *The Worship, the Sacred Ordinances, and the Organisation of the Churches.*

It is necessary to examine the original forms of the worship
and constitution, because of the importance which they acquired
in the following period even for the development of doctrine.

1. In accordance with the purely spiritual idea of God, it
was a fixed principle that only a spiritual worship is well

sitting at the right hand of God are frequently united in the formulæ (Eph. I. 20:
Acts. II. 32 ff.) According to Luke XXIV. 51, and Barn. 15. 9, the ascension
into heaven took place on the day of the resurrection (probably also according to
Joh. XX. 17; see also the fragment of the Gosp. of Peter), and is hardly to be
thought of as happening but once. (Joh. III. 13 : VI. 62; see also Rom. X. 6 f.;
Eph. IV. 9 f.; I Pet. III. 19 f.; very instructive for the origin of the notion).
According to the Valentinians and Ophites, Christ ascended into heaven 18 months
after the resurrection (Iren. I. 3. 2 : 30. 14); according to the Ascension of Isaiah,
545 days (ed. Dillmann, pp. 43, 57 etc.); according to Pistis Sophia 11 years after
the resurrection. The statement that the Ascension took place 40 days after the
resurrection is first found in the Acts of the Apostles. The position of the ἀνελήμφθη
ἐν δόξῃ, in the fragment of an old Hymn, 1 Tim. III. 16, is worthy of note, in
so far as it follows the ὤφθη ἀγγέλοις, ἐκηρύχθη ἐν ἔθνεσιν, ἐπιστεύθη ἐν κόσμῳ.
Justin speaks very frequently of the Ascension into heaven (see also Aristides).
It is to him a necessary part of the preaching about Christ. On the descent into
hell, see the collection of passages in my edition of the Apost. Fathers, III. p. 232.
It is important to note that it is found already in the Gospel of Peter (ἐκήρυξας
τοῖς κοιμωμένοις; ναί), and that even Marcion recognised it (in Iren. I. 27. 3), as
well as the Presbyter of Irenæus (IV. 27. 2), and Ignatius (ad Magn. 9. 3); see also
Celsus in Orig. II. 43. The witnesses to it are very numerous; see Huidekoper,
"The belief of the first three centuries concerning Christ's mission to the under-
world." New York, 1876.

[1] See the Pastoral Epistles, and the Epistles of Ignatius and Polycarp.

[2] The "facts" of the history of Jesus were handed down to the following period
as mysteries predicted in the Old Testament, but the idea of sacrifice was specially
attached to the death of Christ, certainly without any closer definition. It is very
noteworthy that in the Romish baptismal confession, the Davidic Sonship of Jesus,
the baptism, the descent into the under-world, and the setting up of a glorious
Kingdom on the earth, are not mentioned. These articles do not appear even in

pleasing to Him, and that all ceremonies are abolished, ἵνα ὁ καινὸς νόμος τοῦ κυρίου ἡμῶν Ἰησοῦ Χριστοῦ μὴ ἀνθρωποποίητον ἔχῃ τὴν προσφοράν. [1] But as the Old Testament and the Apostolic tradition made it equally certain that the worship of God is a sacrifice, the Christian worship of God was set forth under the aspect of the spiritual sacrifice. In the most general sense it was conceived as the offering of the heart and of obedience, as well as the consecration of the whole personality, body and soul (Rom. XIII. 1) to God. [2] Here, with a change of the figure, the individual Christian and the whole community were described as a temple of God. [3] In a more special sense, prayer as thanksgiving and intercession [4] was regarded as the sacrifice which was to be accompanied, without constraint or ceremony, by fasts and acts of compassionate love. [5] Finally,

the parallel confessions which began to be formed. The hesitancy that yet prevailed here with regard to details is manifest from the fact, for example, that instead of the formula "Jesus was born of (ἐκ) Mary," is found the other, "He was born through (διὰ) Mary," (see Justin, Apol. I. 22, 31-33, 54, 63; Dial. 23, 43, 45, 48, 54, 57, 63, 66, 75, 85, 87, 100, 105, 120, 127). Iren. (I. 7. 2) and Tertull. (de carne 20) first contested the διὰ against the Valentinians.

[1] This was strongly emphasised; see my remarks on Barn. 2. 3. The Jewish cultus is often brought very close to the heathen by Gentile Christian writers. Præd. Petri (Clem. Strom. VI. 5. 41): καινῶς τὸν θεὸν διὰ τοῦ Χριστοῦ σεβόμεθα. The statement in Joh. IV. 24: πνεῦμα ὁ θεός, καὶ τοὺς προσκυνοῦντας αὐτὸν ἐν πνεύματι καὶ ἀληθείᾳ δεῖ προσκυνεῖν, was for long the guiding principle for the Christian worship of God.

[2] Ps. LI. 19 is thus opposed to the ceremonial system (Barn. 2. 10). Polycarp consumed by fire is (Mart. 14. 1) compared to a κριὸς ἐπίσημος ἐκ μεγάλου ποιμνίου εἰς προσφοράν, ὁλοκαύτωμα δεκτὸν τῷ θεῷ ἡτοιμασμένον.

[3] See Barn. 6. 15: 16. 7-9; Tatian Orat. 15; Ignat. ad Eph. 9. 15; Herm. Mand. V. etc. The designation of Christians as priests is not often found.

[4] Justin, Apol. 1. 9: Dial. 117: Ὅτι μὲν οὖν καὶ εὐχαὶ καὶ εὐχαριστίαι, ὑπό τῶν ἀξίων γινόμεναι, τέλειαι μόναι καὶ εὐάρεστοί εἰσι τῷ θεῷ θυσίαι, καὶ αὐτός φημι; see also still the later Fathers; Clem. Strom. VII. 6. 31: ἡμεῖς δι' εὐχῆς τιμῶμεν τὸν θεὸν, καὶ ταύτην τὴν θυσίαν ἀρίστην, καὶ ἁγιωτάτην μετὰ δικαιοσύνης ἀναπέμπομεν τῷ δικαίῳ λόγῳ; Iren. III. 18. 3. Ptolem. ad Floram. 3: προσφορὰς προσφέρειν προσέταξεν ἡμῖν ὁ σωτήρ, ἀλλὰ οὐχὶ τὰς δι' ἀλόγων ζώων ἢ τούτων τῶν θωμιαμάτων ἀλλὰ διὰ πνευματικῶν αἴνων καὶ δοξῶν καὶ εὐχαριστίας καὶ διὰ τῆς εἰς τοὺς πλησίον κοινωνίας καὶ εὐποιίας.

[5] The Jewish regulations about fastings, together with the Jewish system of sacrifice were rejected; but on the other hand, in virtue of words of the Lord, fasts were looked upon as a necessary accompaniment of prayer, and definite arrangements were already made for them (see Barn. 3; Didache 8; Herm. Sim.

prayers offered by the worshipper in the public worship of
the community, and the gifts brought by them, out of which
were taken the elements for the Lord's supper, and which were
used partly in the common meal, and partly in support of
the poor, were regarded as sacrifice in the most special sense
(προσφορά, δῶρα).[1] For the following period, however, it became
of the utmost importance, (1) that the idea of sacrifice ruled
the whole worship, (2) that it appeared in a special manner
in the celebration of the Lord's supper, and consequently
invested that ordinance with a new meaning, (3) that the support of the poor, alms, especially such alms as had been gained
by prayer and fasting, was placed under the category of sacrifice (Heb. XIII. 16); for this furnished the occasion for giving
the widest application to ˌthe idea of sacrifice, and thereby
substituting for the original Semitic Old Testament idea of
sacrifice with its spiritual interpretation, the Greek idea with
its interpretation.[2] It may, however, be maintained that the

---

V. 1. ff. The fast is to have a special value from the fact that whatever one
saved by means of it, is to be given to the poor (see Hermas and Aristides, Apol.
15; "And if any one among the Christians is poor and in want, and they have
not overmuch of the means of life, they fast two or three days, in order that they
may provide those in need with the food they require"). The statement of James
I. 27: θρησκεία καθαρὰ καὶ ἀμίαντος παρὰ τῷ θεῷ καί πατρὶ αὕτη ἐστίν, ἐπισκέπ-
τεσθαι ὀρφανοὺς καὶ χήρας ἐν τῇ θλίψει αὐτῶν, was again and again inculcated in
diverse phraseology (Polycarp. Ep. 4, called the Widows θυσιαστήριον of the community). Where moralistic views preponderated, as in Hermas and 2 Clement, good works
were already valued in detail; prayers, fasts, alms appeared separately, and there
was already introduced, especially under the influence of the so-called deutero-
canonical writings of the Old Testament, the idea of a special meritoriousness of
certain performances in fasts and alms (see 2 Clem. 16. 4). Still, the idea of the
Christian moral life as a whole occupied the foreground (see Didache, cc. 1–5),
and the exhortations to love God and one's neighbour, which, as exhortations to
a moral life, were brought forward in every conceivable relation, supplemented
the general summons to renounce the world, just as the official diaconate of the
churches originating in the cultus prevented the decomposition of them into a
society of ascetics.

[1] For details, see below in the case of the Lord's Supper. It is specially
important that even charity, through its union with the cultus, appeared as sacrificial worship (see *e.g.*, Polyc. Ep. 4. 3).

[2] The idea of sacrifice adopted by the Gentile Christian communities was that
which was expressed in individual prophetic sayings and in the Psalms, a spiritualising of the Semitic Jewish sacrificial ritual, which, however, had not altogether
lost its original features. The entrance of Greek ideas of sacrifice cannot be

changes imposed on the Christian religion by Catholicism, are
at no point so obvious and far-reaching, as in that of sacrifice, and especially in the solemn ordinance of the Lord's
supper, which was placed in such close connection with the
idea of sacrifice.

2. When in the "Teaching of the Apostles," which may
be regarded here as a classic document, the discipline of life
in accordance with the words of the Lord, Baptism, the order
of fasting and prayer, especially the regular use of the Lord's
prayer, and the Eucharist are reckoned the articles on which
the Christian community rests, and when the common Sunday
offering of a sacrifice made pure by a brotherly disposition,
and the mutual exercise of discipline are represented as decisive for the stability of the individual community, [1] we perceive that the general idea of a pure spiritual worship of God
has nevertheless been realised in definite institutions, and that,
above all, it has included the traditional sacred ordinances,
and adjusted itself to them as far as that was possible. [2] This
could only take effect under the idea of the symbolical, and
therefore this idea was most firmly attached to these ordinances. But the symbolical of that time is not to be considered
as the opposite of the objectively real, but as the mysterious,
the God produced (μυστήριον), as contrasted with the natural,
the profanely clear. As to Baptism, which was administered
in the name of the Father, Son and Spirit, though Cyprian,
Ep. 73. 16-18, felt compelled to oppose the custom of baptising
in the name of Jesus, we noted above (Chap. III. p. 161 f.)
that it was regarded as the bath of regeneration, and as renewal
of life, inasmuch as it was assumed that by it the sins of the
past state of blindness were blotted out. [3] But as faith was

---

traced before Justin. Neither was there as yet any reflection as to the connection
of the sacrifice of the Church with the sacrifice of Christ upon the cross.

[1] See my Texte und Unters. z. Gesch. d. Altchristl. Lit .II. 1. 2, p. 88 ff., p. 137 ff.

[2] There neither was a "doctrine" of Baptism and the Lord's Supper, nor was
there any inner connection presupposed between these holy actions. They were
here and there placed together as actions by the Lord.

[3] Melito, Fragm. XII. (Otto. Corp. Apol. IX. p. 418). Δύο συνεστη τὰ ἄφεσιν
ἁμαρτημάτων παρεχόμενα, πάθος διὰ Χριστόν καὶ βάπτισμα.

looked upon as the necessary condition, [1] and as on the other hand, the forgiveness of the sins of the past was in itself deemed worthy of God, [2] the asserted specific result of baptism remained still very uncertain, and the hard tasks which it imposed, might seem more important than the merely retrospective gifts which it proffered. [3] Under such circumstances the rite could not fail to lead believers about to be baptized to attribute value here to the mysterious as such. [4] But that always creates a state of things which not only facilitates, but positively prepares for the introduction of new and strange ideas. For neither fancy nor reflection can long continue in the vacuum of mystery. The names σφραγίς and φωτισμός, which at that period came into fashion for baptism, are instructive, inasmuch as neither of them is a direct designation of the presupposed effect of baptism, the forgiveness of sin, and as, besides, both of them evince a Hellenic conception. Baptism

---

[1] There is no sure trace of infant baptism in this epoch; personal faith is a necessary condition (see Hermas, Vis. III. 7. 3; Justin, Apol. 1. 61). "Prius est prædicare posterius tinguere" (Tertull. "de bapt." 14).

[2] On the basis of repentance. See Praed. Petri in Clem. Strom. VI. 5. 43, 48.

[3] See especially the second Epistle of Clement; Tertull. "de bapt." 15: "Felix aqua quæ semel abluit, quæ ludibrio pecatoribus non est."

[4] The sinking and rising in baptism, and the immersion, were regarded as significant but not indispensable symbols (see Didache. 7). The most important passages for baptism are Didache 7: Barn. 6. 11: 11. 1. 11 (the connection in which the cross of Christ is here placed to the water is important; the tertium comp. is that forgiveness of sin is the result of both); Herm. Vis. III. 3, Sim. IX. 16, Mand. IV. 3 (ἑτέρα μετάνοια οὐκ ἔστιν εἰ μὴ ἐκείνη, ὅτε εἰς ὕδωρ κατέβημεν καὶ ἐλάβομεν ἄφεσιν ἁμαρτιῶν ἡμῶν τῶν προτέρων); 2 Clem. 6. 9: 7. 6: 8. 6. Peculiar is Ignat. ad. Polyc. 6. 2: τὸ βάπτισμα ὑμῶν μενέτω ὡς ὅπλα. Specially important is Justin, Apol I. 61. 65. To this also belong many passages from Tertullian's treatise "de bapt."; a Gnostic baptismal hymn in the third pseudo-Solomonic ode in the Pistis Sophia, p. 131, ed. Schwartze; Marcion's baptismal formula in Irenæus I. 21. 3. It clearly follows from the seventh chapter of the Didache that its author held that the pronouncing of the sacred names over the baptised and over the water was essential, but that immersion was not; see the thorough examination of this passage by Schaff. "The oldest church manual called the teaching of the twelve Apostles" pp. 29-57. The controversy about the nature of John's baptism in its relation to Christian baptism is very old in Christendom; see also Tertull. "de bapt." 10. Tertullian sees in John's baptism only a baptism to repentance, not to forgiveness.

in being called the seal,[1] is regarded as the guarantee of a
blessing, not as the blessing itself, at least the relation to it
remains obscure; in being called enlightenment,[2] it is placed
directly under an aspect that is foreign to it. It would be
different if we had to think of φωτισμός as a gift of the Holy
Spirit, which is given to the baptised as real principle of a
new life and miraculous powers. But the idea of a necessary
union of baptism with a miraculous communication of the
Spirit seems to have been lost very early, or to have become
uncertain, the actual state of things being no longer favourable

[1] In Hermas and 2 Clement. The expression probably arose from the language
of the mysteries: see Appuleius, "de Magia," 55: "Sacrorum pleraque initia in
Græcia participavi. Eorum quædam signa et monumenta tradita mihi a sacerdo-
tibus sedulo conservo." Ever since the Gentile Christians conceived baptism (and
the Lord's Supper) according to the mysteries, they were of course always surprised
by the parallel with the mysteries themselves. That begins with Justin. Tertullian,
"de bapt." 5, says: "Sed enim nationes extraneæ, ab omni intellectu spiritalium
potestatum eadem efficacia idolis suis subministrant. Sed viduis aquis sibi menti-
untur. Nam et sacris quibusdam per lavacrum initiantur, Isidis alicujus aut Mithræ;
ipsos etiam deos suos lavationibus efferunt. Ceterum villas, domos, templa
totasque urbes aspergine circumlatæ aquæ expiant passim. Certe ludis Apollinari-
bus et Eleusiniis tinguuntur, idque se in regenerationem et impunitatem periuriorum
suorum agere præsumunt. Item penes veteres, quisquis se homicidio infecerat,
purgatrices aquas explorabat." De præscr., 40: "Diabolus ipsas quoque res
sacramentorum divinorum idolorum mysteriis æmulatur. Tingit et ipse quosdam,
utique credentes et fideles suos; expositionem delictorum de lavacro repromittit,
et si adhuc memini, Mithras signat illic in frontibus milites suos, celebrat et panis
oblationem et imaginem resurrectionis inducit.... summum pontificem in unius
nuptiis statuit, habet et virgines, habet et continentes." The ancient notion that
matter has a mysterious influence on spirit came very early into vogue in connection with baptism. We see that from Tertullian's treatise on baptism and his
speculations about the power of the water (c. 1 ff.). The water must, of course
have been first consecrated for this purpose (that is, the demons must be
driven out of it). But then it is holy water with which the Holy Spirit is
united, and which is able really to cleanse the soul. See Hatch, "The
influence of Greek ideas, etc.," p. 19. The consecration of the water is
certainly very old: though we have no definite witnesses from the earliest
period. Even for the exorcism of the baptised before baptism I know of no
earlier witness than the Sentent. LXXXVII. episcoporum (Hartel. Opp. Cypr. I.
p. 450, No. 37: "primo per manus impositionem in exorcismo, secundo per
baptismi regenerationem").

[2] Justin is the first who does so (I. 61). The word comes from the Greek
mysteries. On Justin's theory of baptism, see also I. 62. and Von Engelhardt,
"Christenthum Justin's," p. 102 f.

to it; [1] at any rate, it does not explain the designation of baptism as φωτισμός.

As regards the Lord's Supper, the most important point is that its celebration became more and more the central point, not only for the worship of the Church, but for its very life as a Church. The form of this celebration, the common meal, made it appear to be a fitting expression of the brotherly unity of the community (on the public confession before the meal, see Didache, 14, and my notes on the passage). The prayers which it included presented themselves as vehicles for bringing before God, in thanksgiving and intercession, every thing that affected the community; and the presentation of the elements for the holy ordinance was naturally extended to the offering of gifts for the poor brethren, who in this way received them from the hand of God himself. In all these respects, however, the holy ordinance appeared as a sacrifice of the community, and indeed, as it was also named εὐχαριστία, a sacrifice of thanksgiving. [2] As an act of sacrifice, all the

---

[1] Paul unites baptism and the communication of the Spirit: but they were very soon represented apart, see the accounts in the Acts of the Apostles, which are certainly very obscure because the author has evidently never himself observed the descent of the Spirit, or anything like it. The ceasing of special manifestations of the Spirit in and after baptism, and the enforced renunciation of seeing baptism accompanied by special shocks, must be regarded as the first stage in the sobering of the churches.

[2] The idea of the whole transaction of the Supper as a sacrifice is plainly found in the Didache, (c. 14), in Ignatius, and above all in Justin (I. 65 f.). But even Clement of Rome presupposes it, when (in cc. 40-44) he draws a parallel between bishops and deacons and the Priests and Levites of the Old Testament, describing as the chief function of the former (44. 4) προσφέρειν τὰ δῶρα. This is not the place to enquire whether the first celebration had, in the mind of its founder, the character of a sacrificial meal; but, certainly, the idea, as it was already developed at the time of Justin, had been created by the churches. Various reasons tended towards seeing in the Supper a sacrifice. In the first place, Malachi I. 11, demanded a solemn Christian sacrifice : see my notes on Didache, 14. 3. In the second place, all prayers were regarded as sacrifice, and therefore the solemn prayers at the Supper must be specially considered as such. In the third place, the words of institution τοῦτο ποιεῖτε, contained a command with regard to a definite religious action. Such an action, however, could only be represented as a sacrifice, and this the more that the Gentile Christians might suppose that they had to understand ποιεῖν in the sense of θύειν. In the fourth place, payments in kind were necessary for the "agapæ" connected with the Supper, out of which

termini technici which the Old Testament applied to sacrifice could be applied to it, and all the wealth of ideas which the Old Testament connects with sacrifice could be transferred to it. One cannot say that anything absolutely foreign was therewith introduced into the ordinance, however doubtful it may be whether in the idea of its founder the meal was thought of as a sacrificial meal. But it must have been of the most wide-reaching significance, that a wealth of ideas was in this way connected with the ordinance, which had nothing whatever in common either with the purpose of the meal as a memorial of Christ's death, [1] or with the mysterious symbols of the body and blood of Christ. The result was that the one transaction obtained a double value. At one time it appeared as the προσφορά and θυσία of the Church, [2] as the pure sacrifice which is presented to the great king by Christians scattered over the world, as they offer to him their prayers and place before him again what he has bestowed in order to receive it back with thanks and praise. But there is no reference in this to the mysterious words, that the bread and wine are the body of Christ broken and the blood of Christ shed for the for-

---

were taken the bread and wine for the Holy celebration; in what other aspect could these offerings in the worship be regarded than as προσφοραί for the purpose of a sacrifice? Yet the spiritual idea so prevailed that only the prayers were regarded as the θυσία proper, even in the case of Justin (Dial. 117). The elements are only δῶρα, προσφοραί, which obtain their value from the prayers in which thanks are given for the gifts of creation and redemption as well as for the holy meal, and entreaty is made for the introduction of the community into the Kingdom of God (see Didache, 9. 10). Therefore, even the sacred meal itself is called εὐχαριστία (Justin, Apol. I. 66: ἡ τροφὴ αὕτη καλεῖται παρ' ἡμῖν εὐχαριστία. Didache 9. 1: Ignat., because it is τροφὴ εὐχαριστηθεῖσα. It is a mistake to suppose that Justin already understood the body of Christ to be the object of ποιεῖν, and therefore thought of a sacrifice of this body (I. 66). The real sacrificial act in the Supper consists rather, according to Justin, only in the εὐχαριστίαν ποιεῖν, whereby the κοινὸς ἄρτος becomes the ἄρτος τῆς εὐχαριστίας. The sacrifice of the Supper in its essence, apart from the offering of alms, which in the practice of the Church was closely united with it, is nothing but a sacrifice of prayer: the sacrificial act of the Christian here also is nothing else than an act of prayer (see Apol. I. 13, 65–67; Dial. 28, 29, 41, 70, 116–118).

[1] Justin lays special stress on this purpose. On the other hand, it is wanting in the Supper prayers of the Didache, unless c. 9. 2 be regarded as an allusion to it.

[2] The designation θυσία is first found in the Didache, c. 14.

giveness of sin. These words, in and of themselves, must have challenged a special consideration. They called forth the recognition in the sacramental action, or rather in the consecrated elements, of a mysterious communication of God, a gift of salvation, and this is the second aspect. But on a purely spiritual conception of the Divine gift of salvation, the blessings mediated through the Holy Supper could only be thought of as spiritual (faith, knowledge, or eternal life), and the consecrated elements could only be recognised as the mysterious vehicles of these blessings. There was yet no reflection on the distinction between symbol and vehicle; the symbol was rather regarded as the vehicle, and vice versa. We shall search in vain for any special relation of the partaking of the consecrated elements to the forgiveness of sin. That was made impossible by the whole current notions of sin and forgiveness. That on which value was put was the strengthening of faith and knowledge, as well as the guarantee of eternal life; and a meal in which there was appropriated not merely common bread and wine, but a τροφὴ πνευματική, seemed to have a bearing upon these. There was as yet little reflection; but there can be no doubt that thought here moved in a region bounded, on the one hand, by the intention of doing justice to the wonderful words of institution which had been handed down, and on the other hand, by the fundamental conviction that spiritual things can only be got by means of the Spirit.[1] There was thus at-

---

[1] The Supper was regarded as a "Sacrament" in so far as a blessing was represented in its holy food. The conception of the nature of this blessing as set forth in John VI. 27-58, appears to have been the most common. It may be traced back to Ignatius, ad Eph. 20. 2: ἕνα ἄρτον κλῶντες ὅς ἐστιν φάρμακον ἀθανασίας, ἀντίδοτος τοῦ μὴ ἀποθανεῖν ἀλλὰ ζῆν ἐν Ἰησοῦ Χριστοῦ διὰ παντός. Cf. Didache, 10. 3: ἡμῖν ἐχαρίσω πνευματικὴν τροφὴν καὶ ποτὸν καὶ ζωὴν αἰώνιον; also 10. 21: εὐχαριστοῦμέν σοι ὑπὲρ τῆς γνωσεως καὶ πίστεως καὶ ἀθανασίας. Justin Apol. I. 66: ἐκ τῆς τροφῆς ταύτης αἷμα καὶ σάρκες κατὰ μεταβολὴν τρέφονται ἡμῶν (κατὰ μεταβολήν, that is, the holy food, like all nourishment, is completely transformed into our flesh; but what Justin has in view here is most probably the body of the resurrection. The expression, as the context shews, is chosen for the sake of the parallel to the incarnation). Iren. IV. 18. 5: V. 2. 2 f. As to how the elements are related to the body and blood of Christ, Ignatius seems to have expressed himself in a strictly realistic way in several passages, especially ad. Smyr. 7. 1: εὐχαριστίας καὶ προσευχῆς ἀπέχονται διὰ τὸ μὴ ὁμολογεῖν, τὴν εὐχαριστίαν

tached to the Supper the idea of sacrifice, and of a sacred gift guaranteed by God. The two things were held apart, for there is as yet no trace of that conception according to which the body of Christ represented in the bread [1] is the sacrifice offered by the community. But one feels almost called upon here to construe from the premises the later development of the idea, with due regard to the ancient Hellenic ideas of sacrifice.

σάρκα εἶνει τοῦ σωτῆρος ἡμῶν Ἰησοῦ Χριστοῦ, τὴν ὑπὲρ τῶν ἁμαρτιῶν ἡμῶν παθοῦσαν. But many passages shew that Ignatius was far from such a conception, and rather thought as John did. In Trall. 8, faith is described as the flesh, and love as the blood of Christ; in Rom. 7, in one breath the flesh of Christ is called the bread of God, and the blood ἀγάπη ἄφθαρτος. In Philad. 1, we read: αἷμα Ἰ Χρ. ἥτις ἐστὶν χαρὰ αἰώνιος καὶ παράμονος. In Philad. 5, the Gospel is called the flesh of Christ, etc. Höfling is therefore right in saying (Lehre v. Opfer, p. 39): "The Eucharist is to Ignatius σάρξ of Christ, as a visible Gospel, a kind of Divine institution attesting the content of πίστις, viz., belief in the σάρξ παθοῦσα, an institution which is at the same time, to the community, a means of representing and preserving its unity in this belief." On the other hand, it cannot be mistaken that Justin (Apol. I. 66) presupposed the identity, miraculously produced by the Logos, of the consecrated bread and the body he had assumed. In this we have probably to recognise an influence on the conception of the Supper, of the miracle represented in the Greek Mysteries: Οὐχ ὡς κοινὸν ἄρτον οὐδὲ κοινὸν πόμα ταῦτα λαμβάνομεν, ἀλλ' ὃν τρόπον διὰ λόγου θεοῦ σαρκοποιηθεὶς Ἰησοῦς Χριστὸς ὁ σωτὴρ ἡμῶν καὶ σάρκα καὶ αἷμα ὑπὲρ σωτηρίας ἡμῶν ἔσχεν, οὕτως καὶ τὴν δι' εὐχῆς λόγου τοῦ παρ' αὐτοῦ εὐχαριστηθεῖσαν τροφήν, ἐξ ἧς αἷμα καὶ σάρκες κατὰ μεταβολὴν τρέφονται ἡμῶν, ἐκείνου τοῦ σαρκοποιηθέντος Ἰησοῦ καὶ σάρκα καὶ αἷμα ἐδιδάχθημεν εἶναι (See Von Otto on the passage). In the Texte u. Unters. VII. 2. p. 117 ff., I have shewn that in the different Christian circles of the second century, water and only water was often used in the Supper instead of wine, and that in many regions this custom was maintained up to the middle of the third century (see Cypr. Ep. 63). I have endeavoured to make it further probable that even Justin in his Apology describes a celebration of the Lord's Supper with bread and water. The latter has been contested by Zahn, "Bread and wine in the Lord's Supper, in the early Church," 1892, and Jülicher, Zur Gesch. der Abendmahlsfeier in der aeltesten Kirche (Abhandl. f. Weiszäcker, 1892, p. 217 ff.).

---

[1] Ignatius calls the thank-offering the flesh of Christ, but the concept "flesh of Christ" is for him itself a spiritual one. On the contrary, Justin sees in the bread the actual flesh of Christ, but does not connect it with the idea of sacrifice. They are thus both as yet far from the later conception. The numerous allegories which are already attached to the Supper (one bread, equivalent to one community; many scattered grains bound up in the one bread, equivalent to the Christians scattered abroad in the world, who are to be gathered together into the Kingdom of God; one altar, equivalent to one assembly of the community, excluding private worship, etc.), cannot as a group be adduced here.

3. The natural distinctions among men, and the differences
of position and vocation which these involve, were not to be
abolished in the Church, notwithstanding the independence
and equality of every individual Christian, but were to be
consecrated: above all, every relation of natural piety was to
be respected. Therefore the elders also acquired a special
authority, and were to receive the utmost deference and due
obedience. But, however important the organisation that was
based on the distinction between πρεσβύτεροι and νεώτεροι, it
ought not to be considered as characteristic of the Churches,
not even where there appeared at the head of the community a college of chosen elders, as was the case in the
greater communities and, perhaps, soon everywhere. On the
contrary, only an organisation founded on the gifts of the
Spirit (χαρίσματα) bestowed on the Church by God,[1] corresponded to the original peculiarity of the Christian community.
The Apostolic age therefore transmitted a twofold organi
sation to the communities. The one was based on the
διακονία τοῦ λόγου, and was regarded as established directly
by God; the other stood in the closest connection with the
economy of the Church, above all with the offering of gifts, and
so with the sacrificial service. In the first were men speaking
the word of God, commissioned and endowed by God, and bestowed on Christendom, not on a particular community, who
as ἀπόστολοι, προφῆται, and διδάσκαλοι had to spread the Gospel,
that is to edify the Church of Christ. The were regarded
as the real ἡγούμενοι in the communities, whose words given
them by the Spirit all were to accept in faith. In the second
were ἐπίσκοποι, and διάκονοι, appointed by the individual con-
gregation and endowed with the charisms of leading and help-
ing, who had to receive and administer the gifts, to perform
the sacrificial service (if there were no prophets present), and
take charge of the affairs of the community.[2] It lay in the

[1] Cf. for the following my arguments in the larger edition of the "Teaching
of the Apostles" Chap. 5, (Texte u. Unters. II. 1. 2). The numerous recent enquiries
(Loening, Loofs, Réville etc.) will be found referred to in Sohm's Kirchenrecht.
Vol. I. 1892, where the most exhaustive discussions are given.

[2] That the bishops and deacons were, primarily, officials connected with the
cultus is most clearly seen from 1 Clem. 40-44, but also from the connection in

nature of the case that as a rule the ἐπίσκοποι, as independent officials, were chosen from among the elders, and might thus coincide with the chosen πρεσβύτεροι. But a very important development takes place in the second half of our epoch. The prophets and teachers—as the result of causes which followed the naturalising of the Churches in the world—fell more and more into the background, and their function, the solemn service of the word, began to pass over to the officials of the community, the bishops, who already played a great rôle in the public worship. At the same time, however, it appeared more and more fitting to entrust one official, as chief leader (superintendent of public worship), with the reception of gifts and their administration, together with the care of the unity of public worship; that is, to appoint one bishop instead of a number of bishops, leaving, however, as before, the college of presbyters, as προϊστάμενοι τῆς ἐκκλησίας, a kind of senate of the community. [1] Moreover, the idea of the chosen bishops and deacons as the antitypes of the Priests and Levites, had been formed at an early period in connection with the idea of the new sacrifice. But we find also the idea, which

which the 14th Chap. of the Didache stands with the 15th (see the οὖν 15.1), to which Hatch in conversation called my attention. The φιλοξενία and the intercourse with other communities (the fostering of the "unitas") belonged, above all, to the affairs of the Church. Here, undoubtedly, from the beginning lay an important part of the bishop's duties. Ramsay ("The Church in the Roman Empire," p. 361 ff.) has emphasised this point exclusively, and therefore one-sidedly. According to him, the monarchical Episcopate sprang from the officials who were appointed *ad hoc* and for a time, for the purpose of promoting intercourse with other churches.

[1] Sohm (in the work mentioned above) seeks to prove that the monarchical Episcopate originated in Rome and is already presupposed by Hermas. I hold that the proof for this has not been adduced, and I must also in great part reject the bold statements which are fastened on to the first Epistle of Clement. They may be comprehended in the proposition which Sohm, p. 158, has placed at the head of his discussion of the Epistle. "The first Epistle of Clement makes an epoch in the history of the organisation of the Church. It was destined to put an end to the early Christian constitution of the Church." According to Sohm (p. 165), another immediate result of the Epistle was a change of constitution in the Romish Church, the introduction of the monarchical Episcopate. That, however, can only be asserted, not proved; for the proof which Sohm has endeavoured to bring from Ignatius' Epistle to the Romans and the Shepherd of Hermas, is not convincing.

is probably the earlier of the two, that the prophets and
teachers, as the commissioned preachers of the word, are the
priests. The hesitancy in applying this important allegory
must have been brought to an end by the disappearance of
the latter view. But it must have been still more important
that the bishops, or bishop, in taking over the functions of
the old λαλοῦντες τὸν λόγον, who were not Church officials, took
over also the profound veneration with which they were regarded as the special organs of the Spirit. But the condition
of the organisation in the communities about the year 140,
seems to have been a very diverse one. Here and there, no
doubt, the convenient arrangement of appointing only one
bishop was carried out, while his functions had not perhaps
been essentially increased, and the prophets and teachers were
still the great spokesmen. Conversely, there may still have
been in other communities a number of bishops, while the
prophets and teachers no longer played regularly an important rôle. A fixed organisation was reached, and the Apostolic
episcopal constitution established, only in consequence of the
so-called Gnostic crisis, which was epoch-making in every
respect. One of its most important presuppositions, and one
that has struck very deep into the development of doctrine must,
however, be borne in mind here. As the Churches traced
back all the laws according to which they lived, and all the
blessings they held sacred, to the tradition of the twelve
Apostles, because they regarded them as Christian only on
that presupposition, they also in like manner, as far as we can
discover, traced back their organisation of presbyters, i.e., of
bishops and deacons, to Apostolic appointment. The notion
which followed quite naturally, was that the Apostles themselves had appointed the first church officials. [1] That idea may
have found support in some actual cases of the kind, but this
does not need to be considered here; for these cases would
not have led to the setting up of a theory. But the point
in question here is a theory, which is nothing else than an
integral part of the general theory, that the twelve Apostles

---

[1] See, above all, 1 Clem. 42, 44, Acts of the Apostles, Pastoral Epistles, etc.

were in every respect the middle term between Jesus and the present Churches (see above, p. 158). This conception is earlier than the great Gnostic crisis, for the Gnostics also shared it. But no special qualities of the officials, but only of the Church itself, were derived from it, and it was believed that the independence and sovereignty of the Churches were in no way endangered by it, because an institution by Apostles was considered equivalent to an institution by the Holy Spirit, whom they possessed and whom they followed. The independence of the Churches rested precisely on the fact that they had the Spirit in their midst. The conception here briefly sketched was completely transformed in the following period by the addition of another idea—that of Apostolic succession, [1] and then became, together with the idea of the specific priesthood of the leader of the Church, the most important means of exalting the office above the community. [2]

---

[1] This idea is Romish. See Book II. chap 11. C.

[2] We must remember here that besides the teachers, elders and deacons, the ascetics (virgins, widows, celibates, abstinentes) and the martyrs (confessors) enjoyed a special respect in the Churches, and frequently laid hold of the government and leading of them. Hermas enjoins plainly enough the duty of esteeming the confessors higher than the presbyters (Vis. III. 1. 2). The widows were soon entrusted with diaconal tasks connected with the worship, and received a corresponding respect. As to the limits of this, there was, as we can gather from different passages, much disagreement. One statement in Tertullian shews that the confessors had special claims to be considered in the choice of a bishop (adv. Valent. 4: "Speraverat Episcopatum Valentinus, quia et ingenio poterat et eloquio. Sed alium ex martyrii prærogativa loci potitum indignatus de ecclesia authenticæ regulæ abrupit"). This statement is strengthened by other passages; see Tertull. de fuga; 11: "Hoc sentire et facere omnem servum dei oportet, etiam minoris loci, ut maioris fieri possit, si quem gradum in persecutionis tolerantia ascenderit"; see Hippol. in the Arab. canons, and also Achelis, Texte u. Unters. VI. 4. pp. 67, 220: Cypr. Epp. 38. 39. The way in which confessors and ascetics, from the end of the second century, attempted to have their say in the leading of the Churches, and the respectful way in which it was sought to set their claims aside, shew that a special relation to the Lord, and therefore a special right with regard to the community, was early acknowledged to these people, on account of their archievements. On the transition of the old prophets and teachers into wandering ascetics, later into monks, see the Syriac Pseudo-Clementine Epistles, "de virginitate," and my Abhandl i. d. Sitzungsberichten d. K. Pr. Akad. d. Wissensch. 1891, p. 361 ff.

SUPPLEMENTARY.

This review of the common faith and the beginnings of knowledge, worship and organisation in the earliest Gentile Christianity will have shewn that the essential premises for the development of Catholicism were already in existence before the middle of the second century, and before the burning conflict with Gnosticism. We may see this, whether we look at the peculiar form of the *Kerygma*, or at the expression of the idea of tradition, or at the theology with its moral and philosophic attitude. We may therefore conclude that the struggle with Gnosticism hastened the development, but did not give it a new direction. For the Greek spirit, the element which was most operative in Gnosticism, was already concealed in the earliest Gentile Christianity itself; it was the atmosphere which one breathed; but the elements peculiar to Gnosticism were for the most part rejected.[1] We may even go back a step further (see above, pp. 41, 76). The great Apostle to the Gentiles himself, in his epistle to the Romans and in those to the Corinthians, transplanted the Gospel into Greek modes of thought. He attempted to expound it with Greek ideas, and not only called the Greeks to the Old Testament and the Gospel, but also introduced the Gospel as a leaven into the religious and philosophic world of Greek ideas. Moreover, in his pneumatico-cosmic Christology he gave the Greeks an impulse towards a theologoumenon, at whose service they could place their whole philosophy and mysticism. He preached the foolishness of Christ crucified, and yet in doing so proclaimed the wisdom of the nature-vanquishing Spirit, the heavenly Christ. From this moment was established a development which might indeed assume very different forms, but in which all the forces and ideas of Hellenism must gradually pass over to the Gospel. But even with this the last word has not been said; on the contrary, we must remember that the Gospel itself belonged to the fulness of the times, which

[1] See Weizsäcker. Gött. Gel. Anz. 1886, No. 21, whose statements I can almost entirely make my own.

is indicated by the inter-action of the Old Testament and the Hellenic religions (see above, pp. 41, 56).

The documents which have been preserved from the first century of the Gentile Church are, in their relation to the history of Dogma, very diverse. In the Didache we have a Catechism for Christian life dependent on a Jewish Greek Catechism, and giving expression to what was specifically Christian in the prayers and in the order of the Church. The Epistle of Barnabas, probably of Alexandrian origin, teaches the correct, Christian, interpretation of the Old Testament, rejects the literal interpretation and Judaism as of the devil, and in Christology essentially follows Paul. The Romish first Epistle of Clement, which also contains other Pauline reminiscences (reconciliation and justification), represents the same Christology, but it set it in a moralistic mode of thought. This is a most typical writing in which the spirit of tradition, order, stability, and the universal ecclesiastical guardianship of Rome is already expressed. The moralistic mode of thought is classically represented by the Shepherd of Hermas and the second Epistle of Clement, in which, besides, the eschatological element is very prominent. We have in the Shepherd the most important document for the Church Christianity of the age, reflected in the mirror of a prophet who, however, takes into account the concrete relations. The theology of Ignatius is the most advanced, in so far as he, opposing the Gnostics, brings the facts of salvation into the foreground, and directs his Gnosis not so much to the Old Testament as to the history of Christ. He attempts to make Christ κατὰ πνεῦμα and κατὰ σάρκα the central point of Christianity. In this sense his theology and speech is Christocentric, related to that of Paul and the fourth Evangelist, (specially striking is the relationship with Ephesians,) and is strongly contrasted with that of his contemporaries. Of kindred spirit with him are Melito and Irenæus, whose forerunner he is. He is related to them as Methodius at a later period was related to the classical orthodox theology of the fourth and fifth centuries. This parallel is appropriate not merely in point of form: it is rather one and the same tendency of mind which passes over from Ignatius to Melito, Irenæus, Methodius, Athanasius, Gregory of Nyssa (here, however, mixed with Origenic elements), and to Cyril of Alexandria. Its characteristic is that not only does the person of Christ as the God-man form the central point and sphere of theology, but also that all the main points of his history are mysteries of the world's redemption. (Ephes. 19). But Ignatius is also distinguished by the fact that behind all that is enthusiastic, pathetic, abrupt, and again all that pertains to liturgical form, we find in his epistles a true devotion to Christ (ὁ θεός μου). He is laid hold of by Christ: Cf. Ad. Rom. 6: ἐκεῖνον ζητῶ, τὸν ὑπερ ἡμῶν ἀποθανόντα, ἐκεῖνον θέλω, τὸν δι' ἡμᾶς ἀναστάντα; Rom. 7: ὁ ἐμὸς ἔρως ἐσταύρωται καὶ οὐκ ἔστιν ἐν ἐμοὶ πῦρ φιλοῦλον. As a sample of his theological speech and his rule of faith, see ad Smyrn. 1: ἐνόησα ὑμᾶς κατηρτισμένους ἐν ἀκινήτῳ πίστει, ὥσπερ καθηλωμένους ἐν τῷ σταυρῷ τοῦ κυρίου Ἰησοῦ Χριστοῦ σαρκί τε καὶ πνεύματι καὶ ἡδρασμένους ἐν ἀγάπῃ ἐν τῶ αἵματι Χριστοῦ, πεπληροφορημένους εἰς τὸν κυρίου ἡμῶν, ἀληθῶς ὄντα ἐκ γένους Δαβὶδ κατὰ σάρκα, υἱὸν θεοῦ κατὰ θέλημα καὶ δύναμιν θεοῦ, γεγεννημένον ἀληθῶς ἐκ παρθένου, βεβαπτισμένον ὑπὸ Ἰωάννου, ἵνα πληρωθῇ πᾶσα δικαιοσύνη ὑπ' αὐτοῦ, ἀληθῶς ἐπὶ Ποντίου Πιλάτου καὶ Ἡρώδου τετράρχου καθηλωμένον ὑπὲρ ἡμῶν ἐν σαρκί—ἀφ' οὗ καρποῦ ἡμεῖς, ἀπὸ τοῦ θεομακαρίτου αὐτοῦ πάθους—ἵνα ἄρῃ σύσσημον εἰς τοὺς αἰῶνας διὰ τῆς ἀναστάσεως εἰς τοὺς ἁγίους καὶ πιστοὺς αὐτοῦ εἴτε ἐν Ἰουδαίοις εἴτε ἐν ἔθνεσιν ἐν ἑνὶ σώματι τῆς ἐκκλησίας αὐτοῦ. The Epistle of Polycarp is characterised by its dependence on earlier Christian writings (Epistles of Paul, 1 Peter, 1 John), consequently by its conservative attitude with regard to the most valuable traditions of the Apostolic period. The *Kerygma* of Peter exhibits the transition from the early Christian literature to the apologetic (Christ as νόμος and as λόγος).

It is manifest that the lineage, "Ignatius, Polycarp, Melito, Irenæus," is in characteristic contrast with all others, has deep roots in the Apostolic age, as in Paul and in the Johannine writings, and contains in germ important factors of the future formation of dogma, as it appeared in Methodius, Athanasius, Marcellus, Cyril of Jerusalem. It is very doubtful, therefore, whether we are justified in speaking of an Asia

Minor theology. (Ignatius does not belong to Asia Minor.) At any rate, the expression, Asia Minor-Romish Theology, has no justification. But it has its truth in the correct observation, that the standards by which Christianity and Church matters were measured and defined must have been similar in Rome and Asia Minor during the second century. We lack all knowledge of the closer connections. We can only again refer to the journey of Polycarp to Rome, to that of Irenæus by Rome to Gaul, to the journey of Abercius and others. (Cf. also the application of the Montanist communities in Asia Minor for recognition by the Roman bishop.) In all probability, Asia Minor, along with Rome, was the spiritual centre of Christendom from about 60-200; but we have but few means for describing how this centre was brought to bear on the circumference. What we do know belongs more to the history of the Church than to the special history of dogma.

Literature.—The writings of the so-called Apostolic Fathers. See the edition of v. Gebhardt, Harnack, Zahn, 1876. Hilgenfeld, Nov. Test. extra Can. recept. fasc. IV. 2 edit. 1884, has collected further remains of early Christian literature. The Teaching of the twelve Apostles. Fragments of the Gospel and Apocalypse of Peter (my edition, 1893). Also the writings of Justin and other apologists, in so far as they give disclosures about the faith of the communities of his time, as well as statements in Celsus Ἀληθὴς Λόγος, in Irenæus, Clement of Alexandria, and Tertullian. Even Gnostic fragments may be cautiously turned to profit. Ritschl, Entstehung der altkath. Kirche, 2 Aufl. 1857. Pfleiderer, Das Urchristenthum, 1887. Renan, Origins of Christianity, vol. V. V. Engelhardt, Das Christenthum Justin's, d. M. 1878, p. 375 ff. Schenkel, Das Christusbild der Apostel, etc., 1879. Zahn, Gesch. des N.-Tlichen Kanons, 2 Bde. 1888. Behm, Das Christliche Gesetzthum der Apostolischen Väter (Zeitschr. f. kirchl. Wissensch. 1886). Dorner, History of the doctrine of the Person of Christ, 1845. Schultz, Die Lehre von der Gottheit Christi, 1881, p. 22 ff. Höfling, Die Lehre der ältesten Kirche vom Opfer, 1851. Höfling, Das Sacrament d. Taufe, 1848. Kahnis, Die Lehre vom Abendmahl, 1851. Th. Harnack, Der Christliche Gemein degottedienst im Apost. u. Altkath. Zeitalter, 1854. Hatch, Organisation of the Early Church, 1883. My Prolegomena to the Didache (Texte u. Unters. II. Bd. H. 1, 2). Diestel, Gesch. des A. T. in der Christl. Kirche, 1869. Sohm, Kirchenrecht, 1892. Monographs on the Apostolic Fathers: on 1 Clem.: Lipsius, Lightfoot (most accurate commentary), Wrede; on 2 Clem.: A. Harnack (Ztschr. f. K. Gesch. 1887); on Barnabas: J. Müller; on Hermas: Zahn, Hückstädt, Link; on Papias: Weiffenbach, Leimbach, Zahn, Lightfoot; on Ignatius and Polycarp: Lightfoot (accurate commentary) and Zahn; on the Gospel and Apocalypse of Peter: A. Harnack; on the Kerygma of Peter: von Dobschütz; on Acts of Thecla: Schlau.

CHAPTER IV

THE ATTEMPTS OF THE GNOSTICS TO CREATE AN APOSTOLIC
DOGMATIC, AND A CHRISTIAN THEOLOGY; OR, THE
ACUTE SECULARISING OF CHRISTIANITY.

§ 1. *The Conditions for the Rise of Gnosticism.*

THE Christian communities were originally unions for a holy
life on the ground of a common hope, which rested on the
belief that the God who has spoken by the Prophets has sent
his Son Jesus Christ, and through him revealed eternal life,
and will shortly make it manifest. Christianity had its roots
in certain facts and utterances, and the foundation of the
Christian union was the common hope, the holy life in the
Spirit according to the law of God, and the holding fast to
those facts and utterances. There was, as the foregoing chapter
will have shewn, no fixed Didache beyond that.[1] There was
abundance of fancies, ideas, and knowledge, but these had
not yet the value of being the religion itself. Yet the
belief that Christianity guarantees the perfect knowledge, and
leads from one degree of clearness to another, was in operation from the very beginning. This conviction had to be immediately tested by the Old Testament, that is, the task was
imposed on the majority of thinking Christians, by the circumstances in which the Gospel had been proclaimed to them,
of making the Old Testament intelligible to themselves, in

---

[1] We may consider here once more the articles which are embraced in the
first ten chapters of the recently discovered Διδαχὴ τῶν ἀποστόλων, after enume-
rating and describing which, the author continues (11. 1): ὃς ἂν οὖν ἐλθών διδάξῃ
ὑμᾶς ταῦτα πάντα τὰ προειρημένα, δέξασθε αὐτόν.

other words, of using this book as a Christian book, and of finding the means by which they might be able to repel the Jewish claim to it, and refute the Jewish interpretation of it. This task would not have been imposed, far less solved, if the Christian communities in the Empire had not entered into the inheritance of the Jewish propaganda, which had already been greatly influenced by foreign religions (Babylonian and Persian, see the Jewish Apocalypses), and in which an extensive spiritualising of the Old Testament religion had already taken place. This spiritualising was the result of a philosophic view of religion, and this philosophic view was the outcome of a lasting influence of Greek philosophy and of the Greek spirit generally on Judaism. In consequence of this view, all facts and sayings of the Old Testament in which one could not find his way were allegorised. " Nothing was what it seemed, but was only the symbol of something invisible. The history of the Old Testament was here sublimated to a history of the emancipation of reason from passion." It describes, however, the beginning of the historical development of Christianity, that as soon as it wished to give account of itself, or to turn to advantage the documents of revelations which were in its possession, it had to adopt the methods of that fantastic syncretism. We have seen above that those writers who made a diligent use of the Old Testament had no hesitation in making use of the allegorical method. That was required not only by the inability to understand the verbal sense of the Old Testament, presenting diverging moral and religious opinions, but, above all, by the conviction that on every page of that book Christ and the Christian Church must be found. How could this conviction have been maintained unless the definite concrete meaning of the documents had been already obliterated by the Jewish philosophic view of the Old Testament?

This necessary allegorical interpretation, however, brought into the communities an intellectual philosophic element, a γνῶσις, which was perfectly distinct from the Apocalyptic dreams, in which were beheld angel hosts on white horses, Christ with eyes as a flame of fire, hellish beasts, conflict and

victory. [1] In this γνῶσις, which attached itself to the Old
Testament, many began to see the specific blessing which
was promised to mature faith, and through which it was to
attain perfection. What a wealth of relations, hints, and
intuitions seemed to disclose itself, as soon as the Old Testament was considered allegorically, and to what extent had
the way been prepared here by the Jewish philosophic
teachers! From the simple narratives of the Old Testament
had already been developed a theosophy, in which the most
abstract ideas had acquired reality, and from which sounded
forth the Hellenic canticle of the power of the Spirit over
matter and sensuality, and of the true home of the soul.
Whatever in this great adaptation still remained obscure and
unnoticed, was now lighted up by the history of Jesus, his birth,
his life, his sufferings and triumph. The view of the Old Testament as a document of the deepest wisdom, transmitted to
those who knew how to read it as such, unfettered the intellectual
interest which would not rest until it had entirely transferred
the new religion from the world of feelings, actions and hopes,
into the world of Hellenic conceptions, and transformed it
into a metaphysic. In that exposition of the Old Testament
which we find, for example, in the so-called Barnabas, there is
already concealed an important philosophic, Hellenic element,
and in that sermon which bears the name of Clement (the so-
called second Epistle of Clement), conceptions such as that of
the Church, have already assumed a bodily form and been
joined in marvellous connections, while, on the contrary, things
concrete have been transformed into things invisible.

---

[1] It is a good tradition which designates the so-called Gnosticism simply as
Gnosis, and yet uses this word also for the speculations of non Gnostic teachers
of antiquity (*e.g.*, of Barnabas). But the inferences which follow have not been
drawn. Origen says truly (c. Celsus III. 12): "As men, not only the labouring
and serving classes, but also many from the cultured classes of Greece, came to
see something honourable in Christianity, sects could not fail to arise, not simply
from the desire for controversy and contradiction, but because several scholars
endeavoured to penetrate deeper into the truth of Christianity. In this way sects
arose which received their names from men who indeed admired Christianity in
its essence, but from many different causes had arrived at different conceptions
of it."

But once the intellectual interest was unfettered, and the new religion had approximated to the Hellenic spirit by means of a philosophic view of the Old Testament, how could that spirit be prevented from taking complete and immediate possession of it, and where, in the first instance, could the power be found that was able to decide whether this or that opinion was incompatible with Christianity? This Christianity, as it was, unequivocally excluded all polytheism, and all national religions existing in the Empire. It opposed to them the one God, the Saviour Jesus, and a spiritual worship of God. But at the same time it summoned all thoughtful men to knowledge by declaring itself to be the only true religion, while it appeared to be only a variety of Judaism. It seemed to put no limits to the character and extent of the knowledge, least of all to such knowledge as was able to allow all that was transmitted to remain, and at the same time abolish it by transforming it into mysterious symbols. That really was the method which every one must and did apply who wished to get from Christianity more than practical motives and superearthly hopes. But where was the limit of the application? Was not the next step to see in the Evangelic records also new material for spiritual interpretations, and to illustrate from the narratives there, as from the Old Testament, the conflict of the spirit with matter, of reason with sensuality? Was not the conception, that the traditional deeds of Christ were really the last act in the struggle of those mighty spiritual powers whose conflict is delineated in the Old Testament, at least as evident as the other, that those deeds were the fulfilment of mysterious promises? Was it not in keeping with the consciousness possessed by the new religion of being the universal religion, that one should not be satisfied with mere beginnings of a new knowledge, or with fragments of it, but should seek to set up such knowledge in a complete and systematic form, and so to exhibit the best and universal system of life as also the best and universal system of knowledge of the world? Finally, did not the free and yet so rigid forms in which the Christian communities were organised, the union of the mysterious with a wonderful publicity, of the spiritual with

significant rites (baptism and the Lord's Supper), invite men
to find here the realisation of the ideal which the Hellenic
religious spirit was at that time seeking, viz., a communion
which, in virtue of a Divine revelation, is in possession of the
highest knowledge, and therefore leads the holiest life; a
communion which does not communicate the knowledge by
discourse, but by mysterious efficacious consecrations and by
revealed dogmas? These questions are thrown out here in
accordance with the direction which the historical progress of
Christianity took. The phenomenon called Gnosticism gives
the answer to them. [1]

§ 2. *The Nature of Gnosticism.*

The Catholic Church afterwards claimed as her own those
writers of the first century (60-160) who were content with
turning speculation to account only as a means of spiritualising the Old Testament, without, however, attempting a
systematic reconstruction of tradition. But all those who in the
first century undertook to furnish Christian practice with the
foundation of a complete systematic knowledge, she declared false
Christians, Christians only in name. Historical enquiry cannot
accept this judgment. On the contrary, it sees in Gnosticism
a series of undertakings, which in a certain way is analogous
to the Catholic embodiment of Christianity, in doctrine, morals, and worship. The great distinction here consists essentially in the fact that the Gnostic systems represent the acute
secularising or hellenising of Christianity, with the rejection
of the Old Testament; [1] while the Catholic system, on the

---

[1] The majority of Christians in the second century belonged no doubt to the
uncultured classes and did not seek abstract knowledge, nay, were distrustful of
it; see the λόγος ἀληθής of Celsus, especially III. 44, and the writings of the
Apologists. Yet we may infer from the treatise of Origen against Celsus, that the
number of "Christiani rudes" who cut themselves off from theological and philosophic knowledge, was about the year 240 a very large one; and Tertullian says
(Adv. Prax. 3): "Simplices quique, ne dixerim imprudentes et idiotæ, quæ major
semper credentium pars est," cf. de jejun. 11: "Major pars imperitorum apud
gloriosissimam multitudinem psychicorum."

[2] Overbeck (Stud. z. Gesch. d. alten Kirche. p. 184) has the merit of having
first given convincing expression to this view of Gnosticism.

other hand, represents a gradual process of the same kind
with the conservation of the Old Testament. The traditional
religion on being, as it were, suddenly required to recognise
itself in a picture foreign to it, was yet vigorous enough to
reject that picture; but to the gradual, and one might say
indulgent remodelling to which it was subjected, it offered
but little resistance, nay, as a rule, it was never conscious of
it. It is therefore no paradox to say that Gnosticism, which
is just Hellenism, has in Catholicism obtained half a victory.
We have, at least, the same justification for that assertion—
the parallel may be permitted—as we have for recognising
a triumph of 18th century ideas in the first Empire, and a
continuance, though with reservations, of the old régime.

From this point of view the position to be assigned to the
Gnostics in the history of dogma, which has hitherto been
always misunderstood, is obvious. *They were, in short, the
Theologians of the first century.* [1] They were the first to
transform Christianity into a system of doctrines (dogmas).
They were the first to work up tradition systematically. They
undertook to present Christianity as the absolute religion, and
therefore placed it in definite opposition to the other religions,
even to Judaism. But to them the absolute religion, viewed
in its contents, was identical with the result of the philosophy
of religion for which the support of a revelation was to be
sought. They are therefore those Christians who, in a swift
advance, attempted to capture Christianity for Hellenic culture,
and Hellenic culture for Christianity, and who gave up the
Old Testament in order to facilitate the conclusion of the
covenant between the two powers, and make it possible to

---

[1] The ability of the prominent Gnostic teachers has been recognised by the
Church Fathers: see Hieron. Comm. in Osee. II. 10, Opp. VI. 1: "Nullus potest
hæresim struere, nisi qui ardens ingenii est et habet dona naturæ quæ a deo
artifice sunt creata : talis fuit Valentinus, talis Marcion, quos doctissimos legimus,
talis Bardesanes, cujus etiam philosophi admirantur ingenium." It is still more
important to see how the Alexandrian theologians (Clement and Origen) estimated
the exegetic labours of the Gnostics and took account of them. Origen undoubtedly
recognised Herakleon as a prominent exegete, and treats him most respectfully
even where he feels compelled to differ from him. All Gnostics cannot, of course,
be regarded as theologians. In their totality they form the Greek society with a
Christian name.

assert the absoluteness of Christianity.—But the significance of
the Old Testament in the religious history of the world lies just
in this, that, in order to be maintained at all, it required the
application of the allegoric method, that is, a definite proportion
of Greek ideas, and that, on the other hand, it opposed the strongest barrier to the complete hellenising of Christianity.   Neither
the sayings of Jesus, nor Christian hopes, were at first capable of forming such a barrier.   If, now, the majority of Gnostics
could make the attempt to disregard the Old Testament, that
is a proof that, in wide circles of Christendom, people were
at first satisfied with an abbreviated form of the Gospel, containing the preaching of the one God, of the resurrection and
of continence,—a law and an ideal of practical life. [1]   In this
form, as it was realised in life, the Christianity which dispensed
with "doctrines" seemed capable of union with every form
of thoughtful and earnest philosophy, because the Jewish
foundation did not make its appearance here at all.   But the
majority of Gnostic undertakings may also be viewed as
attempts to transform Christianity into a theosophy, that is,
into a revealed metaphysic and philosophy of history, with a
complete disregard of the Jewish Old Testament soil on which
it originated, through the use of Pauline ideas, [2] and under
the influence of the Platonic spirit.   Moreover, comparison is
possible between writers such as Barnabas and Ignatius, and
the so-called Gnostics, to the effect of making the latter appear in possession of a completed theory, to which fragmentary
ideas in the former exhibit a striking affinity.

We have hitherto tacitly presupposed that in Gnosticism
the Hellenic spirit desired to make itself master of Christianity, or more correctly of the Christian communities.   This
conception may be, and really is still contested.   For according to the accounts of later opponents, and on these we are
almost exclusively dependent here, the main thing with the
Gnostics seems to have been the reproduction of Asiatic My-
thologoumena of all kinds, so that we should rather have to

[1]   Otherwise the rise of Gnosticism cannot at all be explained.
[2]   Cf. Bigg, "The Christian Platonists of Alexandria," p. 83: "Gnosticism was
in one respect distorted Paulinism"

see in Gnosticism a union of Christianity with the most remote
Oriental cults and their wisdom. But with regard to the most
important Gnostic systems the words hold true, "The hands
are the hands of Esau, but the voice is the voice of Jacob."
There can be no doubt of the fact, that the Gnosticism which
has become a factor in the movement of the history of dogma,
was ruled in the main by the Greek spirit, and determined
by the interests and doctrines of the Greek philosophy of
religion, [1] which doubtless had already assumed a syncretistic
character. This fact is certainly concealed by the circumstance that the material of the speculations was taken now
from this, and now from that Oriental religious philosophy,
from astrology and the Semitic cosmologies. But that is
only in keeping with the stage which the religious development had reached among the Greeks and Romans of that
time. [2] The cultured, and these primarily come into consideration here, no longer had a religion in the sense of a national
religion, but a philosophy of religion. They were, however,
in search of a religion, that is, a firm basis for the results
of their speculations, and they hoped to obtain it by turning
themselves towards the very old Oriental cults, and seeking
to fill them with the religious and moral knowledge which had
been gained by the Schools of Plato and of Zeno. The union
of the traditions and rites of the Oriental religions, viewed as
mysteries, with the spirit of Greek philosophy is the characteristic of the epoch. The needs, which asserted themselves
with equal strength, of a complete knowledge of the All, of
a spiritual God, a sure and therefore very old revelation,

---

[1] Joel, "Blick in die Religionsgesch." Vol I. pp. 101-170, has justly emphasised
the Greek character of Gnosis, and insisted on the significance of Platonism for
it. "The Oriental element did not always in the case of the Gnostics originate
at first hand, but had already passed through a Greek channel."

[2] The age of the Antonines was the flourishing period of Gnosticism. Marquardt
(Römische .Staatsverwaltung, vol. 3, p. 81) says of this age: "With the Antonines
begins the last period of the Roman religious development, in which two new
elements enter into it. These are the Syrian and Persian deities, whose worship
at this time was prevalent not only in the city of Rome, but in the whole empire,
and at the same time Christianity, which entered into conflict with all ancient
tradition, and in this conflict exercised a certain influence even on the Oriental
forms of worship.

atonement and immortality, were thus to be satisfied at one and the same time. The most sublimated spiritualism enters here into the strangest union with a crass superstition based on Oriental cults. This superstition was supposed to insure and communicate the spiritual blessings. These complicated tendencies now entered into Christianity.

We have accordingly to ascertain and distinguish in the prominent Gnostic schools, which, in the second century on Greek soil, became an important factor in the history of the Church, the Semitic-cosmological foundations, the Hellenic philosophic mode of thought, and the recognition of the redemption of the world by Jesus Christ. Further, we have to take note of the three elements of Gnosticism, viz., the speculative and philosophical, the mystic element connection with worship, and the practical, ascetic. The close connection in which these three elements appear, [1] the total transformation of all ethical into cosmological problems, the upbuilding of a philosophy of God and the world on the basis of a combination of popular Mythologies, physical observations belonging to the Oriental (Babylonian) religious philosophy, and historical events, as well as the idea that the history of religion is the last act in the drama-like history of the Cosmos—all this is not peculiar to Gnosticism, but rather corresponds to a definite stage of the general development. It may, however, be asserted that Gnosticism anticipated the general development, and that not

[1] It is a special merit of Weingarten (Histor. Ztschr. Bd. 45. 1881. p. 441 f.) and Koffmane (De Gnosis nach ihrer Tendenz und Organisation, 1881) to have strongly emphasised the mystery character of Gnosis, and in connection with that, its practical aims. Koffmane, especially, has collected abundant material for proving that the tendency of the Gnostics was the same as that of the ancient mysteries, and that they thence borrowed their organisation and discipline. This fact proves the proposition that Gnosticism was an acute hellenising of Christianity. Koffmane has, however, undervalued the union of the practical and speculative tendency in the Gnostics, and, in the effort to obtain recognition for the mystery character of the Gnostic communities, has overlooked the fact that they were also schools. The union of mystery-cultus and school is just, however, their characteristic. In this also they prove themselves the forerunners of Neoplatonism and the Catholic Church. Moehler in his programme of 1831 (Urspr. d. Gnosticismus Tübingen), vigorously emphasised the practical tendency of Gnosticism, though not in a convincing way. Hackenschmidt (Anfänge des katholischen Kirchenbegriffs, p. 83 f.) has judged correctly.

only with regard to Catholicism, but also with regard to Neoplatonism, which represents the last stage in the inner history
of Hellenism. [1] The Valentinians have already got as far as
Jamblichus.

The name Gnosis, Gnostics, describes excellently the aims
of Gnosticism, in so far as its adherents boasted of the absolute knowledge, and faith in the Gospel was transformed into
a knowledge of God, nature and history. This knowledge,
however, was not regarded as natural, but in the view of the
Gnostics was based on revelation, was communicated and
guaranteed by holy consecrations, and was accordingly cultivated by reflection supported by fancy. A mythology of ideas
was created out of the sensuous mythology of any Oriental
religion, by the conversion of concrete forms into speculative
and moral ideas, such as "Abyss," "Silence," "Logos," "Wisdom," "Life," while the mutual relation and number of these
abstract ideas were determined by the data supplied by the
corresponding concretes. Thus arose a philosophic dramatic
poem similar to the Platonic, but much more complicated,
and therefore more fantastic, in which mighty powers, the
spiritual and good, appear in an unholy union with the material
and wicked, but from which the spiritual is finally delivered
by the aid of those kindred powers which are too exalted to
be ever drawn down into the common. The good and heavenly
which has been drawn down into the material, and therefore really
non-existing, is the human spirit, and the exalted power who
delivers it is Christ. The Evangelic history as handed down
is not the history of Christ, but a collection of allegoric representations of the great history of God and the world. Christ
has really no history. His appearance in this world of mixture
and confusion is his deed, and the enlightenment of the spirit
about itself is the result which springs out of that deed. This

---

[1] We have also evidence of the methods by which ecstatic visions were obtained
among the Gnostics: see the Pistis Sophia, and the important rôle which prophets
and Apocalypses played in several important Gnostic communities (Barcoph and
Barcabbas, prophets of the Basilideans; Martiades and Marsanes among the Ophites;
Philumene in the case of Apelles; Valentinian prophecies; Apocalypses of Zostrian,
Zoroaster, etc.). Apocalypses were also used by some under the names of Old
Testament men of God and Apostles.

enlightenment itself is life. But the enlightenment is dependent on revelation, asceticism and surrender to those mysteries which Christ founded, in which one enters into communion with a *præsens numen*, and which in mysterious ways promote the process of raising the spirit above the sensual. This rising above the sensual is, however, to be actively practised. Abstinence therefore, as a rule, is the watchword. Christianity thus appears here as a speculative philosophy which redeems the spirit by enlightening it, consecrating it, and instructing it in the right conduct of life. The Gnosis is free from the rationalistic interest in the sense of natural religion. Because the riddles about the world which it desires to solve are not properly intellectual, but practical, because it desires to be in the end γνῶσις σωτηρίας, it removes into the region of the supra-rational the powers which are supposed to confer vigour and life on the human spirit. Only a μάθησις, however, united with μυσταγωγία resting on revelation leads thither, not an exact philosophy. Gnosis starts from the great problem of this world, but occupies itself with a higher world, and does not wish to be an exact philosophy, but a philosophy of religion. Its fundamental philosophic doctrines are the following: (1) The indefinable, infinite nature of the Divine primeval Being exalted above all thought. (2) Matter as opposed to the Divine Being, and therefore having no real being, the ground of evil. (3) The fulness of divine potencies, Æons, which are thought of partly as powers, partly as real ideas, partly as relatively independent beings, presenting in gradation the unfolding and revelation of the Godhead, but at the same time rendering possible the transition of the higher to the lower. (4) The Cosmos as a mixture of matter with divine sparks, which has arisen from a descent of the latter into the former, or, as some say, from the perverse, or at least merely permitted undertaking of a subordinate spirit. The Demiurge, therefore, is an evil, intermediate, or weak, but penitent being; the best thing therefore in the world is aspiration. (5) The deliverance of the spiritual element from its union with matter, or the separation of the good from the world of sensuality by the Spirit of Christ which operates through knowledge, ascet-

icism, and holy consecration: thus originates the perfect
Gnostic, the man who is free from the world, and master of
himself, who lives in God and prepares himself for eternity.
All these are ideas for which we find the way prepared in the
philosophy of the time, anticipated by Philo, and represented
in Neoplatonism as the great final result of Greek philosophy.
It lies in the nature of the case that only some men are able
to appropriate the Christianity that is comprehended in these
ideas, viz., just as many as are capable of entering into this
kind of Christianity, those who are spiritual. The others must
be considered as non-partakers of the Spirit from the beginning, and therefore excluded from knowledge as the *profanum vulgus.* Yet some—the Valentinians, for example—made
a distinction in this *vulgus,* which can only be discussed later
on, because it is connected with the position of the Gnostics
towards Jewish Christian tradition.

The later opponents of Gnosticism preferred to bring out
the fantastic details of the Gnostic systems, and thereby
created the prejudice that the essence of the matter lay in
these. They have thus occasioned modern expounders to speculate about the Gnostic speculations in a manner that is
marked by still greater strangeness. Four observations shew
how unhistorical and unjust such a view is, at least with regard to the chief systems. (1) The great Gnostic schools,
wherever they could, sought to spread their opinions. But
it is simply incredible that they should have expected of all
their disciples, male and female, an accurate knowledge of the
details of their system. On the contrary, it may be shewn that
they often contented themselves with imparting consecration, with
regulating the practical life of their adherents, and instructing
them in the general features of their system. [1] (2) We see
how in one and the same school—for example, the Valentinian—the details of the religious metaphysic were very various and changing. (3) We hear but little of conflicts between
the various schools. On the contrary, we learn that the
books of doctrine and edification passed from one school to

---

[1] See Koffmane, before-mentioned work, p. 5 f.

another. [1] (4) The fragments of Gnostic writings which have
been preserved, and this is the most important consideration
of the four, shew that the Gnostics devoted their main strength
to the working out of those religious, moral, philosophical
and historical problems which must engage the thoughtful
of all times. [2] We only need to read some actual Gnostic
document, such as the Epistle of Ptolemæus to Flora, or certain paragraphs of the Pistis Sophia, in order to see that the
fantastic details of the philosophic poem can only, in the case
of the Gnostics themselves, have had the value of liturgical
apparatus, the construction of which was not of course matter
of indifference, but hardly formed the principle interest. The
things to be proved and to be confirmed by the aid of this
or that very old religious philosophy, were certain religious
and moral fundamental convictions, and a correct conception
of God, of the sensible, of the creator of the world, of Christ,
of the Old Testament, and the evangelic tradition. Here were
actual dogmas. But how the grand fantastic union of all the

---

[1] See Fragm. Murat. V. 81 f.; Clem. Strom. VII. 17. 108; Orig. Hom. 34.
The Marcionite Antitheses were probably spread among other Gnostic sects. The
Fathers frequently emphasise the fact that the Gnostics were united against the
Church: Tertullian de præscr. 42: "Et hoc est, quod schismata apud hæreticos
fere non sunt, quia cum sint, non parent. Schisma est enim unitas ipsa." They
certainly also delight in emphasising the contradictions of the different schools ;
but they cannot point to any earnest conflict of these schools with each other.
We know definitely that Bardasanes argued against the earlier Gnostics, and
Ptolemæus against Marcion.

[2] See the collection, certainly not complete, of Gnostic fragments by Grabe
(Spicileg.) and Hilgenfeld (Ketzergeschichte). Our books on the history of Gnosticism take far too little notice of these fragments as presented to us, above all, by
Clement and Origen, and prefer to keep to the doleful accounts of the Fathers
about the "Systems," (better in Heinrici: Valent. Gnosis, 1871). The vigorous
efforts of the Gnostics to understand the Pauline and Johannine ideas, and their
in part surprisingly rational and ingenious solutions of intellectual problems, have
never yet been systematically estimated. Who would guess, for example, from
what is currently known of the system of Basilides, that, according to Clement,
the following proceeds from him, (Strom. IV. 12. 18): ὡς αὐτός φησιν ὁ Βασιλείδης,
ἓν μέρος ἐκ τοῦ λεγομένου θελήματος τοῦ θεοῦ ὑπειλήφαμεν, τὸ ἠγαπηκέναι ἅπαντα.
ὅτι λόγον ἀποσώζουσι πρὸς τὸ πᾶν ἅπαντα· ἕτερον δὲ τὸ μηδενὸς ἐπιθυμεῖν, καὶ τὸ
τρίτον μισεῖν μηδὲ ἕν? and where do we find, in the period before Clement of
Alexandria, faith in Christ united with such spiritual maturity and inner freedom
as in Valentinus, Ptolemæus and Heracleon?

factors was to be brought about, was, as the Valentinian
school shews, a problem whose solution was ever and again
subjected to new attempts. [1] No one to-day can in all respects distinguish what to those thinkers was image and what
reality, or in what degree they were at all able to distinguish
image from reality, and in how far the magic formulæ of their
mysteries were really objects of their meditation. But the
final aim of their endeavours, the faith and knowledge of
their own hearts which they instilled into their disciples, the
practical rules which they wished to give them, and the view
of Christ which they wished to confirm them in, stand out
with perfect clearness. Like Plato, they made their explanation of the world start from the contradiction between sense
and reason, which the thoughtful man observes in himself.
The cheerful asceticism, the powers of the spiritual and the
good which were seen in the Christian communities, attracted
them and seemed to require the addition of theory to practice.
Theory without being followed by practice had long been in
existence, but here was the as yet rare phenomenon of a moral
practice which seemed to dispense with that which was regarded
as indispensable, viz., theory. The philosophic life was already
there; how could the philosophic doctrine be wanting, and after
what other model could the latent doctrine be reproduced than
that of the Greek religious philosophy? [2] That the Hellenic

---

[1] Testament of Tertullian (adv. Valent. 4) shews the difference between the
solution of Valentinus, for example, and his disciple Ptolemæus. "Ptolemæus
nomina et numeros Æonum distinxit in personales substantias, sed extra deum
determinatas, quas Valentinus in ipsa summa divinitatis ut sensus et affectus motus
incluserat." It is, moreover, important that Tertullian himself should distinguish
this so clearly.

[2] There is nothing here more instructive than to hear the judgments of the
cultured Greeks and Romans about Christianity, as soon as they have given up the
current gross prejudices. They shew with admirable clearness the way in which
Gnosticism originated. Galen says (quoted by Gieseler, Church Hist. 1. 1. 4):
"Hominum plerique orationem demonstrativam continuam mente assequi nequeunt,
quare indigent, ut instituantur parabolis. Veluti nostro tempore videmus, homines
illos, qui Christiani vocantur, fidem suam e parabolis petiisse. Hi tamen interdum
talia faciunt, qualia qui vere philosophantur. Nam quod mortem contemnunt, id
quidem omnes ante oculos habemus; item quod verecundia quadam ducti ab usu
rerum venerearam abhorrent. Sunt enim inter eos feminæ et viri, qui per totam

spirit in Gnosticism turned with such eagerness to the Christian communities and was ready even to believe in Christ in order to appropriate the moral powers which it saw operative in them, is a convincing proof of the extraordinary impression which these communities made. For what other peculiarities and attractions had they to offer to that spirit than the certainty of their conviction (of eternal life), and the purity of their life? We hear of no similar edifice being erected in the second century on the basis of any other Oriental cult— even the Mithras cult is scarcely to be mentioned here—as the Gnostic was on the foundation of the Christian.[1] The Christian communities, however, together with their worship of Christ, formed the real solid basis of the greater number and the most important of the Gnostic systems, and in this fact we have, on the very threshold of the great conflict, a triumph of Christianity over Hellenism. The triumph lay in the recognition of what Christianity had already performed as a moral and social power. This recognition found expression in bringing the highest that one possessed as a gift to be consecrated

vitam a concubitu abstinuerint; sunt etiam qui in animis regendis coërcendisque et in accerrimo honestatis studio eo progressi sint, ut nihil cedant vere philosophantibus." Christians, therefore, are philosophers without philosophy. What a challenge for them to produce such, that is to seek out the latent philosophy! Even Celsus could not but admit a certain relationship between Christians and philosophers. But as he was convinced that the miserable religion of the Christians could neither include nor endure a philosophy, he declared that the moral doctrines of the Christians were borrowed from the philosophers (I. 4). In course of his presentation (V. 65 : VI. 12, 15-19, 42 : VII. 27-35) he deduces the most decided marks of Christianity, as well as the most important sayings of Jesus from (misunderstood) statements of Plato and other Greek philosophers. This is not the place to shew the contradictions in which Celsus was involved ·by this. But it is of the greatest significance that even this intelligent man could only see philosophy where he saw something precious. The whole of Christianity from its very origin appeared to Celsus (in one respect) precisely as the Gnostic systems appear to us, that is, these really are what Christianity as such seemed to Celsus to be. Besides, it was constantly asserted up to the fifth century that Christ had drawn from Plato's writings. Against those who made this assertion, Ambrosius (according to Augustine, Ep. 31. c. 8) wrote a treatise, which unfortunately is no longer in existence.

[1] The Simonian system at most might be named, on the basis of the syncretistic religion founded by Simon Magus. But we know little about it, and that little is uncertain. Parallel attempts are demonstrable in the third century on the basis of various "revealed" fundamental ideas (ἡ ἐκ λογίων φιλοσοφία).

by the new religion, a philosophy of religion whose end was plain and simple, but whose means were mysterious and complicated.

§ 3. *History of Gnosticism and the forms in which it appeared.*

In the previous section we have been contemplating Gnosticism as it reached its prime in the great schools of Basilides and Valentinus, and those related to them, [1] at the close of the period we are now considering, and became an important factor in the history of dogma. But this Gnosticism had (1) preliminary stages, and (2) was always accompanied by a great number of sects, schools and undertakings which were only in part related to it, and yet, reasonably enough, were grouped together with it.

To begin with the second point, the great Gnostic schools were flanked on the right and left by a motley series of groups which at their extremities can hardly be distinguished from popular Christianity on the one hand, and from the Hellenic and the common world on the other. [2] On the right were communities such as the Encratites, which put all stress on a strict asceticism, in support of which they urged the example of Christ, but which here and there fell into dualistic ideas. [3] There were, further, whole communities which, for decennia, drew their

---

[1] Among these I reckon those Gnostics whom Irenæus (I. 29–31) has portrayed, as well as part of the so-called Ophites, Peratæ, Sethites and the school of the Gnostic Justin (Hippol. Philosoph. V. 6–28). There is no reason for regarding them as earlier or more Oriental than the Valentinians, as is done by Hilgenfeld against Baur, Möller, and Gruber (the Ophites, 1864). See also Lipsius, "Ophit. Systeme," i. d. Ztschr. f. wiss. Theol. 1863. IV. 1864, I. These schools claimed for themselves the name Gnostic (Hippol. Philosoph V. 6). A part of them, as is specially apparent from Orig. c. Celsus. VI., is not to be reckoned Christian. This motley group is but badly known to us through Epiphanius, much better through the original Gnostic writings preserved in the Coptic language. (Pistis Sophia and the works published by Carl Schmidt. Texte u. Unters. Bd. VIII.) Yet these original writings belong, for the most part, to the second half of the third century (see also the important statements of Porphyry in the Vita Plotini. c. 16), and shew a Gnosticism burdened with an abundance of wild speculations, formulæ, mysteries, and ceremonial. However, from these very monuments it becomes plain that Gnosticism anticipated Catholicism as a ritual system (see below).

[2] On Marcion, see the following Chapter.

[3] We know that from the earliest period (perhaps we might refer even to the

views of Christ from books which represented him as a heavenly
spirit who had merely assumed an apparent body.¹ There
were also individual teachers who brought forward peculiar
opinions without thereby causing any immediate stir in the
Churches.² On the left there were schools such as the Carpocratians, in which the philosophy and communism of Plato

Epistle to the Romans) there were circles of ascetics in the Christian communities
who required of all, as an inviolable law, under the name of Christian perfection,
complete abstinence from marriage, renunciation of possessions, and a vegetarian
diet. (Clem. Strom. III. 6. 49: ὑπὸ διαβόλου ταύτην παραδίδοσθαι δογματίζουσι,
μιμεῖσθαι δ᾽ αὐτοὺς οἱ μεγάλαυχοί φασι τὸν κύριον μήτε γήμαντα, μήτε τι ἐν τῷ
κόσμῳ κτησάμενον μᾶλλον παρὰ τοὺς ἄλλους νενοηκέναι τὸ εὐαγγέλιον καυχόμενοι.—
Here then, already, imitation of the poor life of Jesus, the "Evangelic" life, was
the watchword. Tatian wrote a book, περὶ τοῦ κατὰ τὸν σωτῆρα καταρτισμοῦ, that
is, on perfection according to the Redeemer: in which he set forth the irreconcil-
ability of the worldly life with the Gospel). No doubt now existed in the Churches
that abstinence from marriage, from wine and flesh, and from possessions, was the
perfect fulfilling of the law of Christ (βαστάζειν ὅλον τὸν ζυγὸν τοῦ κύριου). But
in wide circles strict abstinence was deduced from a special charism, all boastful-
ness was forbidden, and the watchword given out: ὅσον δύνασαι ἀγνεύσεις, which
may be understood as a compromise with the worldly life as well as a reminiscence
of a freer morality (see my notes on Didache, c. 6 : 11, 11 and Prolegg. p. 42 ff.).
Still, the position towards asceticism yielded a hard problem, the solution of which
was more and more found in distinguishing a higher and a lower though sufficient
morality, yet repudiating the higher morality as soon as it claimed to be the alone
authoritative one. On the other hand, there were societies of Christian ascetics
who persisted in applying literally to all Christians the highest demands of Christ,
and thus arose, by secession, the communities of the Encratites and Severians.
But in the circumstances of the time even they could not but be touched by the
Hellenic mode of thought, to the effect of associating a speculative theory with
asceticism, and thus approximating to Gnosticism. This is specially plain in Tatian,
who connected himself with the Encratites, and in consequence of the severe asceticism which he prescribed, could no longer maintain the identity of the supreme
God and the creator of the world (see the fragments of his later writings in the
Corp. Apol. ed. Otto. T. VI.). As the Pauline Epistles could furnish arguments to
either side, we see some Gnostics, such as Tatian himself, making diligent use of
them, while others, such as the Severians, rejected them. (Euseb. H. E. IV. 29, 5,
and Orig. c. Cels. V. 65). The Encratite controversy was, on the one hand,
swallowed up by the Gnostic, and on the other hand, replaced by the Montanistic.
The treatise written in the days of Marcus Aurelius by a certain Musanus (where?)
which contains warnings against joining the Encratites (Euseb. H. E. VI. 28) we
unfortunately no longer possess.

¹ See Eusebius, H. E. VI. 12. Docetic elements are apparent even in the
fragment of the Gospel of Peter recently discovered.

² Here, above all, we have to remember Tatian, who in his highly praised
Apology had already rejected altogether the eating of flesh (c. 23) and set up

were taught, the son of the founder and second teacher Epiphanes honoured as a God (at Cephallenia), as Epicurus was in his school, and the image of Jesus crowned along with those of Pythagoras, Plato and Aristotle. [1] On this left flank are, further, swindlers who take their own way, like Alexander of Abonoteichus, magicians, soothsayers, sharpers and jugglers, under the sign-board of Christianity, deceivers and hypocrites who appear using mighty words with a host of unintelligible formulæ, and take up with scandalous ceremonies in order to rob men of their money and women of their honour. [2] All this was afterwards called "Heresy" and "Gnosticism," and is still so called. [3] And these names may be retained, if very peculiar doctrines about the spirit, matter, and the nature of man (c. 12 ff.). The fragments of the Hypotyposes of Clem. of Alex. show how much one had to bear in some rural Churches at the end of the second century.

[1] See Clem. Strom. III. 2. 5; Ἐπιφάνης, υἱὸς Καρποκράτους, ἔζησε τὰ πάντα ἔτη ἑπτακαίδεκα καὶ θεὸς ἐν Σαμῃ τῆς Κεφαλληνίας τετίμηται, ἔνθα αὐτῷ ἱερὸν ῥυτῶν λίθων, βωμοί, τεμένη, μουσεῖον, ᾠκοδόμηταί τε καὶ καθιέρωται, καὶ συνιόντες εἰς τὸ ἱερὸν οἱ Καφαλλῆνες κατὰ νουμηνίαν γενέθλιον ἀποθέωσιν θύουσιν Ἐπιφάνει, σπένδουσί τε καὶ εὐωχοῦνται καὶ ὕμνοι λέγονται. Clement's quotations from the writings of Epiphanes shew him to be a pure Platonist: the proposition that property is theft is found in him. Epiphanes and his father, Carpocrates, were the first who attempted to amalgamate Plato's State with the Christian ideal of the union of men with each other. Christ was to them, therefore, a philosophic Genius like Plato, see Irenæus. I. 25. 5: "Gnosticos autem se vocant, etiam imagines, quasdam quidem depictas, quasdam autem et de reliqua materia fabricatas habent..... et eas coronant, et proponent eas cum imaginibus mundi philosophorum, videlicet cum imagine Pythagoræ et Platonis et Aristotelis et reliquorum, et reliquam observationem circa eas similiter ut gentes faciunt."

[2] See the "Gnostics" of Hermas, especially the false prophet whom he portrays, Maud XI., Lucian's Peregrinus, and the Marcus, of whose doings Irenæus (I. 13 ff.) gives such an abominable picture. To understand how such people were able to obtain a following so quickly in the Churches, we must remember the respect in which the "prophets" were held (see Didache XI.). If one had once given the impression that he had the Spirit, he could win belief for the strangest things, and could allow himself all things possible (see the delineations of Celsus in Orig. c. Cels. VII. 9. 11). We hear frequently of Gnostic prophets and prophetesses: see my notes on Herm. Mand. XI. 1. and Didache XI. 7. If an early Christian element is here preserved by the Gnostic schools, it has undoubtedly been hellenised and secularised as the reports shew. But that the prophets altogether were in danger of being secularised is shewn in Didache XI. In the case of the Gnostics the process is again only hastened.

[3] The name Gnostic originally attached to schools which had so named themselves. To these belonged above all, the so-called Ophites, but not the Valentinians or Basilideans.

we will understand by them nothing else than the world taken into Christianity, all the manifold formations which resulted from the first contact of the new religion with the society into which it entered. To prove the existence of that left wing of Gnosticism is of the greatest interest for the history of dogma, but the details are of no consequence. On the other hand, in the aims and undertakings of the Gnostic right, it is just the details that are of greatest significance, because they shew that there was no fixed boundary between what one may call common Christian and Gnostic Christian. But as Gnosticism, in its contents, extended itself from the Encratites and the philosophic interpretation of certain articles of the Christian proclamation as brought forward without offence by individual teachers in the communities, to the complete dissolution of the Christian element by philosophy, or the religious charlatanry of the age, so it exhibits itself formally also in a long series of groups which comprised all imaginable forms of unions. There were churches, ascetic associations, mystery cults, strictly private philosophic schools, [1] free unions for edification, entertainments by Christian charlatans and deceived deceivers, who appeared as magicians and prophets, attempts at founding new religions after the model and under the influence of the Christian, etc. But, finally, the thesis that Gnosticism is identical with an acute secularising of Christianity in the widest sense of the word, is confirmed by the study of its own literature. The early Christian production

---

[1] Special attention should be given to this form, as it became in later times of the very greatest importance for the general development of doctrine in the Church. The sect of Carpocrates was a school. Of Tatian, Irenæus says (I. 28. 1): Τατίανος ᾿Ιουστίνου ἀκροατὴς |γεγονώς.... μετὰ δὲ τὴν ἐκείνου μαρτυρίαν ἀποστὰς τῆς ἐκκλησίας, οἰήματι διδασκάλου ἐπαρθείς.... ἴδιον χαρακτῆρα διδασκαλείου συνεστήσατο. Rhodon (in Euseb. H. E. V. 13. 4) speaks of a Marcionite διδασκαλεῖον. Other names were: "Collegium" (Tertull. ad Valent. 1); "Secta," the word had not always a bad meaning; αἵρεσις, ἐκκλησία (Clem. Strom. VII. 16. 98; on the other hand, VII. 15. 92: Tertull. de præscr. 42: plerique nec Ecclesias habent); θίασος (Iren. I. 13, 4, for the Marcosians), συναγωγή, σύστημα, διατριβή, αἱ ἀθρώπιναι συνηλύσεις, factiuncula, congregatio, conciliabulum, conventiculum. The mystery-organisation most clearly appears in the Naassenes of Hippolytus, the Marcosians of Irenæus, and the Elkasites of Hippolytus, as well as the Coptic-Gnostic documents that have been preserved. (See Koffmane, above work, pp. 6-22).

of Gospel and Apocalypses was indeed continued in Gnosticism,
yet so that the class of "Acts of the Apostles" was added
to them, and that didactic, biographic and "belles lettres"
elements were received into them, and claimed a very important place. If this makes the Gnostic literature approximate
to the profane, that is much more the case with the scientific theological literature which Gnosticism first produced. Dogmatico-philosophic tracts, theologico-critical treatises, historical
investigations and scientific commentaries on the sacred books,
were, for the first time in Christendom, composed by the
Gnostics, who in part occupied the foremost place in the
scientific knowledge, religious earnestness and ardour of the
age. They form in every respect the counterpart to the
scientific works which proceeded from the contemporary philosophic schools. Moreover, we possess sufficient knowledge of
Gnostic hymns and odes, songs for public worship, didactic
poems, magic formulæ, magic books, etc., to assure us that
Christian Gnosticism took possession of a whole region of the
secular life in its full breadth, and thereby often transformed
the original forms of Christian literature into secular.[1] If,

---

[1] The particulars here belong to church history. Overbeck ("Ueber die Anfänge
der patristischen Litteratur" in d. hist. Ztschr. N. F. Bd. XII. p. 417 ff.) has the
merit of being the first to point out the importance, for the history of the Church,
of the forms of literature as they were gradually received in Christendom. Scientific, theological literature has undoubtedly its origin in Gnosticism. The Old
Testament was here, for the first time, systematically and also in part historically
criticised; a selection was here made from the primitive Christian literature;
scientific commentaries were here written on the sacred books (Basilides and
especially the Valentinians, see Heracleon's comm. on the Gospel of John [in
Origen]; the Pauline Epistles were also technically expounded; tracts were here
composed on dogmatico-philosophic problems (for example, περὶ δικαιοσύνης—περὶ
προσφυοῦς ψυχῆς—ἠθικὰ—περὶ ἐγκρατείας ἢ περὶ εὐνουχίας), and systematic doctrinal
systems already constructed (as the Basilidean and Valentinian); the original form
of the Gospel was here first transmuted into the Greek form of sacred novel and
biography (see, above all, the Gospel of Thomas, which was used by the Marco-
sians and Naassenes, and which contained miraculous stories from the childhood of
Jesus); here, finally, psalms, odes and hymns were first composed (see the Acts of
Lucius, the psalms of Valentinus, the psalms of Alexander the disciple of Valentinus, the poems of Bardesanes). Irenæus, Tertullian and Hippolytus have indeed
noted that the scientific method of interpretation followed by the Gnostics, was
the same as that of the philosophers (e.g., of Philo). Valentinus, as is recognised
even by the Church Fathers, stands out prominent for his mental vigour and

however, we bear in mind how all this at a later period was
gradually legitimised in the Catholic Church, philosophy,
the science of the sacred books, criticism and exegesis, the
ascetic associations, the theological schools, the mysteries, the
sacred formulæ, the superstition, the charlatanism, all kinds
of profane literature, etc., it seems to prove the thesis that the
victorious epoch of the gradual hellenising of Christianity followed the abortive attempts at an acute hellenising.

The traditional question as to the origin and development
of Gnosticism, as well as that about the classification of the
Gnostic systems, will have to be modified in accordance
with the foregoing discussion. As the different Gnostic systems
might be contemporary, and in part were undoubtedly contemporary, and as a graduated relation holds good only between
some few groups, we must, in the classification, limit ourselves
essentially to the features which have been specified in the
foregoing paragraph, and which coincide with the position
of the different groups to the early Christian tradition in its
connection with the Old Testament religion, both as a rule of
practical life, and of the common cultus. [1]

As to the origin of Gnosticism, we see how, even in the
earliest period, all possible ideas and principles foreign to
Christianity force their way into it, that is, are brought in

religious imagination; Heracleon for his exegetic theological ability; Ptolemy for
his ingenious criticism of the Old Testament and his keen perception of the stages
of religious development (see his Epistle to Flora in Epiphanius, hær. 33. c. 7).
As a specimen of the language of Valentinus one extract from a homily may
suffice (in Clem. Strom. IV. 13. 89). 'Απ' ἀρχῆς ἀθάνατοί ἐστε καὶ τέκνα ζωῆς ἐστε
αἰωνίας, καὶ τὸν θάνατον ἠθέλετε μερίσασθαι εἰς ἑαυτούς, ἵνα δαπανήσητε αὐτὸν καὶ
ἀναλώσητε, καὶ ἀποθάνῃ ὁ θάνατος ἐν ὑμῖν καὶ δι' ὑμῶν, ὅταν γὰρ τὸν μὲν κόσμον
λύητε, αὐτοι δὲ μὴ καταλύησθε, κυριεύετε τῆς κρίσεως καὶ τῆς φθορᾶς ἁπάσης.
Basilides falls into the background behind Valentinus and his school. Yet the
Church Fathers, when they wish to summarise the most important Gnostics, usually
mention Simon Magus, Basilides, Valentinus, Marcion (even Apelles). On the
relation of the Gnostics to the New Testament writings and to the New Testament, see Zahn, Gesch. des N. T.-lichen Kanons. I. 2. p. 718.

[1] Baur's classification of the Gnostic systems, which rests on the observation of
how they severally realised the idea of Christianity as the absolute religion in
contrast to Judaism and Heathenism, is very ingenious and contains a great
element of truth. But it is insufficient with reference to the whole phenomenon
of Gnosticism, and has been carried out by Baur by violent abstractions.

under Christian rules, and find entrance, especially in the consideration of the Old Testament.[1] We might be satisfied
with the observation that the manifold Gnostic systems were
produced by the increase of this tendency. In point of fact
we must admit that in the present state of our sources, we
can reach no sure knowledge beyond that. These sources,
however, give certain indications which should not be left
unnoticed. If we leave out of account the two assertions of
opponents, that Gnosticism was produced by demons[2] and
—this, however, was said at a comparatively late period—that
it originated in ambition and resistance to the ecclesiastical
office, the episcopate, we find in Hegesippus, one of the earliest
writers on the subject, the statement that the whole of the
heretical schools sprang out of Judaism or the Jewish sects;
in the later writers, Irenæus, Tertullian and Hippolytus,
that these schools owe most to the doctrines of Pythagoras,
Plato, Aristotle, Zeno, etc.[3] But they all agree in this, that
a definite personality, viz., Simon the Magician, must be regarded
as the original source of the heresy. If we try it by these
statements of the Church Fathers, we must see at once that
the problem in this case is limited—certainly in a proper
way. For after Gnosticism is seen to be the acute secularising of Christianity the only question that remains is, how
are we to account for the origin of the great Gnostic schools,
that is, whether it is possible to indicate their preliminary
stages. The following may be asserted here with some confidence: Long before the appearance of Christianity, combinations of religion had taken place in Syria and Palestine,[4]

---

[1] The question, therefore, as to the time of the origin of Gnosticism as a
complete phenomenon cannot be answered. The remarks of Hegesippus (Euseb.
H. E. IV. 22) refer to the Jerusalem Church, and have not even for that the value
of a fixed datum. The only important question here is the point of time at which
the expulsion or secession of the schools and unions took place in the different
national churches.

[2] Justin Apol. I. 26.

[3] Hegesippus in Euseb. H. E. IV. 22, Iren. II. 14. 1 f., Tertull. de præscr. 7,
Hippol. Philosoph. The Church Fathers have also noted the likeness of the
cultus of Mithras and other deities.

[4] We must leave the Essenes entirely out of account here, as their teaching,
in all probability, is not to be considered syncretistic in the strict sense of the

especially in Samaria, in so far, on the one hand, as the Assyrian
and Babylonian religious philosophy, together with its myths, as
well as the Greek popular religion with its manifold interpretations, had penetrated as far as the eastern shore of the Mediterranean, and been accepted even by the Jews; and, on the
other hand, the Jewish Messianic idea had spread and called
forth various movements. [1] The result of every mixing of
national religions, however, is to break through the traditional,
legal and particular forms. [2] For the Jewish religion syncretism signified the shaking of the authority of the Old
Testament by a qualitative distinction of its different parts,
as also doubt as to the identity of the supreme God with
the national God. These ferments were once more set in
motion by Christianity. We know that in the Apostolic age
there were attempts in Samaria to found new religions, which
were in all probability influenced by the tradition and preaching concerning Jesus. Dositheus, Simon Magus, Cleobius,
and Menander appeared as Messiahs or bearers of the Godhead, and proclaimed a doctrine in which the Jewish faith
was strangely and grotesquely mixed with Babylonian myths,
together with some Greek additions. The mysterious worship,
the breaking up of Jewish particularism, the criticism of the
Old Testament,—which for long had had great difficulty in
retaining its authority in many circles, in consequence of the

---

word, (see Lucius, "Der Essenismus," 1881,) and as we know absolutely nothing
of a greater diffusion of it. But we need no names here, as a syncretistic, ascetic
Judaism could and did arise everywhere in Palestine and the Diaspora.

[1] Freudenthal's "Hellenistische Studien" informs us as to the Samaritan
syncretism; see also Hilgenfeld's "Ketzergeschichte," p. 149 ff. As to the Babylonian mythology in Gnosticism, see the statements in the elaborate article,
"Manichäismus," by Kessler (Real-Encycl. für protest. Theol., 2 Aufl.).

[2] Wherever traditional religions are united under the badge of philosophy a
conservative syncretism is the result, because the allegoric method, that is, the
criticism of all religion, veiled and unconscious of itself, is able to blast rocks
and bridge over abysses. All forms may remain here under certain circumstances,
but a new spirit enters into them. On the other hand, where philosophy is still
weak, and the traditional religion is already shaken by another, there arises the
critical syncretism in which either the gods of one religion are subordinated to
those of another, or the elements of the traditional religion are partly eliminated
and replaced by others. Here, also, the soil is prepared for new religious formations, for the appearance of religious founders.

widened horizon and the deepening of religious feeling,—finally,
the wild syncretism, whose aim, however, was a universal
religion, all contributed to gain adherents for Simon.[1] His
enterprise appeared to the Christians as a diabolical caricature
of their own religion, and the impression made by the success
which Simonianism gained by a vigorous propaganda even
beyond Palestine into the West, supported this idea.[2] We can
therefore understand how, afterwards, all heresies were traced
back to Simon. To this must be added that we can actually
trace in many Gnostic systems the same elements which were
prominent in the religion proclaimed by Simon (the Babylonian and Syrian), and that the new religion of the Simonians,
just like Christianity, had afterwards to submit to be transformed into a philosophic, scholastic doctrine.[3] The formal
parallel to the Gnostic doctrines was therewith established.
But even apart from these attempts at founding new religions,
Christianity in Syria, under the influence of foreign religions
and speculation on the philosophy of religion, gave a powerful
impulse to the criticism of the law and the prophets which

[1] It was a serious mistake of the critics to regard Simon Magus as a fiction,
which, moreover, has been given up by Hilgenfeld (Ketzergeschichte, p. 163 ff.),
and Lipsius (Apocr. Apostelgesch. II. 1),—the latter, however, not decidedly. The
whole figure as well as the doctrines attributed to Simon (see Acts of the Apostles,
Justin, Irenæus, Hippolytus) not only have nothing improbable in them, but suit
very well the religious circumstances which we must assume for Samaria. The
main point in Simon is his endeavour to create a universal religion of the supreme
God. This explains his success among the Samaritans and Greeks. He is really
a counterpart to Jesus, whose activity can just as little have been unknown to him
as that of Paul. At the same time it cannot be denied that the later tradition
about Simon was the most confused and biassed imaginable, or that certain Jewish
Christians at a later period may have attempted to endow the magician with the
features of Paul in order to discredit the personality and teaching of the Apostle.
But this last assumption requires a fresh investigation.

[2] Justin. Apol. I 26: Καὶ σχεδὸν πάντες μὲν Σαμαρεῖς, ὀλίγοι δὲ καὶ ἐν ἄλλοις
ἔθνεσιν, ὡς τὸν πρῶτον θεὸν Σίμωνα ὁμολογοῦντες, ἐκεῖνον καὶ προσκυνοῦσιν (besides
the account in the Philos. and Orig. c. Cels. I. 57: VI. 11). The positive statement of Justin that Simon came even to Rome (under Claudius) can hardly be
refuted from the account of the Apologist himself, and therefore not at all. (See
Renan, " Antichrist ".)

[3] We have it as such in the Μεγάλη Ἀπόφασις which Hippolytus (Philosoph.
VI. 19. 20) made use of. This Simonianism may perhaps have related to the
original, as the doctrines of the Christian Gnostics to the Apostolic preaching.

had already been awakened. In consequence of this, there appeared, about the transition of the first century to the second, a series of teachers who, under the impression of the Gospel, sought to make the Old Testament capable of furthering the tendency to a universal religion, not by allegorical interpretation, but by a sifting criticism. These attempts were of very different kinds. Teachers such as Cerinthus clung to the notion that the universal religion revealed by Christ was identical with undefiled Mosaism, and therefore maintained even such articles as circumcision and the Sabbath commandment, as well as the earthly kingdom of the future. But they rejected certain parts of the law, especially, as a rule, the sacrificial precepts, which were no longer in keeping with the spiritual conception of religion. They conceived the creator of the world as a subordinate being distinct from the supreme God, which is always the mark of a syncretism with a dualistic tendency; introduced speculations about Æons and angelic powers, among whom they placed Christ, and recommended a strict asceticism. When, in their Christology, they denied the miraculous birth, and saw in Jesus a chosen man on whom the Christ, that is, the Holy Spirit, descended at the baptism, they were not creating any innovation, but only following the earliest Palestinian tradition. Their rejection of the authority of Paul is explained by their efforts to secure the Old Testament as far as possible for the universal religion. [1] There were others who rejected all ceremonial commandments as proceeding from the devil, or from some intermediate being, but yet always held firmly that the God of the Jews was the supreme God. But alongside of these stood also decidedly anti-Jewish groups, who seem to have been influenced in part by the preaching of Paul. They advanced much further in the criticism of the Old Testament, and perceived the impossibility of saving it for the Christian universal religion.

---

[1] The Heretics opposed in the Epistle to the Colossians may belong to these. On Cerinthus, see Polycarp in Iren. III. 3. 2, Irenæus (I. 26. 1 : III. 11. 1), Hippolytus and the redactions of the Syntagma, Cajus in Euseb. III. 28. 2, Hilgenfeld, Ketzergeschichte, p. 411 ff. To this category belong also the Ebionites and Elkasites of Epiphanius. (See Chap. 6.)

They rather connected this religion with the cultus-wisdom of
Babylon and Syria, which seemed more adapted for allegorical
interpretations, and opposed this formation to the Old Testament religion. The God of the Old Testament appears here
at best as a subordinate Angel of limited power, wisdom and
goodness. In so far as he was identified with the creator of
the world, and the creation of the world itself was regarded
as an imperfect or an abortive undertaking, expression was
given both to the anti-Judaism and to that religious temper of
the time which could only value spiritual blessing in contrast
with the world and the sensuous. These systems appeared
more or less strictly dualistic, in proportion as they did or
did not accept a slight co-operation of the supreme God in
the creation of man; and the way in which the character and
power of the world-creating God of the Jews was conceived,
serves as a measure of how far the several schools were from
the Jewish religion and the Monism that ruled it. All possible
conceptions of the God of the Jews, from the assumption that
he is a being supported in his undertakings by the supreme
God, to his identification with Satan, seem to have been exhausted in these schools. Accordingly, in the former case,
the Old Testament was regarded as the revelation of a subordinate God, in the latter as the manifestation of Satan, and
therefore the ethic—with occasional use of Pauline formulæ—
always assumed an antinomian form compared with the
Jewish law, in some cases antinomian even in the sense of
libertinism. Correspondingly, the anthropology exhibits man
as bipartite, or even tripartite, and the Christology is strictly
docetic and anti-Jewish. The redemption by Christ is always,
as a matter of course, related only to that element in humanity
which has an affinity with the Godhead. [1]

[1] The two Syrian teachers, Saturninus and Cerdo, must in particular be mentioned here. The first (See Iren. I. 24. 1. 2, Hippolyt. and the redactions of the
Syntagma) was not strictly speaking a dualist, and therefore allowed the God of
the Old Testament to be regarded as an Angel of the supreme God, while at the
same time he distinguished him from Satan. Accordingly, he assumed that the
supreme God co-operated in the creation of man by angel powers—sending a ray
of light, an image of light, that should be imitated as an example and enjoined
as an ideal. But all men have not received the ray of light. Consequently, two

It is uncertain whether we should think of the spread of these doctrines in Syria in the form of a school, or of a cultus; probably it was both. From the great Gnostic systems as formed by Basilides and Valentinus they are distinguished by the fact that they lack the peculiar philosophic, that is Hellenic, element, the speculative conversion of angels and Æons into real ideas, etc. We have almost no knowledge of their effect. This Gnosticism has never directly been a historical factor of striking importance, and the great question is whether it was so indirectly. [1] That is to say, we do not know whether this Syrian Gnosticism was, in the strict sense, the preparatory stage of the great Gnostic schools, so that the schools should be regarded as an actual reconstruction of it. But there can be no doubt that the appearance of the great Gnostic schools in the Empire, from Egypt to Gaul, is contemporaneous with the vigorous projection of Syrian cults westwards, and therefore the assumption is suggested, that the Syrian Christian syncretism was also spread in connection with that projection, and underwent a change corresponding to the new conditions. We know definitely that the Syrian Gnostic, Cerdo, came to Rome, wrought there, and exercised an influ-

---

classes of men stand in abrupt contrast with each other. History is the conflict of the two. Satan stands at the head of the one, the God of the Jews at the head of the other. The Old Testament is a collection of prophecies out of both camps. The truly good first appears in the Æon Christ, who assumed nothing cosmic, did not even submit to birth. He destroys the works of Satan (generation, eating of flesh), and delivers the men who have within them a spark of light. The Gnosis of Cerdo was much coarser. (Iren. I. 27. 1, Hippolyt. and the redactions.) He contrasted the good God and the God of the Old Testament as two primary beings. The latter he identified with the creator of the world. Consequently, he completely rejected the Old Testament and everything cosmic and taught that the good God was first revealed in Christ. Like Saturninus he preached a strict docetism; Christ had no body, was not born, and suffered in an unreal body. All else that the Fathers report of Cerdo's teaching has probably been transferred to him from Marcion, and is therefore very doubtful.

[1] This question might perhaps be answered if we had the Justinian Syntagma against all heresies; but in the present condition of our sources it remains wrapped in obscurity. What may be gathered from the fragments of Hegesippus, the Epistles of Ignatius, the Pastoral Epistles and other documents, such as, for example, the Epistle of Jude, is in itself so obscure, so detached and so ambiguous that it is of no value for historical construction.

ence on Marcion. But no less probable is the assumption
that the great Hellenic Gnostic schools arose spontaneously,
in the sense of having been independently developed out of
the elements to which undoubtedly the Asiatic cults also
belonged, without being influenced in any way by Syrian
syncretistic efforts. The conditions for the growth of such
formations were nearly the same in all parts of the Empire.
The great advance lies in the fact that the religious material
as contained in the Gospel, the Old Testament, and the wisdom connected with the old cults, was philosophically, that
is scientifically, manipulated by means of allegory, and the
aggregate of mythological powers translated into an aggregate
of ideas. The Pythagorean and Platonic, more rarely the
Stoic philosophy, were compelled to do service here. Great
Gnostic schools, which were at the same time unions for worship, first enter into the clear light of history in this form,
(see previous section), and on the conflict with these, surrounded as they were by a multitude of dissimilar and related
formations, depends the progress of the development. [1]

We are no longer able to form a perfectly clear picture of
how these schools came into being, or how they were related
to the Churches. It lay in the nature of the case that
the heads of the schools, like the early itinerant heretical
teachers, devoted attention chiefly, if not exclusively, to
those who were already Christian, that is, to the Christian

---

[1] There are, above all, the schools of the Basilideans, Valentinians and Ophites.
To describe the systems in their full development lies, in my opinion, outside the
business of the history of dogma and might easily lead to the mistake that the
systems as such were controverted, and that their construction was peculiar to
Christian Gnosticism. The construction, as remarked above, is rather that of the
later Greek philosophy, though it cannot be mistaken that, for us, the full parallel
to the Gnostic systems first appears in those of the Neoplatonists. But only
particular doctrines and principles of the Gnostics were really called in question,—
their critique of the world, of providence, of the resurrection, etc.; these therefore
are to be adduced in the next section. The fundamental features of an inner
development can only be exhibited in the case of the most important, viz., the
Valentinian school. But even here we must distinguish an Eastern and a Western
branch. (Tertull. adv. Valent. I.: "Valentiniani frequentissimum plane collegium
inter hæreticos." Iren. l. I.; Hippol. Philos. VI. 35; Orig. Hom. II. 5 in Ezech.
Lomm. XIV. p. 40: "Valentini robustissima secta".)

communities. [1] From the Ignatian Epistles, the Shepherd of
Hermas (Vis. III. 7. 1: Sim. VIII. 6. 5: IX. 19. and especially 22),
and the Didache (XI. 1. 2) we see that those teachers who
boasted of a special knowledge and sought to introduce
"strange" doctrines, aimed at gaining the entire churches.
The beginning, as a rule, was necessarily the formation of
conventicles. In the first period therefore, when there was
no really fixed standard for warding off the foreign doctrines—
Hermas is unable even to characterise the false doctrines—
the warnings were commonly exhausted in the exhortation:
κολλᾶσθε τοῖς ἁγίοις, ὅτι οἱ κολλώμενοι αὐτοῖς ἁγιασθήσονται,
["connect yourselves with the saints, because those who are
connected with them shall be sanctified"]. As a rule, the
doctrines may really have crept in unobserved, and those
gained over to them may for long have taken part in a twofold worship, the public worship of the churches, and the
new consecration. Those teachers must of course have assumed a more aggressive attitude who rejected the Old Testament. The attitude of the Church, when it enjoyed competent
guidance, was one of decided opposition towards unmasked or
recognised false teachers. Yet Irenæus' account of Cerdo in
Rome shews us how difficult it was at the beginning to get
rid of a false teacher. [2] For Justin, about the year 150, the

---

[1] Tertull. de præscr. 42: "De verbi autem administratione quid dicam, cum
hoc sit negotium illis, non ethnicos convertendi, sed nostros evertendi? Hanc magis
gloriam captant, si stantibus ruinam, non si jacentibus elevationem operentur.
Quoniam et ipsum opus eorum non de suo proprio ædificio venit, sed de veritatis
destructione; nostra suffodiunt, ut sua ædificent. Adime illis legem Moysis et
prophetas et creatorem deum, accusationem eloqui non habent." (See adv. Valent.
I. init.) This is hardly a malevolent accusation. The philosophic interpretation
of a religion will always impress those only on whom the religion itself has
already made an impression.

[2] Iren. III. 4. 2: Κέρδων εἰς τὴν ἐκκλησίαν ἐλθὼν καὶ ἐξομολογούμενος, οὕτως
διετέλεσε, ποτὲ μὲν λαθροδιδασκαλῶν ποτὲ δὲ πάλιν ἐξομολογούμενος, ποτὲ δὲ ἐλεγ-
γόμενος ἐφ᾽ οἷς ἐδίδασκε κακῶς, καὶ ἀφιστάμενος τῆς τῶν ἀδελφῶν συνοδίας; see
besides the valuable account of Tertull. de præscr. 30. The account of Irenæus
(I. 13) is very instructive as to the kind of propaganda of Marcus, and the relation
of the women he deluded to the Church. Against actually recognised false teachers
the fixed rule was to renounce all intercourse with them (2 Joh. 10. 11; Iren. ep.
ad Florin on Polycarp's procedure, in Euseb. H. E. V. 20. 7; Iren. III. 3. 4).
But how were the heretics to be surely known?

Marcionites, Valentinians, Basilideans and Saturninians are
groups outside the communities, and undeserving of the name
"Christians." [1] There must therefore have been at that time,
in Rome and Asia Minor at least, a really perfect separation
of those schools from the Churches (it was different in Alexandria). Notwithstanding, this continued to be the region
from which those schools obtained their adherents. For the
Valentinians recognised that the common Christians were much
better than the heathen, that they occupied a middle position
between the "pneumatic" and the "hylic," and might look
forward to a kind of salvation. This admission, as well as
their conforming to the common Christian tradition, enabled
them to spread their views in a remarkable way, and they
may not have had any objection in many cases, to their
converts remaining in the great Church. But can this community have perceived, everywhere and at once, that the
Valentinian distinction of "psychic" and "pneumatic" is not
identical with the scriptural distinction of children and men
in understanding? Where the organisation of the school (the
union for worship) required a long time of probation, where
degrees of connection with it were distinguished, and a strict
asceticism demanded of the perfect, it followed of course that
those on the lower stage should not be urged to a speedy
break with the Church. [2] But after the creation of the

---

[1] Among those who justly bore this name he distinguishes those οἱ ὀρθογνώμενες
κατὰ πάντα χριστανοί εἰσιν (Dial. 80).

[2] Very important is the description which Irenæus (III. 15. 2) and Tertullian
have given of the conduct of the Valentinians as observed by themselves (adv.
Valent. 1). "Valentiniani nihil magis curant quam occultare, quod prædicant; si
tamen prædicant qui occultant. Custodiæ officium conscientiæ officium est (a
comparison with the Eleusinian mysteries follows). Si bona fide quæras, concreto
vultu, suspenso supercilio, Altum est, aiunt. Si subtiliter temptes per ambiguitates
bilingues communem fidem adfirmant. Si scire te subostendas negant quidquid
agnoscunt. Si cominus certes, tuam simplicitatem sua cæde dispergunt. Ne dis-
cipulis quidem propriis ante committunt quam suos fecerint. Habent artificium
quo prius persuadeant quam edoceant." At a later period Dionysius of Alex. in
Euseb. H. E. VII. 7, speaks of Christians who maintain an apparent communion
with the brethren, but resort to one of the false teachers (cf. as to this Euseb.
H. E. VI. 2. 13). The teaching of Bardesanes influenced by Valentinus, who,
moreover, was hostile to Marcionitism, was tolerated for a long time in Edessa
(by the Christian kings), nay, was recognised. The Bardesanites and the "Palutians"
(catholics) were differentiated only after the beginning of the third century.

catholic confederation of churches, existence was made more
and more difficult for these schools. Some of them lived on
somewhat like our freemason-unions; some, as in the East,
became actual sects (confessions), in which the wise and the
simple now found a place, as they were propagated by families.
In both cases they ceased to be what they had been at the
beginning. From about 210 they ceased to be a factor of
the historical development, though the Church of Constantine
and Theodosius was alone really able to suppress them.

§ 4.   *The most important Gnostic Doctrines.*

We have still to measure and compare with the earliest
tradition those Gnostic doctrines which, partly at once and
partly in the following period, became important. Once more,
however, we must expressly refer to the fact that the epoch-
making significance of Gnosticism for the history of dogma
must not be sought chiefly in the particular doctrines, but
rather in the whole way in which Christianity is here conceived
and transformed. The decisive thing is the conversion of the
Gospel into a doctrine, into an absolute philosophy of religion,
the transforming of the *disciplina Evangelii* into an asceticism
based on a dualistic conception, and into a practice of mysteries. [1] We have now briefly to shew, with due regard to
the earliest tradition, how far this transformation was of positive or negative significance for the following period, that is,
in what respects the following development was anticipated by

---

[1] There can be no doubt that the Gnostic propaganda was seriously hindered
by the inability to organise and discipline Churches, which is characteristic of all
philosophic systems of religion. The Gnostic organisation of schools and mysteries
was not able to contend with the episcopal organisation of the Churches; see Ignat.
ad Smyr. 6. 2; Tertull. de præscr. 41. Attempts at actual formation of Churches
were not altogether wanting in the earliest period; at a later period they were forced
on some schools. We have only to read Iren. III. 15. 2 in order to see that these
associations could only exist by finding support in a Church. Irenæus expressly
remarks that the Valentinians designated the Common Christians καθολικοί (com-
munes) καὶ ἐκκλησιαστικοί, but that they, on the other hand, complained that " we
kept away from their fellowship without cause, as they thought like ourselves."

Gnosticism, and in what respects Gnosticism was disavowed by this development. [1]

(1) Christianity, which is the only true and absolute religion, embraces a revealed system of doctrine (positive).

(2) This doctrine contains mysterious powers, which are communicated to men by initiation (mysteries).

(3) The revealer is Christ (positive), but Christ alone, and only in his historical appearance—no Old Testament Christ (negative); this appearance is itself redemption: the doctrine is the announcement of it and of its presuppositions (positive). [2]

(4) Christian doctrine is to be drawn from the Apostolic

---

[1] The differences between the Gnostic Christianity and that of the Church, that is, the later ecclesiastical theology, were fluid, if we observe the following points. (1) That even in the main body of the Church the element of knowledge was increasingly emphasised, and the Gospel began to be converted into a perfect knowledge of the world (increasing reception of Greek philosophy, development of πίστις to γνῶσις). (2) That the dramatic eschatology began to fade away. (3) That room was made for docetic views, and value put upon a strict asceticism. On the other hand we must note: (1) That all this existed only in germ or fragments within the great Church during the flourishing period of Gnosticism. (2) That the great Church held fast to the facts fixed in the baptismal formula (in the *Kerygma*) and to the eschatological expectations, further, to the creator of the world as the supreme God, to the unity of Jesus Christ, and to the Old Testament, and therefore rejected dualism. (3) That the great Church defended the unity and equality of the human race, and therefore the uniformity and universal aim of the Christian salvation. (4) That it rejected every introduction of new, especially of Oriental, Mythologies, guided in this by the early Christian consciousness and a sure intelligence. A deeper, more thorough distinction between the Church and the Gnostic parties hardly dawned on the consciousness of either. The Church developed herself instinctively into an imperial Church, in which office was to play the chief rôle. The Gnostics sought to establish or conserve associations in which the genius should rule, the genius in the way of the old prophets or in the sense of Plato, or in the sense of a union of prophecy and philosophy. In the Gnostic conflict, at least at its close, the judicial priest fought with the virtuoso and overcame him.

[2] The absolute significance of the person of Christ was very plainly expressed in Gnosticism (Christ is not only the teacher of the truth, but the manifestation of the truth), more plainly than where he was regarded as the subject of Old Testament revelation. The pre-existent Christ has significance in some Gnostic schools, but always a comparatively subordinate one. The isolating of the person of Christ, and quite as much the explaining away of his humanity, is manifestly out of harmony with the earliest tradition. But, on the other hand, it must not be denied that the Gnostics recognised redemption in the historical Christ: Christ personally procured it (see under 6, h.).

tradition, critically examined. This tradition lies before us in a series of Apostolic writings, and in a secret doctrine derived from the Apostles (positive). [1]

[1] In this thesis, which may be directly corroborated by the most important Gnostic teachers, Gnosticism shews that it desires *in thesi* (in a way similar to Philo) to continue on the soil of Christianity as a positive religion. Conscious of being bound to tradition, it first definitely raised the question, What is Christianity? and criticised and sifted the sources for an answer to the question. The rejection of the Old Testament led it to that question and to this sifting. It may be maintained with the greatest probability, that the idea of a canonical collection of Christian writings first emerged among the Gnostics (see also Marcion). They really needed such a collection, while all those who recognised the Old Testament as a document of revelation, and gave it a Christian interpretation, did not at first need a new document, but simply joined on the new to the old, the Gospel to the Old Testament. From the numerous fragments of Gnostic commentaries on New Testament writings which have been preserved, we see that these writings then enjoyed canonical authority, while at the same period we hear nothing of such an authority nor of commentaries in the main body of Christendom (see Heinrici, "Die Valentinianische Gnosis, u. d. h. Schrift," 1871). Undoubtedly sacred writings were selected according to the principle of apostolic origin. This is proved by the inclusion of the Pauline Epistles in the collections of books. There is evidence of such having been made by the Naassenes, Peratæ, Valentinians, Marcion, Tatian and the Gnostic Justin. The collection of the Valentinians and the Canon of Tatian must have really coincided with the main parts of the later Ecclesiastical Canon. The later Valentinians accommodated themselves to this Canon, that is, recognised the books that had been added (Tertull. de præscr. 38). The question as to who first conceived and realised the idea of a Canon of Christian writings, Basilides, or Valentinus, or Marcion, or whether this was done by several at the same time, will always remain obscure, though many things favour Marcion. If it should even be proved that Basilides (see Euseb. H. E. IV. 7. 7) and Valentinus himself regarded the Gospels only as authoritative, yet the full idea of the Canon lies already in the fact of their making these the foundation and interpreting them allegorically. The question as to the extent of the Canon afterwards became the subject of an important controversy between the Gnostics and the Catholic Church. The Catholics throughout took up the position that their Canon was the earlier, and the Gnostic collection the corrupt revision of it (they were unable to adduce proof, as is attested by Tertullian's de præscr.). But the aim of the Gnostics to establish themselves on the uncorrupted apostolic tradition gathered from writings, was crossed by three tendencies, which, moreover, were all jointly operative in the Christian communities, and are therefore not peculiar to Gnosticism. (1) By faith in the continuance of prophecy, in which new things are always revealed by the Holy Spirit (the Basilidean and Marcionite prophets). (2) By the assumption of an esoteric secret tradition of the Apostles (see Clem. Strom. VII. 17. 106. 108; Hipp. Philos. VII. 20; Iren. I. 25. 5 : III. 2. 1; Tertull. de præscr. 25. Cf. the Gnostic book, Πίστις Σοφία, which in great part is based on doctrines said to be imparted by Jesus to his disciples after his resurrection). (3) By the inability to oppose the continuous production of Evangelic writings, in

As exoteric it is comprehended in the *regula fidei*[1] other words, by the continuance of this kind of literature and the addition of Acts of the Apostles (Gospel of the Egyptians (?), other Gospels, Acts of John, Thomas, Philip, etc. We know absolutely nothing about the conditions under which these writings originated, the measure of authority which they enjoyed, or the way in which they gained that authority). In all these points which in Gnosticism hindered the development of Christianity to the "religion of a new book," the Gnostic schools shew that they stood precisely under the same conditions as the Christian communities in general (see above Chap. 3. § 2). If all things do not deceive us, the same inner development may be observed even in the Valentinian school as in the great Church, viz., the production of sacred Evangelic and Apostolic writings, prophecy and secret gnosis falling more and more into the background, and the completed Canon becoming the most important basis of the doctrine of religion. The later Valentinians (see Tertull. de præscr. and adv. Valent.) seem to have appealed chiefly to this Canon, and Tatian no less (about whose Canon, see my Texte u. Unters. I. 1. 2. pp. 213-218). But finally we must refer to the fact that it was the highest concern of the Gnostics to furnish the historical proof of the Apostolic origin of their doctrine by an exact reference to the links of the tradition (see Ritschl, Entstehung der altkath. Kirche. 2nd ed. p. 338 f.). Here again it appears that Gnosticism shared with Christendom the universal presupposition that the valuable thing is the Apostolic origin (see above p. 160 f.), but that it first created artificial chains of tradition, and that this is the first point in which it was followed by the Church: (see the appeals to the Apostolic Matthew, to Peter and Paul, through the mediation of "Glaukias" and "Theodas," to James and the favourite disciples of the Lord, in the case of the Naassenes, Ophites, Basilideans and Valentinians, etc.; see, further, the close of the Epistle of Ptolemy to Flora in Epistle H. 33. 7: Μαθήσῃ ἑξῆς καὶ τὴν τούτου ἀρχήν τε καὶ γέννησιν, ἀξιουμένη τῆς ἀποστολικῆς παραδόσεως, ἣ ἐκ διαδοχῆς καὶ ἡμεῖς παρειλήφαμεν, μετὰ καιροῦ [sic] κανονίσαι πάντας τοὺς λόγους τῇ τοῦ σωτῆρος διδασκαλίᾳ, as well as the passages adduced under 2). From this it further follows that the Gnostics may have compiled their Canon solely according to the principle of Apostolic origin. Upon the whole we may see here how foolish it is to seek to dispose of Gnosticism with the phrase, "lawless fancies." On the contrary, the Gnostics purposely took their stand on the tradition—nay, they were the first in Christendom who determined the range, contents and manner of propagating the tradition. They are thus the first Christian theologians.

[1] Here also we have a point of unusual historical importance. As we first find a new Canon among the Gnostics, so also among them (and in Marcion) we first meet with the traditional complex of the Christian *Kerygma* as a doctrinal confession (*regula fidei*), that is, as a confession which, because it is fundamental, needs a speculative exposition, but is set forth by this exposition as the summary of all wisdom. The hesitancy about the details of the *Kerygma* only shews the general uncertainty which at that time prevailed. But again we see that the later Valentinians completely accommodated themselves to the later development in the Church (Tertull. adv. Valent. I.: "communem fidem adfirmant"), that is, attached themselves, probably even from the first, to the existing forms; while in the Marcionite Church a peculiar *regula* was set up by a criticism of the tradition. The *regula*, as a matter of course, was regarded as Apostolic. On Gnostic *regulæ*, see Iren. I. 21.

(positive), as esoteric it is propagated by chosen teachers. [1]

(5) The documents of revelation (Apostolic writings), just because they are such, must be interpreted by means of allegory, that is, their deeper meaning must be extracted in this way (positive). [2]

(6) The following may be noted as the main points in the Gnostic conception of the several parts of the *regula fidei:*

(*a*) The difference between the supreme God and the creator of the world, and therewith the opposing of redemp- tion and creation, and therefore the separation of the Mediator of revelation from the Mediator of creation. [3]

5, 31. 3 : II. præf. : II. 19. 8 : III. 11. 3 : III. 16. 1. 5 : Ptolem. ap. Epiph. h. 33. 7; Tertull. adv. Valent. 1. 4 : de præscr. 42 : adv. Marc. I. 1 : IV. 5. 17; Ep. Petri ad Jacob in Clem. Hom. c. 1. We still possess, in great part verbatim, the *regula* of Apelles, in Epiphan. h. 44. 2. Irenæus (I. 7. 2) and Tertull. (de carne, 20) state that the Valentinian *regula* contained the formula, "*γεννηθέντα διὰ Μαρίας*"; see on this, p. 205. In noting that the two points so decisive for Catholicism, the Canon of the New Testament and the Apostolic *regula*, were first, in the strict sense, set up by the Gnostics on the basis of a definite fixing and systematising of the oldest tradition, we may see that the weakness of Gnosticism here consisted in its inability to exhibit the publicity of tradition and to place its propagation in close connection with the organisation of the churches.

[1] We do not know the relation in which the Valentinians placed the public Apostolic *regula fidei* to the secret doctrine derived from one Apostle. The Church, in opposition to the Gnostics, strongly emphasised the publicity of all tradition. Yet afterwards, though with reservations, she gave a wide scope to the assumption of a secret tradition.

[2] The Gnostics transferred to the Evangelic writings, and demanded as simply necessary, the methods which Barnabas and others used in expounding the Old Testament (see the samples of their exposition in Irenæus and Clement. Heinrici, l. c.). In this way, of course, all the specialities of the system may be found in the docu- ments. The Church at first condemned this method (Tertull. de præscr. 17-19. 39; Iren. I. 8. 9), but applied it herself from the moment in which she had adopted a New Testament Canon of equal authority with that of the Old Testament. How- ever, the distinction always remained, that in the confrontation of the two Testaments with the views of getting proofs from prophecy, the history of Jesus described in the Gospels was not at first allegorised. Yet afterwards the Christological dogmas of the third and following centuries demanded a docetic explanation of many points in that history.

[3] In the Valentinian, as well as in all systems not coarsely dualistic, the Redeemer Christ has no doubt a certain share in the constitution of the highest class of men, but only through complicated mediations. The significance which is attributed to Christ in many systems for the production or organisation of the upper world may be mentioned. In the Valentinian system there are several mediators. It may be noted that the abstract conception of the divine primitive Being seldom called forth a real controversy. As a rule, offence was taken only at the expression.

(*b*) The separation of the supreme God from the God of the Old Testament, and therewith the rejection of the Old Testament, or the assertion that the Old Testament contains no revelations of the supreme God, or at least only in certain parts. [1]

(*c*) The doctrine of the independence and eternity of matter.

(*d*) The assertion that the present world sprang from a fall of man, or from an undertaking hostile to God, and is therefore the product of an evil or intermediate being. [2]

(*e*) The doctrine that evil is inherent in matter and therefore is a physical potence. [3]

[1] The Epistle of Ptolemy to Flora is very instructive here. If we leave out of account the peculiar Gnostic conception, we have represented in Ptolemy's criticism the later Catholic view of the Old Testament, as well as also the beginning of a historical conception of it. The Gnostics were the first critics of the Old Testament in Christendom. Their allegorical exposition of the Evangelic writings should be taken along with their attempts at interpreting the Old Testament literally and historically. It may be noted, for example, that the Gnostics were the first to call attention to the significance of the change of name for God in the Old Testament; see Iren. II. 35. 3. The early Christian tradition led to a procedure directly the opposite. Apelles, in particular, the disciple of Marcion, exercised an intelligent criticism on the Old Testament; see my treatise, "de Apellis gnosi," p. 71 sq., and also Texte u. Unters. VI. 3, p. 111 ff. Marcion himself recognised the historical contents of the Old Testament as reliable and the criticism of most Gnostics only called in question its religious value.

[2] Ecclesiastical opponents rightly put no value on the fact that some Gnostics advanced to Pan-Satanism with regard to the conception of the world, while others beheld a certain *justitia civilis* ruling in the world. For the standpoint which the Christian tradition had marked out, this distinction is just as much a matter of indifference as the other, whether the Old Testament proceeded from an evil, or from an intermediate being. The Gnostics attempted to correct the judgment of faith about the world and its relation to God, by an empiric view of the world. Here again they are by no means "visionaries", however fantastic the means by which they have expressed their judgment about the condition of the world, and attempted to explain that condition. Those, rather, are "visionaries" who give themselves up to the belief that the world is the work of a good and omnipotent Deity, however apparently reasonable the arguments they adduce. The Gnostic (Hellenistic) philosophy of religion at this point comes into the sharpest opposition to the central point of the Old Testament Christian belief, and all else really depends on this. Gnosticism is antichristian so far as it takes away from Christianity its Old Testament foundation, and belief in the identity of the creator of the world with the supreme God. That was immediately felt and noted by its opponents.

[3] The ecclesiastical opposition was long uncertain on this point. It is interesting to note that Basilides portrayed the sin inherent in the child from birth in a

(*f*) The assumption of Æons, that is, real powers and heavenly persons in whom is unfolded the absoluteness of the Godhead. [1]

(*g*) The assertion that Christ revealed a God hitherto unknown.

(*h*) The doctrine that in the person of Jesus Christ—the Gnostics saw in it redemption, but they reduced the person to the physical nature—the heavenly Æon, Christ, and the human appearance of that Æon must be clearly distinguished, and a "distincte agere" ascribed to each. Accordingly, there were some, such as Basilides, who acknowledged no real union between Christ and the man Jesus, whom, besides, they regarded as an earthly man. Others, *e.g.*, part of the Valentinians, among whom the greatest differences prevailed,—see Tertull. adv. Valent. 39—taught that the body of Jesus was

---

way that makes one feel as though he were listening to Augustine (see the fragment from the 23rd book of the Ἐξηγητικά, in Clem., Strom. VI. 12. 83). But it is of great importance to note how even very special later terminologies, dogmas, etc., of the Church, were in a certain way anticipated by the Gnostics. Some samples will be given below; but meanwhile we may here refer to a fragment from Apelles' Syllogisms in Ambrosius (de Parad. V. 28): "Si hominem non perfectum fecit deus, unusquisque autem per industriam propriam perfectionem sibi virtutis adsciscit: nonne videtur plus sibi homo adquirere, quam ei deus contulit?" One seems here to be transferred into the fifth century.

[1] The Gnostic teaching did not meet with a vigorous resistance even on this point, and could also appeal to the oldest tradition. The arbitrariness in the number, derivation and designation of the Æons was contested. The aversion to barbarism also co-operated here, in so far as Gnosticism delighted in mysterious words borrowed from the Semites. But the Semitic element attracted as well as repelled the Greeks and Romans of the second century. The Gnostic terminologies within the Æon speculations were partly reproduced among the Catholic theologians of the third century; most important is it that the Gnostics have already made use of the concept "ὁμοούσιος"; see Iren., I. 5. 1: ἀλλὰ τὸ μὲν πνευματικὸν μὴ δεδυνῆσθαι αὐτὴν μορφῶσαι, ἐπειδὴ ὁμοούσιον ὑπῆρχέν αὐτῇ (said of the Sophia): L. 5. 4, καὶ τοῦτον εἶναι τὸν κατ' εἰκόνα καὶ ὁμοίωσιν γεγονότα· κατ' εἰκόνα μὲν τὸν ὑλικὸν ὑπάρχειν, παραπλήσιον μὲν, ἀλλ' οὐχ ὁμοούσιον τῷ θεῷ καθ' ὁμοίωσιν δὲ τὸν ψυχικόν. I. 5. 5: τὸ δὲ κύημα τῆς μητρὸς τῆς "Ἀχαμώθ," ὁμοούσιον ὑπάρχον τῇ μητρί. In all these cases the word means "of one substance." It is found in the same sense in Clem., Hom. 20. 7: see also Philos. VII. 22; Clem., Exc. Theod. 42· Other terms also which have acquired great significance in the Church since the days of Origen (*e.g.*, ἀγέννητος) are found among the Gnostics, see Ep. Ptol. ad Floram, 5; and Bigg. (l. c. p. 58, note 3) calls attention to the appearance of τρίας in Excerpt. ex. Theod. § 80, perhaps the earliest passage.

a heavenly psychical formation, and sprang from the womb
of Mary only in appearance. Finally, a third party, such as
Saturninus, declared that the whole visible appearance of
Christ was a phantom, and therefore denied the birth of Christ. [1]

[1] The characteristic of the Gnostic Christology is not Docetism in the strict
sense, but the doctrine of the two natures, that is, the distinction between Jesus
and Christ, or the doctrine that the Redeemer as Redeemer was not a man. The
Gnostics based this view on the inherent sinfulness of human nature, and it was
shared by many teachers of the age without being based on any principle (see
above, p. 196 f.). The most popular of the three Christologies briefly characterised
above was undoubtedly that of the Valentinians. It is found, with great variety
of details, in most of the nameless fragments of Gnostic literature that have been
preserved, as well as in Apelles. This Christology might be accommodated to
the accounts of the Gospels and the baptismal confession; (how far is shewn by
the *regula* of Apelles, and that of the Valentinians may have run in similar terms).
It was taught here that Christ had passed through Mary as a channel; from this
doctrine followed very easily the notion of the Virginity of Mary, uninjured even
after the birth—it was already known to Clem. Alex. (Strom. VII. 16. 93). The
Church also, later on, accepted this view. It is very difficult to get a clear idea
of the Christology of Basilides, as very diverse doctrines were afterwards set up
in his school as is shewn by the accounts. Among them is the doctrine, likewise
held by others, that Christ in descending from the highest heaven took to himself
something from every sphere through which he passed. Something similar is
found among the Valentinians, some of whose prominent leaders made a very
complicated phenomenon of Christ, and gave him also a direct relation to the
demiurge. There is further found here the doctrine of the heavenly humanity,
which was afterwards accepted by ecclesiastical theologians. Along with the
fragments of Basilides the account of Clem. Alex. seems to me the most reliable.
According to this, Basilides taught that Christ descended on the man Jesus at the
baptism. Some of the Valentinians taught something similar: the Christology of
Ptolemy is characterised by the union of all conceivable Christology theories.
The different early Christian conceptions may be found in him. Basilides did not
admit a real union between Christ and Jesus; but it is interesting to see how the
Pauline Epistles caused the theologians to view the sufferings of Christ as necessarily based on the assumption of sinful flesh, that is, to deduce from the sufferings
that Christ has assumed sinful flesh. The Basilidean Christology will prove to be
a peculiar preliminary stage of the later ecclesiastical Christology. The anniversary
of the baptism of Christ was to the Basilideans as the day of the ἐπιφάνεια, a
high festival day (see Clem., Strom. I. 21. 146): they fixed it for the 6th (2nd)
January. And in this also the Catholic Church has followed the Gnosis. The
real docetic Christology as represented by Saturninus (and Marcion) was radically
opposed to the tradition, and struck out the birth of Jesus, as well as the first
30 years of his life. An accurate exposition of the Gnostic Christologies, which
would carry us too far here, (see especially Tertull., de carne Christi,) would shew
that a great part of the questions which occupy Church theologians till the present
day were already raised by the Gnostics; for example, what happened to the
body of Christ after the resurrection? (see the doctrines of Apelles and Hermo-

Christ separates that which is unnaturally united, and thus leads everything back again to himself; in this redemption consists (full contrast to the notion of the ἀνακεφαλαίωσις).

(*i*) The conversion of the ἐκκλησία (it was no innovation to regard the heavenly Church as an Æon) into the college of the pneumatic, who alone, in virtue of their psychological endowment, are capable of Gnosis and the divine life, while the

genes); what significance the appearance of Christ had for the heavenly and Satanic powers? what meaning belongs to his sufferings, although there was no real suffering for the heavenly Christ, but only for Jesus? etc. In no other point do the anticipations in the Gnostic dogmatic stand out so plainly; (see the system of Origen; many passages bearing on the subject will be found in the third and fourth volumes of this work, to which readers are referred). The Catholic Church has learned but little from the Gnostics, that is, from the earliest theologians in Christendom, in the doctrine of God and the world, but very much in Christology; and who can maintain that she has ever completely overcome the Gnostic doctrine of the two natures, nay, even Docetism? Redemption viewed in the historical person of Jesus, that is, in the appearance of a Divine being on the earth, but the person divided and the real history of Jesus explained away and made inoperative, is the signature of the Gnostic Christology—this, however, is also the danger of the system of Origen and those systems that are dependent on him (Docetism) as well as, in another way, the danger of the view of Tertullian and the Westerns (doctrine of two natures). Finally, it should be noted that the Gnosis always made a distinction between the supreme God and Christ, but that, from the religious position, it had no reason for emphasising that distinction. For to many Gnostics, Christ was in a certain way the manifestation of the supreme God himself, and therefore in the more popular writings of the Gnostics (see the Acta Johannis) expressions are applied to Christ which seem to identify him with God. The same thing is true of Marcion and also of Valentinus (see his Epistle in Clem., Strom. II. 20. 114: εἷς δὲ ἐστιν ἀγαθός, οὗ πάρουσία ἡ διὰ τοῦ υἱοῦ φανέρωσις). This Gnostic estimate of Christ has undoubtedly had a mighty influence on the later Church development of Christology. We might say without hesitation that to most Gnostics Christ was a πνεῦμα, ὁμοούσιον τῷ πατρί. The details of the life, sufferings and resurrection of Jesus are found in many Gnostics transformed, complemented and arranged in the way in which Celsus (Orig., c. Cels. I. II.) required for an impressive and credible history. Celsus indicates how everything must have taken place if Christ had been a God in human form. The Gnostics in part actually narrate it so. What an instructive coincidence! How strongly the docetic view itself was expressed in the case of Valentinus, and how the exaltation of Jesus above the earthly was thereby to be traced back to his moral struggle, is shewn in the remarkable fragment of a letter (in Clem., Strom. III. 7. 59): Πάντα ὑπομείνας ἠγκρατὴς τὴν θεότητα Ἰησοῦς εἰργάζετο. ἤσθιεν γὰρ καὶ ἔπιεν ἰδίως οὐκ ἀποδιδοὺς τὰ βρώματα, τοσαύτη ἦν αὐτῷ τῆς ἐγκρατείας δύναμις, ὥστε καὶ μὴ φθαρῆναι τὴν τροφὴν ἐν αὐτῷ ἐπεὶ τὸ φθείρεσθαι αὐτὸς οὐκ εἶχεν. In this notion, however, there is more sense and historical meaning than in that of the later ecclesiastical aphtharto-docetism.

others, likewise in virtue of their constitution, as hylic perish. The Valentinians, and probably many other Gnostics also, distinguished between pneumatic, psychic and hylic. They regarded the psychic as capable of a certain blessedness, and of a corresponding certain knowledge of the supersensible, the latter being obtained through Pistis, that is, through Christian faith. [1]

(k) The rejection of the entire early christian eschatology, especially the second coming of Christ, the resurrection of the body, and Christ's Kingdom of glory on the earth; and, in connection with this, the assertion that the deliverance of the spirit from the sensuous can be expected only from the future, while the spirit enlightened about itself already possesses immortality, and only awaits its introduction into the pneumatic pleroma. [2]

---

[1] The Gnostic distinction of classes of men was connected with the old distinction of stages in spiritual understanding, but has its basis in a law of nature. There were again empirical and psychological views—they must have been regarded as very important, had not the Gnostics taken them from the traditions of the philosophic schools—which made the universalism of the Christian preaching of salvation appear unacceptable to the Gnostics. Moreover, the transformation of religion into a doctrine of the school, or into a mystery cult, always resulted in the distinction of the knowing from the *profanum vulgus*. But in the Valentinian assumption that the common Christians as psychical occupy an intermediate stage, and that they are saved by faith, we have a compromise which completely lowered the Gnosis to a scholastic doctrine within Christendom. Whether and in what way the Catholic Church maintained the significance of Pistis as contrasted with Gnosis, and in what way the distinction between the knowing (priests) and the laity was there reached will be examined in its proper place. It should be noted, however, that the Valentinian, Ptolemy, ascribes freedom of will to the psychic (which the pneumatic and hylic lack), and therefore has sketched by way of by-work a theology for the psychical beside that for the pneumatic, which exhibits striking harmonies with the exoteric system of Origen. The denial by Gnosticism of free will, and therewith of moral responsibility, called forth very decided contradiction. Gnosticism, that is, the acute hellenising of Christianity, was wrecked in the Church on free will, the Old Testament and eschatology.

[2] The greatest deviation of Gnosticism from tradition appears in eschatology, along with the rejection of the Old Testament and the separation of the creator of the world from the supreme God. Upon the whole our sources say very little about the Gnostic eschatology. This, however, is not astonishing; for the Gnostics had not much to say on the matter, or what they had to say found expression in their doctrine of the genesis of the world, and that of redemption through Christ. We learn that the *regula* of Apelles closed with the words: ἀνέπτη εἰς οὐρανὸν ὅθεν καὶ ἧκε, instead of ὅθεν ἔρχεται κρῖναι ζῶντας καὶ νεκρούς. We know that Marcion,

In addition to what has been mentioned here, we must finally fix our attention on the ethics of Gnosticism. Like the ethics of all systems which are based on the contrast between the sensuous and spiritual elements of human nature, that of the Gnostics took a twofold direction. On the one hand, it sought to suppress and uproot the sensuous, and thus became strictly ascetic (imitation of Christ as motive of asce-

who may already be mentioned here, referred the whole eschatological expectations of early Christian times to the province of the god of the Jews, and we hear that Gnostics (Valentinians) retained the words σαρκος ἀνάστασιν, but interpreted them to mean that one must rise in this life, that is perceive the truth (thus the "resurrectio a mortuis", that is, exaltation above the earthly, took the place of the "resurrectio mortuorum"; see Iren. II. 31. 2: Tertull., de resurr. carnis, 19). While the Christian tradition placed a great drama at the close of history, the Gnostics regard the history itself as the drama, which virtually closes with the (first) appearing of Christ. It may not have been the opinion of all Gnostics that the resurrection has already taken place, yet for most of them the expectations of the future seem to have been quite faint, and above all without significance. The life is so much included in knowledge, that we nowhere in our sources find a strong expression of hope in a life beyond (it is different in the earliest Gnostic documents preserved in the Coptic language), and the introduction of the spirits into the Pleroma appears very vague and uncertain. But it is of great significance that those Gnostics who, according to their premises, required a real redemption from the world as the highest good, remained finally in the same uncertainty and religious despondency with regard to this redemption, as characterised the Greek philosophers. A religion which is a philosophy of religion remains at all times fixed to this life, however strongly it may emphasise the contrast between the spirit and its surroundings, and however ardently it may desire redemption. The desire for redemption is unconsciously replaced by the thinker's joy in his knowledge, which allays the desire (Iren., III. 15. 2: "Inflatus est iste [scil. the Valentinian proud of knowledge] neque in cœlo, neque in terra putat se esse, sed intra Pleroma introisse et complexum jam angelum suum, cum institorio et supercilio incedit gallinacei elationem habens .... Plurimi, quasi jam perfecti, semetipsos spiritales vocant, et se nosse jam dicunt eum qui sit intra Pleroma ipsorum refrigerii locum"). As in every philosophy of religion, an element of free thinking appears very plainly here also. The eschatological hopes can only have been maintained in vigour by the conviction that the world is of God. But we must finally refer to the fact that, even in eschatology, Gnosticism only drew the inferences from views which were pressing into Christendom from all sides, and were in an increasing measure endangering its hopes of the future. Besides, in some Valentinian circles, the future life was viewed as a condition of education, as a progress through the series of the (seven) heavens; i. e., purgatorial experiences in the future were postulated. Both afterwards, from the time of Origen, forced their way into the doctrine of the Church (purgatory, different ranks in heaven). Clement and Origen being throughout strongly influenced by the Valentinian eschatology.

ticism;[1] Christ and the Apostles represented as ascetics);[2] on the other hand, it treated the sensuous element as indifferent, and so became libertine, that is, conformed to the world. The former was undoubtedly the more common, though there are credible witnesses to the latter; the *frequentissimum collegium* in particular, the Valentinians, in the days of Irenæus and Tertullian, did not vigorously enough prohibit a lax and world-conforming morality;[3] and among the Syrian and Egyptian Gnostics there were associations which celebrated the most revolting orgies.[4] As the early Christian tradition summoned to a strict renunciation of the world and to self-control, the Gnostic asceticism could not but make an impression at the first; but the dualistic basis on which it rested could not fail to excite suspicion as soon as one was capable of examining it.[5]

[1] See the passage Clem., Strom. III. 6, 49, which is given above, p. 239.

[2] Cf. the Apocryphal Acts of Apostles and diverse legends of Apostles (*e.g.*, in Clem. Alex.).

[3] More can hardly be said: the heads of schools were themselves earnest men. No doubt statements such as that of Heracleon seem to have led to laxity in the lower sections of the collegium: ὁμολογίαν εἶναι τὴν μὲν ἐν τῇ πίστει καὶ πολιτείᾳ, τὴν δὲ ἐν φωνῇ· ἡ μὲν οὖν ἐν φωνῇ ὁμολογια καὶ ἐπὶ τῶν ἐξουσιῶν γίνεται, ἥν μόνην ὁμολογίαν ἡγοῦνται εἶναι οἱ πολλοί, οὐχ ὑγιῶς δύνανται δὲ ταύτην τὴν ὁμολογίαν καὶ οἱ ὑποκριταὶ ὁμολογεῖν.

[4] See Epiph. h. 26, and the statements in the Coptic Gnostic works. (Schmidt, Texte u. Unters. VIII. I. 2, p. 566 ff.)

[5] There arose in this way an extremely difficult theoretical problem, but practically a convenient occasion for throwing asceticism altogether overboard, with the Gnostic asceticism, or restricting it to easy exercises. This is not the place for entering into the details. Shibboleths, such as φεύγετε οὐ τὰς φύσεις ἀλλὰ τὰς γνώμας τῶν κακῶν, may have soon appeared. It may be noted here, that the asceticism with gained the victory in Monasticism was not really that which sprang from early Christian, but from Greek impulses, without, of course, being based on the same principle. Gnosticism anticipated the future even here. That could be much more clearly proved in the history of the worship. A few points which are of importance for the history of dogma may be mentioned here: (1) The Gnostics viewed the traditional sacred actions (Baptism and the Lord's Supper) entirely as mysteries, and applied to them the terminology of the mysteries (some Gnostics set them aside as psychic); but in doing so they were only drawing the inference from changes which were then in process throughout Christendom. To what extent the later Gnosticism in particular was interested in sacraments may be studied especially in the Pistis Sophia and the other Coptic works of the Gnostics, which Carl Schmidt has edited; see, for example, Pistis Sophia, p. 233. "Dixit Jesus ad suos μαθήτας: ἀμήν, dixi vobis, haud adduxi quidquam in κόσμον veniens nisi hunc

Literature.—The writings of Justin (his syntagma against here-
sies has not been preserved), Irenæus, Tertullian, Hippolytus,
Clement of Alexandria, Origen, Epiphanius, Philastrius and Theo-
doret; cf. Volkmar, Die Quellen der Ketzergeschichte, 1885.
Lipsius, Zur Quellenkritik des Epiphanios, 1875; also Die
Quellen der ältesten Ketzergeschichte, 1875.

ignem et hanc aquam et hoc vinum et hunc sanguinem." (2) They increased the
holy actions by the addition of new ones, repeated baptisms (expiations), anointing
with oil, sacrament of confirmation (ἀπολύτρωσις); see, on Gnostic sacraments,
Iren. I. 20, and Lipsius, Apokr. Apostelgesch. I. pp. 336-343, and cf. the πυκνῶς
μετανοοῦσι in the delineation of the Shepherd of Hermas. Mand XI. (3) Marcus
represented the wine in the Lord's Supper as actual blood in consequence of the
act of blessing: see Iren., I. 13. 2: ποτήρια οἴνῳ κεκραμένα προσποιούμενος εὐχα-
ριστεῖν, καὶ ἐπὶ πλέον ἐκτείνων τὸν λόγον τῆς ἐπικλήσεως, πορφύρεα καὶ ἐρυθρὰ
ἀναφαίνεσθαι ποιεῖ, ὡς δοκεῖν τὴν ἀπὸ τῶν ὑπὲρ τὰ ὅλα χάριν τὸ αἷμα τὸ ἑαυτῆς
στάζειν ἐν ἐκείνῳ τῷ ποτηρίῳ διὰ τῆς ἐπικλήσεως αὐτοῦ, καὶ ὑπεριμείρεσθαι τοὺς
παρόντας ἐξ ἐκείνου γεύσασθαι τοῦ πόματος, ἵνα καὶ εἰς αὐτοὺς ἐπομβρήσῃ ἡ διὰ τοῦ
μάγου τούτου κληϊζομένη χάρις. Marcus was indeed a charlatan; but religious
charlatanry afterwards became very earnest, and was certainly taken earnestly by
many adherents of Marcus. The transubstantiation idea in reference to the elements in the mysteries is also plainly expressed in the Excerpt. ex. Theodot. § 82:
καὶ ὁ ἄρτος καὶ τὸ ἔλαιον ἁγιάζεται τῇ δυνάμει τοῦ ὀνόματος οὐ τὰ αὐτὰ ὄντα
κατὰ τὸ φαινόμενον οἷα ἐλήφθη, ἀλλὰ δυνάμει εἰς δύναμιν πνευματικὴν μεταβέβληται
(that is, not into a new super-terrestrial material, not into the real body of Christ,
but into a spiritual power) οὕτως καὶ τὸ ὕδωρ καὶ τὸ ἐξορκιζόμενον καὶ τὸ βαπτίσμα
γινόμενον οὐ μόνον χωρεῖ τὸ χεῖρον, ἀλλὰ καὶ ἁγιασμὸν προσλαμβάνει. Irenæus
possessed a liturgical handbook of the Marcionites, and communicates many sacramental formulæ from it (I. c. 13 sq.). In my treatise on the Pistis Sophia (Texte
u. Unters. VII. 2. pp. 59-94) I think I have shewn ("The common Christian and
the Catholic elements of the Pistis Sophia") to what extent Gnosticism anticipated
Catholicism as a system of doctrine and an institute of worship. These results
have been strengthened by Carl Schmidt (Texte u. Unters. VIII. 1. 2). Even
purgatory, prayers for the dead, and many other things raised in speculative
questions and definitely answered, are found in those Coptic Gnostic writings and
are then met with again in Catholicism. One general remark may be permitted
in conclusion. The Gnostics were not interested in apologetics, and that is a very
significant fact. The πνεῦμα in man was regarded by them as a supernatural
principle, and on that account they are free from all rationalism and moralistic
dogmatism. For that very reason they are in earnest with the idea of revelation,
and do not attempt to prove it or convert its contests into natural truths. They
did endeavour to prove that their doctrines were Christian, but renounced all proof
that revelation is the truth (proofs from antiquity). One will not easily find in the
case of the Gnostics themselves the revealed truth described as philosophy, or
morality as the philosophic life. If we compare, therefore, the first and fundamental
system of Catholic doctrine, that of Origen, with the system of the Gnostics, we
shall find that Origen, like Basilides and Valentinus, was a philosopher of revelation, but that he had besides a second element which had its origin in apologetics.

Harnack, Zur Quellenkritik d. Gesch. Gnostic, 1873 (continued i. D. Ztschr. f. d, hist. Theol. 1874, and in Der Schrift de Apellis gnosi monarch. 1874).

Of Gnostic writings we possess the book Pistis Sophia, the writings contained in the Coptic Cod. Brucianus, and the Epistle of Ptolemy to Flora; also numerous fragments, in connection with which Hilgenfeld especially deserves thanks, but which still require a more complete selecting and a more thorough discussion (see Grabe, Spicilegium T. I. II. 1700. Heinrici, Die Valentin. Gnosis, u. d. H. Schrift, 1871).

On the (Gnostic) Apocryphal Acts of the Apostles, see Zahn, Acta Joh. 1880, and the great work of Lipsius, Die apokryphen Apostelgeschichten, I. Vol., 1883; II. Vol., 1887. (See also Lipsius, Quellen d. röm. Petrussage, 1872.)

Neander, Genet. Entw. d. vornehmsten gnostischen Systeme, 1818.

Matter, Hist. crit. du gnosticisme, 2 Vols., 1828.

Baur, Die Christl. Gnosis, 1835.

Lipsius, Der Gnosticismus, in Ersch. und Gruber's Allg. Encykl. 71 Bd. 1860.

Moeller, Geschichte d. Kosmologie i. d. Griech. K. bis auf Origenes. 1860.

King, The Gnostics and their remains, 1873.

Mansel, The Gnostic heresies, 1875.

Jacobi, Art. "Gnosis" in Herzog's Real Encykl. 2nd Edit.

Hilgenfeld, Die Ketzergeschichte des Urchristenthums, 1884, where the more recent special literature concerning individual Gnostics is quoted.

Lipsius, Art. "Valentinus" in Smith's Dictionary of Christian Biography.

Harnack, Art. "Valentinus" in the Encycl. Brit.

Harnack, Pistis Sophia in the Texte und Unters. VII. 2.

Carl Schmidt, Gnostische Schriften in koptischer Sprache aus dem Codex Brucianus (Texte und Unters. VIII. 1. 2).

Joël, Blicke in die Religionsgeschichte zu Anfang des 2 Christl. Jahrhunderts, 2 parts, 1880, 1883.

Renan, History of the Origins of Christianity. Vols. V. VI. VII.

CHAPTER V

MARCION'S ATTEMPT TO SET ASIDE THE OLD TESTAMENT
FOUNDATION OF CHRISTIANITY,
TO PURIFY TRADITION, AND TO REFORM CHRISTENDOM ON
THE BASIS OF THE PAULINE GOSPEL.

MARCION cannot be numbered among the Gnostics in the
strict sense of the word.[1] For (1) he was not guided by any
speculatively scientific, or even by an apologetic, but by a so-
teriological interest.[2] (2) He therefore put all emphasis on
faith, not on Gnosis.[3] (3) In the exposition of his ideas he
neither applied the elements of any Semitic religious wisdom,

[1] He belonged to Pontus and was a rich shipowner: about 139 he came to
Rome already a Christian, and for a short time belonged to the church there. As
he could not succeed in his attempt to reform it, he broke away from it about
144. He founded a church of his own and developed a very great activity. He
spread his views by numerous journeys, and communities bearing his name very
soon arose in every province of the Empire (Adamantius, de recta in deum fide,
Origen, Opp. ed. Delarue I. p. 809: Epiph. h. 42. p. 668. ed. Oehler). They were
ecclesiastically organised (Tertull., de præscr. 41, and adv. Marc. IV. 5) and possessed
bishops, presbyters, etc. (Euseb. H. E. IV. 15. 46: de Mart. Palæst. X. 2: Les Bas
and Waddington, Inscript. Grecq. et Latines rec. en Grêce et en Asie Min. Vol. III.
No. 2558). Justin (Apol. 1. 26) about 150 tells us that Marcion's preaching had
spread κατὰ πᾶν γένος ἀνθρώπων, and by the year 155, the Marcionites were already
numerous in Rome (Iren. III. 34). Up to his death, however, Marcion did not
give up the purpose of winning the whole of Christendom, and therefore again and
again sought connection with it (Iren. I. c.; Tertull., de præscr. 30), likewise his
disciples (see the conversation of Apelles with Rhodon in Euseb. H. E. V. 13. 5,
and the dialogue of the Marcionites with Adamantius). It is very probable that
Marcion had fixed the ground features of his doctrine, and had laboured for its
propagation, even before he came to Rome. In Rome the Syrian Gnostic Cerdo had
a great influence on him, so that we can even yet perceive, and clearly distinguish the Gnostic element in the form of the Marcionite doctrine transmitted to us.

[2] "Sufficit," said the Marcionites, "unicum opsus deo nostro, quod hominem
liberavit summa et præcipua bonitate sua (Tertull. adv. Marc. I. 17).

[3] Apelles, the disciple of Marcion, declared (Euseb. H. E. V. 13. 5) σωθήσεσθαι
τοὺς ἐπὶ τὸν ἐσταυρωμένον ἠλπικότας, μόνον ἐὰν ἐν ἔργοις ἀγαθοῖς εὑρίσκωνται.

nor the methods of the Greek philosophy of religion.¹ (4)
He never made the distinction between an esoteric and an
exoteric form of religion. He rather clung to the publicity
of the preaching, and endeavoured to reform Christendom, in
opposition to the attempts at founding schools for those who

---

¹ This is an extremely important point. Marcion rejected all allegories. (See
Tertull., adv. Marc. II. 19. 21. 22: III. 5. 6. 14. 19: IV. 15. 20: V. 1; Orig.,
Comment. in Matth. T. XV. 3 Opp. III. p. 655: in. ep. ad. Rom. Opp. IV.
p. 494 sq.: Adamant., Sect. I, Orig. Opp. I. pp. 808. 817; Ephr. Syrus. hymn. 36
Edit. Benedict, p. 520 sq.) and describes this method as an arbitrary one. But
that simply means that he perceived and avoided the transformation of the Gospel
into Hellenic philosophy. No philosophic formulæ are found in any of his statements that have been handed down to us. But what is still more important, none
of his early opponents have attributed to Marcion a system, as they did to
Basilides and Valentinus. There can be no doubt that Marcion did not set up
any system (the Armenian, Esnik, first gives a Marcionite system, but that is a
late production, see my essay in the Ztschr. f. wiss. Theol. 1896. p. 80 f.). He
was just as far from having any apologetic or rationalistic interest. Justin (Apol.
I. 58) says of the Marcionites; ἀπόδειξιν μηδεμίαν περὶ ὧν λέγουσιν ἔχουσιν, ἀλλὰ
ἀλόγως ὡς ὑπὸ λύκου ἄρνες συνηπρασμένοι κτλ. Tertullian again and again casts
in the teeth of Marcion that he has adduced no proof. See I. 11 sq.: III. 2. 3.
4: IV. 11: "Subito Christus, subito et Johannes. Sic sunt omnia apud Marcionem,
quæ suum et plenum habent ordinem apud creatorem." Rhodon (Euseb., H. E. V.
13. 4) says of two prominent genuine disciples of Marcion: μὴ εὑρίσκοντες τὴν
διαίρεσιν τῶν πραγμάτων, ὡς οὐδὲ ἐκεῖνος, δυὸ ἀρχὰς ἀπεφήναντο ψιλῶς καὶ ἀναπο-
δείκτως. Of Apelles, the most important of Marcion's disciples who laid aside
the Gnostic, borrows of his master, we have the words (l. c.): μὴ δεῖν ὅλως ἐξετάζειν
τὸν λόγον, ἀλλ᾽ ἕκαστον, ὡς πεπίστευκε, διαμένειν. Σωθήσεσθαι γὰρ τοὺς ἐπὶ τὸν
ἐσταρωμένον ἠλπικότας ἀπεφαίνετο, μόνον ἐὰν ἐν ἔργοις ἀγαθοῖς εὑρίσκωνται . . . . τὸ
δὲ πῶς ἔστι μία ἀρχή, μὴ γινώσκειν ἔλεγεν, οὕτω δὲ κινεῖσθαι μόνον. . . . μὴ ἐπίσ-
τασθαι πῶς εἷς ἐστιν ἀγέννητος θεός, τοῦτο δὲ πιστεύειν. It was Marcion's purpose
therefore to give all value to faith alone, to make it dependent on its own convincing power, and avoid all philosophic paraphrase and argument. The contrast
in which he placed the Christian blessing of salvation, has in principle nothing
in common with the contract in which Greek philosophy viewed the *summum
bonum*. Finally, it may be pointed out that Marcion introduced no new elements
(Æons, Matter, etc.) into his evangelic views, and leant on no Oriental religious
science. The later Marcionite speculations about matter (see the account of Esnik)
should not be charged upon the master himself, as is manifest from the second
book of Tertullian against Marcion. The assumption that the creator of the world
created it out of a *materia subjacens* is certainly found in Marcion (see Tertull.,
I. 15; Hippol., Philos. X. 19); but he speculated no further about it, and that
assumption itself was not rejected, for example, by Clem. Alex. (Strom. II. 16. 74:
Photius on Clement's Hypotyposes). Marcion did not really speculate even about
the good God; yet see Tertull., adv. Marc. I. 14. 15: IV. 7: "Mundus ille
superior"—"cœlum tertium."

knew and mystery cults for such as were in quest of initiation. It was only after the failure of his attempts at reform that he founded churches of his own, in which brotherly equality, freedom from all ceremonies, and strict evangelical discipline were to rule.[1] Completely carried away with the novelty, uniqueness and grandeur of the Pauline Gospel of the grace of God in Christ, Marcion felt that all other conceptions of the Gospel, and especially its union with the Old Testament religion, was opposed to, and a backsliding from, the truth.[2] He accordingly supposed that it was necessary to make the sharp antitheses of Paul, law and gospel, wrath and grace, works and faith, flesh and spirit, sin and righteousness, death and life, that is the Pauline criticism of the Old Testament religion, the foundation of his religious views, and to refer them to two principles, the righteous and wrathful god of the Old Testament, who is at the same time identical with the creator of the world, and the God of the Gospel, quite unknown before Christ, who is only love and mercy.[3] This Paulinism in its religious strength, but without dialectic, without the Jewish Christian view of history, and detached from the soil of the Old Testament, was to him the true Christianity. Marcion, like Paul, felt that the religious value of a statutory law with commandments and ceremonies, was very different from that of a uniform law of love.[4] Accordingly,

---

[1] Tertull., de præscr. 41. sq.; the delineation refers chiefly to the Marcionites (see Epiph. h. 42. c. 3. 4, and Esnik's account) on the Church system of Marcion, see also Tertull., adv. Marc. I. 14, 21, 23, 24, 28, 29: III. 1, 22: IV. 5, 34: V. 7, 10, 15, 18.

[2] Marcion himself originally belonged to the main body of the Church, as is expressly declared by Tertullian and Epiphanius, and attested by one of his own letters.

[3] Tertull., adv. Marc. I. 2. 19: "Separatio legis et evangelii proprium et principale opus est Marcionis . . . ex diversitate sententiarum utriusque instrumenti diversitatem quoque argumentatur deorum." II. 28, 29: IV. 1. 1. 6: "Dispares deos, alterum, judicem, ferum, bellipotentem; alterum mitem, placidum et tantummodo bonum atque optimum." Iren. I. 27. 2.

[4] Marcion maintained that the good God is not to be feared. Tertull., adv. Marc. I. 27: "Atque adeo præ se ferunt Marcionitæ quod deum suum omnino non timeant. Malus autem, inquiunt, timebitur; bonus autem diligitur." To the question why they did not sin if they did not fear their God, the Marcionites answered in the words of Rom. VI. 1. 2. (l. c.).

he had a capacity for appreciating the Pauline idea of faith;
it is to him reliance on the unmerited grace of God which is
revealed in Christ. But Marcion shewed himself to be a Greek
influenced by the religious spirit of the time, by changing the
ethical contrast of the good and legal into the contrast between
the infinitely exalted spiritual and the sensible which is subject to the law of nature, by despairing of the triumph of
good in the world and, consequently, correcting the traditional
faith that the world and history belong to God, by an empirical view of the world and the course of events in it,[1] a
view to which he was no doubt also led by the severity of
the early Christian estimate of the world. Yet to him
systematic speculation about the final causes of the contrast
actually observed, was by no means the main thing. So far
as he himself ventured on such a speculation he seems to
have been influenced by the Syrian Cerdo. The numerous
contradictions which arise as soon as one attempts to reduce
Marcion's propositions to a system, and the fact that his disciples tried all possible conceptions of the doctrine of principles, and defined the relation of the two Gods very differently,
are the clearest proof that Marcion was a religious character,
that he had in general nothing to do with principles, but with
living beings whose power he felt, and that what he ultimately
saw in the Gospel was not an explanation of the world,
but redemption from the world,[2]—redemption from a world
which even in the best that it can offer has nothing that
can reach the height of the blessing bestowed in Christ.[3]

[1] Tertull., adv. Marc. I. 2 : II. 5.

[2] See the passage adduced, p. 267, note 2, and Tertull., I. 19: "Immo inquiunt
Marcionitæ, deus noster, etsi non ab initio, etsi non per conditionem, sed per
semetipsum revelatus est in Christi Jesu." The very fact that different theological
tendencies (schools) appeared within Marcionite Christianity and were mutually
tolerant, proves that the Marcionite Church itself was not based on a formulated
system of faith. Apelles expressly conceded different forms of doctrine in Christendom,
on the basis of faith in the Crucified and a common holy ideal of life (see p. 268).

[3] Tertull. I. 13. "Narem contrahentes impudentissimi Marcionitæ convertuntur
ad destructionem operum creatoris. Nimirum, inquiunt, grande opus et dignum
deo mundus?" The Marcionites (Iren. IV. 34. 1) put the question to their ecclesiastical opponents: "Quid novi attulit dominus veniens?" and therewith caused
them no small embarrassment.

Special attention may be called to the following particulars.

1. Marcion explained the Old Testament in its literal sense and rejected every allegorical interpretation. He recognised it as the revelation of the creator of the world and the god of the Jews, but placed it, just on that account, in sharpest contrast to the Gospel. He demonstrated the contradictions between the Old Testament and the Gospel in a voluminous work (the ἀντιθέσεις). [1] In the god of the former book he saw a being whose character was stern justice, and therefore anger, contentiousness and unmercifulness. The law which rules nature and man appeared to him to accord with the characteristics of this god and the kind of law revealed by him, and therefore it seemed credible to him that this god is the creator and lord of the world (κοτμοκράτωρ). As the law which governs the world is inflexible and yet, on the other hand, full of contradictions, just and again brutal, and as the law of the Old Testament exhibits the same features, so the god of creation was to Marcion a being who united in himself the whole gradations of attributes from justice to malevolence, from obstinacy to inconsistency. [2] Into this conception of the creator of the world, the characteristic of which is that it cannot be systematised, could easily be fitted the Syrian Gnostic theory which regards him as an evil being, because he belongs to this world and to matter. Marcion did not accept it in principle, [3] but touched it lightly and adopted certain inferences. [4] On

---

[1] On these see Tertull. I. 19 : II. 28. 29 : IV. 1. 4. 6 : Epiph.; Hippol. Philos. VII. 30; the book was used by other Gnostics also (it is very probable that 1 Tim. VI. 20, an addition to the Epistle—refers to Marcion's Antitheses). Apelles, Marcion's disciple, composed a similar work under the title of "Syllogismi." Marcion's Antitheses, which may still in part be reconstructed from Tertullian, Epiphanius, Adamantius, Ephraem, etc., possessed canonical authority in the Marcionite church, and therefore took the place of the Old Testament. That is quite clear from Tertull., I. 19 (cf. IV. 1): Separatio legis et Evangelii proprium et principale opus est Marcionis, nec poterunt negare discipuli ejus, quod in summo (suo) instrumento habent, quo denique initiantur et indurantur in hanc hæresim.

[2] Tertullian has frequently pointed to the contradictions in the Marcionite conception of the god of creation. These contradictions, however, vanish as soon as we regard Marcion's god from the point of view that he is like his revelation in the Old Testament.

[3] The creator of the world is indeed to Marcion " malignus," but not " malus."

[4] Marcion touched on it when he taught that the " visibilia " belonged to the

the basis of the Old Testament and of empirical observation, Marcion divided men into two classes, good and evil, though he regarded them all, body and soul, as creatures of the demiurge. The good are those who strive to fulfil the law of the demiurge. These are outwardly better than those who refuse him obedience. But the distinction found here is not the decisive one. To yield to the promptings of Divine grace is the only decisive distinction, and those just men will shew themselves less susceptible to the manifestation of the truly good than sinners. As Marcion held the Old Testament to be a book worthy of belief, though his disciple, Apelles, thought otherwise, he referred all its predictions to a Messiah whom the creator of the world is yet to send, and who, as a warlike hero, is to set up the earthly kingdom of the "just" God. [1]

2. Marcion placed the good God of love in opposition to the creator of the world. [2] This God has only been revealed in Christ. He was absolutely unknown before Christ, [3] and men were in every respect strange to him. [4] Out of pure goodness and mercy, for these are the essential attributes of this God who judges not and is not wrathful, he espoused the cause of those beings who were foreign to him, as he could not bear to have them any longer tormented by their just and yet malevolent lord. [5] The God of love appeared in Christ and proclaimed a new kingdom (Tertull., adv. Marc. III. 24. fin.). Christ called to himself the weary and heavy

---

god of creation, but the "invisibilia" to the good God (I. 16). He adopted the consequences, inasmuch as he taught docetically about Christ, and only assumed a deliverance of the human soul.

[1] See especially the third book of Tertull. adv. Marcion.

[2] "Solius bonitatis," "deus melior," were Marcion's standing expressions for him.

[3] "Deus incognitus" was likewise a standing expression. They maintained against all attacks the religious position that, from the nature of the case, believers only can know God, and that this is quite sufficient (Tertull., I. 11.)

[4] Marcion firmly emphasised this and appealed to passages in Paul; see Tertull. I. 11. 19. 23: "Scio dicturos, atqui hanc esse principalem et perfectam bonitatem, cum sine ullo debito familiaritatis in extraneos voluntaria et libera effunditur, secundum quam inimicos quoque nostros et hoc nomine jam extraneos deligere jubeamur." The Church Fathers therefore declared that Marcion's good God was a thief and a robber. See also Celsus, in Orig. VI. 53.

[5] See Esnik's account, which, however, is to be used cautiously.

laden, [1] and proclaimed to them that he would deliver them
from the fetters of their lord and from the world. He shewed
mercy to all while he sojourned on the earth, and did in
every respect the opposite of what the creator of the world had
done to men. They who believed in the creator of the world
nailed him to the cross. But in doing so they were unconsciously serving his purpose, for his death was the price by
which the God of love purchased men from the creator of the
world. [2] He who places his hope in the Crucified can now
be sure of escaping from the power of the creator of the
world, and of being translated into the kingdom of the good
God. But experience shews that, like the Jews, men who are
virtuous according to the law of the creator of the world,
do not allow themselves to be converted by Christ; it is
rather sinners who accept his message of redemption. Christ,
therefore, rescued from the under-world, not the righteous men
of the Old Testament (Iren. I. 27. 3), but the sinners who
were disobedient to the creator of the world. If the determining thought of Marcion's view of Christianity is here again
very clearly shewn, the Gnostic woof cannot fail to be seen
in the proposition that the good God delivers only the souls,
not the bodies of believers. The antithesis of spirit and matter,
appears here as the decisive one, and the good God of love
becomes the God of the spirit, the Old Testament god the
god of the flesh. In point of fact, Marcion seems to have
given such a turn to the good God's attributes of love and
incapability of wrath, as to make Him the apathetic, infinitely
exalted Being, free from all affections. The contradiction in
which Marcion is here involved is evident, because he taught
expressly that the spirit of man is in itself just as foreign to
the good God as his body. But the strict asceticism which

---

[1] Marcion has strongly emphasised the respective passages in Luke's Gospel: see
his Antitheses, and his comments on the Gospel as presented by Tertullian (l. IV).

[2] That can be plainly read in Esnik, and must have been thought by Marcion
himself, as he followed Paul (see Tertull., l. V. and I. 11). Apelles also emphasised
the death upon the cross. Marcion's conception of the purchase can indeed no
longer be ascertained in its details. But see Adamant., de recta in deum fide,
sect. I. It is one of his theoretic contradictions that the good God who is exalted
above righteousness should yet purchase men.

Marcion demanded as a Christian, could have had no motive
without the Greek assumption of a metaphysical contrast of
flesh and Spirit, which in fact was also apparently the doctrine of Paul.

3. The relation in which Marcion placed the two Gods,
appears at first sight to be one of equal rank. [1] Marcion himself, according to the most reliable witnesses, expressly asserted
that both were uncreated, eternal, etc. But if we look more
closely we shall see that in Marcion's mind there can be no
thought of equality. Not only did he himself expressly declare
that the creator of the world is a self-contradictory being
of limited knowledge and power, but the whole doctrine of
redemption shews that he is a power subordinate to the good
God. We need not stop to enquire about the details, but it
is certain that the creator of the world formerly knew nothing
of the existence of the good God, that he is in the end completely powerless against him, that he is overcome by him, and
that history in its issue with regard to man is determined
solely by its relation to the good God. The just god appears
at the end of history, not as an independent being hostile
to the good God, but as one subordinate to him, [2] so that
some scholars, such as Neander, have attempted to claim for
Marcion a doctrine of one principle, and to deny that he

---

[1] Tertull. I. 6: "Marcion non negat creatorem deum esse."

[2] Here Tertull., I. 27, 28, is of special importance; see also II. 28; IV. 29 (on
Luke XII. 41–46): IV. 30. Marcion's idea was this. The good God does not
judge or punish; but He judges in so far as he keeps evil at a distance from
Him: it remains foreign to Him. "Marcionitæ interrogati quid fiet peccatori
cuique die illo? respondent abici illum quasi ab oculis". " Tranquilitas est et
mansuetudinis segregare solummodo et partem ejus cum infidelibus ponere". But
what is the end of him who is thus rejected? "Ab igne, inquiunt, creatoris
deprehendetur". We might think with Tertullian that the creator of the world
would receive sinners with joy: but this is the god of the law who punishes sinners.
The issue is twofold: the heaven of the good God, and the hell of the creator
of the world. Either Marcion assumed with Paul that no one can keep the law,
or he was silent about the end of the "righteous" because he had no interest in
it. At any rate, the teaching of Marcion closes with an outlook in which the
creator of the world can no longer be regarded as an independent god. Marcion's
disciples (see Esnik) here developed a consistent theory: the creator of the world
violated his own law by killing the righteous Christ, and was therefore deprived
of all his power by Christ.

ever held the complete independence of the creator of the
world, the creator of the world being simply an angel of the
good God. This inference may certainly be drawn with
little trouble, as the result of various considerations, but it is
forbidden by reliable testimony. The characteristic of Marcion's teaching is just this, that as soon as we seek to raise
his ideas from the sphere of practical considerations to that
of a consistent theory, we come upon a tangled knot of contradictions. The theoretic contradictions are explained by
the different interests which here cross each other in Marcion.
In the first place, he was consciously dependent on the Pauline theology, and was resolved to defend everything which
he held to be Pauline. Secondly, he was influenced by the
contrast in which he saw the ethical powers involved. This
contrast seemed to demand a metaphysical basis, and its actual solution seemed to forbid such a foundation. Finally,
the theories of Gnosticism, the paradoxes of Paul, the recognition of the duty of strictly mortifying the flesh, suggested
to Marcion the idea that the good God was the exalted God
of the spirit, and the just god the god of the sensuous, of
the flesh. This view, which involved the principle of a metaphysical dualism, had something very specious about it, and
to its influence we must probably ascribe the fact that Marcion no longer attempted to derive the creator of the world
from the good God. His disciples who had theoretical interests in the matter, no doubt noted the contradictions. In
order to remove them, some of these disciples advanced to
a doctrine of three principles, the good God, the just creator
of the world, the evil god, by conceiving the creator of the
world sometimes as an independent being, sometimes as one
dependent on the good God. Others reverted to the common
dualism, God of the spirit and God of matter. But Apelles,
the most important of Marcion's disciples, returned to the
creed of the one God ($\mu i\alpha$ $\dot{\alpha}\rho\chi\dot{\eta}$), and conceived the creator
of the world and Satan as his angels, without departing from
the fundamental thought of the master, but rather following
suggestions which he himself had given. [1] Apart from Apelles,

[1] Schools soon arose in the Marcionite church, just as they did later on in the

who founded a Church of his own, we hear nothing of the
controversies of disciples breaking up the Marcionite church.
All those who lived in the faith for which the master had
worked—viz., that the laws ruling in nature and history, as
well as the course of common legality and righteousness, are
the antitheses of the act of Divine mercy in Christ, and that
cordial love and believing confidence have their proper contrasts in self-righteous pride and the natural religion of the
heart,—those who rejected the Old Testament and clung solely
to the Gospel proclaimed by Paul, and finally, those who considered that a strict mortification of the flesh and an earnest
renunciation of the world were demanded in the name of the
Gospel, felt themselves members of the same community, and
to all appearance allowed perfect liberty to speculations about
final causes.

4. Marcion had no interest in specially emphasising the
distinction between the good God and Christ, which according to the Pauline Epistles could not be denied. To him
Christ is the manifestation of the good God himself.[1] But

main body of Christendom (see Rhodon in Euseb., H. E. V. 13. 2-4). The
different doctrines of principles which were here developed (two, three, four principles; the Marcionite Marcus's doctrine of two principles in which the creator of
the world is an evil being, diverges furthest from the Master) explain the different
accounts of the Church Fathers about Marcion's teaching. The only one of the
disciples who really seceded from the Master was Appelles (Tertull., de præscr. 30).
His teaching is therefore the more important, as it shews that it was possible to
retain the fundamental ideas of Marcion without embracing dualism. The attitude
of Apelles to the Old Testament is that of Marcion in so far as he rejects the
book. But perhaps he somewhat modified the strictness of the Master. On the
other hand, he certainly designated much in it as untrue and fabulous. It is
remarkable that we meet with a highly honoured prophetess in the environment
of Apelles: in Marcion's church we hear nothing of such, nay, it is extremely
important as regards Marcion that he has never appealed to the Spirit and to
prophets. The "sanctiores feminæ" (Tertull. V. 8) are not of this nature, nor can
we appeal even to V. 15. Moreover, it is hardly likely that Jerome ad Eph. III. 5,
refers to Marcionites. In this complete disregard of early Christian prophecy, and
in his exclusive reliance on literary documents, we see in Marcion a process of
despiritualising, that is, a form of secularisation peculiar to himself. Marcion no
longer possessed the early Christian enthusiasm as, for example, Hermas did.

[1] Marcion was fond of calling Christ "Spiritus salutaris." From the treatise
of Tertullian we can prove both that Marcion distinguished Christ from God, and
that he made no distinction (see, for example, I. 11, 14: II. 27: III. 8, 9, 11:

Marcion taught that Christ assumed absolutely nothing from
the creation of the Demiurge, but came down from heaven in
the 15th year of the Emperor Tiberius, and after the assumption of an apparent body, began his preaching in the synagogue of Capernaum. [1] This pronounced docetism which denies
that Jesus was born, or subjected to any human process of
development, [2] is the strongest expression of Marcion's abhorrence of the world. This aversion may have sprung from the
severe attitude of the early Christians toward the world, but
the inference which Marcion here draws, shews that this
feeling was, in his case, united with the Greek estimate of
spirit and matter. But Marcion's docetism is all the more
remarkable that, under Paul's guidance, he put a high
value on the fact of Christ's death upon the cross. Here
also is a glaring contradiction which his later disciples laboured
to remove. This much, however, is unmistakable, that Marcion succeeded in placing the greatness and uniqueness of
redemption through Christ in the clearest light, and in behold-
ing this redemption in the person of Christ, but chiefly in his
death upon the cross.

5. Marcion's eschatology is also quite rudimentary. Yet he
assumed with Paul that violent attacks were yet in store for
the Church of the good God on the part of the Jewish Christ
of the future, the Antichrist. He does not seem to have taught
a visible return of Christ, but, in spite of the omnipotence
and goodness of God, he did teach a twofold issue of history.
The idea of a deliverance of all men, which seems to follow
from his doctrine of boundless grace, was quite foreign to him.
For this very reason he could not help actually making the
good God the judge, though in theory he rejected the idea,

IV. 7). Here again Marcion did not think theologically. What he regarded as
specially important was that God has revealed himself in Christ, "per semetipsum."
Later Marcionites expressly taught Patripassianism, and have on that account been
often grouped with the Sabellians. But other Christologies also arose in Marcion's
church, which is again a proof that it was not dependent on scholastic teaching,
and therefore could take part in the later development of doctrines.

[1] See the beginning of the Marcionite Gospel.

[2] Tertullian informs us sufficiently about this. The body of Christ was
regarded by Marcion merely as an "umbra", a "phantasma." His disciples
adhered to this, but Apelles first constructed a "doctrine" of the body of Christ.

in order not to measure the will and acts of God by a human standard. Along with the fundamental proposition of Marcion, that God should be conceived only as goodness and grace, we must take into account the strict asceticism which he prescribed for the Christian communities, in order to see that that idea of God was not obtained from antinomianism. We know of no Christian community in the second century which insisted so strictly on renunciation of the world as the Marcionites. No union of the sexes was permitted. Those who were married had to separate ere they could be received by baptism into the community. The sternest precepts were laid down in the matter of food and drink. Martyrdom was enjoined; and from the fact that they were ταλαίπωροι καὶ μισούμενοι in the world, the members were to know that they were disciples of Christ. [1] With all that, the early Christian enthusiasm was wanting.

6. Marcion defined his position in theory and practice towards the prevailing form of Christianity, which, on the one hand, shewed throughout its connection with the Old Testament, and, on the other, left room for a secular ethical code, by assuming that it had been corrupted by Judaism, and therefore needed a reformation. [2] But he could not fail to note that this corruption was not of recent date, but belonged to the oldest tradition itself. The consciousness of this moved him to a historical criticism of the whole Christian tradition. [3] Marcion was the first Christian who undertook such a task. Those writings to which he owed his religious convictions,

---

[1] The strict asceticism of Marcion and the Marcionites is reluctantly acknowledged by the Church Fathers; see Tertull., de præscr. 30: "Sanctissimus magister"; I. 28, "carni imponit sanctitem." The strict prohibition of marriage : I. 29: IV. 11, 17, 29, 34, 38: V. 7, 8, 15, 18; prohibition of food: I. 14; cynical life: Hippol., Philos. VII. 29; numerous martyrs: Euseb., H. E. V. 16. 21, and frequently elsewhere. Marcion named his adherents (Tertull. IV. 9 36) "συνταλαίπωροι καὶ συμμισούμενοι." It is questionable whether Marcion himself allowed the repetition of baptism; it arose in his church. But this repetition is a proof that the prevailing conception of baptism was not sufficient for a vigorous religious temper.

[2] Tertull. I. 20. "Aiunt, Marcionem non tam innovasse regulam separatione legis et evangelii quam retro adulteratam recurrasse"; see the account of Epiphanius, taken from Hippolytus, about the appearance of Marcion in Rome (h. 42. I. 2).

[3] Here again we must remember that Marcion appealed neither to a secret tradition nor to the "Spirit," in order to appreciate the epoch-making nature of his undertaking.

viz., the Pauline Epistles, furnished the basis for it. He found
nothing in the rest of Christian literature that harmonised
with the Gospel of Paul. But he found in the Pauline Epistles
hints which explained to him this result of his observations.
The twelve Apostles whom Christ chose did not understand
him, but regarded him as the Messiah of the god of creation. [1]
And therefore Christ inspired Paul by a special revelation,
lest the Gospel of the grace of God should be lost through
falsifications. [2] But even Paul had been understood only by
few (by none?). His Gospel had also been misunderstood—

---

[1] In his estimate of the twelve Apostles Marcion took as his standpoint Gal. II.
See Tertull. I. 20: IV. 3 (generally IV. 1-6), V. 3; de præscr. 22, 23. He endeavoured to prove from this chapter that from a misunderstanding of the words of
Christ, the twelve Apostles had proclaimed a different Gospel than that of Paul;
they had wrongly taken the Father of Jesus Christ for the god of creation. It is
not quite clear how Marcion conceived the inward condition of the Apostles during
the lifetime of Jesus (see Tertull. III. 22 : IV. 3, 39). He assumed that they were
persecuted by the Jews as the preachers of a new God. It is probable, therefore,
that he thought of a gradual obscuring of the preaching of Jesus in the case of
the primitive Apostles. They fell back into Judaism; see Iren. III. 2. 2. "Apostolos admiscuisse ea quæ sunt legalia salvatoris verbis"; III. 12. 12: "Apostoli
quæ sunt Judæorum sentientes scripserunt" etc.; Tertull. V. 3: "Apostolos vultis
Judaismi magis adfines subintelligi." The expositions of Marcion in Tertull. IV. 9.
11, 13, 21, 24, 39 : V. 13, shew that he regarded the primitive Apostles as out
and out real Apostles of Christ.

[2] The call of Paul was viewed by Marcion as a manifestation of Christ, of
equal value with His first appearance and ministry; see [the account of Esnik.
"Then for the second time Jesus came down to the lord of the creatures in the
form of his Godhead, and entered into judgment with him on account of his
death .... And Jesus said to him: 'Judgment is between me and thee, let no one
be judge but thine own laws .... hast thou not written in this thy law, that he
who killeth shall die?' And he answered, 'I have so written' .... Jesus said to
him, 'Deliver thyself therefore into my hands' .... The creator of the world said,
'Because I have slain thee I give thee a compensation, all those who shall believe
on thee, that thou mayest do with them what thou pleasest.' Then Jesus left him
and carried away Paul, and shewed him the price, and sent him to preach that we
are bought with this price, and that all who believe in Jesus are sold by this just
god to the good one." This is a most instructive account; for it shews that in
the Marcionite schools the Pauline doctrine of reconciliation was transformed into
a drama, and placed between the death of Christ and the call of Paul, and that
the Pauline Gospel was based, not directly on the death of Christ upon the cross,
but a theory of it converted into history. On Paul as the one apostle of the truth,
see Tertull. I. 20 : III. 5, 14 : IV. 2 sq. : IV. 34 : V. I. As to the Marcionite theory
that the promise to send the Spirit was fulfilled in the mission of Paul, an indication
of the want of enthusiasm among the Marcionites, see the following page, note 2.

nay, his Epistles had been falsified in many passages, [1] in order to make them teach the identity of the god of creation and the God of redemption. A new reformation was therefore necessary. Marcion felt himself entrusted with this commission, and the church which he gathered recognised this vocation of his to be the reformer. [2] He did not appeal to a new revelation such as he presupposed for Paul. As the Pauline Epistles and an authentic εὐαγγέλιον κυρίου were in existence, it was only necessary to purify these from interpolations, and restore the genuine Paulinism which was just the Gospel itself. But it was also necessary to secure and preserve this true Christianity for the future. Marcion, in all probability, was the first to conceive and, in great measure, to realise the idea of placing Christendom on the firm foundation of a definite theory of what is Christian—but not of basing it on a theological doctrine—and of establishing this theory by a fixed

---

[1] Marcion must have spoken *ex professo* in his Antitheses about the Judaistic corruptions of Paul's Epistles and the Gospel. He must also have known Evangelic writings bearing the names of the original Apostles, and have expressed himself about them (Tertull. IV. 1-6).

[2] Marcion's self-consciousness of being a reformer, and the recognition of this in his church is still not understood, although his undertaking itself and the facts speak loud enough. (1) The great Marcionite church called itself after Marcion (Adamant., de recta in deum fide. I. 809; Epiph. h. 42, p. 668, ed. Oehler: Μαρκίων σοῦ τὸ ὄνομα ἐπικέκληνται οἱ ὑπὸ σοῦ ἠπατημένοι ὡς σεαυτὸν κηρύξαντος καὶ οὐχὶ Χριστόν. We possess a Marcionite inscription which begins: συναγωγὴ Μαρκιωνιστῶν). As the Marcionites did not form a school, but a church, it is of the greatest value for shewing the estimate of the master in this church, that its members called themselves by his name. (2) The Antitheses of Marcion had a place in the Marcionite canon (see above, p. 272). This canon therefore embraced a book of Christ, Epistles of Paul, and a book of Marcion, and for that reason the Antitheses were always circulated with the canon of Marcion. (3) Origen (in Luc. hom. 25. T. III. p. 962) reports as follows: "Denique in tantam quidam dilectionis audaciam proruperunt, ut nova quædam et inaudita super Paulo monstra confingerent. Alii enim aiunt, hoc quod scriptum est, sedere a dextris salvatoris et sinistris, de Paulo et de Marcione dici, quod Paulus sedet a dextris, Marcion sedet a sinistris. Porro alii legentes: Mittam vobis advocatum Spiritum veritatis, nolunt intelligere tertiam personam a patre et filio, sed Apostolum Paulum." The estimate of Marcion which appears here is exceedingly instructive. (4) An Arabian writer, who, it is true, belongs to a later period, reports that Marcionites called their founder "Apostolorum principem." (5) Justin, the first opponent of Marcion, classed him with Simon Magus and Menander, that is, with demonic founders of religion. These testimonies may suffice.

collection of Christian writings with canonical authority. [1] He
was not a systematic thinker, but he was more; for he was
not only a religious character, but at the same time a man
with an organising talent, such as has no peer in the early
Church. If we think of the lofty demands he made on
Christians, and, on the other hand, ponder the results that
accompanied his activity, we cannot fail to wonder. Wherever Christians were numerous about the year 160, there must
have been Marcionite communities with the same fixed but
free organisation, with the same canon and the same conception
of the essence of Christianity, pre-eminent for the strictness of
their morals and their joy in martyrdom. [2] The Catholic
Church was then only in process of growth, and it was long
ere it reached the solidity won by the Marcionite church
through the activity of one man, who was animated by a
faith so strong that he was able to oppose his conception of
Christianity to all others as the only right one, and who did
not shrink from making selections from tradition instead of
explaining it away. He was the first who laid the firm found-

---

[1] On Marcion's Gospel see the Introductions to the New Testament and Zahn's
Kanonsgeschichte, Bd. I., p. 585 ff. and II., p. 409. Marcion attached no name
to his Gospel, which, according to his own testimony, he produced from the third
one of our Canon (Tertull., adv. Marc. IV. 2. 3. 4). He called it simply εὐαγγέλιον (κυρίου), but held that it was the Gospel which Paul had in his mind when
he spoke of his Gospel. The later Marcionites ascribed the authorship of the
Gospel partly to Paul, partly to Christ himself, and made further changes in it.
That Marcion chose the Gospel called after Luke should be regarded as a make-
shift; for this Gospel, which is undoubtedly the most Hellenistic of the four
Canonical Gospels, and therefore comes nearest to the Catholic conception of
Christianity, accommodated itself in its traditional form but little better than the
other three to Marcionite Christianity. Whether Marcion took it for a basis because
in his time it had already been connected with Paul (or really had a connection
with Paul), or whether the numerous narratives about Jesus as the Saviour of sinners
led him to recognise in this Gospel alone a genuine kernel, we do not know.

[2] The associations of the Encratites and the community founded by Apelles
stood between the main body of Christendom and the Marcionite church. The
description of Celsus (especially V. 61-64 in Orig.) shews the motley appearance
which Christendom presented soon after the middle of the second century. He
there mentions the Marcionites, and a little before (V. 59), the "great Church."
It is very important that Celsus makes the main distinction consist in this, that
some regarded their God as identical with the God of the Jews, whilst others again
declared that "theirs was a different Deity, who is hostile to that of the Jews, and
that it was he who had sent the Son." (V. 61.)

ation for establishing what is Christian, because, in view of the absoluteness of his faith, [1] he had no desire to appeal either to a secret evangelic tradition, or to prophecy, or to natural religion.

Remarks.—The innovations of Marcion are unmistakable. The way in which he attempted to sever Christianity from the Old Testament was a bold stroke which demanded the sacrifice of the dearest possession of Christianity as a religion, viz., the belief that the God of creation is also the God of redemption. And yet this innovation was partly caused by a religious conviction, the origin of which must be sought not in heathenism, but on Old Testament and Christian soil. For the bold Anti-judaist was the disciple of a Jewish thinker, Paul, and the origin of Marcion's antinomianism may be ultimately found in the prophets. It will always be the glory of Marcion in the early history of the Church that he, the born heathen, could appreciate the religious criticism of the Old Testament religion as formerly exercised by Paul. The antinomianism of Marcion was ultimately based on the strength of his religious feeling, on his personal religion as contrasted with all statutory religion. That was also its basis in the case of the prophets and of Paul, only the statutory religion, which was felt to be a burden and a fetter, was different in each case. As regards the prophets, it was the outer sacrificial worship, and the deliverance was the idea of Jehovah's righteousness. In the case of Paul, it was the pharisaic treatment of the law, and the deliverance was righteousness by faith. To Marcion it was the sum of all that the past had described as a revelation of God: only what Christ had given him was of real value to him. In this conviction he founded a Church. Before him there was no such thing in the sense of a community firmly united by a fixed conviction, harmoniously organised, and spread over the whole world. Such a

---

[1] One might be tempted to comprise the character of Marcion's religion in the words, "The God who dwells in my breast can profoundly excite my inmost being. He who is throned above all my powers can move nothing outwardly." But Marcion had the firm assurance that God has done something much greater than move the world: he has redeemed men from the world, and given them the assurance of this redemption, in the midst of all oppression and enmity which do not cease.

Church the Apostle Paul had in his mind's eye, but he was
not able to realise it. That in the century of the great
mixture of religion the greatest apparent paradox was actually
realised—namely, a Paulinism with two Gods and without the
Old Testament; and that this form of Christianity first resulted
in a church which was based not only on intelligible words,
but on a definite conception of the essence of Christianity as
a religion, seems to be the greatest riddle which the earliest
history of Christianity presents. But it only seems so. The
Greek, whose mind was filled with certain fundamental features
of the Pauline Gospel (law and grace), who was therefore convinced that in all respects the truth was there, and who on
that account took pains to comprehend the real sense of
Paul's statements, could hardly reach any other results than
those of Marcion. The history of Pauline theology in the
Church, a history first of silence, then of artificial interpretation,
speaks loudly enough. And had not Paul really separated
Christianity as religion from Judaism and the Old Testament?
Must it not have seemed an inconceivable inconsistency, if
he had clung to the special national relation of Christianity
to the Jewish people, and if he had taught a view of history
in which for pædagogic reasons indeed, the Father of mercies
and God of all comfort had appeared as one so entirely
different? He who was not capable of translating himself
into the consciousness of a Jew, and had not yet learned the
method of special interpretation, had only the alternative, if
he was convinced of the truth of the Gospel of Christ as
Paul had proclaimed it, of either giving up this Gospel against
the dictates of his conscience, or striking out of the Epistles
whatever seemed Jewish. But in this case the god of creation
also disappeared, and the fact that Marcion could make this
sacrifice proves that this religious spirit, with all his energy,
was not able to rise to the height of the religious faith which
we find in the preaching of Jesus.

In basing his own position and that of his church on Paulinism, as he conceived and remodelled it, Marcion connected
himself with that part of the earliest tradition of Christianity
which is best known to us, and has enabled us to understand

his undertaking historically as we do no other. Here we have the means of accurately indicating what part of this structure of the second century has come down from the Apostolic age and is really based on tradition, and what has not. Where else could we do that? But Marcion has taught us far more. He does not impart a correct understanding of early Christianity, as was once supposed, for his explanation of that is undoubtedly incorrect, but a correct estimate of the reliability of the traditions that were current in his day alongside of the Pauline. There can be no doubt that Marcion criticised tradition from a dogmatic stand-point. But would his undertaking have been at all possible if at that time a reliable tradition of the twelve Apostles and their teaching had existed and been operative in wide circles? We may venture to say no. Consequently, Marcion gives important testimony against the historical reliability of the notion that the common Christianity was really based on the tradition of the twelve Apostles. It is not surprising that the first man who clearly put and answered the question, "What is Christian?" adhered exclusively to the Pauline Epistles, and therefore found a very imperfect solution. When more than 1600 years later the same question emerged for the first time in scientific form, its solution had likewise to be first attempted from the Pauline Epistles, and therefore led at the outset to a one-sidedness similar to that of Marcion. The situation of Christendom in the middle of the second century was not really more favourable to a historical knowledge of early Christianity than that of the 18th century, but in many respects more unfavourable. Even at that time, as attested by the enterprise of Marcion, its results, and the character of the polemic against him, there were besides the Pauline Epistles no reliable documents from which the teaching of the twelve Apostles could have been gathered. The position which the Pauline Epistles occupy in the history of the world is, however, described by the fact that every tendency in the Church which was unwilling to introduce into Christianity the power of Greek mysticism, and was yet no longer influenced by the early Christian eschatology, learned from the Pauline Epistles a Christianity which, as a religion, was peculiarly vigorous. But that position is further described by the fact that every tendency which courageously disregards spurious traditions is compelled to turn to the Pauline Epistles, which, on the one hand, present such a profound type of Christianity, and on the other darken and narrow the judgment about the preaching of Christ himself by their complicated theology. Marcion was the first, and for a long time the only Gentile Christian who took his stand on Paul. He was no moralist, no Greek mystic, no Apocalyptic enthusiast, but a religious character, nay, one of the few pronouncedly typical religious characters whom we know in the early Church before Augustine. But his attempt to resuscitate Paulinism is the first great proof that the conditions under which this Christianity originated do not repeat themselves, and that therefore Paulinism itself must receive a new construction if one desires to make it the basis of a Church. His attempt is a further proof of the unique value of the Old Testament to early Christendom, as the only means at that time of defending Christian monotheism. Finally, his attempt confirms the experience that a religious community can only be founded by a religious spirit who expects nothing from the world.

Nearly all ecclesiastical writers, from Justin to Origen, opposed Marcion. He appeared already to Justin as the most wicked enemy. We can understand this, and we can quite as well understand how the Church Fathers put him on a level with Basilides and Valentinus, and could not see the difference between them. Because Marcion elevated a better God above the god of creation, and consequently robbed the Christian God of his honour, he appeared to be worse than a heathen (Sentent. episc. LXXXVII., in Hartel's edition of Cyprian, I. p. 454; "Gentiles quamvis idola colant, tamen summum deum patrem creatorem cognoscunt et confitentur [!]; in hunc Marcion, blasphemat, etc."), as a blaspheming emissary of demons, as the first-born of Satan (Polyc., Justin, Irenæus). Because he rejected the allegoric interpretation of the Old Testament, and explained its predictions as referring to a Messiah of the Jews who was yet to come, he seemed to be a Jew (Tertull., adv. Marc. III.). Because he deprived Christi-

anity of the apologetic proof (the proof from antiquity) he
seemed to be a heathen and a Jew at the same time (see my
Texte u. Unters. I. 3, p. 68; the antitheses of Marcion became very important for the heathen and Manichæan assaults
on Christianity). Because he represented the twelve Apostles
as unreliable witnesses, he appeared to be the most wicked
and shameless of all heretics. Finally, because he gained so
many adherents, and actually founded a church, he appeared
to be the ravening wolf (Justin, Rhodon), and his church as
the spurious church. (Tertull., adv. Marc. IV. 5.) In Marcion
the Church Fathers chiefly attacked what they attacked in
all Gnostic heretics, but here error shewed itself in its worst
form. They learned much in opposing Marcion (see Bk. II.).
For instance, their interpretation of the *regula fidei* and of
the New Testament received a directly Antimarcionite expression in the Church. One thing, however, they could not learn
from him, and that was how to make Christianity into a philosophic system. He formed no such system, but he has
given a clearly outlined conception, based on historic documents, of Christianity as the religion which redeems the world.

   Literature.—All anti-heretical writings of the early Church,
but especially Justin, Apol. I. 26, 58; Iren. I. 27; Tertull.,
adv. Marc. I—V.; de præscr.; Hippol., Philos.; Adamant., de
recta in deum fidei; Epiph. h. 42; Ephr. Syr.; Esnik. The
older attempts to restore the Marcionite Gospel and Aposto-
licum have been antiquated by Zahn's Kanonsgeschichte, l. c.
Hahn (Regimonti, 1823) has attempted to restore the Antitheses. We are still in want of a German monograph on Marcion
(see the whole presentation of Gnosticism by Zahn, with his
Excursus, l. c.). Hilgenfeld, Ketzergesch. p. 316 f. 522 f.; cf. my
work, Zur Quellenkritik des Gnosticismus, 1873; de Apelles
Gnosis Monarchia, 1874; Beiträge z. Gesch. der Marcionit-
ischen Kirchen (Ztschr. f. wiss. Theol. 1876). Marcion's Commentar zum Evangelium (Ztschr. f. K. G. Bd. IV. 4). Apelles
Syllogismen in the Texte u. Unters. VI. H. 3. Zahn, die
Dialoge des Adamantius in the Ztschr. f. K-Gesch. IX. p.
193 ff. Meyboom, Marcion en de Marcionieten, Leiden, 1888.

CHAPTER VI

APPENDIX: THE CHRISTIANITY OF THE JEWISH CHRISTIANS.

1. ORIGINAL Christianity was in appearance Christian Judaism, the creation of a universal religion on Old Testament soil. It retained, therefore, so far as it was not hellenised, which never altogether took place, its original Jewish features. The God of Abraham, Isaac and Jacob was regarded as the Father of Jesus Christ, the Old Testament was the authoritative source of revelation, and the hopes of the future were based on the Jewish ones. The heritage which Christianity took over from Judaism shews itself on Gentile Christian soil, in fainter or distincter form, in proportion as the philosophic mode of thought already prevails, or recedes into the background. [1] To describe the appearance of the Jewish, Old Testament, heritage in the

---

[1] The attitude of the recently discovered "Teaching of the twelve Apostles" is strictly universalistic, and hostile to Judaism as a nation, but shews us a Christianity still essentially uninfluenced by philosophic elements. The impression made by this fact has caused some scholars to describe the treatise as a document of Jewish Christianity. But the attitude of the Didache is rather the ordinary one of universalistic early Christianity on the soil of the Græco-Roman world. If we describe this as Jewish Christian, then from the meaning which we must give to the words "Christian" and "Gentile Christian," we tacitly legitimise an undefined and undefinable aggregate of Greek ideas, along with a specifically Pauline element, as primitive Christianity, and this is perhaps not the intended, but yet desired, result of the false terminology. Now, if we describe even such writings as the Epistle of James and the Shepherd of Hermas as Jewish Christian, we therewith. reduce the entire early Christianity, which is the creation of a universal religion on the soil of Judaism, to the special case of an indefinable religion. The same now appears as one of the particular values of a completely indeterminate magnitude. Hilgenfeld (Judenthum und Judenchristenthum, 1886; cf. also Ztschr. f. wiss. Theol. 1886 H. 4.) advocates another conception of Jewish Christianity in opposition to the following account. Zahn. Gesch. des N.T.-lich. Kanons, II. p. 668 ff. has a different view still.

Christian faith, so far as it is a religious one, by the name
Jewish Christianity, beginning at a certain point quite arbitrarily chosen, and changeable at will, must therefore necessarily lead to error, and it has done so to a very great extent.
For this designation makes it appear as though the Jewish
element in the Christian religion were something accidental,
while it is rather the case that all Christianity, in so far as
something alien is not foisted into it, appears as the religion
of Israel perfected and spiritualised. We are therefore not
justified in speaking of Jewish Christianity where a Christian
community, even one of Gentile birth, calls itself the true
Israel, the people of the twelve tribes, the posterity of Abraham; for this transfer is based on the original claim of Christianity and can only be forbidden by a view that is alien to
it. Just as little may we designate Jewish Christian the mighty
and realistic hopes of the future which were gradually repressed
in the second and third centuries. They may be described
as Jewish, or as Christian; but the designation Jewish Christian
must be rejected; for it gives a wrong impression as to the
historic right of these hopes in Christianity. The eschatological ideas of Papias were not Jewish Christian, but Christian;
while, on the other hand, the eschatological speculations of
Origen were not Gentile Christian, but essentially Greek. Those
Christians who saw in Jesus the man chosen by God and
endowed with the Spirit, thought about the Redeemer not in
a Jewish Christian, but in a Christian manner. Those of Asia
Minor who held strictly to the 14th of Nisan as the term of
the Easter festival, were not influenced by Jewish Christian,
but by Christian or Old Testament considerations. The author
of the "Teaching of the Apostles," who has transferred the
rights of the Old Testament priests with respect to the first
fruits to the Christian prophets, shews himself by such transference not as a Jewish Christian, but as a Christian. There
is no boundary here; for Christianity took possession of the
whole of Judaism as religion, and it is therefore a most arbitrary view of history which looks upon the Christian appropriation of the Old Testament religion, after any point, as no
longer Christian, but only Jewish Christian. Wherever the

universalism of Christianity is not violated in favour of the Jewish nation, we have to recognise every appropriation of the Old Testament as Christian. Hence this proceeding could be spontaneously undertaken in Christianity, as was in fact done.

2. But the Jewish religion is a national religion, and Christianity burst the bonds of nationality, though not for all who recognised Jesus as Messiah. This gives the point at which the introduction of the term "Jewish Christianity" is appropriate. [1] It should be applied exclusively to those Christians who really maintained in their whole extent, or in some measure, even if it were to a minimum degree, the national and political forms of Judaism and the observance of the Mosaic law in its literal sense, as essential to Christianity, at least to the Christianity of born Jews, or who, though rejecting these forms, nevertheless assumed a prerogative of the Jewish people even in Christianity (Clem., Homil. XI. 26: ἐὰν ὁ ἀλλόφυλος τὸν νόμον πράξῃ, Ἰουδαῖός ἐστιν, μὴ πράξας δέ ῞Ελλην; "If the foreigner observe the law he is a Jew, but if not he is a Greek"). [2] To this Jewish Christianity is opposed, not Gentile Christianity, but the Christian religion, in so far as it is conceived as universalistic and anti-national in the strict sense of the term (Presupp. § 3), that is, the main body of Christendom in so far as it has freed itself from Judaism as a nation. [3]

It is not strange that this Jewish Christianity was subject to all the conditions which arose from the internal and external position of the Judaism of the time; that is, different tenden-

---

[1] Or even Ebionitism; the designations are to be used as synonymous.

[2] The more rarely the right standard has been set up in the literature of Church history for the distinction of Jewish Christianity, the more valuable are those writings in which it is found. We must refer, above all, to Diestel, Geschichte des A. T. in der Christl. Kirche, p. 44, note 7.

[3] See Theol. Lit. Ztg. 1883. Col. 409 f. as to the attempt of Joël to make out that the whole of Christendom up to the end of the first century was strictly Jewish Christian, and to exhibit the complete friendship of Jews and Christians in that period ("Blicke in die Religionsgesch." 2 Abth. 1883). It is not improbable that Christians like James, living in strict accordance with the law, were for the time being respected even by the Pharisees in the period preceding the destruction of Jerusalem But that can in no case have been the rule. We see from Epiph. h. 29. 9. and from the Talmud what was the custom at a later period.

cies were necessarily developed in it, according to the measure
of the tendencies (or the disintegrations) which asserted themselves in the Judaism of that time. It lies also in the nature
of the case that, with one exception, that of Pharisaic Jewish
Christianity, all other tendencies were accurately parallelled in
the systems which appeared in the great, that is, anti-Jewish
Christendom. They were distinguished from these, simply by
a social and political, that is, a national element. Moreover,
they were exposed to the same influences from without as the
synagogue and as the larger Christendom, till the isolation
to which Judaism as a nation, after severe reverses condemned
itself, became fatal to them also. Consequently, there were
besides Pharisaic Jewish Christians, ascetics of all kinds who
were joined by all those over whom Oriental religious wisdom
and Greek philosophy had won a commanding influence. (See
above, p. 242 f.)

In the first century these Jewish Christians formed the
majority in Palestine, and perhaps also in some neighbouring
provinces. But they were also found here and there in the West.

Now the great question is whether this Jewish Christianity
as a whole, or in certain of its tendencies, was a factor in the
development of Christianity to Catholicism. This question is
to be answered in the negative, and quite as much with regard
to the history of dogma as with regard to the political history
of the Church. From the stand-point of the universal history
of Christianity, these Jewish Christian communities appear as
rudimentary structures which now and again, as objects of
curiosity, engaged the attention of the main body of Christendom in the East, but could not exert any important influence
on it, just because they contained a national element.

The Jewish Christians took no considerable part in the Gnostic
controversy, the epoch-making conflict which was raised within
the pale of the larger Christendom about the decisive question,
whether and to what extent the Old Testament should remain
a basis of Christianity, although they themselves were no less
occupied with the question.[1] The issue of this conflict in

---

[1] There were Jewish Christians who represented the position of the great Church
with reference to the Old Testament religion, and there were some who criticised

favour of that party which recognised the Old Testament in its full extent as a revelation of the Christian God, and asserted the closest connection between Christianity and the Old Testament religion, was so little the result of any influence of Jewish Christianity, that the existence of the latter would only have rendered that victory more difficult unless it had already fallen into the background as a phenomenon of no importance.[1] How completely insignificant it was is shewn not only by the limited polemics of the Church Fathers, but perhaps still more by their silence, and the new import which the reproach of Judaising obtained in Christendom after the middle of the second century. In proportion as the Old Testament, in opposition to Gnosticism, became a more conscious and accredited possession in the Church, and at the same time, in consequence of the naturalising of Christianity in the world, the need of regulations, fixed rules, statutory enactments etc., appeared as indispensable, it must have been natural to use the Old Testament as a holy code of such enactments. This procedure was no falling away from the original anti-Judaic attitude, provided nothing national was taken from the book, and some kind of spiritual interpretation given to what had been borrowed. The "apostasy" rather lay simply in the changed needs. But one now sees how those parties in the Church, to which for any reason this progressive legislation was distasteful, raised the reproach of "Judaising,"[2] and

the Old Testament like the Gnostics. Their contention may have remained as much an internal one as that between the Church Fathers and Gnostics (Marcion) did, so far as Jewish Christianity is concerned. Their may have been relations between Gnostic Jewish Christians and Gnostics not of a national Jewish type, in Syria and Asia Minor, though we are completely in the dark on the matter.

[1] From the mere existence of Jewish Christians, those Christians who rejected the Old Testament might have argued against the main body of Christendom and put before it the dilemma: either Jewish Christian or Marcionite. Still more logical indeed was the dilemma: either Jewish, or Marcionite Christian.

[2] So did the Montanists and Antimontanists mutually reproach each other with Judaising (see the Montanist writings of Tertullian). Just in the same way the arrangements as to worship and organisation, which were ever being more richly developed, were described by the freer parties as Judaising, because they made appeal to the Old Testament, though, as regards their contents, they had little in common with Judaism. But is not the method of claiming Old Testament authority for the regulations rendered necessary by circumstances nearly as

further, how conversely the same reproach was hurled at
those Christians who resisted the advancing hellenising of
Christianity, with regard, for example, to the doctrine of God,
eschatology, Christology, etc.[1] But while this reproach is
raised, there is nowhere shewn any connection between those
described as Judaising Christians and the Ebionites. That they
were identified off-hand is only a proof that "Ebionitism"
was no longer known. That "Judaising" within Catholicism
which appears, on the one hand, in the setting up of a Catholic
ceremonial law (worship, constitution, etc.), and on the other,
in a tenacious clinging to less hellenised forms of faith and
hopes of faith, has nothing in common with Jewish Christianity, which desired somehow to confine Christianity to the
Jewish nation.[2] Speculations that take no account of history
may make out that Catholicism became more and more Jewish
Christian. But historical observation, which reckons only with
concrete quantities, can discover in Catholicism, besides Christianity, no element which it would have to describe as Jewish
Christian. It observes only a progressive hellenising, and in
consequence of this, a progressive spiritual legislation which

---

old as Christianity itself? Against whom the lost treatise of Clement of Alexandria
"κανὼν ἐκκλησιαστικὸς ἢ πρὸς τοὺς Ἰουδαίζοντας" (Euseb. H. E. VI. 13. 3.) was
directed, we cannot tell. But as we read, Strom., VI. 15. 125, that the Holy
Scriptures are to be expounded according to the ἐκκλησιαστικός κανὼν, and then
find the following definition of the Canon: κανὼν δὲ ἐκκλησιαστικός ἡ συνωδία καὶ
συμφωνία νόμου τε καὶ προφητῶν τῇ κατὰ τὴν τοῦ κυρίου παρουσίαν παραδιδομένῃ
διαθήκῃ, we may conjecture that the Judaisers were those Christians who, in principle or to some extent, objected to the allegorical interpretation of the Old
Testament. We have then to think either of Marcionite Christians or of "Chiliasts,"
that is, the old Christians who were still numerous in Egypt about the middle of
the third century (see Dionys. Alex. in Euseb., H. E. VII. 24). In the first case,
the title of the treatise would be paradoxical. But perhaps the treatise refers to
the Quarto-decimans, although the expression κανὼν ἐκκλησιαστικός seems too pon-
derous for them (see, however, Orig., Comm. in Matth. n. 76, ed. Delarue III.,
p. 895). Clement may possibly have had Jewish Christians before him. See Zahn,
Forschungen, vol. III., p. 37 f.

[1] Cases of this kind are everywhere, up to the fifth century, so numerous that
they need not be cited. We may only remind the reader that the Nestorian
Christology was described by its earliest and its latest opponents as Ebionitic.

[2] Or were those western Christians Ebionitic who, in the fourth century, still
clung to very realistic Chiliastic hopes, who, in fact, regarded their Christianity as
consisting in these?

utilizes the Old Testament, a process which went on for centuries according to the same methods which had been employed in the larger Christendom from the beginning.[1] Baur's brilliant attempt to explain Catholicism as a product of the mutual conflict and neutralising of Jewish and Gentile Christianity, (the latter, according to Baur, being equivalent to Paulinism) reckons with two factors, of which the one had no significance at all, and the other only an indirect effect, as regards the formation of the Catholic Church. The influence of Paul in this direction is exhausted in working out the universalism of the Christian religion, for a Greater than he had laid the foundation for this movement, and Paul did not realise it by himself alone. Placed on this height Catholicism was certainly

---

[1] The hellenising of Christianity went hand in hand with a more extensive use of the Old Testament; for, according to the principles of Catholicism, every new article of the Church system must be able to legitimise itself as springing from revelation. But, as a rule, the attestation could only be gathered from the Old Testament, since religion here appears in the fixed form of a secular community. Now the needs of a secular community for outward regulations gradually became so strong in the Church as to require palpable ceremonial rules. But it cannot be denied that from a certain point of time, first by means of the fiction of Apostolic constitutions (see my edition of the Didache, Prolegg. p. 239 ff.), and then without this fiction, not, however, as a rule, without reservations, ceremonial regulations were simply taken over from the Old Testament. But this transference (see Bk. II.) takes place at a time when there can be absolutely no question of an influence of Jewish Christianity. Moreover, it always proves itself to be catholic by the fact that it did not in the least soften the traditional anti-Judaism. On the contrary, it attained its full growth in the age of Constantine. Finally, it should not be overlooked that at all times in antiquity certain provincial churches were exposed to Jewish influences, especially in the East and in Arabia, that they were therefore threatened with being Judaised, or with apostasy to Judaism, and that even at the present day certain Oriental Churches shew tokens of having once been subject to Jewish influences (see Serapion in Euseb. H. E. VI. 12. 1, Martyr. Pion., Epiph. de mens. et pond 15. 18; my Texte u. Unters. I. 3. p. 73 f., and Wellhausen, Skizzen und Vorarbeiten, Part. 3. p. 197 ff.; actual disputations with Jews do not seem to have been common, though see Tertull., adv. Jud. and Orig. c. Cels. I. 45, 49, 55 : II. 31. Clement also keeps in view Jewish objections). This Jewish Christianity, if we like to call it so, which in some regions of the East was developed through an immediate influence of Judaism on Catholicism, should not, however, be confounded with the Jewish Christianity which is the most original form in which Christianity realised itself. This was no longer able to influence the Christianity which had shaken itself free from the Jewish nation (as to futile attempts, see below), any more than the protecting covering stripped from the new shoot can ever again acquire significance for the latter.

developed by means of conflicts and compromises, not, however, by conflicts with Ebionitism, which was to all intents
and purposes discarded as early as the first century, but as
the result of the conflict of Christianity with the united
powers of the world in which it existed, on behalf of its own
peculiar nature as the universal religion based on the Old
Testament. Here were fought triumphant battles, but here
also compromises were made which characterise the essence
of Catholicism as Church and as doctrine. [1]

A history of Jewish Christianity and its doctrines does not
therefore, strictly speaking, belong to the history of dogma,
especially as the original distinction between Jewish Christianity and the main body of the Church lay, as regards its
principle, not in doctrine, but in policy. But seeing that the
opinions of the teachers in this Church regarding Jewish
Christianity throw light upon their own stand-point, also that
up till about the middle of the second century Jewish Christians
were still numerous and undoubtedly formed the great major-

---

[1] What is called the ever-increasing "legal" feature of Gentile Christianity and
the Catholic Church is conditioned by its origin, in so far as its theory is rooted
in that of Judaism spiritualised and influenced by Hellenism. As the Pauline conception of the law never took effect, and a criticism of the Old Testament religion
which is just law, neither understood nor ventured upon in the larger Christendom
—the forms were not criticised, but the contents spiritualised—so the theory that
Christianity is promise and spiritual law is to be regarded as the primitive one.
Between the spiritual law and the national law there stand indeed ceremonial laws
which, without being spiritually interpreted, could yet be freed from the national
application. It cannot be denied that the Gentile Christian communities and the
incipient Catholic Church were very careful and reserved in their adoption of such
laws from the Old Testament, and that the later Church no longer observed this
caution. But still it is only a question of degree, for there are many examples of
that adoption in the earliest period of Christendom. The latter had no cause for
hurry in utilizing the Old Testament so long as there was no external or internal
policy, or so long as it was still in embryo. The decisive factor lies here again
in enthusiasm and not in changing theories. The basis for these was supplied
from the beginning. But a community of individuals under spiritual excitement
builds on this foundation something different from an association which wishes to
organise and assert itself as such on earth. (The history of Sunday is specially
instructive here; see Zahn, Gesch. des Sonntags, 1878, as well as the history of
the discipline of fasting, see Linsenmayr, Entwickelung der Kirchl. Fastendisciplin.
1877, and Die Abgabe des Zehnten. In general, cf. Ritschl., Entstehung der Altkath.
Kirche, 2 edit. pp. 312 ff. 331 ff. 1 Cor. IX. 9, may be noted).

ity of believers in Palestine,[1] and finally, that attempts—
unsuccessful ones indeed—on the part of Jewish Christianity
to bring Gentile Christians under its sway did not cease till
about the middle of the third century, a short sketch may
be appropriate here.[2]

[1] Justin, Apol. I. 53, Dial. 47; Euseb., H. E. IV. 5; Sulpic. Sev., Hist. Sacr.
II. 31; Cyrill, Catech. XIV. 15. Important testimonies in Origen, Eusebius, Epiphanius and Jerome.

[2] No Jewish Christian writings have been transmitted to us, even from the earliest
period; for the Apocalypse of John which describes the Jews as a synagogue of
Satan is not a Jewish Christian book (III. 9 especially, shews that the author knows
of only one covenant of God, viz., that with the Christians). Jewish Christian
sources lie at the basis of our synoptic Gospels, but none of them in their present
form is a Jewish Christian writing. The Acts of the Apostles is so little Jewish
Christian, its author seemingly so ignorant of Jewish Christianity, at least so unconcerned with regard to it that to him the spiritualised Jewish law, or Judaism
as a religion which he connects as closely as possible with Christianity, is a factor
already completely detached from the Jewish people (see Overbeck's Commentar z.
Apostelgesch. and his discussion in the Ztschr. f. wiss. Theol. 1872. p. 305 ff.).
Measured by the Pauline theology we may indeed, with Overbeck, say of the
Gentile Christianity, as represented by the Author of the Acts of the Apostles, that
it already has germs of Judaism and represents a falling off from Paulinism; but
these expressions are not correct, because they have at least the appearance of
making Paulinism the original form of Gentile Christianity. But as this can neither
be proved nor believed, the religious attitude of the Author of the Acts of the
Apostles must have been a very old one in Christendom. The Judaistic element
was not first introduced into Gentile Christianity by the opponents of Paul, who
indeed wrought in the national sense, and there is even nothing to lead to the
hypothesis that the common Gentile Christian view of the Old Testament and of
the law should be conceived as resulting from the efforts of Paul and his opponents,
for the consequent effect here would either have been null, or a strengthening of
the Jewish Christian thesis. The Jewish element, that is the total acceptance of
the Jewish religion *sub specie aeternitatis et Christi*, is simply the original Christianity of the Gentile Christians itself considered as theory. Contrary to his own
intention, Paul was compelled to lead his converts to this Christianity, for only
for such Christianity was "the time fulfilled" within the empire of the world.
The Acts of the Apostles gives eloquent testimony to the pressing difficulties which
under such circumstances stand in the way of a historical understanding of the
Gentile Christians in view of the work and the theology of Paul. Even the
Epistle to the Hebrews is not a Jewish Christian writing; but there is certainly a
peculiar state of things connected with this document. For, on the one hand, the
author and his readers are free from the law, a spiritual interpretation is given to
the Old Testament religion which makes it appear to be glorified and fulfilled in
the work of Christ, and there is no mention of any prerogative of the people of
Israel. But, on the other hand, because the spiritual interpretation, as in Paul, is
here teleological, the author allows a temporary significance to the cultus as literally
understood, and therefore by his criticism he conserves the Old Testament religion

Justin vouches for the existence of Jewish Christians, and distinguishes between those who would force the law even on Gentile

for the past, while declaring that it was set aside as regards the present by the
fulfilment of Christ. The teleology of the author, however, looks at everything
only from the point of view of shadow and reality, an antithesis which is at the
service of Paul also, but which in his case vanishes behind the antithesis of law
and grace. This scheme of thought which is to be traced back to a way of
looking at things which arose in Christian Judaism, seeing that it really distinguishes
between old and new, stands midway between the conception of the Old Testament religion entertained by Paul, and that of the common Gentile Christian as
it is represented by Barnabas. The author of the Epistle to the Hebrews undoubtedly knows of a twofold convenant of God. But the two are represented as
stages, so that the second is completely based on the first. This view was more
likely to be understood by the Gentile Christians than the Pauline, that is, with
some seemingly slight changes, to be recognised as their own. But even it at first
fell to the ground, and it was only in the conflict with the Marcionites that some
Church Fathers advanced to views which seem to be related to those of the Epistle
to the Hebrews. Whether the author of this Epistle was a born Jew or a Gentile
—in the former case he would far surpass the Apostle Paul in his freedom from
the national claims—we cannot, at any rate, recognise in it a document containing
a conception which still prizes the Jewish nationality in Christianity, nay, not even
a document to prove that such a conception was still dangerous. Consequently,
we have no Jewish Christian memorial in the New Testament at all, unless it be
in the Pauline Epistles. But as concerns the early Christian literature outside the
Canon, the fragments of the great work of Hegesippus are even yet by some
investigators claimed for Jewish Christianity. Weizsäcker (Art. "Hegesippus" in
Herzog's R. E. 2 edit.) has shewn how groundless this assumption is. That
Hegesippus occupied the common Gentile Christian position is certain from un-
equivocal testimony of his own. If, as is very improbable, we were obliged to
ascribe to him a rejection of Paul, we should have to refer to Euseb. H. E. IV.
29. 5. (Σευηριανοὶ βλασφημοῦντες Παῦλον τὸν ἀπόστολον ἀθετοῦσιν αὐτοῦ τὰς ἐπιστολὰς μηδὲ τὰς πράξεις τῶν ἀποστόλων καταδεχόμενοι, but probably the Gospels;
these Severians therefore, like Marcion, recognised the Gospel of Luke, but rejected
the Acts of the Apostles), and Orig. c. Cels. V. 65: (εἰσὶ γὰρ τινες αἱρέσεις τὰς
Παύλου ἐπιστολὰς τοῦ ἀποστόλου μὴ προσιέμεναι ὥσπερ Ἐβιωναῖοι ἀμφότεροι καὶ
οἱ καλούμενοι Ἐγκρατηταί). Consequently, our only sources of knowledge of Jewish
Christianity in the post-Pauline period are merely the accounts of the Church Fathers
and some additional fragments (see the collection of fragments of the Ebionite
Gospel and that to the Hebrews in Hilgenfeld, Nov. Test. extra can. rec. fasc. IV.
Ed. 2, and in Zahn, l. c. II. p. 642 ff.). We know better, but still very imperfectly,
certain forms of the syncretistic Jewish Christianity, from the Philosoph. of Hippolytus and the accounts of Epiphanius, who is certainly nowhere more incoherent
than in the delineation of the Jewish Christians, because he could not copy original
documents here, but was forced to piece together confused traditions with his own
observations. See below on the extensive documents which are even yet, as they
stand, treated as records of Jewish Christianity, viz., the Pseudo-Clementines. Of
the pieces of writing whose Jewish Christian origin is controverted, in so far as
they may be simply Jewish, I say nothing.

Christians and would have no fellowship with such as did not observe it, and those who considered that the law was binding only on people of Jewish birth and did not shrink from fellowship with Gentile Christians who were living without the law. How the latter could observe the law and yet enter into intercourse with those who were not Jews is involved in obscurity, but these he recognises as partakers of the Christian salvation and therefore as Christian brethren, though he declares that there are Christians who do not possess this large-heartedness. He also speaks of Gentile Christians who allowed themselves to be persuaded by Jewish Christians into the observance of the Mosaic law, and confesses that he is not quite sure of the salvation of these. This is all we learn from Justin,[1] but it is instructive enough. In the first place, we can see that the question is no longer a burning one: "Justin here represents only the interests of a Gentile Christianity whose stability has been secured." This has all the more meaning that in the Dialogue Justin has not in view an individual Christian community, or the communities of a province, but speaks as one who surveys the whole situation of Christendom.[2] The very fact that Justin has devoted to the whole question only one chapter of a work containing 142, and the magmanimous way in which he speaks, shew that the phenomena in question have no longer any importance for the main body of Christendom. Secondly, it is worthy of notice that Justin distinguishes two tendencies in Jewish Christianity. We observe these two tendencies in the Apostolic age (Presupp. § 3); they had therefore maintained themselves to his time. Finally, we must not overlook the circumstance that he adduces only the ἔννομος πολιτεία, "legal polity," as characteristic of this Jewish Christianity. He speaks only incidentally of a difference in doctrine, nay, he manifestly presupposes that the διδάγματα Χριστοῦ, "teachings of Christ," are essentially found among them just as among the Gentile Christians; for he regards the more liberal among them as friends and brethren.[3]

---

[1] As to the chief localities where Jewish Christians were found, see Zahn, Kanonsgesch. II. p. 648 ff.

[2] Dialogue 47.

[3] Yet it should be noted that the Christians who, according to Dial. 48, denied

The fact that even then there were Jewish Christians here and there who sought to spread the ἔννομος πολιτεία among Gentile Christians has been attested by Justin and also by other contemporary writers.[1] But there is no evidence of this propaganda having acquired any great importance. Celsus also knows Christians who desire to live as Jews according to the Mosaic law (V. 61), but he mentions them only once, and otherwise takes no notice of them in his delineation of, and attack on, Christianity. We may perhaps infer that he knew of them only from hearsay, for he simply enumerates them along with the numerous Gnostic sects. Had

the pre-existence of Christ and held him to be a man are described as Jewish Christians. We should read in the passage in question, as my recent comparison of the Parisian codex shews, ἀπὸ τοῦ ὑμετέρου γένους. Yet Justin did not make this a controversial point of great moment.

[1] The so-called Barnabas is considerably older than Justin. In his Epistle (4. 6) he has in view Gentile Christians who have been converted by Jewish Christians, when he utters a warning against those who say ὅτι α διαθήκη ἐκείνων (the Jews) καὶ ἡμῶν (ἐστιν). But how great the actual danger was cannot be gathered from the Epistle. Ignatius in two Epistles (ad Magn. 8—10: ad Philad. 6. 9) opposes Jewish Christian intrigues, and characterises them solely from the point of view that they mean to introduce the Jewish observance of the law. He opposes them with a Pauline idea (Magn. 8. 1: εἰ γὰρ μέχρι νῦν κατὰ νόμον, Ἰουδαϊσμὸν ζῶμεν ὁμολογοῦμεν χάριν μὴ εἰληφέναι), as well as with the common Gentile Christian assumption that the prophets themselves had already lived κατὰ Χριστόν. These Judaists must be strictly distinguished from the Gnostics whom Ignatius elsewhere opposes (against Zahn, Ignat. v. Ant. p. 356 f.). The dangers from this Jewish Christianity cannot have been very serious, even if we take Magn. 11. 1, as a phrase. There was an active Jewish community in Philadelphia (Rev. III. 9), and so Jewish Christian plots may have continued longer there. At the first look it seems very promising that in the old dialogue of Aristo of Pella a Hebrew Christian, Jason, is put in opposition to the Alexandrian Jew, Papiscus. But as the history of the little book proves, this Jason must have essentially represented the common Christian and not the Ebionite conception of the Old Testament and its relation to the Gospel, etc.; see my Texte u. Unters. I. 1. 2. p. 115 ff.; I. 3. pp. 115—130. Testimony as to an apostasy to Judaism is occasionally though rarely given; see Serapion in Euseb., H. E. VI. 12, who addresses a book to one Domninus, ἐκπεπτωκότα παρὰ τὸν τοῦ διωγμοῦ καιρὸν ἀπὸ τῆς εἰς Χριστὸν πίστεως ἐπὶ τὴν Ἰουδαϊκὴν ἐθελοθρησκείαν; see also Acta Pionii, 13. 14. According to Epiphanius, de mens et pond. 14. 15, Acquila, the translator of the Bible, was first a Christian and then a Jew. This account is perhaps derived from Origen, and is probably reliable. Likewise according to Epiphanius (l. c. 17. 18), Theodotion was first a Marcionite and then a Jew. The transition from Marcionitism to Judaism (for extremes meet) is not in itself incredible.

this keen observer really known them he would hardly have passed them over, even though he had met with only a small number of them. [1] Irenæus placed the Ebionites among the heretical schools, [2] but we can see from his work that in his day they must have been all but forgotten in the West. [3] This was not yet the case in the East. Origen knows of them. He knows also of some who recognise the birth from the Virgin. He is sufficiently intelligent and acquainted with history to judge that the Ebionites are no school, but, as believing Jews, are the descendants of the earliest Christians, in fact he seems to suppose that all converted Jews have at all times observed the law of their fathers. But he is far from judging of them favourably. He regards them as little better than the Jews ('Ιουδαῖοι καὶ οἱ ὀλίγῳ διαφέροντες αὐτῶν Ἐβιωναῖοι,

---

[1] It follows from c. Cels. II. 1—3, that Celsus could hardly have known Jewish Christians.

[2] Iren. 26. 2: III. 11. 7: III. 15. 1, 21. 1: IV. 33. 4: V. 1. 3. We first find the name Ebionæi, the poor, in Irenæus. We are probably entitled to assume that this name was given to the Christians in Jerusalem as early as the Apostolic age, that is, they applied it to themselves (poor in the sense of the prophets and of Christ, fit to be received into the Messianic kingdom). It is very questionable whether we should put any value on Epiph. h. 30. 17.

[3] When Irenæus adduces as the points of distinction between the Church and the Ebionites, that besides observing the law and repudiating the Apostle Paul, the latter deny the Divinity of Christ and his birth from the Virgin and reject the New Testament Canon (except the Gospel of Matthew), that only proves that the formation of dogma has made progress in the Church. The less was known of the Ebionites from personal observation, the more confidently they were made out to be heretics who denied the Divinity of Christ and rejected the Canon. The denial of the Divinity of Christ and the birth from the Virgin was, from the end of the second century, regarded as the Ebionite heresy *par excellence*, and the Ebionites themselves appeared to the Western Christians, who obtained their information solely from the East, to be a school like those of the Gnostics, founded by a scoundrel named Ebion for the purpose of dragging down the person of Jesus to the common level. It is also mentioned incidentally, that this Ebion had commanded the observance of circumcision and the Sabbath; but that is no longer the main thing (see Tertull, de carne 14, 18, 24: de virg. vel. 6: de præscr. 10. 33; Hippol., Syntagma, [Pseudo-Tertull, 11; Philastr. 37; Epiph. h. 30]; Hippol., Philos. VII. 34. The latter passage contains the instructive statement that Jesus by his perfect keeping of the law became the Christ). This attitude of the Western Christians proves that they no longer knew Jewish Christian communities Hence it is all the more strange that Hilgenfeld (Ketzergesch. p. 422 ff.) has in all earnestness endeavoured to revive the Ebion of the Western Church Fathers.

"Jews and Ebionites who differ little from them"). Their rejection of Paul destroys the value of their recognition of Jesus as Messiah. They appear only to have assumed Christ's name, and their literal exposition of the Scripture is meagre and full of error. It is possible that such Jewish Christians may have existed in Alexandria, but it is not certain. Origen knows nothing of an inner development in this Jewish Christianity.[1] Even in Palestine, Origen seems to have occupied himself personally with these Jewish Christians, just as little as Eusebius.[2] They lived apart by themselves and were not aggressive. Jerome is the last who gives us a clear and certain account of them.[3] He, who associated with them, assures us that their attitude was the same as in the second century, only they seem to have made progress in the recognition of the birth from the Virgin and

[1] See Orig. c. Cels. II. 1 : V. 61, 65 : de princip. IV. 22; hom. in Genes. III. 15 (Opp. II. p. 65) : hom. in Jerem. XVII. 12 (III. p. 254): in Matth. T. XVI. 12 (III. p. 494), T. XVII. 12 (III. p. 733); cf. Opp. III. p. 895 : hom. in Lc. XVII. (III. p. 952). That a portion of the Ebionites recognised the birth from the Virgin was according to Origen frequently attested. That was partly reckoned to them for righteousness and partly not, because they would not admit the pre-existence of Christ. The name "Ebionites" is interpreted as a nickname given them by the Church "beggarly" in the knowledge of scripture, and particularly of Christology.

[2] Eusebius knows no more than Origen (H. E. III. 27) unless we specially credit him with the information that the Ebionites keep along with the Sabbath also the Sunday. What he says of Symmachus, the translator of the Bible, and an Ebionite, is derived from Origen (H. E. VI. 17). The report is interesting, because it declares that Symmachus *wrote* against Catholic Christianity, especially against the Catholic Gospel of Matthew (about the year 200). But Symmachus is to be classed with the Gnostics, and not with the common type of Jewish Christianity (see below). We have also to thank Eusebius (H. E. III. 5. 3) for the information that the Christians of Jerusalem fled to Pella, in Peræa, before the destruction of that city. In the following period the most important settlements of the Ebionites must have been in the countries east of the Jordan, and in the heart of Syria (see Jul. Afric. in Euseb., H. E. I. 7. 14 : Euseb., de loc. hebr. in Lagarde, Onomast. p. 301; Epiph., h. 29. 7 : h. 30. 2). This fact explains how the bishops in Jerusalem and the coast towns of Palestine came to see very little of them. There was a Jewish Christian community in Beroea with which Jerome had relations (Jerom., de Vir. inl. 3).

[3] Jerome correctly declares (Ep. ad. August. 122. c. 13, Opp. I. p. 746), "(Ebionitæ) credentes in Christo propter hoc solum a patribus anathematizati sunt, quod legis cæremonias Christi evangelio miscuerunt, et sic nova confessa sunt, ut vetera non omitterent."

in their more friendly position towards the Church.¹ Jerome
at one time calls them Ebionites and at another Nazarenes,
thereby proving that these names were used synonymously.²
There is not the least ground for distinguishing two clearly
marked groups of Jewish Christians, or even for reckoning
the distinction of Origen and the Church Fathers to the account of Jewish Christians themselves, so as to describe as
Nazarenes those who recognised the birth from the Virgin
and who had no wish to compel the Gentile Christians to
observe the law, and the others as Ebionites. Apart from
syncretistic or Gnostic Jewish Christianity, there is but one
group of Jewish Christians holding various shades of opinion,
and these from the beginning called themselves Nazarenes
as well as Ebionites. From the beginning, likewise, one
portion of them was influenced by the existence of a great
Gentile Church which did not observe the law. They acknowledged the work of Paul and experienced in a slight degree
influences emanating from the great Church.³ But the gulf

¹ Ep. ad August. l. c.; Quid dicam de Hebionitis, qui Christianos esse se
simulant? usque hodie per totas orientis synagogas inter Judæos (!) hæresis est, que
dicitur Minæorum et a Pharisæis nunc usque damnatur, quos vulgo Nazaræos
nuncupant, qui credunt in Christum filium dei natum de Virgine Maria et eum
dicunt esse, qui sub pontio Pilato passus est et resurrexit, in quem et nos credimus;
sed dum volunt et Judæi esse et Christiani, nec Judæi sunt nec Christiani." The
approximation of the Jewish Christian conception to that of the Catholics shews itself
also in their exposition of Isaiah IX. 1. f. (see Jerome on the passage). But we
must not forget that there were such Jewish Christians from the earliest times. It
is worthy of note that the name Nazarenes, as applied to Jewish Christians, is
found in the Acts of the Apostles XXIV. 5, in the Dialogue of Jason and Papiscus,
and then first again in Jerome.

² Zahn, l. c. p. 648 ff. 668 ff. has not convinced me of the contrary, but I
confess that Jerome's style of expression is not everywhere clear.

³ Zahn, (l. c.) makes a sharp distinction between the Nazarenes, on the one
side, who used the Gospel of the Hebrews, acknowledged the birth from the
Virgin, and in fact the higher Christology to some extent, did not repudiate Paul,
etc., and the Ebionites on the other, whom he simply identifies with the Gnostic
Jewish Christians, if I am not mistaken. In opposition to this, I think I must
adhere to the distinction as given above in the text and in the following: (1)
Non-Gnostic, Jewish Christians (Nazarenes, Ebionites), who appeared in various
shades, according to their doctrine and attitude to the Gentile Church, and whom,
with the Church Fathers, we may appropriately classify as strict or tolerant (exclusive or liberal). (2) Gnostic or syncretistic Judæo-Christians who are also
termed Ebionites.

which separated them from that Church did not thereby become narrower. That gulf was caused by the social and
political separation of these Jewish Christians, whatever mental
attitude, hostile or friendly, they might take up to the
great Church. This Church stalked over them with iron feet,
as over a structure which in her opinion was full of contradictions throughout ("Semi-christiani"), and was disconcerted
neither by the gospel of these Jewish Christians nor by anything else about them. [1] But as the Synagogue also vigorously
condemned them, their position up to their extinction was a
most tragic one. These Jewish Christians, more than any other
Christian party, bore the reproach of Christ.

The Gospel, at the time when it was proclaimed among
the Jews, was not only law, but theology, and indeed syncretistic theology. On the other hand, the temple service
and the sacrificial system had begun to lose their hold in
certain influential circles. [2] We have pointed out above
(Presupp. §§ 1. 2. 5) how great were the diversities of Jewish sects,
and that there was in the Diaspora, as well as in Palestine
itself, a Judaism which, on the one hand, followed ascetic
impulses, and on the other, advanced to a criticism of the
religious tradition without giving up the national claims. It
may even be said that in theology the boundaries between
the orthodox Judaism of the Pharisees and a syncretistic
Judaism were of an elastic kind. Although religion, in those

---

[1] This Gospel no doubt greatly interested the scholars of the Catholic Church
from Clement of Alexandria onwards. But they have almost all contrived to
evade the hard problem which it presented. It may be noted, incidentally, that
the Gospel of the Hebrews, to judge from the remains preserved to us, can neither
have been the model nor the translation of our Matthew, but a work independent
of this, though drawing from the same sources, representing perhaps to some
extent an earlier stage of the tradition. Jerome also knew very well that the
Gospel of the Hebrews was not the original of the canonical Matthew, but he
took care not to correct the old prejudice. Ebionitic conceptions, such as that of
the female nature of the Holy Spirit, were of course least likely to convince the
Church Fathers. Moreover, the common Jewish Christians hardly possessed a
Church theology, because for them Christianity was something entirely different
from the doctrine of a school. On the Gospel of the Hebrews, see Handmann
(Texte u. Unters V. 3), Resch, Agrapha (l. c. V. 4), and Zahn, l. c. p. 642 ff.

[2] We have as yet no history of the sacrificial system and the views as to sacrifice in the Græco-Roman epoch of the Jewish Nation. It is urgently needed.

circles, seemed to be fixed in its legal aspect, yet on its theological side it was ready to admit very diverse speculations,
in which angelic powers especially played a great rôle. [1]
That introduced into Jewish monotheism an element of differ-
entiation, the results of which were far-reaching. The field
was prepared for the formation of syncretistic sects. They
present themselves to us on the soil of the earliest Christianity, in the speculations of those Jewish Christian teachers
who are opposed in the Epistle to the Colossians, and in the
Gnosis of Cerinthus (see above, p. 247). Here cosmological
ideas and myths were turned to profit. The idea of God
was sublimated by both. In consequence of this, the Old
Testament records were subjected to criticism, because they
could not in all respects be reconciled with the universal religion which hovered before men's minds. This criticism was
opposed to the Pauline in so far as it maintained, with the
common Jewish Christians and Christendom as a whole, that
the genuine Old Testament religion was essentially identical
with the Christian. But while those common Jewish Christians drew from this the inference that the whole of the Old
Testament must be adhered to in its traditional sense and
in all its ordinances, and while the larger Christendom secured
for itself the whole of the Old Testament by deviating
from the ordinary interpretation, those syncretistic Jewish
Christians separated from the Old Testament, as interpolations, whatever did not agree with their purer moral conceptions and borrowed speculations. Thus, in particular, they got
rid of the sacrificial ritual and all that was connected with
it by putting ablutions in their place. First the profanation,
and afterwards the abolition of the temple worship after
the destruction of Jerusalem, may have given another new
and welcome impulse to this by coming to be regarded
as its Divine confirmation (Presupp. § 2). Christianity now

---

[1] We may remind readers of the assumptions, that the world was created by
angels, that the law was given by angels, and similar ones which are found in
the theology of the Pharisees. Celsus (in Orig. I. 26 : V. 6) asserts generally that
the Jews worshipped angels, so does the author of the Prædicatio Petri, as well
as the apologist Aristides. Cf. Joël, Blicke in die Religionsgesch. I Abth., a book
which is certainly to be used with caution (see Theol. Lit. Ztg. 1881. Coll. 184 ff.).

appeared as purified Mosaism. In these Jewish Christian undertakings we have undoubtedly before us a series of peculiar
attempts to elevate the Old Testament religion into the universal one, under the impression of the person of Jesus; attempts, however, in which the Jewish religion, and not the
Jewish people, was to bear the costs by curtailment of its
distinctive features. The great inner affinity of these attempts
with the Gentile Christian Gnostics has already been set forth.
The firm partition wall between them, however, lies in the
claim of these Jewish Christians to set forth the pure Old
Testament religion, as well as in the national Jewish colouring
which the constructed universal religion was always to preserve. This national colouring is shewn in the insistance upon
a definite measure of Jewish national ceremonies as necessary
to salvation, and in the opposition to the Apostle Paul, which
united the Gnostic Judæo-Christians with the common type,
those of the strict observance. How the latter were related
to the former, we do not know, for the inner relations here
are almost completely unknown to us. [1]

Apart from the false doctrines opposed in the Epistle to
the Colossians, and from Cerinthus, this syncretistic Jewish
Christianity which aimed at making itself a universal religion
meets us in tangible form only in three phenomena: [2] in the
Elkesaites of Hippolytus and Origen; in the Ebionites with
their associates of Epiphanius, sects very closely connected,
in fact to be viewed as one party of manifold shades; [3] and

[1] No reliance can be placed on Jewish sources, or on Jewish scholars, as a
rule. What we find in Joël, l. c. I. Abth. p. 101 ff. is instructive. We may
mention Grätz, Gnosticismus und Judenthum (Krotoschin, 1846), who has called
attention to the Gnostic elements in the Talmud, and dealt with several Jewish
Gnostics and Antignostics, as well as with the book of Jezira. Grätz assumes that
the four main dogmatic points in the book Jezira, viz., the strict unity of the
deity, and, at the same time, the negation of the demiurgic dualism, the creation
out of nothing with the negation of matter, the systematic unity of the world and
the balancing of opposites, were directed against prevailing Gnostic ideas.

[2] We may pass over the false teachers of the Pastoral Epistles, as they cannot
be with certainty determined, and the possibility is not excluded that we have
here to do with an arbitrary construction; see Holtzman, Pastoralbriefe, p. 150 f.

[3] Orig. in Euseb. VI. 38; Hippol., Philos. IX. 13 ff., X. 29; Epiph., h. 30,
also h. 19. 53; Method., Conviv. VIII. 10. From the confused account of Epipha-

in the activity of Symmachus.[1] We observe here a form of
religion as far removed from that of the Old Testament as from
the Gospel, subject to strong heathen influences, not Greek, but
Asiatic, and scarcely deserving the name "Christian," because it
appeals to a new revelation of God which is to complete that
given in Christ. We should take particular note of this in
judging of the whole remarkable phenomenon. The question
in this Jewish Christianity is not the formation of a philosophic
school, but to some extent the establishment of a kind of
new religion, that is, the completion of that founded by Christ,
undertaken by a particular person basing his claims on a
revealed book which was delivered to him from heaven. This
book which was to form the complement of the Gospel, possessed, from the third century, importance for all sections of
Jewish Christians so far as they, in the phraseology of Epiphanius, were not Nazarenes.[2] The whole system reminds

nius, who called the common Jewish Christians Nazarenes, the Gnostic type
Ebionites and Sampsæi, and their Jewish forerunners Osseni, we may conclude,
that in many regions where there were Jewish Christians they yielded to the
propaganda of the Elkesaite doctrines, and that in the fourth century there was
no other syncretistic Jewish Christianity besides the various shades of Elkesaites.

[1] I formerly reckoned Symmachus, the translator of the Bible, among the
common Jewish Christians; but the statements of Victorinus Rhetor on Gal. I. 19.
II. 26 (Migne T. VIII. Col. 1155. 1162) shew that he has a close affinity with the
Pseudo-Clementines, and is also to be classed with the Elkesaite Alcibiades.
"Nam Jacobum apostolum Symmachiani faciunt quasi duodecimum et hunc secuntur,
qui ad dominum nostrum Jesum Christum adjungunt Judaismi observationem,
quamquam etiam Jesum Christum fatentur; dicunt enim eum ipsum Adam esse et
esse animam generalem, et aliæ hujusmodi blasphemiæ." The account given by
Eusebius, H. E. VI. 17 (probably on the authority of Origen, see also Demonstr.
VII. 1) is important : Τῶν γε μὲν ἑρμηνευτῶν αὐτῶν δὴ τούτων ἰστέον, Ἐβιωναίου
τὸν Σύμμαχον γεγονέναι. . . . καὶ ὑπομνήματα δὲ τοῦ Συμμάχου εἰσέτι νῦν φέρεται,
ἐν οἷς δοκεῖ πρὸς τὸ κατὰ Ματθαῖον ἀποτεινόμενος εὐαγγέλιον τὴν δεδηλωμένην αἵρεσιν
κρατύνειν. Symmachus therefore adopted an aggressive attitude towards the great
Church, and hence we may probably class him with Alcibiades who lived a little
later. Common Jewish Christianity was no longer aggressive in the second century.

[2] Wellhausen (l. c. Part III. p. 206) supposes that Elkesai is equivalent to
Alexius. That the receiver of the "book" was a historical person is manifest
from Epiphanius' account of his descendants (h. 19 2: 53. 1). From Hipp.
Philosoph. IX. 16, p. 468, it is certainly probable, though not certain, that the
book was produced by the unknown author as early as the time of Trajan. On
the other hand, the existence of the sect itself can be proved only at the beginning
of the third century, and therefore we have the possibility of an ante-dating of
the "book". This seems to have been Origen's opinion.

one of Samaritan Christian syncretism; [1] but we must be on
our guard against identifying the two phenomena, or even
regarding them as similar. These Elkesaite Jewish Christians
held fast by the belief that Jesus was the Son of God, and
saw in the "book" a revelation which proceeded from him.
They did not offer any worship to their founder, [2] that is, to
the receiver of the "book," and they were, as will be shewn,
the most ardent opponents of Simonianism. [3]

Alcibiades of Apamea, one of their disciples, came from the
East to Rome about 220-230, and endeavoured to spread the
doctrines of the sect in the Roman Church. He found the
soil prepared, inasmuch as he could announce from the "book"
forgiveness of sins to all sinful Christians, even the grossest
transgressors, and such forgiveness was very much needed.
Hippolytus opposed him, and had an opportunity of seeing the
book and becoming acquainted with its contents. From his
account and that of Origen we gather the following: (1) The
sect is a Jewish Christian one, for it requires the νόμου πολιτεία
(circumcision and the keeping of the Sabbath), and repudiates
the Apostle Paul; but it criticises the Old Testament and rejects
a part of it. (2) The objects of its faith are the "Great and
most High God," the Son of God (the "Great King"), and
the Holy Spirit (thought of as female); Son and Spirit appear
as angelic powers. Considered outwardly, and according to

---

[1] Epiph. (h. 53. 1) says of the Elkesaites: οὔτε χριστιανοὶ ὑπάρχοντες οὔτε
Ἰουδαῖοι οὔτε Ἕλληνες, ἀλλὰ μέσον ἁπλῶς ὑπάρχοντες. He pronounces a similar
judgment as to the Samaritan sects (Simonians), and expressly (h. 30. 1) connects
the Elkesaites with them.

[2] The worship paid to the descendants of this Elkesai, spoken of by Epiphanius, does not, if we allow for exaggerations, go beyond the measure of honour
which was regularly paid to the descendants of prophets and men of God in the
East. Cf. the respect enjoyed by the blood relations of Jesus and Mohammed.

[3] It the "book" really originated in the time of Trajan, then its production
keeps within the frame-work of common Christianity, for at that time there were
appearing everywhere in Christendom revealed books which contained new
instructions and communications of grace. The reader may be reminded, for
example, of the Shepherd of Hermas. When the sect declared that the "book"
was delivered to Elkesai by a male and a female angel, each as large as a
mountain, that these angels were the Son of God and the Holy Spirit, etc., we
have, apart from the fantastic colouring, nothing extraordinary.

his birth, Christ is a mere man, but with this peculiarity,
that he has already been frequently born and manifested
(πολλάκις γεννηθέντα καὶ γεννώμενον πεφηνέναι καὶ φύεσθαι, ἀλλάσ-
σοντα γενέσεις καὶ μετενσωματούμενον, cf. the testimony of Victorinus as to Symmachus). From the statements of Hippolytus
we cannot be sure whether he was identified with the Son of
God, [1] at any rate the assumption of repeated births of Christ
shews how completely Christianity was meant to be identified
with what was supposed to be the pure Old Testament religion. (3) The "book" proclaimed a new forgiveness of sin,
which, on condition of faith in the "book" and a real change
of mind, was to be bestowed on every one, through the medium of washings, accompanied by definite prayers which are
strictly prescribed. In these prayers appear peculiar Semitic
speculations about nature ("the seven witnesses: heaven,
water, the holy spirits, the angels of prayer, oil, salt,
earth"). The old Jewish way of thinking appears in the
assumption that all kinds of sickness and misfortune are punish-
ments for sin, and that these penalties must therefore be
removed by atonement. The book contains also astrological
and geometrical speculations in a religious garb. The main
thing, however, was the possibility of a forgiveness of sin, ever
requiring to be repeated, though Hippolytus himself was unable to point to any gross laxity. Still, the appearance of
this sect represents the attempt to make the religion of Christian Judaism palatable to the world. The possibility of repeated forgiveness of sin, the speculations about numbers, ele-

---

[1] It may be assumed from Philos. X. 29 that, in the opinion of Hyppolytus,
the Elkesaites identified the Christ from above with the Son of God, and assumed
that this Christ appeared on earth in changing and purely human forms, and will
appear again (αὐτὸν δὲ μεταγγιζόμενον ἐν σώμασι πολλοῖς πολλάκις καὶ νῦν δὲ ἐν
τῷ Ἰησοῦ, ὁμοίως ποτὲ μὲν ἐκ τοῦ θεοῦ γεγενῆσθαι, ποτὲ δὲ πνεῦμα γεγονέναι, ποτὲ
δὲ ἐκ παρθένου, ποτὲ δὲ οὐ καὶ τοῦτον δὲ μετέπειτα ἀεὶ ἐν σώματι μεταγγίζεσθαι
καὶ ἐν πολλοῖς κατὰ καιροὺς δείκνυσθαι). As the Elkesaites (see the account by
Epiphanius) traced back the incarnations of Christ to Adam, and not merely to
Abraham, we may see in this view of history the attempt to transform Mosaism
into the universal religion. But the Pharisaic theology had already begun with
these Adam-speculations, which are always a sign that the religion in Judaism is
feeling its limits too narrow. The Jews in Alexandria were also acquainted with
these speculations.

ments, and stars, the halo of mystery, the adaptation to the
forms of worship employed in the "mysteries," are worldly
means of attraction which shew that this Jewish Christianity
was subject to the process of acute secularization. The Jewish
mode of life was to be adopted in return for these concessions.
Yet its success in the West was of small extent and short-lived.

Epiphanius confirms all these features, and adds a series of
new ones. In his description, the new forgiveness of sin is
not so prominent as in that of Hippolytus, but it is there.
From the account of Epiphanius we can see that these syncretistic Judæo-Christian sects were at first strictly ascetic and
rejected marriage as well as the eating of flesh, but that they
gradually became more lax. We learn here that the whole
sacrificial service was removed from the Old Testament by
the Elkesaïtes and declared to be non-Divine, that is non-
Mosaic, and that fire was consequently regarded as the impure
and dangerous element, and water as the good one.[1] We
learn further, that these sects acknowledged no prophets and
men of God between Aaron and Christ, and that they completely adapted the Hebrew Gospel of Matthew to their own
views.[2] In addition to this book, however, (the Gospel of
the 12 Apostles), other writings, such as Περίοδοι Πέτρου διὰ
Κλήμεντος 'Αναβαθμοὶ 'Ιακώβου and similar histories of Apostles,
were held in esteem by them. In these writings the Apostles
were represented as zealous ascetics, and, above all, as vege-
tarians, while the Apostle Paul was most bitterly opposed.
They called him a Tarsene, said he was a Greek, and heaped
on him gross abuse. Epiphanius also dwells strongly upon
their Jewish mode of life (circumcision, Sabbath), as well as
their daily washings,[1] and gives some information about the

---

[1] In the Gospel of these Jewish Christians Jesus is made to say (Epiph. h. 30. 16)
ἦλθον καταλῦσαι τὰς θυσίας, καὶ ἐὰν μὴ παύσησθε τοῦ θύειν, οὐ παύσεται ἀφ' ὑμῶν ἡ
ὀργή. We see the essential progress of this Jewish Christianity within Judaism in the
opposition in principle to the whole sacrificial service (vid. also Epiph., h. 19. 3).

[2] On this new Gospel see Zahn, Kanongesch. II. p. 724.

[3] It is incorrect to suppose that the lustrations were meant to take the place of
baptism, or were conceived by these Jewish Christians as repeated baptisms. Their
effect was certainly equal to that of baptism. But it is nowhere hinted in our
authorities that they were on that account made equivalent to the regular baptism.

constitution and form of worship of these sects (use of baptism :
Lord's Supper with bread and water). Finally, Epiphanius
gives particulars about their Christology. On this point there
were differences of opinion, and these differences prove that
there was no Christological dogma. As among the common
Jewish Christians, the birth of Jesus from the Virgin was a
matter of dispute. Further, some identified Christ with Adam,
others saw in him a heavenly being (ἄνωθεν ὄν), a spiritual
being, who was created before all, who was higher than all
angels and Lord of all things, but who chose for himself the
upper world; yet this Christ from above came down to this
lower world as often as he pleased. He came in Adam, he
appeared in human form to the patriarchs, and at last appeared
on earth as a man with the body of Adam, suffered, etc.
Others again, as it appears, would have nothing to do with
these speculations, but stood by the belief that Jesus was the
man chosen by God, on whom, on account of his virtue, the
Holy Spirit—ὅπερ ἐστίν ὁ Χριστός—descended at the baptism. [1]
(Epiph. h. 30. 3, 14, 16). The account which Epiphanius gives
of the doctrine held by these Jewish Christians regarding the
Devil, is specially instructive (h. 30. 16): Δύο δὲ τινας συνιστῶσιν
ἐκ θεοῦ τεταγμένους, ἕνα μὲν τὸν Χριστὸν, ἕνα δὲ τὸν διάβολον.
καὶ τὸν μὲν Χριστὸν λέγουσι τοῦ μέλλοντος αἰῶνος εἰληφέναι τὸν
κλῆρον, τὸν δὲ διάβολον τοῦτον πεπιστεῦσθαι ὃν αἰῶνα, ἐκ προσταγῆς
δῆθεν τοῦ παντοκράτορος κατὰ αἴτησιν ἑκατέρων αὐτῶν. Here we
have a very old Semitico-Hebraic idea preserved in a very
striking way, and therefore we may probably assume that in
other respects also, these Gnostic Ebionites preserved that
which was ancient. Whether they did so in their criticism
of the Old Testament, is a point on which we must not
pronounce judgment.

We might conclude by referring to the fact that this syn-

---

[1] The characteristic here, as in the Gentile Christian Gnosis, is the division of
the person of Jesus into a more or less indifferent medium, and into the Christ.
Here the factor constituting his personality could sometimes be placed in that
medium, and sometimes in the Christ spirit, and thus contradictory formulæ could
not but arise. It is therefore easy to conceive how Epiphanius reproaches these
Jewish Christians with a denial, sometimes of the Divinity, and sometimes of the
humanity of Christ (see h. 30 14).

cretistic Jewish Christianity, apart from a well-known missionary effort at Rome, was confined to Palestine and the neighbouring countries, and might consider it proved that this
movement had no effect on the history and development of
Catholicism [1] were it not for two voluminous writings which
still continue to be regarded as monuments of the earliest
epoch of syncretistic Jewish Christianity. Not only did Baur
suppose that he could prove his hypothesis about the origin
of Catholicism by the help of these writings, but the attempt
has recently been made on the basis of *the Pseudo-Clementine
Recognitions and Homilies*, for these are the writings in question,
to go still further and claim for Jewish Christianity the glory
of having developed by itself the whole doctrine, worship and
constitution of Catholicism, and of having transmitted it to
Gentile Christianity as a finished product which only required
to be divested of a few Jewish husks. [2] It is therefore necessary to subject these writings to a brief examination. Everything depends on the time of their origin, and the tendencies
they follow. But these are just the two questions that are
still unanswered. Without depreciating those worthy men
who have earnestly occupied themselves with the Pseudo-Clementines, [3] it may be asserted, that in this region everything

---

[1] This syncretistic Judaism had indeed a significance for the history of the
world, not, however, in the history of Christianity, but for the origin of Islam.
Islam, as a religious system, is based partly on syncretistic Judaism (including the
Zabians, so enigmatic in their origin), and, without questioning Mohammed's
originality, can only be historically understood by taking this into account. I
have endeavoured to establish this hypothesis in a lecture printed in MS. form,
1877. Cf. now the conclusive proofs in Wellhausen, l. c. Part III. p. 197–212.
On the Mandeans, see Brandt, Die Mandäische Religion, 1889; (also Wellhausen
in d. deutschen Lit. Ztg., 1890 No. I. Lagarde i. d. Gött. Gel. Anz., 1890, No. 10).

[2] See Bestmann, Gesch. der Christl. Sitte, Bd. II. 1 Part: Die judenchristliche
Sitte, 1883; also, Theol. Lit. Ztg., 1883. Col. 269 ff. The same author, Der Ur-
sprung der Katholischen Christenthums und des Islams, 1884; also Theol. Lit.
Ztg. 1884, Col. 291 ff.

[3] See Schliemann, Die Clementinen, etc., 1844; Hilgenfeld, Die Clementinischen
Recogn. u. Homil, 1848; Ritschl, in d. Allg. Monatschrift f. Wissensch. u. Litt.,
1852. Uhlhorn, Die Homil. u. Recogn., 1854; Lehmann, Die Clement. Schriften,
1869; Lipsius, in d. Protest. K. Ztg., 1869, p. 477 ff.; Quellen der Römische
Petrussage, 1872. Uhlhorn, in Herzog's R. Encykl. (Clementinen) 2 Edit. III. p. 286,
admits: "There can be no doubt that the Clementine question still requires further

is as yet in darkness, especially as no agreement has been reached even in the question of their composition. No doubt such a result appears to have been pretty nearly arrived at as far as the time of composition is concerned, but that estimate (150-170, or the latter half of the second century) not only awakens the greatest suspicion, but can be proved to be wrong. The importance of the question for the history of dogma does not permit the historian to set it aside, while, on the other hand, the compass of a manual does not allow us to enter into an exhaustive investigation. The only course open in such circumstances is briefly to define one's own position.

1. The Recognitions and Homilies, in the form in which we have them, do not belong to the second century, but at the very earliest to the first half of the third. There is nothing, however, to prevent our putting them a few decades later. [1]

discussion. It can hardly make any progress worth mentioning until we have collected better the material, and especially till we have got a corrected edition with an exhaustive commentary. The theory of the genesis, contents and aim of the pseudo-Clementine writings unfolded by Renan (Orig. T. VII. p. 74–101) is essentially identical with that of German scholars. Langen (die Clemensromane, 1890) has set up very bold hypotheses, which are based on the assumption that Jewish Christianity was an important church factor in the second century, and that the pseudo-Clementines are comparatively old writings.

[1] There is no external evidence for placing the pseudo-Clementine writings in the second century. The oldest witness is Origen (IV. p. 401, Lommatzsch); but the quotation: "Quoniam opera bona, quæ fiunt ab infidelibus, in hoc sæculo iis prosunt," etc., is not found in our Clementines, so that Origen appears to have used a still older version. The internal evidence all points to the third century (canon, composition, theological attitude, etc.). Moreover, Zahn, (Gött. Gel. Anz. 1876. No. 45) and Lagarde have declared themselves in favour of this date; while Lipsius (Apokr. Apostelgesch. II. 1) and Weingarten (Zeittafeln, 3 Edit. p. 23) have recently expressed the same opinion. The Homilies presuppose (1) Marcion's Antitheses, (2) Apelles' Syllogisms, (3) perhaps Callistus' edict about penance (see III. 70) and writings of Hippolytus (see also the expression ἐπίσκοπος ἐπισκόπων. Clem. ep. ad Jacob I., which is first found in Tertull., de pudic. I.). (4) The most highly developed form of polemic against heathen mythology. (5) The complete development of church apologetics, as well as the conviction that Christianity is identical with correct and absolute knowledge. They further presuppose a time when there was a lull in the persecution of Christians, for the Emperor, though pretty often referred to, is never spoken of as a persecutor, and when the cultured heathen world was entirely disposed in favour of a eclectic monotheism. More-

2. They were not composed in their present form by heretical Christians, but most probably by Catholics. Nor do they aim at forming a theological system, [1] or spreading the views of a sect. Their primary object is to oppose Greek polytheism, immoral mythology, and false philosophy, and thus to promote edification. [2]

3. In describing the authors as Catholic, we do not mean that they were adherents of the theology of Irenæus or Origen. The instructive point here, rather, is that they had as yet no fixed theology, and therefore could without hesitation regard and use all possible material as means of edification. In like manner, they had no fixed conception of the Apostolic age, and could therefore appropriate motley and dangerous material. Such Christians, highly educated and correctly trained too, were still to be found, not only in the third century, but even later. But the authors do not seem to have been free from a bias, inasmuch as they did not favour the Catholic, that is the Alexandrian, apologetic theology which was in process of formation

4. The description of the Pseudo-Clementine writings, naturally derived from their very form, as "edifying, didactic romances for the refutation of paganism," is not inconsistent with the idea that the authors at the same time did their utmost to oppose heretical phenomena, especially the Marcionite church and Apelles, together with heresy and heathenism in general, as represented by Simon Magus.

over, the remarkable Christological statement in Hom. XVI. 15. 16. points to the third century, in fact probably even presupposes the theology of Origen; Cf. the sentence: τοῦ πατρὸς τὸ μή γεγεννῆσθαι ἐστιν, υἱοῦ δὲ τὸ γεγεννῆσθαι λεννητὸν δὲ ἀγεννήτῳ ἤ καὶ αὐτυγεννήτῳ οὐ συνκρίνεται.. Finally, the decided repudiation of the awakening of Christian faith by visions and dreams, and the polemic against these is also no doubt of importance for determining the date; see XVII. 14-19. Peter says, § 18: τὸ ἀδιδάκτως ἄνευ ὀπτασίας καὶ ὀνείρων μαθεῖν ἀποκάλυψίς ἐστιν, he had already learned that at his confession (Matt. XVI). The question, ἔι τις δὶ ὀπτασίαν πρὸς διδασκαλίαν σοφισθῆναι δύναται, is answered in the negative, § 19.

[1] This is also acknowledged in Koffmane, Die Gnosis, etc., p. 33.

[2] The Homilies, as we have them, are mainly composed of the speeches of Peter and others. These speeches oppose polytheism, mythology and the doctrine of demons, and advocate monotheism, ascetic morality and rationalism. The polemic against Simon Magus almost appears as a mere accessory.

5. The objectionable materials which the authors made use of were edifying for them, because of the position assigned therein to Peter, because of the ascetic and mysterious elements they contained, and the opposition offered to Simon, etc. The offensive features, so far as they were still contained in these sources, had already become unintelligible and harmless. They were partly conserved as such and partly removed.

6. The authors are to be sought for perhaps in Rome, perhaps in Syria, perhaps in both places, certainly not in Alexandria.

7. The main ideas are: (1) The monarchy of God. (2) the syzygies (weak and strong). (3) Prophecy (the true Prophet). (4) Stoical rationalism, belief in providence, good works, φιλαν-θρωπία, etc. = Mosaism. The Homilies are completely saturated with stoicism, both in their ethical and metaphysical systems, and are opposed to Platonism, though Plato is quoted in Hom. XV. 8, as Ἑλλήνων τοφός τις (a wise man of the Greeks). In addition to these ideas we have also a strong hierarchical tendency. The material which the authors made use of was in great part derived from syncretistic Jewish Christian tradition, in other words, those histories of the Apostles were here utilised which Epiphanius reports to have been used by the Ebionites (see above). It is not probable, however, that these writings in their original form were in the hands of the narrators; the likelihood is that they made use of them in revised forms.

8. It must be reserved for an accurate investigation to ascertain whether those modified versions which betray clear marks of Hellenic origin were made within syncretistic Judaism itself, or whether they are to be traced back to Catholic writers. In either case, they should not be placed earlier than about the beginning of the third century, but in all probability one or two generations later still.

9. If we adopt the first assumption, it is most natural to think of that propaganda which, according to the testimony of Hippolytus and Origen, Jewish Christianity attempted in Rome in the age of Caracalla and Heliogabalus, through the medium of the Syrian, Alcibiades. This coincides with the last

great advance of Syrian cults into the west, and is at the
same time the only one known to us historically. But it is
further pretty generally admitted that the immediate sources
of the Pseudo-Clementines already presuppose the existence of
Elkesaite Christianity. We should accordingly have to assume
that in the West this Christianity made greater concessions
to the prevailing type, that it gave up circumcision and accommodated itself to the Church system of Gentile Christianity, at the same time withdrawing its polemic against Paul.

10. Meanwhile the existence of such a Jewish Christianity
is not as yet proved, and therefore we must reckon with the
possibility that the remodelled form of the Jewish Christian
sources, already found in existence by the revisers of the
Pseudo-Clementine Romances, was solely a Catholic literary
product. In this assumption, which commends itself both as
regards the aim of the composition and its presupposed conditions, we must remember that, from the third century
onwards, Catholic writers systematically corrected, and to a
great extent reconstructed, the heretical histories which were
in circulation in the churches as interesting reading, and that
the extent and degree of this reconstruction varied exceedingly, according to the theological and historical insight of
the writer. The identifying of pure Mosaism with Christianity
was in itself by no means offensive when there was no further
question of circumcision. The clear distinction between the
ceremonial and moral parts of the Old Testament, could no
longer prove an offence after the great struggle with Gnosticism. [1] The strong insistance upon the unity of God, and the
rejection of the doctrine of the Logos, were by no means
uncommon in the beginning of the third century; and in the

---

[1] This distinction can also be shewn elsewhere in the Church of the third
century. But I confess I do not know how Catholic circles got over the fact
that, for example, in the third book of the Homilies many passages of the old
Testament are simply characterised as untrue, immoral and lying. Here the
Homilies remind one strongly of the Syllogisms of Apelles, the author of which,
in other respects, opposed them in the interest of his doctrine of creating angels.
In some passages the Christianity of the Homilies really looks like a syncretism
composed of the common Christianity, the Jewish Christian Gnosticism, and the
criticism of Apelles. Hom. VIII. 6–8 is also highly objectionable.

speculations about Adam and Christ, in the views about God and the world and such like, as set before us in the immediate sources of the Romances, the correct and edifying elements must have seemed to outweigh the objectionable. At any rate, the historian who, until further advised, denies the existence of a Jewish Christianity composed of the most contradictory elements, lacking circumcision and national hopes, and bearing marks of Catholic and therefore of Hellenic influence, judges more prudently than he who asserts, solely on the basis of Romances which are accompanied by no tradition and have never been the objects of assault, the existence of a Jewish Christianity accommodating itself to Catholicism which is entirely unattested.

11. Be that as it may, it may at least be regarded as certain that the Pseudo-Clementines contribute absolutely nothing to our knowledge of the origin of the Catholic Church and doctrine, as they shew at best in their immediate sources a Jewish Christianity strongly influenced by Catholicism and Hellenism.

12. They must be used with great caution even in seeking to determine the tendencies and inner history of syncretistic Jewish Christianity. It cannot be made out with certainty, how far back the first sources of the Pseudo-Clementines date, or what their original form and tendency were. As to the first point, it has indeed been said that Justin, nay, even the author of the Acts of the Apostles, presupposes them, and that the Catholic tradition of Peter in Rome and of Simon Magus are dependent on them (as is still held by Lipsius); but there is so little proof of this adduced that in Christian literature up to the end of the second century (Hegesippus?) we can only discover very uncertain traces of acquaintance with Jewish Christian historical narrative. Such indications can only be found to any considerable extent in the third century, and I do not mean to deny that the contents of the Jewish Christian histories of the Apostles contributed materially to the formation of the ecclesiastical legends about Peter. As is shewn in the Pseudo-Clementines, these histories of the Apostles especially opposed Simon Magus and

his adherents (the new Samaritan attempt at a universal religion), and placed the authority of the Apostle Peter against them. But they also opposed the Apostle Paul, and seem to have transferred Simonian features to Paul, and Pauline features to Simon. Yet it is also possible that the Pauline traits found in the magician were the outcome of the redaction, in so far as the whole polemic against Paul is here struck out, though certain parts of it have been woven into the polemic against Simon. But probably the Pauline features of the magician are merely an appearance. The Pseudo-Clementines may to some extent be used, though with caution, in determining the doctrines of syncretistic Jewish Christianity. In connection with this we must take what Epiphanius says as our standard. The Pantheistic and Stoic elements which are found here and there must of course be eliminated. But the theory of the genesis of the world from a change in God himself (that is from a προβολή), the assumption that all things emanated from God in antitheses (Son of God—Devil; heaven—earth; male—female; male and female prophecy), nay, that these antitheses are found in God himself (goodness, to which corresponds the Son of God—punitive justice, to which corresponds the Devil), the speculations about the elements which have proceeded from the one substance, the ignoring of freedom in the question about the origin of evil, the strict adherence to the unity and absolute causality of God, in spite of the dualism, and in spite of the lofty predicates applied to the Son of God—all this plainly bears the Semitic-Jewish stamp.

We must here content ourselves with these indications. They were meant to set forth briefly the reasons which forbid our assigning to syncretistic Jewish Christianity, on the basis of the Pseudo-Clementines, a place in the history of the genesis of the Catholic Church and its doctrine.

Bigg, The Clementine Homilies (Studia Biblica et Eccles. II., p. 157 ff.), has propounded the hypothesis that the Homilies are an Ebionitic revision of an older Catholic original (see p. 184: "The Homilies as we have it, is a recast of an orthodox work by a highly unorthodox editor." P. 175: "The Homilies

are surely the work of a Catholic convert to Ebionitism, who
thought he saw in the doctrine of the two powers the only
tenable answer to Gnosticism. We can separate his Catholicism from his Ebionitism just as surely as his Stoicism ").
This is the opposite of the view expressed by me in the text.
I consider Bigg's hypothesis well worth examining, and at
first sight not improbable; but I am not able to enter into
it here.

APPENDIX I.

On the Conception of Pre-existence.

ON account of the importance of the question, we may be
here permitted to amplify a few hints given in Chap. II., § 4,
and elsewhere, and to draw a clearer distinction between the
Jewish and Hellenic conceptions of pre-existence.

According to the theory held by the ancient Jews and by
the whole of the Semitic nations, everything of real value
that from time to time appears on earth has its existence in
heaven. In other words, it exists with God, that is God possesses a knowledge of it; and for that reason it has a real
being. But it exists beforehand with God in the same way
as it appears on earth, that is with all the material attributes
belonging to its essence. Its manifestation on earth is merely
a transition from concealment to publicity (φανεροῦσθαι). In
becoming visible to the senses, the object in question assumes
no attribute that it did not already possess with God. Hence
its material nature is by no means an inadequate expression
of it, nor is it a second nature added to the first. The truth
rather is that what was in heaven before is now revealing
itself upon earth, without any sort of alteration taking place
in the process. There is no *assumptio naturæ novæ*, and no
change or mixture. The old Jewish theory of pre-existence
is founded on the religious idea of the omniscience and omnipotence of God, that God to whom the events of history do
not come as a surprise, but who guides their course. As the
whole history of the world and the destiny of each individual
are recorded on his tablets or books, so also each thing is
ever present before him. The decisive contrast is between
God and the creature. In designating the latter as "foreknown"
by God, the primary idea is not to ennoble the creature, but

rather to bring to light the wisdom and power of God. The ennobling of created things by attributing to them a pre-existence is a secondary result (see below).

According to the Hellenic conception, which has become associated with Platonism, the idea of pre-existence is independent of the idea of God; it is based on the conception of the contrast between spirit and matter, between the infinite and finite, found in the cosmos itself. In the case of all spiritual beings, life in the body or flesh is at bottom an inadequate and unsuitable condition, for the spirit is eternal, the flesh perishable. But the pre-temporal existence, which was only a doubtful assumption as regards ordinary spirits, was a matter of certainty in the case of the higher and purer ones. They lived in an upper world long before this earth was created, and they lived there as spirits without the "polluted garment of the flesh." Now if they resolved for some reason or other to appear in this finite world, they cannot simply become visible, for they have no "visible form." They must rather "assume flesh," whether they throw it about them as a covering, or really make it their own by a process of transformation or mixture. In all cases—and here the speculation gave rise to the most exciting problems—the body is to them something inadequate which they cannot appropriate without adopting certain measures of precaution, but this process may indeed pass through all stages, from a mere seeming appropriation to complete union. The characteristics of the Greek ideas of pre-existence may consequently be thus expressed. First, the objects in question to which pre-existence is ascribed are meant to be ennobled by this attribute. Secondly, these ideas have no relation to God. Thirdly, the material appearance is regarded as something inadequate. Fourthly, speculations about *phantasma, assumptio naturæ humanæ, transmutatio, mixtura, duæ naturæ*, etc., were necessarily associated with these notions.

We see that these two conceptions are as wide apart as the poles. The first has a religious origin, the second a cosmological and psychological; the first glorifies God, the second the created spirit.

However, not only does a certain relationship in point of form exist between these speculations, but the Jewish conception is also found in a shape which seems to approximate still more to the Greek one.

Earthly occurrences and objects are not only regarded as "foreknown" by God before being seen in this world, but the latter manifestation is frequently considered as the copy of the existence and nature which they possess in heaven, and which remains unalterably the same, whether they appear upon earth or not. That which is before God experiences no change. As the destinies of the world are recorded in the books, and God reads them there, it being at the same time a matter of indifference, as regards this knowledge of his, when and how they are accomplished upon earth, so the Tabernacle and its furniture, the Temple, Jerusalem, etc., are before God and continue to exist before him in heaven, even during their appearance on earth and after it.

This conception seems really to have been the oldest one. Moses is to fashion the Temple and its furniture according to the pattern he saw on the Mount (Exod. XXV. 9. 40: XXVI. 30: XXVII. 8: Num. VIII. 4). The Temple and Jerusalem exist in heaven, and they are to be distinguished from the earthly Temple and the earthly Jerusalem; yet the ideas of a φανεροῦσθαι of the thing which is in heaven and of its copy appearing on earth, shade into one another and are not always clearly separated.

The classing of things as original and copy was at first no more meant to glorify them than was the conception of a preexistence they possessed within the knowledge of God. But since the view which in theory was true of everything earthly, was, as is naturally to be expected, applied in practice to nothing but valuable objects—for things common and ever recurring give no impulse to such speculations—the objects thus contemplated were ennobled, because they were raised above the multitude of the commonplace. At the same time the theory of original and copy could not fail to become a starting point for new speculations, as soon as the contrast between the spiritual and material began to assume importance among the Jewish people.

That took place under the influence of the Greek spirit; and was perhaps also the simultaneous result of an intellectual or moral development which arose independently of that spirit. Accordingly, a highly important advance in the old ideas of pre-existence appeared in the Jewish theological literature belonging to the time of the Maccabees and the following decades. To begin with, these conceptions are now applied to persons, which, so far as I know, was not the case before this (individualism). Secondly, the old distinction of original and copy is now interpreted to mean that the copy is the inferior and more imperfect, that in the present æon of the transient it cannot be equivalent to the original, and that we must therefore look forward to the time when the original itself will make its appearance, (contrast of the material and finite and the spiritual).

With regard to the first point, we have not only to consider passages in Apocalypses and other writings in which pre-existence is attributed to Moses, the patriarchs, etc., (see above, p. 102), but we must, above all, bear in mind utterances like Ps. CXXXIX. 15, 16. The individual saint soars upward to the thought that the days of his life are in the book of God, and that he himself was before God, whilst he was still unperfect. But, and this must not be overlooked, it was not merely his spiritual part that was before God, for there is not the remotest idea of such a distinction, but the whole man, although he is בָּשָׂר.

As regards the second point, the distinction between a heavenly and an earthly Jerusalem, a heavenly and an earthly Temple, etc., is sufficiently known from the Apocalypses and the New Testament. But the important consideration is that the sacred things of earth were regarded as objects of less value, instalments, as it were, pending the fulfilment of the whole promise. The desecration and subsequent destruction of sacred things must have greatly strengthened this idea. The hope of the heavenly Jerusalem comforted men for the desecration or loss of the earthly one. But this gave at the same time the most powerful impulse to reflect whether it

was not an essential feature of this temporal state, that everything high and holy in it could only appear in a meagre and
inadequate form. Thus the transition to Greek ideas was
brought about. The fulness of the time had come when the
old Jewish ideas, with a slightly mythological colouring, could
amalgamate with the ideal creations of Hellenic philosophers.

These, however, are also the general conditions which gave
rise to the earliest Jewish speculations about a personal Messiah, except that, in the case of the Messianic ideas within
Judaism itself, the adoption of specifically Greek thoughts, so
far as I am able to see, cannot be made out.

Most Jews, as Trypho testifies in Justin's Dialogue 49, conceived the Messiah as a man. We may indeed go a step
further and say that no Jew at bottom imagined him otherwise; for even those who attached ideas of pre-existence to
him, and gave the Messiah a supernatural background, never
advanced to speculations about assumption of the flesh, incarnation, two natures and the like. They only transferred in a
specific manner to the Messiah the old idea of pre-terrestrial
existence with God, universally current among the Jews. Before
the creation of the world the Messiah was hidden with God,
and, when the time is fulfilled, he makes his appearance. This
is neither an incarnation nor a humiliation, but he appears on
earth as he exists before God, viz., as a mighty and just king,
equipped with all gifts. The writings in which this thought
appears most clearly are the Apocalypse of Enoch (Book of
Similitudes, Chap. 46-49) and the Apocalypse of Esra (Chap.
12-14). Support to this idea, if anything more of the kind
had been required, was lent by passages like Daniel VII. 13 f.
and Micah, V. 1. Nowhere do we find in Jewish writings a
conception which advances beyond the notion that the Messiah
is the man who is with God in heaven; and who will make
his appearance at his own time. We are merely entitled to
say that, as the same idea was not applied to all persons with
the same certainty, it was almost unavoidable that men's minds
should have been led to designate the Messiah as the man from
heaven. This thought was adopted by Paul (see below), but I
know of no *Jewish* writing which gave clear expression to it.

Jesus Christ designated himself as the Messiah, and the first of his disciples who recognised him as such were native Jews. The Jewish conceptions of the Messiah consequently passed over into the Christian community. But they received an impulse to important modifications from the living impression conveyed by the person and destiny of Jesus. Three facts were here of pre-eminent importance. First, Jesus appeared in lowliness, and even suffered death. Secondly, he was believed to be exalted through the resurrection to the right hand of God, and his return in glory was awaited with certainty. Thirdly, the strength of a new life and of an indissoluble union with God was felt issuing from him, and therefore his people were connected with him in the closest way.

In some old Christian writings found in the New Testament and emanating from the pen of native Jews, there are no speculations at all about the pre-temporal existence of Jesus as the Messiah, or they are found expressed in a manner which simply embodies the old Jewish theory and is merely distinguished from it by the emphasis laid on the exaltation of Jesus after death through the resurrection. I. Pet. i. 18 ff. is a classic passage: ἐλυτρώθητε τιμίῳ αἵματι ὡς ἀμνοῦ ἀμώμου καὶ ἀσπίλου Χριστοῦ, προεγνωσμένου μὲν πρὸ καταβολῆς κόσμου, φανερωθέντος δὲ ἐπ᾽ ἐσχάτου τῶν χρόνων δι᾽ ὑμᾶς τοὺς δι᾽ αὐτοῦ πιστοὺς εἰς θεὸν τὸν ἐγείραντα αὐτὸν ἐκ νεκρῶν καὶ δόξαν αὐτῷ δόντα, ὥστε τὴν πίστιν ὑμῶν καὶ ἐλπίδα εἶναι εἰς θεόν. Here we find a conception of the pre-existence of Christ which is not yet affected by cosmological or psychological speculation, which does not overstep the boundaries of a purely religious contemplation, and which arose from the Old Testament way of thinking, and the living impression derived from the person of Jesus. He is "foreknown (by God) before the creation of the world," not as a spiritual being without a body, but as a Lamb without blemish and without spot; in other words, his whole personality together with the work which it was to carry out, was within God's eternal knowledge. He "was manifested in these last days for our sake," that is, he is now visibly what he already was before God. What is meant here is not an incarnation, but a *revelatio*. Finally, he appeared in order that our faith and hope should now be firmly directed to the living God, *that* God who raised him from the dead and gave him honour. In the last clause expression is given to the specifically Christian thought, that the Messiah Jesus was *exalted* after crucifixion and death; from this, however, no further conclusions are drawn.

But it was impossible that men should everywhere rest satisfied with these utterances, for the age was a theological one. Hence the paradox of the suffering Messiah, the certainty of his glorification through the resurrection, the conviction of his specific relationship to God, and the belief in the real union of his Church with him did not seem adequately expressed by the simple formulæ προεγνωσμένος, φανερωθείς. In reference to all these points, we see even in the oldest Christian writings, the appearance of formulæ which fix more precisely the nature of his pre-existence, or in other words his heavenly existence. With regard to the first and second points there arose the view of humiliation and exaltation, such as we find in Paul and in numerous writings after him. In connection with the third point the concept "Son of God" was thrust into the fore-ground, and gave rise to the idea of the image of God (2 Cor. IV. 4; Col. I. 15; Heb. I. 2; Phil. II. 6). The fourth point gave occasion to the formation of theses, such as we find in Rom. VIII. 29: πρωτότοκος ἐν πολλοῖς ἀδελφοῖς, Col. I. 18: πρωτότοκος ἐκ τῶν νεκρῶν (Rev. I. 5), Eph. II. 6: συνήγειρεν καὶ συνεκάθισεν ἐν τοῖς ἐπουρανίοις ἡμᾶς ἐν Χριστῷ Ἰησοῦ, I. 4: ὁ θεὸς ἐξελέξατο ἡμᾶς ἐν Χριστῷ πρὸ καταβολῆς κόσμου, I. 22: ὁ θεὸς ἔδωκεν τὸν Χριστὸν κεφαλὴν ὑπὲρ πάντα τῇ ἐκκλησίᾳ ἥτις ἐστὶν τὸ σῶμα αὐτοῦ, etc. This purely religious view of the Church, according to which all that is predicated of Christ is also applied to his followers, continued a considerable time. Hermas declares that the Church is older than the world, and that the world was created for its sake (see above, p. 103), and the author of the so-called 2nd Epistle of Clement declares (Chap. 14) .... ἐσόμεθα ἐκ τῆς ἐκκλησίας τῆς πρώτης τῆς πνευματικῆς, τῆς πρὸ ἡλίου καὶ σελήνης ἐκτισμένης ....., οὐκ οἴομαι δὲ ὑμᾶς ἀγνοεῖν, ὅτι ἐκκλησία ζῶσα σῶμα ἐστι Χριστοῦ. λέγει γὰρ ἡ γραφή. Ἐποίησεν ὁ θεὸς τὸν ἄνθρωπον ἄρσεν καὶ θῆλυ. τὸ ἄρσεν ἐστιν ὁ Χριστὸς τὸ θῆλυ ἡ ἐκκλησία. Thus Christ and his Church are inseparably connected. The latter is to be conceived as pre-existent quite as much as the former; the Church was also created before the sun and the moon, for the world was created for its sake. This conception of the Church illustrates a final group of utterances about the pre-existent Christ, the origin of which might easily be misinterpreted unless we bear in mind their reference to the Church. In so far as he is προεγνωσμένος πρὸ καταβολῆς κόσμου, he is the ἀρχὴ τῆς κτίσεως τοῦ θεοῦ (Rev. III. 14), the πρωτότοκος πάσης κτίσεως, etc. According to the current conception of the time, these expressions mean exactly the same as the simple προεγνωσμένος πρὸ καταβολῆς κόσμου, as is proved by the parallel formulæ referring to the Church. Nay, even the further advance to the idea that the world was created by him (Cor. Col. Eph. Heb.) need not yet necessarily be a μετάβασις εἰς ἄλλο γένος; for the beginning of things (ἀρχή) and their purpose form the real force to which their origin is due (principle ἀρχή). Hermas indeed calls the Church older than the world simply because "the world was created for its sake."

All these further theories which we have quoted up to this time need in no sense alter the original conception, so long as they appear in an isolated form and do not form the basis of fresh speculations. They may be regarded as the working out of the original conception attaching to Jesus Christ προεγνωσμένος πρὸ καταβολῆς κόσμου, φανερωθείς κ.τ.λ.; and do not really modify this religious view of the matter. Above all, we find in them as yet no certain transition to the Greek view which splits up his personality into a heavenly and an earthly portion; it still continues to be the complete Christ to whom all the utterances apply. But, beyond doubt, they already reveal the strong impulse to conceive the Christ that had appeared as a divine being. He had not been a transitory phenomenon, but has ascended into heaven and still continues to live. This post-existence of his gave to the ideas of his pre-existence a support and a concrete complexion which the earlier Jewish theories lacked.

We find the transition to a new conception in the writings of Paul. But it is important to begin by determining the re-

lationship between his Christology and the views we have been
hitherto considering. In the Apostle's clearest trains of thought
everything that he has to say of Christ hinges on his death
and resurrection. For this we need no proofs, but see, more
especially Rom. I. 3 f.: περὶ τοῦ υἱοῦ αὐτοῦ, τοῦ γενομένου ἐκ
σπέρματος Λαυεὶδ κατὰ σάρκα, τοῦ ὁρισθέντος υἱοῦ θεοῦ ἐν δυνάμει
κατὰ πνεῦμα ἀγιωσύνης ἐκ ἀναστάσεως νεκρῶν, Ἰησοῦ Χριστοῦ τοῦ
κυρίου ἡμῶν. What Christ became and his significance for us
now are due to his death on the cross and his resurrection.
He condemned sin in the flesh and was obedient unto death.
Therefore he now shares in the δόξα of God. The exposition
in I Cor. XV. 45, also (ὁ ἔσχατος Ἀδὰμ εἰς πνεῦμα ζωοποιοῦν,
ἀλλ' οὐ πρῶτον τὸ πνευματικὸν ἀλλὰ τὸ ψυχικόν, ἔπειτα τὸ πνευ-
ματικόν. ὁ πρῶτος ἄνθρωπος ἐκ γῆς χοϊκός ὁ δεύτερος ἄνθρωπος ἐξ
οὐρανοῦ) is still capable of being understood as to its fundamental features, in a sense which agrees with the conception
of the Messiah, as κατ' ἐξοχήν, the man from heaven who was
hidden with God. There can be no doubt, however, that this
conception, as already shewn by the formulæ in the passage
just quoted, formed to Paul the starting-point of a speculation,
in which the original theory assumed a completely new shape.
The decisive factors in this transformation were the Apostle's
doctrine of "spirit and flesh," and the corresponding conviction that the Christ who is not be known "after the flesh,"
is a spirit, namely, the mighty spiritual being (πνεῦμα ζωοποιοῦν),
who has condemned sin in the flesh, and thereby enabled
man to walk not after the flesh, but after the spirit.

According to one of the Apostle's ways of regarding the
matter, Christ, after the accomplishment of his work, became
the πνεῦμα ζωοποιοῦν through the resurrection. But the belief
that Jesus always stood before God as the heavenly man,
suggested to Paul the other view, that Christ was always a
"spirit," that he was sent down by God, that the flesh is
consequently something inadequate and indeed hostile to him,
that he nevertheless assumed it in order to extirpate the sin
dwelling in the flesh, that he therefore humbled himself by
appearing, and that this ·humiliation was the deed he performed.

This view is found in 2 Cor. VIII. 9: Ἰησοῦς Χριστὸς δι' ὑμᾶς ἐπτώχευσεν πλούσιος ὤν; in Rom. VIII. 3: ὁ θεὸς τὸν ἑαυτοῦ υἱὸν πέμψας ἐν ὁμοιώματι σαρκὸς ἁμαρτίας καὶ περὶ ἁμαρτίας κατέκρινε τὴν ἁμαρτίαν ἐν τῇ σαρκί; and in Phil. II. 5 f.: Χριστὸς Ἰησοῦς ἐν μορφῇ θεοῦ ὑπάρχων . . . . . ἑαυτὸν ἐκένωσεν μορφὴν δούλου λαβών, ἐν ὁμοιώματι ἀνθρώπων γενόμενος, καὶ σχήματι εὑρεθεὶς ὡς ἄνθρωπος ἐταπείνωσεν ἑαυτὸν κ. τ. λ. In both forms of thought Paul presupposes a real exaltation of Christ. Christ receives after the resurrection more than he ever possessed (τὸ ὄνομα τὸ ὑπὲρ πᾶν ὄνομα). In this view Paul retains a historical interpretation of Christ, even in the conception of the πνεῦμα Χριστός. But whilst many passages seem to imply that the work of Christ began with suffering and death, Paul shews in the verses cited, that he already conceives the appearance of Christ on earth as his moral act, as a humiliation, purposely brought about by God and Christ himself, which reaches its culminating point in the death on the cross. Christ, the divine spiritual being, is sent by the Father from heaven to earth, and of his own free will he obediently takes this mission upon himself. He appears in the ὁμοίωμα σαρκὸς ἁμαρτίας, dies the death of the cross, and then, raised by the Father, ascends again into heaven in order henceforth to act as the κύριος ζώντων and νεκρῶν, and to become to his own people the principle of a new life in the spirit.

Whatever we may think about the admissibility and justification of this view, to whatever source we may trace its origin and however strongly we may emphasise its divergencies from the contemporaneous Hellenic ideas, it is certain that it approaches very closely to the latter; for the distinction of spirit and flesh is here introduced into the concept of pre-existence, and this combination is not found in the Jewish notions of the Messiah.

Paul was the first who limited the idea of pre-existence by referring it solely to the spiritual part of Jesus Christ, but at the same time gave life to it by making the pre-existing Christ (the spirit) a being who, even during his pre-existence, stands independently side by side with God.

He was also the first to designate Christ's σάρξ as "assumpta," and to recognise its assumption as in itself a humiliation. To him the appearance of Christ was no mere φανεροῦσθαι, but a κενοῦσθαι, ταπεινοῦσθαι, πτωχεύειν.

These outstanding features of the Pauline Christology must have been intelligible to the Greeks, but, whilst embracing these, they put everything else in the system aside, Χριστὸς ὁ κύριος ὁ σώσας ἡμᾶς, ὢν μὲν τὸ πρῶτον πνεῦμα, ἐγένετο σάρξ καὶ οὕτως ἡμᾶς ἐκάλεσεν, says 2 Clem. (9. 5), and that is also the Christology of 1 Clement, Barnabas and many other Greeks. From the sum total of Judæo-Christian speculations they only borrowed, in addition, the one which has been already mentioned: the Messiah as προεγνωσμένος πρὸ καταβολῆς κόσμου is for that very reason also ἡ ἀρχὴ τῆς κτίσεως τοῦ θεοῦ, that is the beginning, purpose and principle of the creation The Greeks, as the result of their cosmological interest, embraced this thought as a fundamental proposition. The complete Greek Christology then is expressed as follows: Χριστὸς, ὁ σώσας ἡμᾶς, ὢν μὲν τὸ πρῶτον πνεῦμα καὶ πάσης κτίσεως ἀρχὴ, ἐγένετο σάρξ καὶ οὕτως ἡμᾶς ἐκάλεσεν. *That is the fundamental, theological and philosophical creed on which the whole Trinitarian and Christological speculations of the Church of the succeeding centuries are built, and it is thus the root of the orthodox system of dogmatics;* for the notion that Christ was the ἀρχὴ πάσης κτίσεως necessarily led in some measure to the conception of Christ as the Logos. For the Logos had long been regarded by cultured men as the beginning and principle of the creation. [1]

---

[1] These hints will have shewn that Paul's theory occupies a middle position between the Jewish and Greek ideas of pre-existence. In the canon, however, we have another group of writings which likewise gives evidence of a middle position with regard to the matter, I mean the Johannine writings. If we only possessed the prologue to the Gospel of John with its "ἐν ἀρχῇ ἦν ὁ λόγος" the "πάντα δι᾽ αὐτοῦ ἐγένετο" and the "ὁ λόγος σάρξ ἐγένετο," we could indeed point to nothing but Hellenic ideas. But the Gospel itself, as is well known, contains very much that must have astonished a Greek, and is opposed to the philosophical idea of the Logos. This occurs even in the thought, "ὁ λόγος σάρξ ἐγένετο," which in itself is foreign to the Logos conception. Just fancy a proposition like the one in VI. 44, οὐδεὶς δύναται ἐλθεῖν πρὸς με, ἐὰν μὴ ὁ πατὴρ ὁ πέμψας με ἑλκύσῃ αὐτὸν, or in V. 17. 21, engrafted on Philo's system, and consider the revolution it would have caused there. No doubt the prologue to some extent contains the

With this transition the theories concerning Christ are removed from Jewish and Old Testament soil, and also that of religion (in the strict sense of the word), and transplanted to the Greek one. Even in his pre-existent state Christ is an independent power existing side by side with God. The pre-

themes set forth in the presentation that follows, but they are worded in such a way that one cannot help thinking the author wished to prepare Greek readers for the paradox he had to communicate to them, by adapting his prologue to their mode of thought. Under the altered conditions of thought which now prevail, the prologue appears to us the mysterious part, and the narrative that follows seems the portion that is relatively more intelligible. But to the original readers, if they were educated Greeks, the prologue must have been the part most easily understood. As nowadays a section on the nature of the Christian religion is usually prefixed to a treatise on dogmatics, in order to prepare and introduce the reader, so also the Johannine prologue seems to be intended as an introduction of this kind. It brings in conceptions which were familiar to the Greeks, in fact it enters into these more deeply than is justified by the presentation which follows; for the notion of the incarnate Logos is by no means the dominant one here. Though faint echoes of this idea may possibly be met with here and there in the Gospel—I confess I do not notice them—the predominating thought is essentially the conception of Christ as the Son of God, who obediently executes what the Father has shewn and appointed him. The works which he does are allotted to him, and he performs them in the strength of the Father. The whole of Christ's farewell discourses and the intercessory prayer evince no Hellenic influence and no cosmological speculation whatever, but shew the inner life of a man who knows himself to be one with God to a greater extent than any before him, and who feels the leading of men to God to be the task he had received and accomplished. In this consciousness he speaks of the glory he had with the Father before the world was (XVII. 4 f.: ἐγώ σε ἐδόξασα ἐπὶ τῆς γῆς, τὸ ἔργον τελειώσας ὃ δέδωκάς μοι ἵνα ποιήσω· καὶ νῦν δόξασον με σύ, πάτερ, παρὰ σεαυτῷ τῇ δόξῃ ᾗ εἶχον πρὸ τοῦ τὸν κόσμον εἶναι, παρὰ σοι). With this we must compare verses like III. 13: οὐδεὶς ἀναβέβηκεν εἰς τὸν οὐρανὸν εἰ μὴ ὁ ἐκ τοῦ οὐρανοῦ καταβάς, ὁ υἱὸς τοῦ ἀνθρῶπου, and III. 31: ὁ ἄνωθεν ἐρχόμενος ἐπάνω πάντων ἐστιν. ὁ ὢν ἐκ τῆς γῆς ἐκ τῆς γῆς ἐστιν καὶ ἐκ τῆς γῆς λαλεῖ ὁ ἐκ τοῦ οὐρανοῦ ἐρχόμενος ἐπάνω πάντων ἐστιν (see also I. 30 : VI. 33, 38, 41 f. 50 f. 58, 62 : VIII. 14, 58; XVII. 24). But though the pre-existence is strongly expressed in these passages, a separation of πνεῦμα (λόγος) and σάρξ in Christ is nowhere assumed in the Gospel except in the prologue. It is always Christ's whole personality to which every sublime attribute is ascribed. The same one who "can do nothing of himself" is also the one who was once glorious and will yet be glorified. This idea, however, can still be referred to the προεγνωσμένος πρὸ καταβολῆς κόσμου, although it gives a peculiar δόξα with God to him who was foreknown of God, and the oldest conception is yet to be traced in many expressions, as, for example, I. 31: κἀγὼ οὐκ ᾔδειν αὐτὸν, ἀλλ' ἵνα φανερωθῇ τῷ Ἰσραὴλ διὰ τοῦτο ἦλθον, V. 19: οὐ δύναται ὁ υἱὸς ποιεῖν ἀφ' ἑαυτοῦ οὐδὲν ἂν μή τι βλέπῃ τὸν πατέρα ποιοῦντας, V. 36 : VIII. 38: ἃ ἐγὼ ἑώρακα παρὰ τῷ πατρὶ λαλῶ, VIII. 40: τὴν ἀλήθειαν ὑμῖν λελάληκα ἣν ἤκουσα παρὰ τοῦ θεοῦ, XII. 49 : XV. 15: πάντα ἃ ἤκουσα παρὰ τοῦ πατρός μου ἐγνώρισα ὑμῖν.

existence does not refer to his whole appearance, but only to
a part of his essence; it does not primarily serve to glorify
the wisdom and power of the God who guides history, but
only glorifies Christ, and thereby threatens the monarchy of
God. [1] The appearance of Christ is now an "assumption of
flesh," and immediately the intricate questions about the connection of the heavenly and spiritual being with the flesh
simultaneously arise and are at first settled by the theories of
a naive docetism. But the flesh, that is the human nature
created by God, appears depreciated, because it was reckoned
as something unsuitable for Christ, and foreign to him as a
spiritual being. Thus the Christian religion was mixed up
with the refined asceticism of a perishing civilization, and a
foreign substructure given to its system of morality, so earnest
in its simplicity. [2] But the most questionable result was the
following. Since the predicate "Logos," which at first, and
for a long time, coincided with the idea of the reason ruling
in the cosmos, was considered as the highest that could be
given to Christ, the holy and divine element, namely, the
power of a new life, a power to be viewed and laid hold of
in Christ, was transformed into a cosmic force and thereby
secularised.

In the present work I have endeavoured to explain fully
how the doctrine of the Church developed from these premises
into the doctrine of the Trinity and of the two natures. I
have also shewn that the imperfect beginnings of Church doctrine, especially as they appear in the Logos theory derived
from cosmology, were subjected to wholesome corrections—
by the Monarchians, by Athanasius, and by the influence of

---

[1] This is indeed counterbalanced in the fourth Gospel by the thought of the
complete community of love between the Father and the Son, and the pre-existence
and descent of the latter here also tend to the glory of God. In the sentence "God
so loved the world," etc., that which Paul describes in Phil. II. becomes at the
same time an act of God, in fact the act of God. The sentence "God is love"
sums up again all individual speculations, and raises them into a new and most
exalted sphere.

[2] If it had been possible for speculation to maintain the level of the Fourth
Gospel, nothing of that would have happened; but where were there theologians
capable of this?

biblical passages which pointed in another direction. Finally, the Logos doctrine received a form in which the idea was deprived of nearly all cosmical content. Nor could the Hellenic contrast of "spirit" and "flesh" become completely developed in Christianity, because the belief in the bodily resurrection of Christ, and in the admission of the flesh into heaven, opposed to the principle of dualism a barrier which Paul as yet neither knew nor felt to be necessary. The conviction as to the resurrection of the flesh proved the hard rock which shattered the energetic attempts to give a completely Hellenic complexion to the Christian religion.

The history of the development of the ideas of pre-existence is at the same time the criticism of them, so that we need not have recourse to our present theory of knowledge which no longer allows such speculations. The problem of determining the significance of Christ through a speculation concerning his natures, and of associating with these the concrete features of the historical Christ, was originated by Hellenism. But even the New Testament writers, who appear in this respect to be influenced in some way by Hellenism, did not really speculate concerning the different natures, but, taking Christ's spiritual nature for granted, determined his religious significance by his moral qualities—Paul by the moral act of humiliation and obedience unto death, John by the complete dependence of Christ upon God and hence also by his obedience, as well as the unity of the love of Father and Son. There is only one idea of pre-existence which no empiric contemplation of history and no reason can uproot. This is identical with the most ancient idea found in the Old Testament, as well as that prevalent among the early Christians, and consists in the religious thought that God the Lord directs history. In its application to Jesus Christ, it is contained in the words we read in 1 Pet. I. 20: προεγνωσμένος μὲν πρὸ καταβολῆς κόσμου, φανερωθεὶς δὲ δι' ὑμᾶς τοὺς δι' αὐτοῦ πιστοὺς εἰς θεὸν τὸν ἐγείραντα αὐτὸν ἐκ νεκρῶν καὶ δόξαν αὐτῷ δόντα, ὥστε τὴν πίστιν ὑμῶν καὶ ἐλπίδα εἶναι εἰς θεόν.

APPENDIX II.

Liturgy and the Origin of Dogma.

THE reader has perhaps wondered why I have made so little reference to Liturgy in my description of the origin of dogma. For according to the most modern ideas about the history of religion and the origin of theology, the development of both may be traced in the ritual. Without any desire to criticise these notions, I think I am justified in asserting that this is another instance of the exceptional nature of Christianity. For a considerable period it possessed no ritual at all, and the process of development in this direction had been going on, or been completed, a long time before ritual came to furnish material for dogmatic discussion.

The worship in Christian Churches grew out of that in the synagogues, whereas there is no trace of its being influenced by the Jewish Temple service (Duchesne, Origines du Culte Chrétien, p. 45 ff.). Its oldest constituents are accordingly prayer, reading of the scriptures, application of scripture texts, and sacred song. In addition to these we have, as specifically Christian elements, the celebration of the Lord's Supper, and the utterances of persons inspired by the Spirit. The latter manifestations, however, ceased in the course of the second century, and to some extent as early as its first half. The religious services in which a ritual became developed were prayer, the Lord's Supper and sacred song. The Didache had already prescribed stated formulæ for prayer. The ritual of the Lord's Supper was determined in its main features by the memory of its institution. The sphere of sacred song remained the most unfettered, though here also, even at an early period —no later in fact than the end of the first and beginning of the second century—a fixed and a variable element were distinguished; for responsory hymns, as is testified by the Epistle of Pliny and the still earlier Book of Revelation, require to follow a definite arrangement. But the whole, though perhaps already fixed during the course of the second century, still bore the stamp of spirituality and freedom. It was really worship in spirit and in truth, and this and no other was the light in which the Apologists, for instance, regarded it. Ritualism did not begin to be a power in the Church till the end of the second century; though it had been cultivated by the " Gnostics " long before, and traces of it are found at an earlier period in some of the older Fathers, such as Ignatius.

Among the liturgical fragments still preserved to us from the first three centuries two strata may de distinguished. Apart from the responsory hymns in the Book of Revelation, which can hardly represent fixed liturgical pieces, the only portions of the older stratum in our possession are the Lord's Prayer, originating with Jesus himself and used as a liturgy, together with the sacramental prayers of the Didache. These prayers exhibit a style unlike any of the liturgical formulæ of later times; the prayer is exclusively addressed to God, it returns thanks for knowledge and life; it speaks of Jesus the $\pi\alpha\hat{\iota}\varsigma\ \theta\epsilon o\hat{\upsilon}$ (Son of God) as the mediator; the intercession refers exclusively to the Church, and the supplication is for the gathering together of the Church, the hastening of the coming of the kingdom and the destruction of the world. No direct mention is made of the death and resurrection of Christ. These prayers are the peculiar property of the Christian Church. It cannot, however, be said that they exercised any important influence on the history of dogma. The thoughts contained in them perished in their specific shape; the measure of permanent importance they attained in a more general form, was not preserved to them through these prayers.

The second stratum of liturgical pieces dates back to the great prayer with which the first Epistle of Clement ends, for in many respects this prayer, though some expressions in it remind us of the older type ($\delta\iota\acute{\alpha}\ \tau o\hat{\upsilon}\ \mathring{\eta}\gamma\alpha\pi\eta\mu\acute{\epsilon}\nu o\upsilon\ \pi\alpha\iota\delta\acute{o}\varsigma\ \sigma o\upsilon$ Ἰησοῦν Χριστοῦ, "through thy beloved son Jesus Christ "), already exhibits the characteristics of the later liturgy, as is shewn, for example, by a comparison of the liturgical prayer in the Constitutions of the Apostles (see Lightfoot's edition and my own). But this piece shews at the same time that the liturgical prayers, and consequently the liturgy also, sprang from those in the synagogue, for the similarity is striking. Here we find a connection resembling that which exists between the Jewish "Two Ways" and the Christian instruction of catechumens. If this observation is correct, it clearly explains the cautious use of historical and dogmatic material in the oldest liturgies — a precaution not to their disadvantage. As in the prayers of the synagogue, so also in Christian Churches, all sorts of matters were not submitted to God or laid bare before Him, but the prayers serve as a religious ceremony, that is, as adoration, petition and intercession. Σὺ εἶ ὁ θεὸς μόνος καὶ Ἰησοῦς Χριστὸς ὁ παῖς σου καὶ ἡμεῖς λαός σου καὶ πρόβατα τῆς νομῆς σου, (thou art God alone and Jesus Christ is thy son, and we are thy people and the sheep of thy pasture). In this confession, and expressive Christian modification of that of the synagogue, the whole liturgical ceremony is epitomised. So far as we can assume and conjecture from the scanty remains of Ante-Nicene liturgy, the character of the ceremony was not essentially altered in this respect. Nothing containing a specific dogma or theological speculation was admitted. The number of sacred ceremonies, already considerable in the second century, (how did they arise?) was still further increased in the third; but the accompanying words, so far as we know, expressed nothing but adoration, gratitude, supplication and intercession. The relations expressed in the liturgy became more comprehensive, copious and detailed; but its fundamental character was not changed. The history of dogma in the first three centuries is not reflected in their liturgy.

APPENDIX III.

The Historical Significance and Position of Neoplatonism.

THE political history of the ancient world ends with the
Empire of Diocletian and Constantine, which has not only
Roman and Greek, but also Oriental features. The history of
ancient philosophy ends with the universal philosophy of Neoplatonism, which assimilated the elements of most of the
previous systems, and embodied the result of the history of
religion and civilisation in East and West. But as the Roman
Byzantine Empire is at one and the same time a product of
the final effort and the exhaustion of the ancient world, so
also Neoplatonism is, on one side, the completion of ancient
philosophy, and, on another, its abolition. Never before in the
Greek and Roman theory of the world did the conviction of
the dignity of man and his elevation above nature attain so
certain an expression as in Neoplatonism; and never before
in the history of civilisation did its highest exponents, notwithstanding all their progress in inner observation, so much under-
value the sovereign significance of real science and pure knowledge as the later Neoplatonists did. Judged from the stand-point
of pure science, of empirical knowledge of the world, the
philosophy of Plato and Aristotle marks a momentous turning-
point, the post-Aristotelian a retrogression, the Neoplatonic a
complete declension. But judging from the stand-point of religion
and morality, it must be admitted that the ethical temper which
Neoplatonism sought to beget and confirm was the highest
and purest which the culture of the ancient world produced.
This necessarily took place at the expense of science: for on

the soil of polytheistic natural religions, the knowledge of nature must either fetter and finally abolish religion, or be fettered and abolished by religion. Religion and ethic, however, proved the stronger powers. Placed between these and the knowledge of nature, philosophy, after a period of fluctuation finally follows the stronger force. Since the ethical itself, in the sphere of natural religions, is unhesitatingly conceived as a higher kind of "nature," conflict with the empirical knowledge of the world is unavoidable. The higher "physics," for that is what religious ethics is here, must displace the lower or be itself displaced. Philosophy must renounce its scientific aspect, in order that man's claim to a supernatural value of his person and life may be legitimised.

It is an evidence of the vigour of man's moral endowments that the only epoch of culture which we are able to survey in its beginnings, its progress, and its close, ended not with materialism, but with the most decided idealism. It is true that in its way this idealism also denotes a bankruptcy; as the contempt for reason and science, and these are contemned when relegated to the second place, finally leads to barbarism, because it results in the crassest superstition, and is exposed to all manner of imposture. And, as a matter of fact, barbarism succeeded the flourishing period of Neoplatonism. Philosophers themselves no doubt found their mental food in the knowledge which they thought themselves able to surpass; but the masses grew up in superstition, and the Christian Church, which entered on the inheritance of Neoplatonism, was compelled to reckon with that and come to terms with it. Just when the bankruptcy of the ancient civilisation and its lapse into barbarism could not have failed to reveal themselves, a kindly destiny placed on the stage of history barbarian nations, for whom the work of a thousand years had as yet no existence. Thus the fact is concealed, which, however, does not escape the eye of one who looks below the surface, that the inner history of the ancient world must necessarily have degenerated into barbarism of its own accord, because it ended with the renunciation of this world. There is no desire either to enjoy it, to master it, or to know it as it really is. A new world is disclosed for which everything is given up, and men are ready to sacrifice insight and understanding, in order to possess this world with certainty; and, in the light which radiates from the world to come, that which in this world appears absurd becomes wisdom, and wisdom becomes folly.

Such is Neoplatonism. The pre-Socratic philosophers, declared by the followers of Socrates to be childish, had freed themselves from theology, that is the mythology of the poets, and constructed a philosophy from the observation of nature, without troubling themselves about ethics and religion. In the systems of Plato and Aristotle physics and ethics were to attain to their rights, though the latter no doubt already occupied the first place; theology, that is popular religion, continues to be thrust aside. The post-Aristotelian philosophers of all parties were already beginning to withdraw from the objective world. Stoicism, indeed, seems to fall back into the materialism that prevailed before Plato and Aristotle; but the ethical dualism which dominated the mood of the Stoic philosophers did not in the long run tolerate the materialistic physics; it sought and found help in the metaphysical dualism of the Platonists, and at the same time reconciled itself to the popular religion by means of allegorism, that is it formed a new theology. But it did not result in permanent philosophic creations. A one-sided development of Platonism produced the various forms of scepticism which sought to abolish confidence in empirical knowledge. Neoplatonism, which came last, learned from all schools. In the first place, it belongs to the series of post-Aristotelian systems and, as the philosophy of the subjective, it is the logical completion of them. In the second place, it rests on scepticism; for it also, though not at the very beginning, gave up both confidence and pure interest in empirical knowledge. Thirdly, it can boast of the name and authority of Plato; for in metaphysics it consciously went back to him and expressly opposed the metaphysics of the Stoics. Yet on this very point it also learned something from the Stoics; for the Neoplatonic conception of the action of God on the world, and of the nature and origin of matter, can only be explained by reference to the dynamic pantheism of the Stoics. In other

respects, especially in psychology, it is diametrically opposed
to the Stoa, though superior. Fourthly, the study of Aristotle
also had an influence on Neoplatonism. That is shewn not
only in the philosophic methods of the Neoplatonists, but also,
though in a subordinate way, in their metaphysics. Fifthly,
the ethic of the Stoics was adopted by Neoplatonism, but this
ethic necessarily gave way to a still higher view of the conditions of the spirit. Sixthly and finally, Christianity also,
which Neoplatonism opposed in every form (especially in that
of the Gnostic philosophy of religion), seems not to have been
entirely without influence. On this point we have as yet no
details, and these can only be ascertained by a thorough examination of the polemic of Plotinus against the Gnostics.

Hence, with the exception of Epicureanism, which Neoplatonism dreaded as its mortal enemy, every important system
of former times was drawn upon by the new philosophy. But
we should not on that account call Neoplatonism an eclectic
system in the usual sense of the word. For in the first place,
it had one pervading and all-predominating interest, the religious; and in the second place, it introduced into philosophy
a new supreme principle, the super-rational, or the super-essen-
tial. This principle should not be identified with the "Ideas"
of Plato or the "Form" of Aristotle. For as Zeller rightly
says: "In Plato and Aristotle the distinction of the sensuous
and the intelligible is the strongest expression for belief in
the truth of thought; it is only sensuous perception and sensuous existence whose relative falsehood they presuppose; but
of a higher stage of spiritual life lying beyond idea and thought,
there is no mention. In Neoplatonism, on the other hand, it
is just this super-rational element which is regarded as the
final goal of all effort, and the highest ground of all existence;
the knowledge gained by thought is only an intermediate stage
between sensuous perception and the super-rational intuition;
the intelligible forms are not that which is highest and last,
but only the media by which the influences of the formless
original essence are communicated to the world. This view
therefore presupposes not merely doubt of the reality of sensuous existence and sensuous notions, but absolute doubt,

aspiration beyond all reality. The highest intelligible is not that which constitutes the real content of thought, but only that which is presupposed and earnestly desired by man as the unknowable ground of his thought." Neoplatonism recognised that a religious ethic can be built neither on sense-perception nor on knowledge gained by the understanding, and that it cannot be justified by these; it therefore broke both with intellectual ethics and with utilitarian morality. But for that very reason, having as it were parted with perception and understanding in relation to the ascertaining of the highest truth, it was compelled to seek for a new world and a new function in the human spirit, in order to ascertain the existence of what it desired, and to comprehend and describe that of which it had ascertained the existence. But man cannot transcend his psychological endowment. An iron ring incloses him. He who does not allow his thought to be determined by experience falls a prey to fancy, that is thought which cannot be suppressed assumes a mythological aspect: superstition takes the place of reason, dull gazing at something incomprehensible is regarded as the highest goal of the spirit's efforts, and every conscious activity of the spirit is subordinated to visionary conditions artificially brought about. But that every conceit may not be allowed to assert itself, the gradual exploration of every region of knowledge according to every method of acquiring it, is demanded as a preliminary —the Neoplatonists did not make matters easy for themselves,—and a new and mighty principle is set up which is to bridle fancy, viz., *the authority of a sure tradition.* This authority must be superhuman, otherwise it would not come under consideration; it must therefore be divine. On divine disclosures, that is revelations, must rest both the highest super-rational region of knowledge and the possibility of knowledge itself. In a word, the philosophy which Neoplatonism represents, whose final interest is the religious, and whose highest object is the super-rational, must be a *philosophy of revelation.*

In the case of Plotinus himself and his immediate disciples, this does not yet appear plainly. They still shew confidence in the

objective presuppositions of their philosophy; and have, especially
in psychology, done great work and created something new.   But
this confidence vanishes in the later Neoplatonists.   Porphyry, before he became a disciple of Plotinus, wrote a book περὶ τῆς ἐκλογίων
Φιλοσοφίας; as a philosopher he no longer required the " λόγια."
But the later representatives of the system sought for their philosophy revelations of the Godhead.   They found them in the religious traditions and cults of all nations.   Neoplatonism learned
from the Stoics to rise above the political limits of nations and
states, and to widen the Hellenic consciousness to a universally
human one.   The spirit of God has breathed throughout the
whole history of the nations, and the traces of divine revelation
are to be found everywhere.   The older a religious tradition or
cultus is, the more worthy of honour, the more rich in thoughts
of God it is.   Therefore the old Oriental religions are of special
value to the Neoplatonists.   The allegorical method of interpreting myths, which was practised by the Stoics in particular,
was accepted by Neoplatonism also.   But the myths, spiritually
explained, have for this system an entirely different value from
what they had for the Stoic philosophers.   The latter adjusted themselves to the myths by the aid of allegorical explanation; the later Neoplatonists, on the other hand, (after
a selection in which the immoral myths were sacrificed, see,
e.g., Julian) regarded them as *the proper material and sure
foundation of philosophy*.   Neoplatonism claims to be not only
the absolute *philosophy*, completing all systems, but at the
same time the absolute *religion*, confirming and explaining all
earlier religions.   A rehabilitation of all ancient religions is
aimed at (see the philosophic teachers of Julian and compare his
great religious experiment); each was to continue in its traditional form, but at the same time each was to communicate
the religious temper and the religious knowledge which Neoplatonism had attained, and each cultus is to lead to the high
morality which it behoves man to maintain.   In Neoplatonism
the psychological fact of the longing of man for something
higher, is exalted to the all-predominating principle which explains the world.   Therefore the religions, though they are to be
purified and spiritualised, become the foundation of philosophy.

The Neoplatonic philosophy therefore presupposes the religious syncretism of the third century, and cannot be understood without it. The great forces which were half unconsciously at work in this syncretism, were reflectively grasped by Neoplatonism. It is the final fruit of the developments resulting from the political, national and religious syncretism which arose from the undertakings of Alexander the Great and the Romans.

Neoplatonism is consequently a stage in the history of religion; nay, its significance in the history of the world lies in the fact that it is so. In the history of science and enlightenment it has a position of significance only in so far as it was the necessary transition stage through which humanity had to pass, in order to free itself from the religion of nature and the depreciation of the spiritual life, which oppose an insurmountable barrier to the highest advance of human knowledge. But as Neoplatonism in its philosophical aspect means the abolition of ancient philosophy, which, however, it desired to complete, so also in its religious aspect it means the abolition of the ancient religions which it aimed at restoring. For in requiring these religions to mediate a definite religious knowledge, and to lead to the highest moral disposition, it burdened them with tasks to which they were not equal, and under which they could not but break down. And in requiring them to loosen, if not completely destroy, the bond which was their only stay, namely, the political bond, it took from them the foundation on which they were built. But could it not place them on a greater and firmer foundation? Was not the Roman Empire in existence, and could the new religion not become dependent on this in the same way as the earlier religions had been dependent on the lesser states and nations? It might be thought so, but it was no longer possible. No doubt the political history of the nations round the Mediterranean, in their development into the universal Roman monarchy, was parallel to the spiritual history of these nations in their development into monotheism and a universal system of morals; but the spiritual development in the end far outstripped the political: even the Stoics attained to a height which the political development could only partially reach. Neoplatonism did indeed attempt to gain a connection with the Byzantine Roman Empire: one noble monarch, Julian, actually perished as a result of this endeavour: but even before this the profounder Neoplatonists discerned that their lofty religious philosophy would not bear contact with the despotic Empire, because it would not bear any contact with the "world" (plan of the founding of Platonopolis). Political affairs are at bottom as much a matter of indifference to Neoplatonism as material things in general. The idealism of the new philosophy was too high to admit of its being naturalised in the despirit-ualised, tyrannical and barren creation of the Byzantine Empire, and this Empire itself needed unscrupulous and despotic police officials, not noble philosophers. Important and instructive, therefore, as the experiments are, which were made from time to time by the state and by individual philosophers, to unite the monarchy of the world with Neoplatonism, they could not but be ineffectual.

But, and this is the last question which one is justified in raising here, why did not Neoplatonism create an independent religious community? Since it had already changed the ancient religions so fundamentally, in its purpose to restore them; since it had attempted to fill the old naive cults with profound philosophic ideas, and to make them exponents of a high mo-rality; why did it not take the further step and create a religious fellowship of its own? Why did it not complete and confirm the union of gods by the founding of a church which was destined to embrace the whole of humanity, and in which, beside the one ineffable Godhead, the gods of all nations could have been worshipped? Why not? The answer to this question is at the same time the reply to another, viz., Why did the christian church supplant Neoplatonism? Neoplatonism lacked three elements to give it the significance of a new and permanent religious system. Augustine in his confessions (Bk. VII. 18—21) has excellently described these three elements. First and above all, it lacked a religious founder; secondly, it was unable to give any answer to the question, how one could permanently maintain the mood of blessedness and peace; thirdly, it lacked the means of winning those who could not speculate. The "people" could not learn the philosophic exercises which it recommended as the condition of attaining the enjoyment of the highest good; and the way by which even the "people" can attain to the highest good was hidden from it. Hence these "wise and prudent" remained a school. When Julian attempted to interest the common uncultured man in the doctrines and worship of this school, his reward was mockery and scorn.

Not as philosophy and not as a new religion did Neoplatonism become a decisive factor in history, but, if I may say so, as a frame of mind. [1] The feeling that there is an eternal highest good which lies beyond all outer experience and is not even the intelligible, this feeling, with which was united the conviction of the entire worthlessness of everything earthly, was produced and fostered by Neoplatonism. But it was unable to describe the contents of that highest being and highest good, and therefore it was here compelled to give itself entirely up to fancy and æsthetic feeling. Therefore it was forced to trace out "mysterious ways to that which is within," which, however, led nowhere. It transformed thought into a dream of feeling; it immersed itself in the sea of emotions; it viewed the old fabled world of the nations as the reflection of a higher reality, and transformed reality into poetry; but in spite of all these efforts it was only able, to use the words of Augustine, to see from afar the land which it desired. It broke this world into fragments; but nothing remained to it, save a ray from a world beyond, which was only an indescribable "something."

[1] Excellent remarks on the nature of Neoplatonism may be found in Eucken, Gött. Gel. Anz., 1 März, 1884. p. 176 ff.: this sketch was already written before I saw them. "We find the characteristic of the Neoplatonic epoch in the effort to make the inward, which till then had had alongside of it an independent outer world as a contrast, the exclusive and all-determining element. The movement which makes itself felt here, outlasts antiquity and prepares the way for the modern period; it brings about the dissolution of that which marked the culminating point of ancient life, that which we are wont to call specifically classic. The life of the spirit, till then conceived as a member of an ordered world and subject to its laws, now freely passes beyond these bounds, and attempts to mould, and even to create, the universe from itself. No doubt the different attempts to realise this desire reveal, for the most part, a deep gulf between will and deed; usually ethical and religious requirements of the naive human consciousness must replace universally creative spiritual power, but all the insufficient and unsatisfactory elements of this period should not obscure the fact that, in one instance, it reached the height of a great philosophic achievement, in the case of Plotinus."

And yet the significance of Neoplatonism in the history of our moral culture has been, and still is, immeasurable. Not only because it refined and strengthened man's life of feeling and sensation, not only because it, more than anything else, wove the delicate veil which even to-day, whether we be religious or irreligious, we ever and again cast over the offensive impression of the brutal reality, but, above all, because it begat the consciousness that the blessedness which alone can satisfy man is to be found somewhere else than in the sphere of knowledge. That man does not live by bread alone is a truth that was known before Neoplatonism; but it proclaimed the profounder truth, which the earlier philosophy had failed to recognise, that man does not live by knowledge alone. Neoplatonism not only had a propadeutic significance in the past, but continues to be, even now, the source of all the moods which deny the world and strive after an ideal, but have not power to raise themselves above æsthetic feeling, and see no means of getting a clear notion of the impulse of their own heart and the land of their desire.

Historical Origin of Neoplatonism.

The forerunners of Neoplatonism were, on the one hand, those Stoics who recognise the Platonic distinction of the sensible and supersensible world, and on the other, the so-called Neopythagoreans and religious philosophers, such as Posidonius, Plutarch of Chæronea, and especially Numenius of Apamea. [1] Nevertheless, these cannot be regarded as the actual Fathers of Neoplatonism; for the philosophic method was still very imperfect in comparison with the Neoplatonic, their principles were uncertain, and the authority of Plato was not yet regarded as placed on an unapproachable height. The Jewish and Christian philosophers of the first and second centuries stand very much nearer the later Neoplatonism than Numenius. We would probably see this more clearly if we knew the development of Christianity in Alexandria in the second century. But, un-

---

[1] Plotinus, even in his lifetime, was reproached with having borrowed most of his system from Numenius. Porphyry, in his "Vita Plotini," defended him against this reproach.

fortunately, we have only very meagre fragments to tell us of this. First and above all, we must mention Philo. This philosopher who interpreted the Old Testament religion in terms of Hellenism had, in accordance with his idea of revelation, already maintained that the Divine Original Essence is supra-rational, that only ecstasy leads to Him, and that the materials for religious and moral knowledge are contained in the oracles of the Deity. The religious ethic of Philo, a combination of Stoic, Platonic, Neopythagorean and Old Testament gnomic wisdom, already bears the marks which we recognise in Neo-platonism. The acknowledgment that God was exalted above all thought was a sort of tribute which Greek philosophy was compelled to pay to the national religion of Israel, in return for the supremacy which was here granted to the former. The claim of positive religion to be something more than an intellectual conception of the universal reason was thereby justified. Even religious syncretism is already found in Philo; but it is something essentially different from the later Neo-platonic, since Philo regarded the Jewish cult as the only valuable one, and traced back all elements of truth in the Greeks and Romans to borrowings from the books of Moses.

The earliest Christian philosophers, especially Justin and Athenagoras, likewise prepared the way for the speculations of the later Neoplatonists by their attempts, on the one hand, to connect Christianity with Stoicism and Platonism, and on the other, to exhibit it as supra-Platonic. The method by which Justin, in the introduction to the Dialogue with Trypho, attempts to establish the Christian knowledge of God, that is the knowledge of the truth, on Platonism, Scepticism and "Revelation," strikingly reminds us of the later methods of the Neoplatonists. Still more is one reminded of Neoplatonism by the speculations of the Alexandrian Christian Gnostics, especially of Valentinus and the followers of Basilides. The doctrines of the Basilidians(?) communicated by Hippolytus (Philosoph. VII. c. 20 sq.), read like fragments from the didactic writings of the Neoplatonists: Ἐπεὶ οὐδὲν ἦν οὐκ ὕλη, οὐκ οὐσία, οὐκ ἀνούσιον, οὐκ ἁπλοῦν, οὐκ σύνθετον, οὐκ ἀνόητον, οὐκ ἀναίσθητον, οὐκ ἄνθρωπος......οὐκ ὢν θεὸς ἀνοήτως, ἀναισθήτως ἀβούλως ἀπροαιρέτως, ἀπαθῶς, ἀνεπιθυ-

μήτιος κόσμον ἠθέλησε ποιῆσαι...... Οὕτως οὐκ ὢν θεὸς ἐποίησε κόσμον οὐκ ὄντα ἐξ οὐκ ὄντων, καταβαλόμενος καὶ ὑποστήσας σπέρμα
τι ἓν ἔχον πᾶσαν ἐν ἑαυτῷ τῆς τοῦ κόσμου πανσπερμίαν. Like the
Neoplatonists, these Basilidians did not teach an emanation from
the Godhead, but a dynamic mode of action of the Supreme
Being. The same can be asserted of Valentinus who also
places an unnamable being above all, and views matter not as
a second principle, but as a derived product. The dependence
of Basilides and Valentinus on Zeno and Plato is, besides, undoubted. But the method of these Gnostics in constructing
their mental picture of the world and its history was still an
uncertain one. Crude primitive myths are here received, and
naively realistic elements alternate with bold attempts at
spiritualising. While therefore, philosophically considered, the
Gnostic systems are very unlike the finished Neoplatonic ones,
it is certain that they contained almost all the elements of
the religious view of the world which we find in Neoplatonism.

But were the earliest Neoplatonists really acquainted with
the speculations of men like Philo, Justin, Valentinus and
Basilides? Were they familiar with the Oriental religions, especially with the Jewish and the Christian? And, if we must
answer these questions in the affirmative, did they really learn
from these sources?

Unfortunately, we cannot at present give certain, and still less
detailed, answers to these questions. But, as Neoplatonism originated in Alexandria, as Oriental cults confronted every one
there, as the Jewish philosophy was prominent in the literary
market of Alexandria, and that was the very place where scientific
Christianity had its headquarters, there can, generally speaking,
be no doubt that the earliest Neoplatonists had some acquaintance
with Judaism and Christianity. In addition to that, we have
the certain fact that the earliest Neoplatonists had discussions
with (Roman) Gnostics (see Carl Schmidt, Gnostische Schriften
in koptischer Sprache, pp. 603—665, and that Porphyry entered
into elaborate controversy with Christianity. In comparison
with the Neoplatonic philosophy, the system of Philo and the
Gnostics appears in many respects an anticipation which had
a certain influence on the former, the precise nature of which

has still to be ascertained. But the anticipation is not wonderful, for the religious and philosophic temper which was only gradually produced on Greek soil, existed from the first in such philosophers as took their stand on the ground of a revealed religion of redemption. Iamblichus and his followers first answer completely to the Christian Gnostic schools of the second century; that is to say, Greek philosophy, in its immanent development, did not attain till the fourth century the position which some Greek philosophers who had accepted Christianity, had already reached in the second. The influence of Christianity—both Gnostic and Catholic—on Neoplatonism was perhaps very little at any time, though individual Neoplatonists since the time of Amelius employed Christian sayings as oracles, and testified their high esteem for Christ.

Sketch of the History and Doctrines of Neoplatonism.

Ammonius Saccas (died about 245), who is said to have been born a Christian, but to have lapsed into heathenism, is regarded as the founder of the Neoplatonic school in Alexandria. As he has left no writings, no judgment can be formed as to his teaching. His disciples inherited from him the prominence which they gave to Plato and the attempts to prove the harmony between the latter and Aristotle. His most important disciples were Origen the Christian, a second heathen Origen, Longinus, Herennius, and, above all, Plotinus. The latter was born in the year 205, at Lycopolis in Egypt, laboured from 224 in Rome, and found numerous adherents and admirers, among others the Emperor Galienus and his consort, and died in lower Italy about 270. His writings were arranged by his disciple Porphyry, and edited in six Enneads.

The Enneads of Plotinus are the fundamental documents of Neoplatonism. The teaching of this philosopher is mystical, and, like all mysticism, it falls into two main portions. The first and theoretic part shews the high origin of the soul, and how it has departed from this its origin. The second and practical part points out the way by which the soul can again be raised to the Eternal and the Highest. As the soul with

its longings aspires beyond all sensible things and even beyond
the world of ideas, the Highest must be something above
reason. The system therefore has three parts. I. The Original
Essence. II. The world of ideas and the soul. III. The world
of phenomena. We may also, in conformity with the thought
of Plotinus, divide the system thus: A. The supersensible world
(1. The Original Essence; 2. the world of ideas; 3. the soul).
B. The world of phenomena. The Original Essence is the One
in contrast to the many; it. is the Infinite and Unlimited
in contrast to the finite; it is the source of all being, therefore the absolute causality and the only truly existing; but
it is also the Good, in so far as everything finite is to find
its aim in it and to flow back to it. Yet moral attributes
cannot be ascribed to this Original Essence, for these would
limit it. It has no attributes at all: it is a being without
magnitude, without life, without throught; nay, one should not,
properly speaking, even call it an existence; it is something
above existence, above goodness, and at the same time the
operative force without any substratum. As operative force
the Original Essence is continually begetting something else,
without itself being changed or moved or diminished. This
creation is not a physical process, but an emanation of force;
and because that which is produced has any existence only
in so far as the originally Existent works in it, it may be
said that Neoplatonism is dynamical Pantheism. Everything
that has being is directly or indirectly a production of the
"One." In this "One" everything so far as it has being, is
Divine, and God is all in all. But that which is derived is
not like the Original Essence itself. On the contrary, the
law of decreasing perfection prevails in the derived. The latter
is indeed an image and reflection of the Original Essence,
but the wider the circle of creations extends the less their
share in the Original Essence. Hence the totality of being
forms a gradation of concentric circles which finally lose themselves almost completely in non-being, in so far as in the last
circle the force of the Original Essence is a vanishing one.
Each lower stage of being is connected with the Original
Essence only by means of the higher stages; that which is

inferior receives a share in the Original Essence only through the medium of these. But everything derived has one feature, viz., a longing for the higher; it turns itself to this so far as its nature allows it.

The first emanation of the Original Essence is the Νοῦς; it is a complete image of the Original Essence and archetype of all existing things; it is being and thought at the same time, World of ideas and Idea. As image the Νοῦς is equal to the Original Essence, as derived it is completely different from it. What Plotinus understands by Νοῦς is the highest sphere which the human spirit can reach (κόσμος νοητός) and at the same time pure thought itself.

The soul which, according to Plotinus, is an immaterial substance like the Νοῦς, [1] is an image and product of the immovable Νοῦς. It is related to the Νοῦς as the latter is to the Original Essence. It stands between the Νοῦς and the world of phenomena. The Νοῦς penetrates and enlightens it, but it itself already touches the world of phenomena. The Νοῦς is undivided, the soul can also preserve its unity and abide in the Νοῦς; but it has at the same time the power to unite itself with the material world and thereby to be divided. Hence it occupies a middle position. In virtue of its nature and destiny it belongs, as the single soul (soul of the world), to the supersensible world; but it embraces at the same time the many individual souls; these may allow themselves to be ruled by the Νοῦς, or they may turn to the sensible and be lost in the finite.

The soul, an active essence, begets the corporeal or the world of phenomena. This should allow itself to be so ruled by the soul that the manifold of which it consists may abide in fullest harmony. Plotinus is not a dualist like the majority of Christian Gnostics. He praises the beauty and glory of the world. When in it the idea really has dominion over matter, the soul over the body, the world is beautiful and good. It is the image of the upper world, though a shadowy one, and the gradations' of better or worse in it are necessary to the harmony of the whole. But, in point of fact, the unity and har-

---

[1] On this sort of Trinity, see Bigg, " The Christian Platonists of Alexandria," p. 248 f.

mony in the world of phenomena disappear in strife and opposition. The result is a conflict, a growth and decay, a seeming
existence. The original cause of this lies in the fact that a
substratum, viz., matter, lies at the basis of bodies. Matter
is the foundation of each (τὸ βάθος ἑκάστου ἡ ὕλη); it is the
obscure, the indefinite, that which is without qualities, the
μὴ ὄν. As devoid of form and idea it is the evil, as capable
of form the intermediate.

The human souls that are sunk in the material have been
ensnared by the sensuous, and have allowed themselves to be
ruled by desire. They now seek to detach themselves entirely
from true being, and striving after independence fall into an
unreal existence. Conversion therefore is needed, and this is
possible, for freedom is not lost.

Now here begins the practical philosophy. The soul must
rise again to the highest on the same path by which it descended: it must first of all return to itself. This takes place
through virtue, which aspires to assimilation with God and
leads to Him. In the ethics of Plotinus all earlier philosophic
systems of virtue are united and arranged in graduated order.
Civic virtues stand lowest, then follow the purifying, and finally
the deifying virtues. Civic virtues only adorn the life, but do
not elevate the soul as the purifying virtues do; they free
the soul from the sensuous and lead it back to itself and
thereby to the Νοῦς. Man becomes again a spiritual and permanent being, and frees himself from every sin, through asceticism. But he is to reach still higher; he is not only to be
without sin, but he is to be "God." That takes place through
the contemplation of the Original Essence, the One, that is
through ecstatic elevation to Him. This is not mediated by
thought, for thought reaches only to the Νοῦς, and is itself
only a movement. Thought is only a preliminary stage towards
union with God. The soul can only see and touch the Original
Essence in a condition of complete passivity and rest. Hence,
in order to attain to this highest, the soul must subject itself
to a spiritual "Exercise." It must begin with the contemplation of material things, their diversity and harmony, then
retire into itself and sink itself in its own essence, and thence

mount up to the Νοῦς, to the world of ideas; but, as it still does not find the One and Highest Essence there, as the call always comes to it from there: "We have not made ourselves" (Augustine in the sublime description of Christian, that is Neoplatonic, exercises), it must, at it were, lose sight of itself in a state of intense concentration, in mute contemplation and complete forgetfulness of all things. It can then see God, the source of life, the principle of being, the first cause of all good, the root of the soul. In that moment it enjoys the highest and indescribable blessedness; it is itself, as it were, swallowed up by the deity and bathed in the light of eternity.

Plotinus, as Porphyry relates, attained to this ecstatic union with God four times during the six years he was with him. To Plotinus this religious philosophy was sufficient; he did not require the popular religion and worship. But yet he sought their support. The Deity is indeed in the last resort only the Original Essence, but it manifests itself in a fulness of emanations and phenomena. The Νοῦς is, as it were, the second God; the λόγοι which are included in it are gods; the stars are gods etc. A strict monotheism appeared to Plotinus a poor thing. The myths of the popular religion were interpreted by him in a particular sense, and he could justify even magic, soothsaying and prayer. He brought forward reasons for the worship of images, which the Christian worshippers of images subsequently adopted. Yet, in comparison with the later Neoplatonists, he was free from gross superstition and wild fanaticism. He cannot, in the remotest sense, be reckoned among the "deceivers who were themselves deceived," and the restoration of the ancient worship of the Gods was not his chief aim.

Among his disciples the most important were Amelius and Porphyry. Amelius changed the doctrine of Plotinus in some points, and even made use of the prologue of the Gospel of John. Porphyry has the merit of having systematized and spread the teaching of his master, Plotinus. He was born at Tyre, in the year 233; whether he was for some time a Christian is uncertain; from 263-268 he was a pupil of Plotinus at Rome; before that he wrote the work περὶ τῆς ἐκ λογίων φιλο-σοφίας, which shews that he wished to base philosophy on revelation; he lived a few years in Sicily, (about 270) where he wrote his "fifteen books against the Christians"; he then returned to Rome, where he laboured as a teacher, edited the works of Plotinus, wrote himself a series of treatises, married in his old age, the Roman Lady Marcella, and died about the year 303. Porphyry was not an original, productive thinker, but a diligent and thorough investigator, characterized by great learning, by the gift of an acute faculty for philological and historical criticism, and by an earnest desire to spread the true philosophy of life, to refute false doctrines, especially those of the Christians, to ennoble man and draw him to that which is good.   That a mind so free and noble surrendered itself entirely to the philosophy of Plotinus and to polytheistic mysticism, is a proof that the spirit of the age works almost irresistibly, and that religious mysticism was the highest possession of the time. The teaching of Porphyry is distinguished from that of Plotinus by the fact that it is still more practical and religious.   The aim of philosophy, according to Porphyry, is the salvation of the soul.   The origin and the guilt of evil lie not in the body, but in the desires of the soul.   The strictest asceticism (abstinence from cohabitation, flesh and wine) is therefore required in addition to the knowledge of God.   During the course of his life Porphyry warned men more and more decidedly against crude popular beliefs and immoral cults. "The ordinary notions of the Deity are of such a kind that it is more godless to share them than to neglect the images of the gods."   But freely as he criticised the popular religions, he did not wish to give them up.   He contended for a pure worship of the many gods, and recognised the right of every old national religion, and the religious duties of their professors.   His work against the Christians is not directed against Christ, or what he regarded as the teaching of Christ, but against the Christians of his day, and against the sacred books which, according to Porphyry, were written by impostors and ignorant people.   In his acute criticism of the genesis or what was regarded as Christianity in his day, he spoke bitter and earnest truths, and therefore acquired the name of the fiercest and most formidable of all the enemies of Christians.   His work was destroyed (condemned by an edict of Theodosius II. and Valentinian, of the year 448), and even the writings in reply (by Methodius, Eusebius, Apollinaris, Philostorgius, etc.,) have not been preserved. Yet we possess fragments in Lactantius, Augustine, Macarius Magnes and others, which attest how thoroughly Porphyry studied the Christian writings and how great his faculty was for true historical criticism.

Porphyry marks the transition to the Neoplatonism which subordinated itself entirely to the polytheistic cults, and which strove, above all, to defend the old Greek and Oriental religions against the formidable assaults of Christianity. Iamblichus, the disciple of Porphyry (died 330), transformed Neoplatonism "from a philosophic theorem into a theological doctrine." The doctrines peculiar to Iamblichus can no longer be deduced from scientific, but only from practical motives. In order to justify superstition and the ancient cults, philosophy in Iamblichus becomes a theurgic mysteriosophy, spiritualism. Now appears that series of "Philosophers" in whose case one is frequently unable to decide whether they are deceivers or deceived, "decepti deceptores," as Augustine says. A mysterious mysticism of numbers plays a great rôle. That which is absurd and mechanical is surrounded with the halo of the sacramental; myths are proved by pious fancies and pietistic considerations with a spiritual sound; miracles, even the most foolish, are believed in and are performed. The philosopher becomes the priest of magic, and philosophy an instrument of magic. At the same time the number of Divine Beings is infinitely increased by the further action of unlimited speculation. But this fantastic addition which Iamblichus makes to the inhabitants of Olympus is the very fact which proves that Greek philosophy has here returned to mythology, and that the religion of nature was still a power. And yet no one can deny that, in the fourth century, even the noblest and choicest minds were found among the Neoplatonists. So great was the declension that this Neoplatonic philosophy was still the protecting roof for many influential and earnest thinkers, although swindlers and hypocrites also concealed themselves under this roof. In relation to some points of doctrine, at any rate, the dogmatic of Iamblichus marks an advance.

Thus, the emphasis he lays on the idea that evil has its seat in the will, is an important fact; and in general the significance he assigns to the will is perhaps the most important advance in psychology, and one which could not fail to have great influence on dogmatic also (Augustine). It likewise deserves to be noted that Iamblichus disputed Plotinus' doctrine of the divinity of the human soul.

The numerous disciples of Iamblichus (Aedesius, Chrysantius, Eusebius, Priscus, Sopater, Sallust and especially Maximus, the most celebrated) did little to further speculation; they occupied themselves partly with commenting on the writings of the earlier philosophers (particularly Themistius), partly as missionaries of their mysticism. The interests and aims of these philosophers are best shewn in the treatise "De mysteriis Ægyptiorum." Their hopes were strengthened when their disciple Julian, a man enthusiastic and noble, but lacking in intellectual originality, ascended the imperial throne, 361 to 363. This emperor's romantic policy of restoration, as he himself must have seen, had, however, no result, and his early death destroyed every hope of supplanting Christianity.

But the victory of the Church in the age of Valentinian and Theodosius, unquestionably purified Neoplatonism. The struggle for dominion had led philosophers to grasp at and unite themselves with everything that was hostile to Christianity. But now Neoplatonism was driven out of the great arena of history. The Church and its dogmatic, which inherited its estate, received along with the latter superstition, polytheism, magic, myths and the apparatus of religious magic. The more firmly all this established itself in the Church and succeeded there, though not without finding resistance, the freer Neoplatonism becomes. It does not by any means give up its religious attitude or its theory of knowledge, but it applies itself with fresh zeal to scientific investigations and especially to the study of the earlier philosophers. Though Plato remains the divine philosopher, yet it may be noticed how, from about 400, the writings of Aristotle were increasingly read and prized. Neoplatonic schools continue to flourish in the chief cities of the empire up to the beginning of the fifth century, and in this period they are at the same time the places where the theologians of the Church are formed. The noble Hypatia, to whom Synesius, her enthusiastic disciple, who was afterwards a bishop, raised a splendid monument, taught in Alexandria. But from the beginning of the fifth century ecclesiastical fanaticism ceased to tolerate heathenism. The murder of Hypatia put an end to philosophy in Alexandria, though the Alexandrian school maintained itself in a feeble form till the middle of the sixth century. But in one city of the East, removed from the great highways of the world, which had become a provincial city and possessed memories which the Church of the fifth century felt itself too weak to destroy, viz., in Athens, a Neoplatonic school continued to flourish. There, among the monuments of a past time, Hellenism found its last asylum. The school of Athens returned to a more strict philosophic method and to learned studies. But as it clung to religious philosophy and undertook to reduce the whole Greek tradition, viewed in the light of Plotinus' theory, to a comprehensive and strictly articulated system, a philosophy arose here which may be called scholastic. For every philosophy is scholastic which considers fantastic and mythological material as a *noli me tangere*, and treats it in logical categories and distinctions by means of a complete set of formulæ. But to these Neoplatonists the writings of Plato, certain divine oracles, the Orphic poems, and much else which were dated back to the dim and distant past, were documents of standard authority and inspired divine writings. They took from them the material of philosophy, which they then treated with all the instruments of dialectic.

The most prominent teachers at Athens were Plutarch (died 433), his disciple Syrian (who, as an exegete of Plato and Aristotle, is said to have done important work, and who deserves notice also because he very vigorously emphasised the freedom of the will), but, above all, Proclus (411-485). Proclus is the great scholastic of Neoplatonism. It was he "who fashioned the whole traditional material into a powerful system with religious warmth and formal clearness, filling up the gaps and reconciling the contradictions by distinctions and specu-

lations." "Proclus," says Zeller, "was the first who, by the
strict logic of his system, formally completed the Neoplatonic
philosophy and gave it, with due regard to all the changes
it had undergone since the second century, that form in which
it passed over to the Christian and Mohammedan middle ages.
Forty-four years after the death of Proclus the school of Athens
was closed by Justinian (in the year 529); but in the labours of
Proclus it had completed its work, and could now really retire
from the scene. It had nothing new to say; it was ripe for
death, and an honourable end was prepared for it. The words
of Proclus, the legacy of Hellenism to the Church and to the
middle ages, attained an immeasurable importance in the
thousand years which followed. They were not only one of
the bridges by which the philosophy of the middle ages returned
to Plato and Aristotle, but they determined the scientific
method of the next thirty generations, and they partly produced, partly strengthened and brought to maturity the mediæval
Christian mysticism in East and West.

The disciples of Proclus—Marinus, Asclepiodotus, Ammonius,
Zenodotus, Isidorus, Hegias, Damascius—are not regarded as
prominent. Damascius was the last head of the school at
Athens. He, Simplicius, the masterly commentator on Aristotle,
and five other Neoplatonists migrated to Persia after Justinian
had issued the edict closing the school. They lived in the
illusion that Persia, the land of the East, was the seat of wisdom,
righteousness and piety. After a few years they returned
with blasted hopes to the Byzantine kingdom.

At the beginning of the sixth century Neoplatonism died
out as an independent philosophy in the East; but almost
at the same time, and this is no accident, it conquered
new regions in the dogmatic of the Church through the
spread of the writings of the pseudo-Dionysius; it began
to fertilize Christian mysticism, and filled the worship with a
new charm.

In the West, where, from the second century, we meet with
few attempts at philosophic speculation, and where the necessary conditions for mystical contemplation were wanting, Neoplatonism only gained a few adherents here and there. We

know that the rhetorician, Marius Victorinus, (about 350) translated the writings of Plotinus. This translation exercised decisive
influence on the mental history of Augustine, who borrowed
from Neoplatonism the best it had, its psychology, introduced
it into the dogmatic of the Church, and developed it still further.
It may be said that Neoplatonism influenced the West at first
only through the medium or under the cloak of ecclesiastical
theology. Even Boethius—we can now regard this as certain—
was a Catholic Christian. But in his mode of thought he was
certainly a Neoplatonist. His violent death in the year 525,
marks the end of independent philosophic effort in the West.
This last Roman philosopher stood indeed almost completely
alone in his century, and the philosophy for which he lived
was neither original nor firmly grounded and methodically
carried out.

Neoplatonism and Ecclesiastical Dogmatic.

The question as to the influence which Neoplatonism had
on the history of the development of Christianity is not easy
to answer; it is hardly possible to get a clear view of the
relation between them. Above all, the answers will diverge
according as we take a wider or a narrower view of so-called
"Neoplatonism." If we view Neoplatonism as the highest
and only appropriate expression for the religious hopes and
moods which moved the nations of Græco-Roman Empire
from the second to the fifth centuries, the ecclesiastical dogmatic which was developed in the same period may appear
as a younger sister of Neoplatonism which was fostered by
the elder one, but which fought and finally conquered her.
The Neoplatonists themselves described the ecclesiastical theologians as intruders who appropriated Greek philosophy, but
mixed it with foreign fables. Hence Porphyry said of Origen
(in Euseb., H. E. VI. 19): "The outer life of Origen was that
of a Christian and opposed to the law; but, in regard to his
views of things and of the Deity, he thought like the Greeks,
inasmuch as he introduced their ideas into the myths of other
peoples." This judgment of Porphyry is at any rate more

just and appropriate than that of the Church theologians about
Greek philosophy, that it had stolen all its really valuable
doctrines from the ancient sacred writings of the Christians.
It is, above all, important that the affinity of the two sides
was noted. So far, then, as both ecclesiastical dogmatic and
Neoplatonism start from the feeling of the need of redemption,
so far as both desire to free the soul from the sensuous, so
far as they recognise the inability of man to attain to blessedness and a certain knowledge of the truth without divine
help and without a revelation, they are fundamentally related.
It must no doubt be admitted that Christianity itself was already
profoundly affected by the influence of Hellenism when it began
to outline a theology; but this influence must be traced back
less to philosophy than to the collective culture and to all
the conditions under which the spiritual life was enacted. When
Neoplatonism arose ecclesiastical Christianity already possessed
the fundamental features of its theology, that is, it had developed
these, not by accident, contemporaneously and independent of
Neoplatonism. Only by identifying itself with the whole history of Greek philosophy, or claiming to be the restoration of
pure Platonism, was Neoplatonism able to maintain that it had
been robbed by the church theology of Alexandria. But that
was an illusion. Ecclesiastical theology appears, though our
sources here are unfortunately very meagre, to have learned
but little from Neoplatonism even in the third century, partly
because the latter itself had not yet developed into the form
in which the dogmatic of the church could assume its doctrines,
partly because ecclesiastical theology had first to succeed in
its own region, to fight for its own position and to conquer
older notions intolerable to it. Origen was quite as independent
a thinker as Plotinus; but both drew from the same tradition.
On the other hand, the influence of Neoplatonism on the Oriental
theologians was very great from the fourth century. The more
the Church expressed its peculiar ideas in doctrines which,
though worked out by means of philosophy, were yet unacceptable to Neoplatonism (the christological doctrines), the more
readily did theologians in all other questions resign themselves
to the influence of the latter system. The doctrines of the

incarnation, of the resurrection of the body, and of the creation of the word, in time formed the boundary lines between the dogmatic of the Church and Neoplatonism; in all else ecclesiastical theologians and Neoplatonists approximated so closely that many among them were completely at one. Nay, there were Christian men, such as Synesius, for example, who in certain circumstances were not found fault with for giving a speculative interpretation of the specifically Christian doctrines. If in any writing the doctrines just named are not referred to, it is often doubtful whether it was composed by a Christian or a Neoplatonist. Above all, the ethical rules, the precepts of the right life, that is asceticism, were always similar. Here Neoplatonism in the end celebrated its greatest triumph. It introduced into the Church its entire mysticism, its mystic exercises, and even the magical ceremonies as expounded by Iamblichus. The writings of the pseudo-Dionysius contain a Gnosis in which, by means of the doctrines of Iamblichus and doctrines like those of Proclus, the dogmatic of the Church is changed into a scholastic mysticism with directions for practical life and worship. As the writings of this pseudo-Dionysius were regarded as those of Dionysius the disciple of the Apostle, the scholastic mysticism which they taught was regarded as apostolic, almost as a divine science. The importance which these writings obtained first in the East, then from the ninth or the twelfth century also in the West, cannot be too highly estimated. It is impossible to explain them here. This much only may be said, that the mystical and pietistic devotion of to-day, even in the Protestant Church, draws its nourishment from writings whose connection with those of the pseudo-Areopagitic can still be traced through its various intermediate stages.

In antiquity itself Neoplatonism influenced with special directness one Western theologian, and that the most important, viz., Augustine. By the aid of this system Augustine was freed from Manichæism, though not completely, as well as from scepticism. In the seventh Book of his confessions he has acknowledged his indebtedness to the reading of Neoplatonic writings. In the most essential doctrines, viz., those about God, matter, the relation of God to the world, freedom and evil, Augustine always remained dependent on Neoplatonism; but, at the same time, of all theologians in antiquity he is the one who saw most clearly and shewed most plainly wherein Christianity and Neoplatonism are distinguished. The best that has been written by a Father of the Church on this subject, is contained in Chapters 9-21 of the seventh Book of his confessions.

The question why Neoplatonism was defeated in the conflict with Christianity, has not as yet been satisfactorily answered by historians. Usually the question is wrongly stated. The point here is not about a Christianity arbitrarily fashioned, but only about Catholic Christianity and Catholic theology. This conquered Neoplatonism after it had assimilated nearly every-thing it possessed. Further, we must note the place where the victory was gained. The battle-field was the empire of Constantine, Theodosius and Justinian. Only when we have considered these and all other conditions are we entitled to enquire in what degree the specific doctrines of Christianity contributed to the victory, and what share the organisation of the Church had in it. Undoubtedly, however, we must always give the chief prominence to the fact that the Catholic dogmatic excluded polytheism in principle, and at the same time found a means by which it could represent the faith of the cultured mediated by science as identical with the faith of the multitude resting on authority.

In the theology and philosophy of the middle ages mysticism was the strong opponent of rationalistic dogmatism; and, in fact, Platonism and Neoplatonism were the sources from which, in the age of the Renaissance and in the following two centuries, empiric science developed itself in opposition to the rationalistic dogmatism which disregarded experience. Magic, astrology, alchemy, all of which were closely connected with Neoplatonism, gave an effective impulse to the observation of nature and consequently to natural science, and finally prevailed over formal and barren rationalism. Consequently, in the history of science, Neoplatonism has attained a significance and performed services of which men like Iamblichus and Proclus never ventured to dream. In point of fact, actual history is often more wonderful and capricious than legends and fables.

Literature.—The best and fullest account of Neoplatonism, to which I have been much indebted in preparing this sketch, is Zeller's Die Philosophie der Griechen, III. Theil, 2 Abtheilung (3 Auflage, 1881) pp. 419-865. Cf. also Hegel, Gesch. d. Philos. III. 3 ff. Ritter, IV. pp. 571-728: Ritter et Preller, Hist. phil. græc. et rom. § 531 ff. The Histories of Philosophy by Schwegler, Brandis, Brucker, Thilo, Strümpell, Ueberweg (the most complete survey of the literature is found here), Erdmann, Cousin, Prantl. Lewes. Further: Vacherot, Hist. de l'école d'Alexandria, 1846, 1851. Simon, Hist. de l'école d'Alexandria, 1845. Steinhart, articles "Neuplatonismus," "Plotin," "Porphyrius," "Proklus" in Pauly, Realencyclop. des klass. Alterthums. Wagenmann, article "Neuplatonismus" in Herzog, Realencyklopädie f. protest. Theol. T. X. (2 Aufl.) pp. 519-529. Heinze, Lehre vom Logos, 1872, p. 298 f. Richter, Neuplatonische Studien, 4 Hefte.

Heigl, Der Bericht des Porphyrios über Origenes, 1835. Redepenning, Origenes I. p. 421 f. Dehaut, Essai historique sur la vie et la doctrine d'Ammonius Saccas, 1836. Kirchner, Die Philosophie des Plotin, 1854. (For the biography of Plotinus, cf. Porphyry, Eunapius, Suidas; the latter also in particular for the later Neoplatonists.) Steinhart, De dialectica Plotini ratione, 1829, and Meletemata Plotiniana, 1840. Neander, Ueber die welthistorische Bedeutung des 9ten Buchs in der 2ten Enneade des Plotinos, in the Adhandl. der Berliner Akademie, 1843. p. 299 f. Valentiner, Plotin u. s. Enneaden, in the Theol. Stud. u. Kritiken, 1864, H. 1. On Porphyrius, see Fabricius, Bibl. gr. V. p. 725 f. Wolff, Porph. de philosophia ex oraculis haurienda librorum reliquiæ, 1856. Müller, Fragmenta hist. gr. III. 688 f. Mai, Ep. ad Marcellam, 1816. Bernays, Theophrast. 1866. Wagenmann, Jahrbücher für Deutsche Theol. Th. XXIII. (1878) p. 269 f. Richter, Zeitschr. f. Philos. Th. LII. (1867) p. 30 f. Hebenstreit, de Iamblichi doctrina, 1764. Harless, Das Buch von den ägyptischen Mysterien, 1858. Meiners, Comment. Societ. Götting. IV. p. 50 f. On Julian, see the catalogue of the rich literature in the Realencyklop. f. prot. Theol. Th. VII. (2 Aufl.) p. 287; and Neumann, Juliani libr. c. Christ. quæ supersunt, 1880. Hoche, Hypatia, in "Philologus," Th. XV.

(1860) p. 435 f. Bach, De Syriano philosopho, 1862. On Proclus, see the Biography of Marinus and Freudenthal in "Hermes" Th. XVI. p. 214 f. On Boethius, cf. Nitzsch, Das System des Boëthius, 1860. Usener, Anecdoton Holderi, 1877.

On the relation of Neoplatonism to Christianity and its significance in the history of the world, cf. the Church Histories of Mosheim, Gieseler, Neander, Baur; also the Histories of Dogma by Baur and Nitzsch. Also Löffler, Der Platonismus, der Kirchenväter, 1782. Huber, Die Philosophie der Kirchenväter, 1859. Tzschirner, Fall des Heidenthums, 1829. Burckhardt, Die Zeit Constantin's des Grossen, p. 155 f. Chastel, Hist. de la destruction du Paganisme dans l'empire d'Orient, 1850. Beugnot, Hist. de la destruction du Paganisme en Occident. 1835. E. v. Lasaulx, Der Untergang des Hellenismus, 1854. Bigg, The Christian Platonists of Alexandria, 1886. Réville, La réligion à Rome sous les Sévères, 1886. Vogt, Neuplatonismus und Christenthum, 1836. Ullmann, Einfluss des Christenthums auf Porphyrius, in Stud. und Krit., 1832.

On the relation of Neoplatonism to Monasticism, cf. Keim, Aus dem Urchristenthum, 1178, p. 204 f. Carl Schmidt, Gnostische Schriften in Koptischer Sprache, 1892 (Texte u. Unters., VIII. 1. 2). See, further, the Monographs on Origen, the later Alexandrians, the three Cappadocians, Theodoret, Synesius, Marius Victorinus, Augustine, Pseudo-Dionysius, Maximus, Scotus Erigena and the Mediæval Mystics. Special prominence is due to Jahn, Basilius Plotinizans, 1838. Dorner, Augustinus, 1875. Bestmann, Qua ratione Augustinus notiones philos. Græcæ adhibuerit, 1877. Loesche, Augustinus Plotinizans, 1881. Volkmann, Synesios, 1869.

On the after effects of Neoplatonism on Christian Dogmatic, see Ritschl, Theologie und Metaphysik. 2 Aufl. 1887.